D0886668

Teacher Behavior and Pupil Self-Concept

Teacher Behavior and Pupil Self-Concept

MARILYNN M. KASH
The Research and Development Center for Teacher Education

GARY D. BORICH
The University of Texas at Austin

WITH THE ASSISTANCE OF
SUSAN K. MADDEN AND KATHLEEN S. FENTON

ADDISON-WESLEY PUBLISHING COMPANY
Reading, Massachusetts • Menlo Park, California
London • Amsterdam • Don Mills, Ontario • Sydney

This book is in the
Addison-Wesley Series in Education

Excerpts in this book from:

All God's Dangers: The Life of Nate Shaw, by Theodore Rosengarten, are reprinted by permission of Alfred A. Knopf, Inc. Copyright © 1974 by Theodore Rosengarten.

I Know Why the Caged Bird Sings, by Maya Angelou, are reprinted by permission of Random House, Inc. Copyright © 1969 by Maya Angelou.

The Autobiography of Eleanor Roosevelt are reprinted by permission of Harper & Row, Publishers, Inc. Copyright © 1937, 1949, 1958, 1960, and 1961 by Anna Eleanor Roosevelt.

ISBN 0-201-00843-2
ABCDEFGHIJ-MA-798

ACKNOWLEDGMENTS

The authors would like to express their appreciation to the National Institute of Education, Division of Teaching, for supporting the Evaluation of Teaching Project at the Research and Development Center for Teacher Education, The University of Texas at Austin, in the course of which many of the concepts and ideas in this book were developed.

The authors also wish to acknowledge their appreciation to Linda Borchardt for her contributions and services during the writing of this book.

CONTENTS

Prologue

THE PHILOSOPHY, PERSPECTIVE, AND PURPOSE OF THIS BOOK

> ... America, compared to every other country in Western civilization, large or small, has the most *explicitly expressed* system of general ideals in reference to human interrelations. This body of ideals is more widely understood and appreciated than similar ideals are anywhere else. The American Creed is not merely—as in some other countries —the implicit background of the nation's political and judicial order as it functions. To be sure, the political creed of America is not very satisfactorily effectuated in actual social life. But as principles which *ought* to rule, the Creed has been made conscious to everyone in American society
>
> G. Myrdal, 1962. An American dilemma, p. 3.

Our success in perpetuating what Myrdal calls the American Creed throughout our history and throughout our multifarious society is due in no small part to our system of public education. From two centuries marked by accelerated social, political, and technological change, public education has emerged as our most stable institution and the prime repository for and principal transmitter of the nation's traditions. Yet our success in preserving the traditional belief in the value of the individual and our own particular social and political concepts of individualism (Lukes 1973) may in fact be jeopardizing the American Creed.

American society has moved steadily in the direction of traditionalizing and secularizing (that is, separating from its religious foundation) the concept of the individual as inherently valuable, a concept which originated in Western philosophy, Western Christian theology, and the European experience (Morris 1972). Our Founding Fathers could ". . . hold these Truths to be self-evident, that all Men are created equal, that they are endowed by their Creator with certain unalienable Rights, that among these are Life, Liberty, and the Pursuit of Happiness . . . ." But the self-evidence of these truths has apparently escaped succeeding generations of Americans who associate equality and individual rights not with humanity but with United States citizenship. Today neither Christian nor humanist ethics can guarantee realization of the American Creed for every citizen. We now rely on the Constitution of the United States as the embodiment of the American Creed and the guarantor of our rights. The con-

1

cept of the individual as a valuable being possessed of certain inalienable rights forms the basis of the political ideology, the social philosophy and, most important, the law of the United States.

But there is real danger in separating a stated value from its conceptual and experiential origins. As it became secularized and traditionalized, the concept of inherent individual worth also became vulnerable to the erosive power of cynicism, pragmatism, and dogmatism. Early in our national history the belief that all men are *created* equal and endowed by their *Creator* with certain inalienable rights provided consolation for those who experienced social or political oppression—because the conditions in which individuals lived were not considered the measure of their inherent value. In other words, those who suffered political injustice or social abasement were able to preserve their feeling of inherent worth by way of a sustaining belief in the value of the individual, a belief reinforced by religious convictions. But as the tenets of the American Creed became separated from their theological and philosophical foundations, the value of individuals and their endowment with personal rights came to be associated with the *secular* power provided by the Constitution, and thus, in the public mind, became subject to the operating interpretations of that document's provisions. When individual worth is perceived as dependent on secular power, the conditions in which one lives—whether one experiences justice or injustice, poverty or wealth, social acceptance or social oppression—can be interpreted as an index of personal value and a determinant of personal rights. Shorn of its theological and philosophical underpinnings, the American Creed cannot protect one's self-concept from the pervasive assumption that social conditions indicate personal worth. When secular institutionalization of the American Creed exacts a toll in self-concept, the Creed itself is subverted.

Various individuals and minorities in our society experience conditions that constantly attest to their disinheritance and limited worth. Some of the defeated have come to accept themselves as they are defined by their circumstances. Others who have not succumbed to the paralysis induced by such acceptance have found avenues of violence and force through which to make their claims on society. Still others retreat from secular life and form religious or pseudoreligious sects through which to reestablish their sense of personal value, control the conditions for worthiness, and condemn secular society which has in one way or another devalued and disinherited them.

If the devalued, disinherited, and disillusioned in our society are to be restored, they must be allowed to experience their inherent value and their personal, inalienable rights in the secular world. This can be done only by changing the circumstances, and the experiences of their daily lives—in short, by implementing the American Creed as the measure and goal of national life.

On the one hand, then, secularization of the American Creed has ensured preservation of its tenets in the political and social foundations of this nation.

Yet, on the other hand, secularization has transformed our national belief in the individual's inherent worth from a theological and philosophical abstraction to a concrete reality, evidence of which is assumed to be in one's social and political condition. Our system of public education, which is based on the values represented in the American Creed, is a concrete, social, and political manifestation of our beliefs. However, this system of public education reflects the apportionment of individual value and personal rights that accompanied secularization of the American Creed. While public schooling is the one nearly universal experience of all United States citizens and an integral part of our mutually shared national life, it is also an essential component of each *individual's personal experience* and, as such, contributes to one's concept of self-value, understanding of individual rights, and personal belief in the American Creed.

Like other traditions, the American Creed serves to maintain and propagate our national culture. The values, ideals, and beliefs expressed in the American Creed, along with other national traditions, constitute an established core of symbolically preserved experience and knowledge which must be transmitted to, and adopted by, successive generations in order to ensure continuation of our culture. But it is not enough to simply transmit knowledge—to speak of Founding Fathers and battlefield sacrifices in our nation's past. In order to retain their function in the culture, traditions and beliefs must be *experienced* by individuals within that culture. A belief that is not implemented ceases to function as an integrative cultural force and becomes inert knowledge. A tradition which has been transmitted and adopted but cannot be practiced due to prevailing circumstances and conditions creates dissonance within the cultural body which can be resolved only by altering the impeding circumstances and conditions to allow implementation. Of course, the dissonance can be eased by dissolving the tradition—but since this threatens the values, ideals, and beliefs which constitute the American Creed, it is not a pleasant alternative.

When the values of the American Creed are no longer applied as the standard by which to measure the experience of all members of our entire culture, when the ideals of the American Creed are no longer used as the goals and directives of our national life, the creed will no longer be the source of social conflicts or political problems. The American Creed with its traditional values and beliefs will cease to function intact as the dynamic, integrative force of our culture.

While our educational system has achieved respectable success in conveying our cultural values, ideals, and beliefs in the past, it is now being pressed to function not merely as a transmitting agent, but also as an *institutional manifestation* of our traditional beliefs. We are being asked to examine the experience of public schooling and to measure that experience against our national values and ideals. We are being asked to assess the extent to which we, as

Americans and educators, have implemented our traditional belief in the personal rights of each individual and the unconditional nature of individual value. Royce Van Norman of Johns Hopkins University (1966, pp. 315–316) made this assessment of the situation:

> **Is it not ironical that in a planned society of controlled workers given compulsory assignments, where religious expression is suppressed, the press controlled, and all media of communication censored, where a puppet government is encouraged but denied any real authority, where a great attention is given to efficiency and character reports, and attendance at cultural assemblies is compulsory, where it is avowed that all will be administered to each according to abilities, and where those who flee are tracked down, returned, and punished for trying to escape—in short in the milieu of the typical large American secondary school—we attempt to teach "the democratic system"?**

There is no reason to infer from this rather severe description of public education that implementation of the American Creed within the school system would require turning classrooms over to the students, or dispensing with public school altogether. Neither of these actions would reflect the pupil's inherent value or alter the circumstances that perhaps prevent him or her from experiencing, adopting, and implementing our cultural traditions.

There are a good many things our future citizens need to know before they are prepared to assume the responsibilities of adulthood and citizenship. Skills, tools, and knowledge must be acquired and mastered at certain levels of competency. But there is no basis in either our political ideology or our social philosophy for exacting such competency as a condition of a child's inherent worth. Our traditional beliefs must be realized and felt in each child's school experience. And in the teacher-pupil relationship we have, first and foremost, an opportunity to express the basic tenet of our founding principles —that the individual has inherent value.

It is precisely at this juncture that our interest in the effects of teacher behavior on pupil self-concept is focused. We are certainly aware that much of the very limited interest in the effect of schooling on pupil self-concept arises from the hypothesis that a positive self-concept, particularly a positive concept of self-as-student, leads to greater *academic* achievement. If this hypothesis can be proven, it will surely heighten and hasten interest in the relationship between teacher behavior and pupil self-concept. But suppose it cannot be satisfactorily proven at the present time, under present conditions?

Why confine interest in teacher behavior and pupil self-concepts to this one particular hypothesis? Public education in our country is, after all, an enforced and formative cultural experience. As a nation with a unique concept of the individual's inherent value, with "the *most explicitly expressed* system of general ideals in reference to human interrelations," we can (and should) easily justify research on the relationship between teacher behavior and pupil self-concept on the basis of our traditional concern for individuals. We should be interested in knowing how, or even if, the experience of public education can be made more consonant with our values and ideals. And, we should hope to learn whether or not public schooling can become an effective instrument for promulgating belief in the value of the individual.

Our feeling that the affective aspects of the learning process warrant attention is influenced by our philosophy of education. That philosophy is well to the right of radical reformers such as Ivan Illich who suggests "deschooling" (1971), and considerably left of the fundamentalist philosophy of Max Rafferty (Postman and Weingartner 1973). Though our middle-of-the-road position permits occasional veering to either side, most educators will recognize our moderation and find it compatible with their own. We have a healthy respect for the "fundamentals," however, not as the ends of education but as the means for acquiring education. Our concept of individualism in education is tempered by our view of education as a socializing process. Our preference for less autocratic, more student-centered learning situations recognizes that for some students a more structured, teacher-dominated environment may be temporarily essential. We support the concept of community participation in and control of public education, but only insofar as the participating citizenry can accept professional guidance and national, rather than parochial, standards for public education. Our desire for educational innovation and experimentation is countered by our concern that such enterprises recognize the basic rights of individuals. We believe that our educational system must change in order to meet the needs of our changing society, but we are concerned that change be founded in a knowledge of the learning process. We also hope that change will be responsibly implemented in order to preserve and perpetuate our democratic heritage.

In keeping with this philosophy of education for a free society, we have no alternative but to accept the less than perfect conditions for controlled, experimental research in our educational institutions. Because the goals of educational research and the needs of individual investigators often conflict, particularly in the affective area of beliefs and values, the classroom is not an ideal research setting. The control and manipulation required in experimental studies are more easily achieved in a laboratory situation using animal subjects than in a community setting using human beings, since in the latter case the rights of individuals must be protected and the consent of the subjects must be obtained. However, because we feel that education should promote democratic ideals, we accept these imperfect conditions and the limitations they place upon the findings of research studies conducted in the real world rather than the laboratory.

We are aware of the dangers involved in a purely pragmatic approach dictated by the circumstances of educational research in our society, but we believe that educational research, like medical research, has a two-pronged purpose: (1) to pursue identification of causative factors toward the ultimate goal of prediction and treatment in the best tradition of pure science, and (2) to provide, in the meantime, supportive and ameliorating information and techniques to those actively engaged in the art of educating.

It is the intent of this book to serve the second purpose of educational research; and it is this intent, along with our recognition of the constraints placed upon experimentation in the real world, that has caused us to assume a liberal and accepting attitude toward the research undertaken to date in the area of teacher behavior and pupil self-concept. This attitude is warranted, considering the state of the art and the current level of knowledge in this area. All teacher behavior and pupil self-concept research, whether descriptive, correlational, or experimental, is still in the process of discovering the nature of the subject itself. While plateaus of understanding are occasionally reached, there is still no consensus among researchers about what should be studied or how. Under these circumstances, it is difficult to determine what constitutes a major study of minor importance or a minor study of major importance without falling back on the criteria of institutional dominance, investigator prominence, or popular appeal of the study.

This situation is complicated by the fact that we have no precise language for defining either the subject or the process of affective research or for communicating the results. Investigators reporting research on teacher behavior and its relationship to pupil self-concept must stand on the same argument Lewis Carroll's Humpty Dumpty offered to Alice:

> **"When I use a word," Humpty Dumpty said, in rather a scornful tone, "it means just what I choose it to mean—neither more nor less."**
> **"The question is," said Alice, "whether you** *can* **make words mean so many different things."**
> **"The question is," said Humpty Dumpty, "which is to be master —that's all."**

The absence of common definitions has had two important effects on research related to teacher behavior and its affective dimensions. First, it has tended to make each study specific to the particular research situation, thereby limiting its generalizability; and second, it has reduced the impact of findings from such studies by generating extended debates over terminology used and interpretations made. One of the most obvious causes for the language problem encountered by researchers in the affective domain is the prevalence of adjectives in the working vocabulary of this area. As Humpty Dumpty points out, "adjectives you can do anything with."

Our position includes recognition, but no final resolution, of these problems. We have, instead, simply selected those studies which we feel contribute to the knowledge of our subject and presented each one using the terms, definitions, criteria, and measurements provided by the investigator. Having presented the study, we have then allowed ourselves the license of interpreting the author in accordance with our own operational definitions, leaving the reader at liberty to disagree with either the original investigator or the authors of this book, or both. We have made no effort to determine the importance of the reported research to the study of teacher behavior and pupil self-concept. Our evaluative efforts have been limited to study design or concept and interpretation. In these areas we have exercised a somewhat more critical attitude and applied more stringent criteria in judging the merit of each study or program and the value of reported findings.

An assessment of the methodological strengths and weaknesses of these studies has been articulated in a series of related books and articles for readers who wish to pursue this topic further. Borich (1977b) has described the major sources of invalidity in the measurement of classroom behavior, Borich and Madden (1977) have compiled a sourcebook detailing the reliability, validity, and other psychometric characteristics of many of the instruments used in the studies reported in this volume, and Borich (1977a) has detailed many of the methodological and design problems found by researchers studying teacher behavior. The preparation of these documents has allowed us, in part, to devote the present volume to the substantive concepts and interpretations of the studies reported.

The research studies included in this book necessarily focus on teacher behaviors selected and defined by individual researchers. These variables by no means represent all the teaching behaviors that could or should be investigated. The affective variables measured in the pupil population, likewise chosen by individual researchers, also reflect the particular definitions and hypotheses of these investigators.

The educational programs and projects included in this volume have all been reported in popular and professional literature by their designers or implementors. We have carefully adhered to the original report for information about the design, implementation, and results of these programs and projects. When a report included an overt statement of affective objectives, or outcomes intended or perceived by the program developer, we used that statement and our operational definitions to place the report in the chapter which, according to our conceptual framework, was most appropriate. When no overt statement of purpose was supplied, the program or project was incorporated according to our interpretation of its intent.

We would like to encourage the reader to use any suggestions or criticisms we have made with regard to the research studies and programs included in this book. We are confident that fresh and interesting hypotheses, as well as improved research designs and methodologies, will be developed. We are hopeful that new projects and programs for incorporating affective objectives into the educational curriculum will be created by our readers. Whether new research and development projects result directly from this book or from serendipitous inspiration received while examining its contents, we hope that our efforts will generate contributions to the study of teacher behavior and its relationship to pupil self-concept.

REFERENCES

Borich, G. D. 1977a. *The appraisal of teaching: concepts and process.* Reading, Mass.: Addison-Wesley.

————. 1977b. Sources of invalidity in measuring classroom behavior. *Instructional Science* **6.**

————, and S. K. Madden 1977. *Evaluating classroom instruction: a sourcebook of instruments.* Reading, Mass.: Addison-Wesley.

Illich, I. 1971. *Deschooling society.* New York: Harper & Row.

Lukes, S. 1972. *Individualism.* New York: Harper Torch Books, Harper & Row.

Morris, C. 1972. *The discovery of the individual 1050–1200.* New York: Harper Torch Books, Harper & Row.

Myrdal, G. 1962. *An American dilemma.* New York: Harper & Row.

Postman, N., and C. Weingartner 1973. *The school book.* New York: Delacorte Press.

Van Norman, R. 1966. School administration: thoughts on organization and purpose. *Phi Delta Kappan* **47:**315–16.

CHAPTER 1
A Theoretical Framework and Organizational Schema

Successful experiences in school are no guarantee of a generally positive self-concept, but they increase the probabilities that such will be the case. In contrast, unsuccessful experiences in school guarantee that the individual will develop a negative academic self-concept and increase the probabilities that he will have a generally negative self-concept.

Benjamin Bloom 1973. Facts and feelings in the classroom, *p. 142.*

Concern for pupil self-concept, general or academic, is not shared by all educators; nor is professional interest in the affective aspects of the learning process motivated primarily by concern for the emotional development of pupils.

To many educators, the feelings, attitudes, values, self-concepts, and concerns of pupils are relevant to the learning process only when they serve cognitive objectives. Professional interest in the affective aspects of education is generally prompted by the pragmatic desire to equip educators with more carrots and sticks to use in herding pupils along on the daily trek toward cognitive achievement. Accordingly, affective objectives often function only as the spoonful of sugar that makes the medicine go down. This limited, palliative application of the affective element in education is denounced by its critics as "catering to" and "mollycoddling" pupils. It is interesting that these critics rarely object to the use of pupil fear (fear of failure, fear of punishment, and fear of public humiliation)—an equally blatant and manipulative harnessing of affective elements for cognitive purposes.

This view of affect as the servant of cognition, though dominant, is not universal. There are educators, generally classed as "humanistic," who consider objectives in the Affective Domain (Krathwohl, Bloom, and Masia 1964), as well as pupil values, concerns, and self-concept, valid educational objectives in their own right. These educators regard attention to pupil affect not only as a means to motivate students toward higher academic achievement,

9

but also as a desirable and legitimate educational goal in itself. Since cognitive knowledge alone is insufficient to produce behavioral change, and since behavioral change is the best evidence of learning, they propose that cognition and affect be engaged as equal and complementary forces to effect such change among pupils (Weinstein and Fantini 1970).

The extent to which the cognitive and affective aspects of learning have been considered as complementary forces of learning is indicated by the focus in recent years on individual differences in learners. This focus is highlighted by the prevailing concerns for individualized instruction, learning disorders, and the disadvantaged learner (Sperry 1972). Behind these concerns is an awareness of individual learning styles, individual potential, and individual experiences as contributing factors to the learning performances of pupils. Research on individual differences of personality, intelligence, and social background (the learner as person) and their effect on the learning styles seen in differential responses to instructional styles and differential responses to expectancies (the learner as learner) has contributed to the knowledge and understanding of this complementary relationship that exists between the cognitive and affective aspects of learning performances.

The "humanistic" position, however, is not adequately represented in educational research related to pupil self-concept. At present virtually all such research strongly reflects the position that the affective dimensions should serve the cognitive in the learning process. As they are currently formulated, research questions deal primarily with improving the cognitive product of the system. Therefore, investigation in the affective area has centered around an attempt to identify teacher behaviors that motivate or facilitate the academic achievement of pupils. The problems of public education, as they are presently perceived, dictate that educational research focus on finding immediate, remedial solutions that can be implemented in the existing educational structure and that can accommodate the variety of social, political, and economic conditions characterizing local school systems.

Several factors may account for the "expedient" and "one-sided" quality of the research. One of these, of course, is prevailing values. The belief that pupil self-concept is not a legitimate concern of public education, or that affective dimensions warrant consideration only when they serve cognitive objectives, may have influenced the amount of research, the kind of research, and the funds available for research in the affective area. Even more determinant, however, is the prevailing concept of learning (and educating) as a solely cognitive endeavor. Before we can begin to progress in researching the affective aspects of the learning experience, we must acknowledge that learning is indeed composed of *both* affective and cognitive elements. We need an holistic concept of education, a concept that deals with the phenomenon of schooling as an experience of the *total* person. The categorization of educational objectives into Cognitive, Affective, and Psychomotor Domains (Bloom,

Engelhart, Furst, Hill, and Krathwohl 1956) does not imply that the actual experience of learning is in reality a fragmented and disparate activity. Educational objectives can be established for any of the three domains, but the actual experience of learning these objectives is felt by the total person and affects the total "self." It is the process of learning cognitive, affective, or psychomotor objectives that ultimately contributes to the self-concept of the learner. Each event in the educational experience has potential for self-concept change or reinforcement, whether that event is one of success or failure.

This holistic concept of learning gives us a perspective from which to view the pupil self-concept research. In order to examine the relationship between teacher behavior and pupil self-concept, however, we must also utilize existing theories of human development, learning, social interaction, and self-concept development. In addition, we require an operational definition of the psychological construct "self-concept" that explains both the process and the product of self-conceptualizing.

With these needs in mind, we have devised a model of teacher/pupil interaction that relates existing theories to the learning situation and includes an operational definition of "self-concept" derived from theory and from previously described constructs of "self."

THEORETICAL FRAMEWORK

For thou has granted to man that he should come to self-knowledge through the knowledge of others, and that he should believe many things about himself on the authority of the womenfolk. Now, clearly, I had life and being; and, as my infancy closed, I was already learning signs by which my feelings could be communicated to others.

St. Augustine, 1955. Augustine: confessions and enchiridion, *p. 36.*

The research hypothesis that teacher behavior affects pupil self-concept assumes that teachers are influential in the lives of pupils. This hypothesis also assumes that "self-concept," understood as a psychological realization of the abstract "self," is acquired through social interaction and is subject to change through experience. These assumptions, in turn, imply that there is a psychological event occurring in an interaction that is specifically related to the formation of a psychological concept of the "self." Finally, the words "teacher" and "pupil" imply a power structure characterizing the relationship between these two roles and influencing the psychological events occurring in teacher/pupil interaction.

These assumptions, inherent in the hypothesis that teacher behavior affects pupil self-concept, evoke the "self" theories of social interactionists and social psychologists, particularly that advanced by G. H. Mead (1934). Mead theorized that the "self" is a social product formed through the processes of internalizing and organizing psychological experiences. These psychological experiences are the result of the individual's exploration of his physical environment and the reflections of "self" he has received from those persons he considers "significant others."

Mead's theory appears to accommodate the hypothesis (and its concomitant assumptions) that teacher behavior affects pupil self-concept. Applying this theory to the learning situation, the pupil may be viewed as the "developing self," gradually forming a concept of self through interaction with "significant others" (in this case, teachers) and the environment (the school). Within this interaction, or "behavioral dialogue," are psychological experiences in which the teacher (or school environment) reflects to the pupil an image of his or her "self." If the pupil values this image (that is, does indeed consider the teacher a significant other), the pupil will internalize the psychological experience to influence the development of his or her self-concept.

This application of Mead's theory to the teacher/pupil relationship summarizes our theoretical framework. It is supplemented, however, with a model of self-concept which we have used to interpret and categorize the teacher behavior and pupil self-concept research. Each component of our theoretical framework is briefly defined below and, along with our self-concept model, more fully explained on the following pages.

The Developing Self

The developing self is a term intended to convey a dynamic concept of "self," a concept always subject to change through the impact of further psychological experiences.

The Performing Self

The performing self is the concept of "self-as-doer," the self exhibiting behaviors and producing products.

The Significant Other

The significant other is an individual selected and unconditionally valued by the developing self as a source of self-reflection and an interpreter of the behavioral dialogue.

The Salient Other

The salient other is an individual, selected and/or accepted by the developing self and conditionally valued for a *specific* reflection of the "self" and for interpretation of *specific* events in the behavioral dialogue.

The Environment

The environment consists of the physical milieu in which the developing self exists and in which the behavioral dialogue occurs. This physical milieu includes the body of the developing self under certain conditions and all human beings who do not function as significant or salient others.

Psychological Experience

A psychological experience occurs when the developing self receives, responds to, values, and internalizes the reflective, interpretive, or informative stimuli offered by significant/salient others or the environment, incorporating these stimuli as aspects of self-concept which influence behavior, beliefs, and attitudes.

The Behavioral Dialogue

The behavioral dialogue is a psychosocial concept of dyadic interaction encompassing the phenomenal field, or subjective reality (Rogers 1959), of both the developing self and the significant/salient others. It also contains the observable, objective reality that can be perceived and described as the behavior of the participants in the dialogue. All psychological experiences having impact on the developing self occur within the behavioral dialogues the individual experiences. Interactions between the developing self and the environment are also considered dialogical and therefore may produce psychological experiences that contribute to the formation of self-concept.

THE ROLE OF THE SIGNIFICANT OTHER

The role of the significant other is one of reflection, but not in the sense of casual mirroring. The child, seeking an image of "self," *selects* a significant other and *values* the representation of the self reflected by that significant other. The accuracy of the reflected image is dependent upon the capabilities of the significant other; unfortunately, accurate reflection is not a major or even a minor consideration in selecting and valuing a significant other, at least not until the image-seeking developing self acquires an experiential level of sophistication.

The selection of the significant other appears to be forced by limited options: the choice must be made from those persons having potential for interaction with the image-seeking self. The most important point, however, concerning the selection and valuing of a significant other is that the process rests solely and unequivocally with the developing, image-seeking self. Becoming a significant other in a child's life is not simply a matter of assuming the role. One is *chosen* a significant other and denied the option of declining the honor. While willingness to act as a significant other may improve, and unwillingness impair, one's performance in that capacity, the role is always conferred, never assumed.

To function properly, a significant other requires not only the opportunity and capacity to interact with the developing self (*constancy*), but also the ability to reflect a stable, integrated image of the developing self (*consistency*). But here again, accuracy is not the criterion used by the child in placing value on the reflection supplied by the significant other. To the child, the image reflected by the significant other always has impact, though it can be incorporated into the developing self-concept only if it is consistent, stable, and basically noncontradictory. The significant other may be uniformly accepting, consistently reflecting a positive image to the child, or constantly rejecting, regularly reflecting a negative image. In either case, the reflected image becomes a prime source of psychological experiences considered necessary to the formation of a self-concept.

In addition to reflecting an image of the child, the significant other also interprets experiences and events for the child. Since these interpretations are shaped by the perceptual reality of the significant other, the experiences and behaviors of the developing self are initially explained from the perspective of the significant other. The behavioral cues exhibited by the developing self acquire meaning, or content, according to their interpretation by the significant other. In this interpretive role, the significant other helps the child associate behavioral cues with verbal symbols. This allows the child to assume increased participation in the ongoing dialogue between self and environment. If, however, the significant other gives inconsistent interpretations, refuses to accept cues for interpretation, or stifles participation by the developing self, the dialogue becomes a monologue by the significant other which inhibits and/or negatively influences the child's self-concept formation.

The quality of the significant other's performance in this interpretative role affects the child's ability to form cognitive constructs and to devise an organized schema for the child's own behaviors. If, in interpreting events, the significant other provides cognitive material for differentiation as well as association processes, the significant other supplies the child with psychological experiences that enable the child to assume increased participation and initiative in the dialogue through which the "self" is developed.

THE ROLE OF THE SALIENT OTHER

The role of "salient other" also involves reflection and interpretation for the developing self, but in a more limited way. First, a salient other is selected and valued less for himself or herself than for the "position" the salient other occupies—that is, what he or she can "do" for the developing self. Salient others are often selected from the environment to meet needs unfulfilled by significant others, but they are valued merely for the function they perform. In fact, salient others may be chosen to serve specific, sometimes temporary, needs that arise in the course of the child's physical, emotional, and intellectual growth. They do not, however, acquire the blanket acceptance and unconditional value bestowed upon significant others.

The selection of a salient other is, again, made by the developing self alone and is subject to the same constraints that limit the choice of a significant other. Need may force selection on the basis of expediency, rather than quality of performance; environmental limitations, such as availability of others, may also influence the choice. In any case, once salient others are selected, the reflections and interpretations they provide become a source of psychological experiences which may be internalized and organized by the child to help form a self-concept—functioning in exactly the same manner as those provided by a significant other.

THE ROLE OF THE ENVIRONMENT

The environment, acting in concert with significant others to provide reflections for self-concept formation, offers the child the psychological experiences of exploration, limitation, and self-impact. When either one of these sources fails to perform its function, the child relies on the more constant and consistent reflection supplied by the remaining source. The nature of the source, i.e., whether it is "good" or "bad," does not affect its functioning. The image reflected by a hostile or rejecting environment is as effective a contributor to self-concept as that reflected by a warm and accepting environment. However, we would expect differences in the end product, the self-concept, emerging from two so different environments.

The child must accept the opportunities the environment offers for exploring, testing, and experiencing, and the reflections it provides of success, failure, and self-impact until he or she has sufficient experience and independence to alter that environment, or leave it altogether. At birth, infants are dependent not only on the external environment, but also the "environment" of their own bodies. The child's success or failure in mastering these environments contributes to a sense of adequacy or inadequacy, competence or incompetence, that is incorporated into the child's developing self-concept. Experiences within these environments also contribute to what Erikson (1963) calls a basic sense of trust or mistrust. The child who trusts the environment can be open, accepting, autonomous, and explorative, and through these behaviors continue to acquire the confidence and competence which reinforce a positive self-concept. The child who mistrusts the environment due to negative psychological experiences in early years will tend to limit self-initiated activities which could provide him or her with new experiences and positive reflections of the performing self. These self-imposed limitations reinforce the already negative and perhaps unrealistic self-concept the child has acquired through earlier psychological experiences.

The environment, then, like the significant other, serves two main functions in self-concept formation: (1) reflection—receiving and responding to the developing self—and (2) interpretation—mediating between the developing self and selected phenomena or stimuli to provide information, meaning, value, and content. The reflections and interpretations from these two sources supply psychological experiences which the child internalizes and organizes into cognitive constructs and reference systems that form self-concept and direct behavior.

But all the reflections and interpretations of the self are not automatically internalized. The physiological state of the individual affects the course of internalization and organization, limiting and ordering the stimuli that can be processed at various stages of physical and psychological development.

INTERNALIZING AND ORGANIZING

Internalization is described by Krathwohl, Bloom, and Masia (1964, pp. 27–28) as:

> **the process by which a given phenomenon or value passes from a level of bare awareness to a position of some power to guide or control the behavior of a person . . . the process by which the phenomenon or value successively and pervasively becomes a part of the individual.**

Krathwohl *et al.* divide this process into five steps representing discernible levels of internalization: (1) *Receiving,* (2) *Responding,* (3) *Valuing,* (4) *Organizing,* and (5) *Characterization by a value or value complex.*

Examining the role of the significant other in relation to the processes of internalization and self-concept development, we can see that the developing self in accepting the reflections and interpretations of self in the significant other is exhibiting *Receiving* behavior. In turn, desire for attention and approval from the significant other prompts a compliant, *Responding* behavior. The developing self is beginning to internalize the reflections of "self" and the interpretations of experience supplied by the significant other. At this level of internalization, however, the process does not yet affect self-concept formation. Like the physical symptoms of chills and fever, *Receiving* and *Responding* behaviors indicate the onset of change in the individual, but do not, by themselves, produce such change. For this reason, we cannot identify a significant or salient other simply by noting the individual to whom the developing self is attending and responding.

In forming a concept of "self," the crucial stage in the process of internalization is *Valuing.* This level is characterized by acceptance, preference, and commitment (conviction). The developing self accepts, prefers, and believes the reflections and interpretations received from the significant other because the source is valued. This does not mean that the developing self automatically internalizes *all* reflective and interpretive stimuli provided by the significant other. It simply means that the developing self values the significant other unconditionally. And only after this unconditional commitment is made will the developing self complete the internalization process and incorporate the significant other's reflections and interpretations into an evolving self-concept.

THE BEHAVIORAL DIALOGUE

Tell me, good Brutus, can you see your face?

No, Cassius; for the eye sees not itself,
But by reflection, by some other things.

Tis just.
And it is very much lamented, Brutus,
That you have no such mirrors as will turn
Your hidden worthiness into your eye,
That you might see your shadow.

Therefore, good Brutus, be prepar'd to hear;
And since you know you cannot see yourself
So well as by reflection, I, your glass,
Will modestly discover to yourself
That of yourself which you yet know not of.

William Shakespeare, Julius Caesar: *I: ii*

The interactive process through which the individual forms a self-concept is the final component of our theoretical framework for examining the relationship between teacher behavior and pupil self-concept. Our model of interaction, which we call the Behavioral Dialogue, may be used to study the interactive process in any context, among any group of individuals, though in this case it is applied to the pupil, the teacher, and the school environment.

The behavioral dialogue is a dyadic relationship, with the developing self on one side and significant/salient others and the environment on the other. Within the behavioral dialogue the developing self is engaged in the processes of internalizing and organizing; the significant/salient others and the environment are engaged in the processes of reflecting and interpreting. Theoretically, every interaction within the behavioral dialogue may produce a psychological experience affecting self-concept formation in the developing self.

Since the behavioral dialogue represents a unit of *interaction,* the psychological dynamics occurring within it can be graphically portrayed only in terms of their achieved or anticipated effects on the participants. Like the before and after pictures of the proud dieter or the skinny weakling turned majestic muscle man, a graphic portrayal of the behavioral dialogue necessarily

BASIC ELEMENTS OF THE BEHAVIORAL DIALOGUE

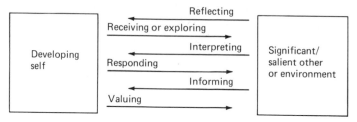

focuses on the status of the participants before and after the interaction. The "after" status of the developing self should indicate the occurrence of receiving, responding, and valuing, while that of the significant/salient other (or the environment) should show evidence of reflecting or interpreting behavior. The interaction itself is a moving picture, and, as in television's instant replay of sports events, the minute the motion is stopped for examination, the action is lost.

The psychological events occurring within the behavioral dialogue can be evaluated according to Rogers' (1959) theory of self and interpretation of interactive events. The teacher's role as significant/salient other in the behavioral dialogue resembles that of a Rogerian therapist in one major respect: the teacher must feel and demonstrate unconditional acceptance of the pupil as a person, just as the therapist feels "unconditional positive regard" for the patient. In order to do this, the teacher must feel secure and nondefensive about his or her own personal and professional role in the relationship.

The extent to which teachers accept themselves, their role, and the pupil determines the extent to which they can, if nominated, function *positively* in the role of significant/salient other. Teachers who can express unconditional acceptance of pupils have acquired both self-knowledge and awareness. Through self-knowledge they recognize their own values and the biases that might color their perception of others; and through self-awareness they can assess the effects of their behavior on pupils. Teachers who are comfortable and nondefensive in their role can acknowledge their own limitations while accepting those of their pupils. They do not perceive pupils as an extension of themselves or as a reflection of their personal and professional adequacy. Instead they see pupils as individuals engaged in a learning process and understand that pupils' performances and products reflect the nature of their previous experiences. Teachers' unconditional acceptance of themselves and their students allows them to be sympathetic toward and supportive of pupils and at the same time constructively critical of their performances and products. In other words, they are able to use their power as significant others to produce *positive* change in pupils. In discussing this aspect of the physician's role in guiding a client toward self-correction, Freud (1963, p. 158) commented,

> ... it is not the same thing to know a thing in oneself and to hear it from someone outside oneself; the physician takes the part of this significant outsider; he makes use of the influence which one human being can exercise over another.

Teachers also make use of this influence—and the extent to which they accept themselves and their pupils determines whether its effect will be positive or negative.

The dialogue between pupil and teacher is more extensive, multifaceted, and uncontrolled than that between Rogerian therapists and their clients. Classroom dialogues are often subject to influences beyond the control of both teacher and pupil. And the degree to which a classroom dialogue is positive or therapeutic depends on the teacher's ability to personally and professionally respond to the cognitive and affective needs of pupils *within the structure and constraints of the classroom*. While our theoretical framework assumes that teachers function as significant or salient others in the lives of their pupils, we must take care to give them neither all the credit nor all the blame for the self-concepts of those pupils. We must remember that other factors also affect pupil self-concept. Biological and sociological factors, for example, interact with the psychological experiences from which self-concept is acquired. This interaction of "nature and nurture" in shaping one's life and self-concept is illustrated particularly well by the self-appraisal of Nate Shaw, a poor black sharecropper whose insights appear throughout this volume:

> I just happen to be one of a different spirit. I've learned many a thing that's profitable to me, and I've learned a heap that aint profitable, but to learn anything at all is a blessin. And I've learned that whatever is in a person, a heap of his conditions is created in him by his life, and for the rest, he's born that way. In many cases I got a quick thought and a quick mind. So definitely until sometimes I think I harms myself, I acts too quickly. I can't help it though, I was natured that way.
>
> *Nate Shaw in T. Rosengarten, 1974.* All God's dangers: the life of Nate Shaw, *p. 546.*

THE SELF AND SELF-CONCEPT

Because the role of significant other is usually filled by a parent, we generally look for the source of early self-concepts in the values, attitudes, and behaviors of the parents. The child's teachers and peers, however, may also serve as significant or salient others.

In examining the relationship between teacher behavior and pupil self-concept, we are indeed assuming that teachers function as significant or salient others. We are suggesting that their reflections and interpretations of the pupil's "self" form the content of psychological experiences which the pupil will internalize, organize, and incorporate into a self-concept. Considering this broad assumption in relation to the function of significant and salient others, it is apparent that the pupil's needs and values determine whether or not the teacher will serve in that role. Furthermore, the pupil's values and physiological state will determine which teacher behaviors will contribute to the pupil's psychological experiences and in turn affect the development of self-concept. Theoretically, then, in order to identify teacher behaviors associated with pupil self-concept we must start by hypothesizing relationships between specific teacher behaviors and pupil values—relationships that will have predictable effects on pupil self-concept.

To establish a basis from which to hypothesize such relationships and from which to examine pupil values in reference to pupil self-concepts, we must first have an operating definition of "self-concept."

When we theorize that a concept of "self" is acquired by an individual through relationships with others and the environment, we are utilizing the theoretical constructs of the self-as-process, the self-as-doer, and the self-as-object. Though the self-as-process and the self-as-doer are often used to describe the same phenomena, we are separating these phenomena into two categories and using both terms: self-as-process refers to the psychological processes of thinking, feeling, remembering, perceiving, while self-as-doer describes the physical acts or mechanical performances that are observed, reflected, and evaluated by the "self" and others. The self-as-object is generally defined as the attitudes, feelings, and thoughts about one's self. The self-as-doer participates in a relationship; the self-as-process experiences the relationship; and the perceptions of the self-as-doer and the feelings of the self-as-process become attitudes and beliefs about the self-as-object. A concept of self is a product of psychological processes applied to psychological experiences, a product which in turn affects the individual's response to new processes and experiences. Most of us employ the concepts of self-as-process, self-as-doer, and self-as-object in everyday conversation. And most of us demonstrate that our current self-concept is an active participant in the formation of tomorrow's self-concept. The phrases, "I think," "I feel," "I am," "I can," "I'm a person who," "If I can . . . today, then tomorrow I will be . . . ," all reflect the concepts of self-as-process, self-as-doer, and self-as-object, and demonstrate that the present concept of self actively guides and directs future behavior.

The "self" defined as both process and product becomes the foundation on which to build both a general theory of self-concept formation and an operating definition of the self-concept as product. Like a model of biological cell division, a theory of self-concept formation describes a *process;* like a model of a cell, the definition of the self-concept describes a *form* without specifying its characteristic uniqueness. But, can the psychological construct of "self-concept," which is first of all considered unique to every individual, be represented as having *constant* elements of form that, as in the cell, allow for uniqueness and specialization?

In discussing problems of personality theory, Kluckholn reportedly observed that "a man is in some respects like all other men, in other respects like some other men, and in still other respects like no other man" (Wepman and Heine 1963). In presenting a general theory of self-concept formation, we propose to define the construct of self-concept at its most general level, focusing on those aspects wherein it appears to be alike in all persons. With this purpose in mind, we reviewed a broad range of "self" and "personality" theories and found in Allport's (1961) concept of the evolving senses of self a model of "self" adaptable to our needs in that they provided inclusive categories that together adequately illustrate the form—the components—of a general self-concept. Allport identifies the rudimentary senses of self as seven aspects that emerge in a developmental sequence:

First three years of life	Aspect 1: Sense of bodily self
	Aspect 2: Sense of continuing self-identity
	Aspect 3: Self-esteem, pride
Four to six	Aspect 4: The extension of self
	Aspect 5: The self-image
Six to twelve	Aspect 6: The self as rational coper
Adolescence	Aspect 7: Propriate striving

The developmental sequences, stages, processes and hierarchies of other theorists were then aligned to establish rough parallels so that we could examine the definitions and descriptions within these parallels for evidence of the physiological and psychological states of the theoretical "self," i.e., the identified nature, and the environmental conditions and behaviors of significant others described and implied, i.e., the elements of nurture, that would create the behavioral dialogues from which the senses of self would theoretically be conceived.

In many instances comparative references creating these parallels were provided by the authors themselves. For example, Krathwohl *et al.* (1964) compared the levels of internalization with the stages of moral development in Peck and Havighurst's (1960) study of character types. Peck and Havighurst have made comparisons between the stages of moral development represented in their character typology and the stages of Freud's theory of psychosexual development which is also a reference for Erikson's (1963)

Table 1.1 Parallel of infancy across theories

	Age	**Allport** Emerging sense of self	**Freud** Psycho-sexual stages	**Erikson** Eight stages of man	**Peck-Havighurst** Character typology	**Krathwohl** et al. Internalizing
Infancy	Birth	Sense of bodily self	Oral	Oral-sensory Basic trust vs. mis-trust		
	1				Amoral	Receiving
				Muscular-anal		
	2	Sense of self-identity	Anal	Autonomy vs. shame		
					Expedient	
						Responding
	3	Sense of self-esteem	Phallic	Locomotor-genital Initiative vs. guilt		

epigenetic theory of the ages of man. Table 1.1 illustrates the process of paralleling the infancy period across these theories.

The experiences of the infant, whether referenced to body zones, cognitive processes, or physiological needs, occur within the behavioral dialogue as we have defined it, and the behavior of significant others, such as the nursing or toilet-training mother, contain reflections, responses, and interpretations of the ingestive, biting, retentive, and eliminative activities of the developing self. We can infer from each theory the ideal model who proceeds apace with standards of physical, cognitive, or psychosexual and social development. We can also infer from each theory the nature of the condition or experience that produces those effects wherein some persons are like or unlike the ideal model. The physical, experiential, and environmental differences and deficiencies that result in character types, personality traits, and behavioral patterns described by theorists must be considered a part of self-concept development.

The self-conceptualizations that emerged from this process of examining and applying the construct of the behavioral dialogue to a variety of theories fell into categories roughly similar to those proposed by Allport. Our model of the General Self-Concept uses five of Allport's category titles, adapting them by reordering and redefining the content of each category in accordance with our own theory.

THE GENERAL SELF-CONCEPT

The General Self-Concept consists of five senses of self: The Sense of Bodily Self, the Sense of Self-Identity, the Sense of Self-Extension, the Sense of Self-Esteem, and the Sense of Self-Image.

This model of the General Self-Concept represents components of a psychological form that are consistent and common to all self-concepts. It may be considered a psychological outline providing the major heading and five subheadings designed to cover the topic. As an outline, it is an appropriate and useful tool for describing the psychological construct of self-concept, either collectively or individually. Using the descriptive content of each category we can identify beliefs about the self that differentiate individuals, characterize groups, or apply to large populations. Just as the biological form of the human body allows us to describe each human being as like all others in some respects, like some others in some respects, and unlike any other in some respects, the model of the General Self-Concept, with its five senses of self, allows us to describe the similarities between, differences among, and idiosyncrasies of pupil self-concepts.

It is difficult to visually represent the General Self-Concept without losing the interactive, interrelated, and interdependent nature of the component senses. The Sense of Bodily Self can be described as the dominant sense of self that emerges first in an individual's life, and should be viewed as the primary or central core of the conceptualized self. The senses of self are generally acquired in a developmental sequence, but the incomplete circles in the model (Fig. 1.1) suggest that in a normal, healthy individual, no sense of self is ever "finished" or entirely separated from the other senses.

Although these five senses of self are truly divisible only as psychological abstractions, we can find examples of our own behaviors and those reported

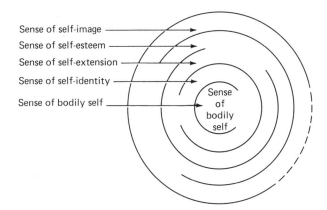

Fig. 1.1 The general self-concept as five senses of self.

in literature that illustrate the presence and functioning of one or more identifiable senses of self as we have defined them. To test the utility of our model
as a tool for describing and organizing self-conceptualizations, we applied it
to the autobiographical writings of individuals who represent a broad spectrum
of physical and social phenomena and experiences. Quotations from the
writings of these individuals are used throughout the following chapters to
confirm the presence of the five senses of self in very different personalities,
with very different values, and different experiences. These individuals are
alike in that each one of them has achieved sufficient recognition of individual
contributions to warrant the publication of their autobiographical writings.
But the diversity in the nature of their achievements and the values represented in their public recognition cover the broadest spectrum to be found in
the literature.

Below are definitions of the five categories of self-concept, each illustrated
with an autobiographical example. These definitions and illustrations are not
intended to describe fully the process or products of self-concept formation.
They are meant only to clarify the categories of general self-concept, each of
which is more fully discussed in the remaining chapters.

The Bodily Self

The sense of self differentiated from others and the environment (individuality);
the sense of self as a physical entity having form, substance, and appearance; the
sense of a continuing self with a general sense of security–insecurity for the self,
acceptance–rejection of the self, and trust–mistrust of others and the environment.

Helen Keller:

**I do not remember when I first realized that I was different from other
people; but I knew it before my teacher came to me. I had noticed
my mother and my friends did not use signs as I did when they wanted
anything done, but talked with their mouths. Sometimes I stood between two persons who were conversing and touched their lips.**

**Two little children were seated on the veranda steps one hot July
afternoon. One was black as ebony, with little bunches of fuzzy hair
tied with shoestrings sticking out all over her head like corkscrews.
The other was white, with long golden curls. One child was six years
old, the other two or three years older. The younger child was blind
—that was I—and the other was Martha Washington.**

Helen Keller, 1968. The story of my life, pp. 20, 24–25.

Self-Identity

The sense of self affiliated with others and the environment, having social membership and role identity; the sense of self as both subject and object; the sense of self
as related to others by communication.

Nate Shaw:

It's stamped in me, in my mind, the way I been treated, the way I have seed other colored people treated—couldn't never go by what you think or say, had to come up to the white man's orders.

Nate Shaw in T. Rosengarten, 1974. All God's dangers: The life of Nate Shaw, *p. 109.*

Self-Extension

The sense of self as doer, learner, and knower expressed as a Performing Self; the sense of self-representation and self-sustention through behaviors of the Performing Self; the sense of an unknown self experienced in the feelings of the self and confronted in behavior.

St. Augustine:

In the declamation, the boy won most applause who most strikingly reproduced the passions of anger and sorrow according to the "character" of the persons presented and who clothed it all in the most suitable language. What is it now to me, O my true Life, my God, that my declaiming was applauded above that of many of my classmates and fellow students?

St. Augustine, 1955. Augustine: confessions and enchiridion, *46–47.*

Nate Shaw:

He didn't know what was in me but I was growin to knowledge every day. Had no book learnin to speak of but I got to where I thought I could do anything just as good as anybody else.

Nate Shaw in T. Rosengarten, 1974. All God's dangers, the life of Nate Shaw, *p. 53.*

Self-Esteem

The sense of self-affirmation, recognition, and confirmation of impact on others and the environment.

Nate Shaw:

I've gotten along in this world by studying the races and knowin that I was one of the underdogs. I was under many rulins. . . . I got tired of it but no help did I know; weren't nobody to back me up. . . . I've taken every kind of insult and went on. Still, I always knowed to give the white man his time of day or else he's ready to knock me in the head. I just aint goin to go nobody's way against my own self. First thing of all—I care for myself and respect myself.

Nate Shaw in T. Rosengarten, 1974. All God's dangers, the life of Nate Shaw, *p. 545.*

Self-Image

The sense of past and present value-based images of self; the sense of a value-based Ideal Self.

Nate Shaw:

I was a poor young colored man but I had the strength of a man who comes to know himself, all in me from my toes to my head. I meant right and no wrong; I meant to get up and out of that old rut and act a man. I didn't want to marry no man and no woman's daughter, take her off and perish her to death because I couldn't support her, just an old hack through the world.

Nate Shaw in T. Rosengarten, 1974. All God's dangers, the life of Nate Shaw, *p. 82.*

The autobiographies from which the quotations above are drawn are those of three unique and diverse individuals. St. Augustine's *Confessions,* written A.D. 398, is commonly credited as the first autobiographical writing. His attempt to chronicle his long spiritual and intellectual journey to Christianity provides unusually clear examples of the five components of self-concept. As the most promising of three children in a lower middle-class Roman family, St. Augustine was given a liberal education, at some expense to his parents, in the hope that he would become a professional teacher, lawyer, or administrator. His writings indicate that his mother most assuredly played the role of the significant other in his life. Because St. Augustine was an unusually gifted man of another age and culture, his self-reporting offers an interesting contrast to that of other more contemporary authors.

Helen Keller (*The story of my life,* 1968) was born in 1880 into a comfortable, Southern family living in Tuscumbia, Alabama. Her father was a captain in the Confederate Army and the owner of a small plantation. In the twentieth month of her life, Helen Keller contracted an illness that left her deaf and blind. Three months before her seventh birthday Anne Sullivan arrived to begin teaching her. Writings by Miss Sullivan, included in Helen Keller's autobiography, have provided us with interesting illustrations of a teacher functioning as a significant other in a child's life. Helen Keller's experiences were, by virtue of her family's financial and social position, very broad. But her access to these experiences was extremely limited due to her physical deprivation. The concepts of self reported by Helen Keller are those she was able to acquire from physically restricted exploration of a broad cultural environment and limited access to many sources of reflection and interpretation.

All God's dangers, the life of Nate Shaw, (T. Rosengarten 1974) is rich in examples of the five senses of self. Nate Shaw, an uneducated black man, born in Alabama in 1885, never learned to read or write. His spoken recollections were tape recorded, transcribed, and edited by Theodore Rosengarten to produce an autobiography which retains Nate Shaw's unique form of self-expression and his great gift for narration. Born into a poor sharecropper's family, Nate Shaw lived virtually all of his life in one small area of rural Alabama. Although he speaks admiringly of his mother, it was clearly Nate's father who played the role of significant other in his life while his white employers and his environment served as salient others. His illiteracy obscures neither his intelligence nor his keen insight. In contrast to the deprivations of Helen Keller, Nate Shaw's deprivations were environmental and social, rather than physical. Because Helen Keller and Nate Shaw were both born in Alabama in the 1880s, yet lived such different lives, their autobiographies provide interesting comparisons and particularly good support for our representation of the self-concept. The "self" reflected and interpreted to a blind, deaf, intelligent, educated white girl from an upper-class family, and the "self" reflected to an intelligent black youth from an impoverished sharecropper's family, though very different, can both be accommodated by our five-category General Self-Concept model.

There are other dimensions of individual nature and nurture represented in the autobiographies of Maya Angelou (1969), a black woman, author, actor, and dancer with both rural and urban background experiences; Eleanor Roosevelt (1961) a white woman from the upper social class, with a famous family name and identity; Muhammad Ali (1975), a black man whose physical prowess and personal convictions gained the attention of people all over the world; Bertrand Russell (1967), a man with special talents and a unique British background; and Lawrence Welk (1971), the son of German emigrants whose "Champagne Music" became the symbol of his personal and national success and acceptance. Within the self-reporting of these and many others we have found support for the commonality of the General Self-Concept and have used examples of this support liberally throughout the chapters of this book.

We have presented the General Self-Concept as a psychological construct which incorporates the theoretical concepts of the self-as-process, the self-as-object, and the self-as-doer. Hereafter, we will use the terms "self-concept" and "general self-concept" interchangeably to represent this construct. We have identified and defined the Senses of Bodily Self, Self-Identity, Self-Extension, Self-Esteem, and Self-Image as the five components of the General Self-Concept. Each of these five senses of self is also a concept of self and is defined the same way whether described as a concept or a sense of self.

THE ORGANIZATIONAL SCHEMA

When we began reviewing the research on teacher behaviors related to pupil self-concept, we defined teacher behaviors very broadly. We were interested in all teacher traits—interaction patterns, instructional styles, and self-reported or behaviorally manifested attitudes, values, and beliefs about pupils, pupil roles, and teacher roles. The term "self-concept" was also broadly defined to include not only research relating specifically to self-concept, but also that relating to any of the innumerable self-construct terms (self-confidence, self-evaluation, self-acceptance) or to any pupil-referenced variable in the affective domain. Even within this broad scope, however, we found few research studies relating teacher behavior to pupil affective variables. This scarcity, along with the wide applicability of our theoretical framework, prompted us to expand our research base to include any study suggesting a promising teacher variable, regardless of whether or not the study had been conducted in a classroom situation.

Organizing such a broad range of studies—an already challenging task—was further complicated by the fact that self-construct terms are used interchangeably in the literature. Furthermore, investigators often fail to clearly define their interpretations of these terms. However, after examining the literature, we concluded that the terms self-concept, self-image, self-perception, and self-identity, are generally used to represent an individual's total concept of self or the systems of beliefs, attitudes, and hypotheses that individuals hold about themselves. Self-esteem, self-value, and self-worth usually refer to a self-judgment made in accordance with internalized standards and values. Self-perception, qualified as realistic or unrealistic, self-awareness, and self-knowledge generally represent a comparison between the individual's internalized measure of self and some external standard. The ideal self usually indicates an hypothesized model of the individual's self projected in accordance with the self's values and ideals. Finally, the psychological construct of "self" is generally and broadly assumed to be an holistic representation of the self-as-process, the self-as-object, and the self-as-doer, without reference to the conflicts among "self" theorists over the properties of the self (Allport 1961; Buhler 1962; Chein 1944; Erikson 1963; Koffka 1935; Lundholm 1940; Rogers 1959; Sherif and Cantril 1947; Sullivan 1953; Snygg and Combs 1949; and Symonds 1951).

Though we were able to make these generalizations, the lack of consistency in the use and interpretation of the self-construct terms dictated that we examine each study and classify it according to our own model of the General Self-Concept. In some instances, simply applying the definitions of the five senses of self to the descriptions and interpretations of a self-construct term was sufficient to determine whether, for example, a described change in self-perception actually referred to a change in general self-concept or to a change in one or more of the five senses of self. However, when descriptions and definitions were insufficient or unclear, we applied our theoretical framework to the reported interaction to identify the nature of the psychological experience described and then related the affective variable thus identified to the definitions of the five senses of self in order to determine the proper category for the study. Of course, this categorization process was not nearly as simple and clear-cut as it sounds, and we suspect that we may have made some quantum leaps of faith in determining the intent of certain investigators. However, the free hand we have taken with the research was dictated by its own limitations and deemed necessary in order to organize what had initially seemed a totally unmanageable array of studies.

Having classified all studies into the proper self-concept categories, we then linked the teacher behavior variables named in these studies to the assumed values of the pupil in order to hypothesize a relationship between specific teacher behaviors and the self-concept of the student.

For each category of the General Self-Concept we asked the question, "Which of the teacher behaviors reported in the literature would be valued by the developing self?" The answer to this question came from our review of the content emphases provided by self-concept, child development, and personality theories (e.g., Adler 1927; Sullivan 1953; Murray 1938; Rogers 1959; Peck and Havighurst 1960; Freud 1963; and Erikson 1963) that had provided environmental variables, social experiences, and "significant others" behaviors which, by virtue of their affective content, could be theoretically related to a particular sense of the self-concept.

Through this process, a number of variables relating to one or more of the five senses of self had been identified, including behaviors that indicated specific states of the self-concept. For purposes of illustration, variables relating to one of the five senses of self—the Sense of Bodily Self—are charted in Table 1.2. The Sense of Bodily Self is defined in terms of three components (A, B, and C), and therefore, the variables are listed under the particular component(s) to which they relate.

In answer to our original question—"Which specific behaviors (conditions, experiences) related to the sense of bodily self would be valued by the developing self?"—we can now hypothesize several value relationships.

For example, the developing self theoretically would value behaviors of significant/salient others reflecting his or her appearance (2B in Table 1.2), since these behaviors provide psychological experiences from which to form a concept of his or her physical form. The effect of these behaviors on the concept of Bodily Self could be positive or negative, depending on the nature of the reflection. In the same way, it can be hypothesized that the behaviors listed in block 2A of the chart would be similarly valued since they affect the developing self's sense of individuality. And the behaviors under 2C would also be valued since they act upon the feelings of physical and psychological safety which are necessary for a positive sense of continuing self. In this same vein, behaviors under both 2A and 2C—behaviors that reflect acceptance, rejection, or indifference to the developing self but have no apparent relationship to his or her behavior—say, in effect, "There's something good about you," or

Table 1.2 Hypothesized variables affecting the sense of bodily self

Type of variables	Three components of the sense of bodily self		
	A. Sense of self differentiated from others and environment	B. Sense of self as having physical form and attributes	C. Sense of a continuous self
1. Experience and environmental behaviors			Physical comfort/ discomfort Safety/danger Nurturance/ deprivation Known/unknown
2. Reflecting, interpreting, and informing behaviors of significant/ salient others	Accepting/rejecting/ignoring (unrelated to developing self's performance), i.e., attending, responding, fairness, unfairness, hostility. Individuality/ mechanical processing Controlling	Physical attributes (i.e., size, sex, ethnicity, appearance, race, age, intelligence, health, habits)	Accepting/ rejecting/ ignoring (unrelated to developing self's performance), i.e., attending, responding, fairness, unfairness, hostility. Individualizing/ mechanical processing Controlling
3. Behaviors of developing self related to sense of bodily self	Stress, anxiety	Withdrawal/ aggression	Stress, anxiety Dependency Withdrawal/ aggression Conformance

"There's something wrong or bad about you." Though such behaviors may also affect the Sense of Self-Esteem, theoretically they are more strongly related to the general sense of well-being or the general state of anxiety and insecurity that determines the sense of continuing self.

Similar hypotheses can be posited for all cells on the chart. Such hypotheses help to identify the focal area of self for measuring and evaluating self-concept change and also provide a basis for planning and testing therapeutic psychological experience.

When teacher behavior variables are charted in this way, it is apparent that they often affect more than one of the senses of self. The teacher's praise of a pupil's performance could, for example, affect the pupil's Sense of Bodily Self if the praise were given for a *physical* performance. Or the praise could influence the Sense of Self-Identity by giving the pupil a special, identifying quality—or the Sense of Self-Extension by increasing the pupil's perception of self as a performer. However, because praise is most clearly related to Sense of Self-Esteem, if we were measuring pupil change due to teacher praise, we would focus our measurement on the pupil's Sense of Self-Esteem. Although problems in categorizing teacher behaviors are certain to arise, our theoretical framework offers a rational basis for classifying variables and serves as a source of alternative hypotheses for testing as well.

The theories on which our self-concept framework is based are those used to explain *developmental* concepts, and we suspect it may be difficult to disregard the developmental aspects of the sense of self labels when they are used as a classification system. However, as a category, the Sense of Self-Esteem includes *all* investigations related to that sense of self, regardless of the age, sex, socioeconomic status, or other defined characteristics of the pupil population studied.

At the beginning of each chapter devoted to a Sense of Self, we have supplied a process definition which offers a theory of self-concept development. We have also related teacher variables, conditions and experiences, and pupil behaviors to each of these definitions. If you are a teacher or are studying to be a teacher, you will probably be dismayed to find that most of the "knowledge" on which we have based our suggestions for affective teaching practices is still largely theoretical. If you are a researcher, you may be overjoyed to find an area of educational research in which so much remains to be done. As Hamlet said, "There are more things in heaven and earth, Horatio, than are dreamt of in your philosophy." There are a great many more things in the area of teacher behavior and pupil self-concept than we have covered in this book. We do believe, however, that our theoretical framework can be used to generate enough hypotheses to keep teachers and researchers busy for some time.

REFERENCES

Adler, A. 1927. *Practice and theory of individual psychology.* New York: Harcourt, Brace, and World.

Ali, M. 1975. *The greatest, Muhammad Ali.* With Richard Durham. New York: Random House.

Allport, G. W. 1961. *Pattern and growth in personality*. New York: Holt, Rinehart and Winston.

Angelou, M. 1969. *I know why the caged bird sings*. New York: Random House.

Bloom, B. S. 1973. Individual differences in achievement. In L. J. Rubin (ed.), *Facts and feelings in the classroom*. New York: Viking.

————, M. D. Engelhart, E. J. Furst, W. H. Hill, and D. R. Krathwohl 1956. *Taxonomy of educational objectives: the classification of educational goals. Handbook I: Cognitive domain*. New York: McKay.

Buhler, C. 1962. Genetic aspects of the self. In E. Harms (ed.), *Fundamentals of psychology: the psychology of the self*. Annals New York Academic Sciences **96:** 730–764.

Chein, I. 1944. The awareness of self and the structure of the ego. *Psychology Review* **51:** 304–314.

Erikson, E. H. 1963. *Childhood and society*. (2nd ed. rev.) New York: Norton.

Freud, S. 1963. *Character and culture*. Philip Rieff (ed.) New York: Collier Books.

Keller, H. 1968. *The story of my life*. New York: Lancer.

Koffka, K. 1935. *Principles of gestalt psychology*. New York: Harcourt, Brace, and World.

Krathwöhl, D. R., B. S. Bloom, and B. B. Masia (eds.) 1964. *Taxonomy of educational objectives: the classification of educational goals. Handbook II: Affective domain*. New York: McKay.

Lundholm, H. 1940. Reflections upon the nature of the psychological self. *Psychology Review* **47:** 110–127.

Mead, G. H. 1934. *Mind, self, and society from the standpoint of a social behaviorist*. Chicago: University of Chicago Press.

Murray, H. A. (and collaborators) 1938. *Explorations in personality*. New York: Oxford.

Peck, R. F., R. J. Havighurst, R. Cooper, J. Lilienthal, and D. More, 1960. *The psychology of character development*. New York: Wiley.

Rogers, C. R. 1959. A theory of therapy, personality and interpersonal relationships, as developed in the client-centered framework. In S. Koch (ed.), *Psychology: a study of science* (Vol. 3). New York: McGraw-Hill, 1959.

Roosevelt, E. 1961. *Autobiography of Eleanor Roosevelt*. New York: Harper & Row.

Rosengarten, T. 1974. *All God's dangers: the life of Nate Shaw*. New York: Knopf.

Russell, B. 1967. *The autobiography of Bertrand Russell*. Boston: Little, Brown.

Sherif, M., and H. Cantril 1947. *The psychology of ego-involvements*. New York: Wiley.

Snygg, D., and A. W. Combs 1949. *Individual behavior*. New York: Harper.

Sperry, L. 1972. *Learning performance and individual differences.* Glenview, Ill.: Scott, Foresman.

St. Augustine 1955. *Augustine: confessions and enchiridion.* Vol. VII. Albert Cook Outler (ed.). Philadelphia: The Westminster Press.

Sullivan, H. S. 1953. *The interpersonal theory of psychiatry.* New York: Norton.

Symonds, P. M. 1951. *The ego and the self.* New York: Appleton-Century-Crofts.

Weinstein, G., and M. D. Fantini (eds.) 1970. *Toward humanistic education: a curriculum of affect.* New York: Praeger.

Welk, L. 1971. *Wunnerful, wunnerful! The autobiography of Lawrence Welk.* With Bernice McGeehan. Englewood Cliffs, N.J.: Prentice-Hall.

Wepman, J. M., and R. W. Heine (eds.) 1963. Introduction to *Concepts of personality.* Chicago: Aldine.

CHAPTER 2

The Teacher as Significant Other and Controller of Pupil Environment

Every person who will ever occupy a bed in a mental hospital, every parent, every professional man, every criminal, every priest, was once in some teacher's first grade. Somewhere, sometime, everyone in our society has known a teacher who might have influenced him. The teacher's opportunity for impact is thus both broad and deep.

Fuller, Bown, and Peck 1967. Creating climates for growth, *p. 5.*

What could weigh more heavily on the dedicated and caring teacher than the implications of the statement above? Almost every adult can tell a story beginning "I had a teacher who. . . ." and go on to recite the remembered vices or virtues—the impact—of an individual whose name he or she cannot recall or "will never forget." This impact is not only assumed by society and recalled by former pupils, it is also felt by teachers themselves. While it is unrealistic to assume that teachers are constantly preoccupied with the long-term consequences of a child's classroom experience, many have, like Ginott (1972, pp. 16–17), sensed at least an immediate, day-to-day power over pupils:

> **I have come to a frightening conclusion. I am the decisive element in the classroom. It is my personal approach that creates the climate. It is my daily mood that makes the weather. As a teacher I possess tremendous power to make a child's life miserable or joyous. I can be a tool of torture or an instrument of inspiration. I can humiliate or humor, hurt or heal. In all situations it is my response that decides whether a crisis will be escalated or de-escalated, a child humanized or de-humanized.**

This power to "humiliate or humor, hurt or heal" is clearly illustrated by Branan (1972), who reports that college students, asked to describe their most negative and growth-inhibiting experiences, overwhelmingly listed interpersonal situations, the great majority of which involved interaction with a

35

teacher. (Parents came in a distant second.) The incidents described, which concerned humiliation in front of the class, embarrassment, unfairness in evaluation, and destruction of self-confidence, occurred more often in high school than college and more often in elementary school than junior high.

Such documentation of the teacher's influence is, however, unnecessary. It is both theoretically and popularly accepted that teachers have the power and position to affect the self-concept development of pupils. In our society, the relationship between pupil and teacher is the only child-adult relationship that approximates the expanse of time, stability of place, constancy of function, and variety of opportunity for interaction that characterize the parent–child dyad. Perhaps it is the similarity of these two relationships that has led to a persistent belief in the teacher's ability to influence the "character" development of pupils as well as their acquisition of academic knowledge.

The hypothesis that teachers function as significant or salient others, informing pupils, interpreting events for them, reflecting images to them, and shaping the school environment, appears to be popularly accepted. This being the case, we should step beyond assumptions, personal memories, expert admonitions, and attitudes of "kismet" toward teaching, and test this hypothesis. If parents, pupils, psychologists, teachers and other educators all believe that teachers influence the process of self-concept development (and there is sufficient evidence in educational literature to affirm that this is, indeed, the case), they should be willing to cooperate with researchers in an attempt to identify the personal attributes and professional behaviors that affect the teacher's performance as significant other and controller of pupil environment.

TEACHERS AS A RESEARCH POPULATION

Excluding private school teachers, we are considering a population of over two million individuals teaching in public school classrooms located in urban, suburban and rural settings throughout the nation.

Approximately two-thirds of these teachers are female, and the remaining male third is concentrated primarily at the secondary or high school level. Beyond the secondary level, teaching ceases to be a predominantly female occupation, and proportional sex representation figures are completely reversed (National Education Association 1971).

As this shift indicates, teaching reflects the social and economic values of our society, including an hierarchical concept of the worth of education and educators. The stereotypes, "pretty young schoolmarm" and "old maid schoolteacher," reflect the female's social role and occupational opportunity, rather than aptitudes and characteristics that distinguish teachers and the teaching profession. In fact, we dare to suggest that the female's selection of teaching as a career is *still* influenced to a greater extent by socially determined limitations of choice and opportunity than by personality characteristics or particular aptitudes. And the same social and economic values that dispose females toward teaching may have the opposite effect on males, causing them to bypass teaching and to select a profession considered more appropriate for men from the generally broader spectrum of occupational opportunities open to them.

However, the social conditions influencing career choice and pursuit are rapidly changing, and research on teacher personality and behavior conducted prior to 1960 (Ryans 1960; Peterson 1964) cannot be assumed to apply to the current teacher population. Hopefully, continued research will identify what Biddle (1964) terms "main sequence variables" and Borich and Madden (1977) term "preoperational variables"—i.e., formative experiences, personality characteristics and teaching behaviors, the immediate and long-term classroom effects of which persist across time and changing teacher populations.

Research efforts to discriminate between teachers and the general population are well chronicled by Getzels and Jackson (1963). Though the studies they report measure a variety of personality characteristics on a variety of instruments, none successfully differentiates teachers from the general population. Attempts to predict teaching success from personality traits and to identify "good" or "effective" teachers have to date produced a collection of variables so general that they apply to any "nice" person. In the opinion of Getzels and Jackson, these results are neither helpful nor informative. Yet, we must expect results like these as long as the "good" teacher is conceptualized in terms of a single model, equally "effective" with all pupils, in all subjects, at all levels, for all psychomotor, cognitive, and affective objectives, in all teaching-learning situations. It should be no surprise that the only variables generalizing across all of these factors are those which characterize the nice, helpful, socially acceptable individual who is appreciated by most people, everywhere. If an equally global and unitary concept were applied to the definition of a master marksman, and performance criteria ignored, the definition would be similarly broadened to become "a person with a gun and good vision," two essential but not delimiting or distinguishing characteristics of the marksman.

What is needed to remedy this situation, according to Getzels and Jackson, is the identification of "specific and distinctive" components of the teacher's personality. In pursuit of this end, these authors note three obstacles to such identification: (1) definitions, (2) instrumentation, and (3) criteria. In a more recent evaluation of teacher behavior research, Ornstein (1971) found these obstacles still unsurmounted; and our own review of the research on teacher behavior and pupil self-concept was no more encouraging. Yet, recognizing the limitations of the research and operating from the theoretical position that teachers function as significant others and therefore affect the self-concept development of pupils, we can examine the studies presented herein and attempt to interpret the results in light of that theory.

THE TEACHER AS SIGNIFICANT OTHER

By the time a child reaches school age, a developmentally and experientially limited concept of self is already formed and operating. Even those children who, in ever increasing numbers at ever decreasing ages, are placed in nursery schools and day-care centers have operating self-concepts subject to the formative influences of their daily psychological experiences.

Regardless of the age at which a child enters an educational system, such exposure expands the psychological experiences available to the child and extends his or her behavioral dialogue to include teachers and the new learning environment. Thus, important new contributors to the developing self-concept are introduced into the child's life.

Among the adults involved in caring for and educating children there appears to be an understanding that the mantle of authority over a child, previously held exclusively by the parents and delegated to others only at their discretion, is now shared with individuals having societal, rather than personal, parental designation and endorsement. Should it then be assumed that the parental role of significant other in the child's life is also shared by the teacher or caretaker?

If we maintain the theoretical posture that the developing self alone decides who shall function as a significant other, the answer to this question is a qualified "No." Teachers and other adults will not automatically become significant others unless:

1. The level of the child's self-concept development dictates a need for continuing, total functioning of a significant other. This condition, similar to that in which the child chose the first significant other, forces a selection from what may be a very limited field. Placed in a new environment, the child must make a new selection, and the teacher may be the only possible candidate.

2. The parental significant others have generalized their roles to include other adults so that the child may indiscriminately accept all authoritative adults as significant others.

However, if neither of these conditions prevails, the extent to which the teacher functions as a significant or salient other may be determined by the degree of similarity between home and school. If the teacher's values, attitudes, beliefs, and perception of the child produce a reflection of the child consistent with that supplied by the parents, the teacher's functioning as a significant or salient other may be enhanced. Similarly, when the teacher *models* beliefs consonant with those of the parents—which is the case, for example, when poorly educated parents value education—the teacher's role as a significant other may be strengthened through parental support, though perhaps confined to the one shared value.

However, if the parents' values, attitudes, and beliefs conflict with those of the teacher, or if their perception and reflection of the developing self differs materially from the teacher's, the continuum from familial to institutional setting is broken, and the teacher's function as a significant or salient other may be curtailed or completely negated. Or, when new psychological experiences and positive reflections are acquired in school, the child may form concepts, beliefs, and behavioral schema that conflict with those previously absorbed in the familial setting, in which case the role of the parents as significant others may be considerably weakened.

Although breaks in the psychological continuum from home to school most commonly issue from perceptual differences between parents and teachers, they may also arise from socioeconomic or ethnic differences between the two environments. The child may find that goal-achieving behavior considered acceptable in one environment is frowned upon in the other. Accordingly, the reflected self the child perceives may change from one setting to the other, causing the child considerable internal conflict, which may be expressed behaviorally. A similar conflict may occur when the child receives divergent reflections of self from different teachers.

Individuals faced with inconsistent reflections of self can, theoretically, reduce the conflict they are experiencing by devaluing any of the dissonant reflecting sources, that is, by terminating the functions of a previously designated significant other. The source providing the more positive reflection of self, currently consonant with the child's evolving value system, better serves the needs of the developing self and is consequently more likely to be retained in resolving the conflict. In any case, when dissonance is experienced by the child as the result of two materially different self-reflections, the battle between the two reflections affects the process of self-concept development. A change in the image reflected to the child can produce a positive or negative alteration in the developing self-concept.

It can be assumed that teachers generally intend their behaviors to have a positive effect on pupils and that negative consequences of their actions are therefore inadvertent. Intent, however, does not matter to the child. It is the teacher's *behavior* to which the child responds. Therefore, teachers who are conscious of the impact of their behaviors increase the likelihood that their effects on pupils' self-concepts will be more positive. Yet, it is not enough merely to recognize one's power. The teachers must also see within that power the *means* to bring about positive pupil change. The teacher who recognizes the potential for making positive changes that is *built into* the teaching role and knows how to realize it is more likely to effect such changes. In other words, it is primarily a teacher's perception of the teaching task (including an awareness of pupil needs and pupil values) and the performance of the teaching role, that determines the degree to which a teacher will function positively in the capacity of a significant/salient other.

The effect of a teacher's perception of role and task on subsequent performance is clearly illustrated by Anne Sullivan's approach to Helen Keller, her blind and deaf pupil.

Anne Sullivan arrived to begin her teaching task three months before Helen Keller's seventh birthday. At this time Miss Sullivan perceived Helen, who had been blind and deaf since she was 20 months old, as "unresponsive and even impatient of caresses from anyone except her mother." She further described her pupil as "very quick-tempered and wilful," and observed that "nobody except her brother James has attempted to control her." Miss Sullivan tried to establish a relationship with Helen in the environment of the family home, but failed. She finally received permission, as a last resort, to take her pupil to a small cottage on the family estate where the two of them lived in relative isolation. Under these circumstances, Anne Sullivan was able to establish a relationship with Helen and in the process to become one of the world's most successful and acknowledged teachers. Using a brief item from her account of this experience and other knowledge of events and circumstances gained from Miss Keller's autobiography, we would like to reconstruct and interpret the interaction between Helen and Miss Sullivan according to our theoretical framework (Keller 1968, p. 361):

> ... I have thought about it a great deal, and the more I think, the more certain I am that obedience is the gateway through which knowledge, yes, and love, too, enter the mind of the child. As I wrote you, I meant to go slowly at first. I had an idea that I could win the love and confidence of my little pupil by the same means that I should use if she could see and hear. But I soon found that I was cut off from all the usual approaches to the child's heart. She accepted everything I did for her as a matter of course, and refused to be caressed, and there was no way of appealing to her affection or sympathy or childish love of approbation. She would or she wouldn't and there was an end of it. Thus it is, we study, plan and prepare ourselves for a task, and when the hour for action arrives, we find that the system we have followed with such labour and pride does not fit the occasion; and then there's nothing for us to do but rely on something within us, some innate capacity for knowing and doing, which we did not know we possessed until the hour of our great need brought it to light.

In this brief self-report we see a glimpse of Miss Sullivan's value system, her perception of the teaching task, and her perception of herself performing that task. We also see the operation of her beliefs, attitudes, and values on her perception of children in general and of children in the pupil role. She valued the teaching profession. She had prepared herself for her career with "labour" and "pride." She had acquired the means of winning "the love and confidence" of pupils, an indication of the way in which she perceived the teaching role and the needs and values of pupils. She proposed to use these means with her new pupil, apparently assuming that her initial caring and attending behaviors toward Helen would be received and valued (would, in other words, convey a positive reflection of self to this blind, deaf child). But Helen "accepted everything I did for her as a matter of course, and refused to be caressed" and "there was no way of appealing to her affection or sympathy or childish love of approbation." In the terms of our theoretical framework, there was no behavioral dialogue between teacher and pupil. Although Miss Sullivan wished to be a salient other and Helen had a pressing need for reflection, interpretation, and information, their interaction did not constitute a behavioral dialogue. Miss Sullivan tried to stimulate what she believed was Helen's value system, but Helen, though receiving some of Miss Sullivan's overtures, did not respond to or value these stimuli. At this time Miss Sullivan was valued neither for herself nor for the functions she performed, and, consequently, there was no behavioral dialogue from which Helen could gain new psychological experiences.

In order to change this situation, Miss Sullivan, trusting her "innate capacity for knowing and doing," suggested the following program for Helen (Keller 1968, p. 362):

> **I had a good, frank talk with Mrs. Keller, and explained to her how difficult it was going to be to do anything with Helen under the existing circumstances. I told her that in my opinion the child ought to be separated from the family for a few weeks at least—that she must learn to depend on and obey me before I could make any headway.**

The separation of Helen from her usual environment and from her "significant others" (her mother, father, and brother) created a deliberate break in the psychological and experiential continuum which normally extends from the home to the learning situation. It caused, as one might expect, a few days of total disorientation and despondence for Helen.

This removal from the home environment also made Helen totally dependent upon Miss Sullivan, who became the child's only source of reflection, interpretation, and information, though at a very primitive level. After several days, Helen's dependency elevated Miss Sullivan to the position of salient other, valued for the functions she performed. At this point Helen began the internalization process which ultimately produced the "obedient" behavior recognized by Miss Sullivan as the "gateway through which knowledge, yes, and love, too, enter the mind of the child."

This "obedience" appears to incorporate the first three levels of the internalization process. The pupil receives, responds to, and values the stimuli offered by the teacher. Helen, in order to regain her equilibrium after being uprooted from her home environment, was forced to accept and depend upon Miss Sullivan, who was her only source of psychological experiences (apart from the new and strange environment to which she had little physical access). Helen's dependence prompted the receiving, responding, and ultimately valuing behaviors that formed a "light yoke" over her. After a few days alone with Helen, Miss Sullivan reported, "You will be glad to hear that my experiment is working out finely. I have not had any trouble at all with Helen, either yesterday or today." Seven days later she added (Keller, p. 365):

> She lets me kiss her now, and when she is in a particularly gentle mood, she will sit in my lap for a minute or two; but she does not return my caresses. The great step—the step that counts—has been taken. The little savage has learned her first lesson in obedience, and finds the yoke easy. It now remains my pleasant task to direct and mould the beautiful intelligence that is beginning to stir in the child-soul.

Experiencing a break in the continuum from home to learning situation, Helen found the new reflections and interpretations of her behavior totally at variance with those she had previously received. But she did find within these new reflections consistent acceptance of herself as a person. Miss Sullivan carefully differentiated between acceptance of Helen's behavior and acceptance of Helen as an individual.

The conditions under which Miss Sullivan began teaching her pupil were extraordinary, and her pupil was extraordinary. But there are some features of this extraordinary experience that apply to ordinary teaching situations as well.

Miss Sullivan deliberately interrupted the continuum between Helen's home and learning environments and used Helen's dependency to establish a behavioral dialogue through which she ultimately gave her pupil independence. We have discussed the fact that pupils in public school classrooms sometimes experience a similar break in the home-to-school continuum, particularly those from other than middle-class families or from minority racial and ethnic groups. We have also noted that in such situations pupils may experience a difference between the self reflected in the home and that reflected in the classroom. These dissonant reflections can cause the pupil conflict, which may be behaviorally expressed as disruptive, disoriented, or dependent conduct. Such behavior, however, can be used as the basis for a behavioral dialogue. Miss Sullivan, for example, used Helen's dependence as the foundation for a relationship in which she could gain the child's confidence. She accepted Helen as an individual while Helen had her tantrums. She was supportive when Helen was despondent and unresponsive. In other words, she looked for an approach "to the child's heart."

Unlike Helen Keller, most school-age (and even preschool-age) children have acquired a system of values, social behaviors, and communication skills that almost automatically place the teacher in the role of salient other. To the majority of pupils, the word "teacher" conveys a function that will be performed for them and an authority that will be exercised over them. These pupils have already acquired and assigned varying degrees of value to the concepts of learning and authority. Since most middle-class children are taught to value these concepts highly, they are able to accept the teacher in the role of salient or significant other at the onset of the relationship. A behavioral dialogue often begins almost immediately between these pupils and the teacher, thus establishing early in the school year a source of psychological experiences that will affect their self-concepts. Some pupils, of course, may value authority but not learning, (or at least not "school"). For these pupils teachers become salient others only because they are valued as authority figures; but this valuing, though limited, provides sufficient basis for a behavioral dialogue between pupil and teacher. Once accepted as a salient other, the teacher can affect not only the pupil's self-concept but also the pupil's value system, and in so doing perhaps bring about a positive value for the learning experience.

Pupils who value neither authority nor learning—or who interpret these concepts in a manner inconsistent with the teacher's role, (who, for example, view authority in terms of physical power or personal dominance) do not provide the teacher with a "ready-made" entrance to their value system. And if teachers are ever to function as salient others in the lives of these pupils, they must find access to the pupils' values. When all other avenues are closed to teachers, they can often find such access in their role as controller of pupil environment.

THE TEACHER AS CONTROLLER OF PUPIL ENVIRONMENT

The pupil who does not accept the teacher as a significant or salient other may instead seek a reflected image in the environment of the classroom. Yet the pupil will find that the teacher is the dominant influence on this environment. It is the teacher's role to plan, organize, and manage the events occurring in the classroom. Teachers' perceptions of their role and performance of that role dictate the emotional climate of the classroom and direct the pupils' energies toward teacher-determined objectives.

We have already noted that the environment, physical and human, is an important component of each person's behavioral dialogue. Teachers alter neither the role nor the functioning of the environment in the process of self-concept formation. But they do influence the nature of the environment, and in turn the nature of the reflections, interpretations, and information transferred in the behavioral dialogue between pupil and environment. Pupils who value neither teacher-represented authority nor school-represented learning are not apt to find themselves positively reflected in an environment structured to reinforce the teacher's authoritarian role and the teacher's cognitive learning objectives. If such pupils cannot physically or emotionally withdraw from the psychological experiences incurred in this hostile atmosphere, they will continue to receive negative reflections of their impact on the environment and reinforcement of their negative estimation of authority and learning.

Teachers, however, can reach pupils like this by altering the classroom environment. Using their ability to control or influence classroom climate, teachers can not only extend their functions as salient others for pupils who accept them in that role but also gain access to the values of other pupils for whom they wish to function as salient others. By discovering and utilizing what these pupils *do* value highly, teachers can create environmental experiences that offer positive reflections of these children. The environment offers teachers several avenues through which to channel their influence: they can alter the human or personal environment, affect the interpretations supplied by the physical environment, or use classroom conditions to convey information that would be rejected by the pupil if received directly from an authoritarian source. In other words, teachers who are not valued for themselves or for their functions can still have impact on the self-concept of a pupil through their impact—planned or unplanned—on the pupil's environment.

If it appears that we are suggesting a means by which pupil values can be used to facilitate pupil control and manipulation, we can only conclude that our perception of the teaching task differs from that of the reader. Though we do acknowledge that in most classrooms pupil values are indeed used to achieve teacher control, we do not endorse this practice. It is our conviction that pupil values should be perceived, to paraphrase Anne Sullivan, as the gateway through which teachers, as significant and salient others, can reach and positively influence pupil self-concept.

Anne Sullivan's remarkable "innate capacity for knowing and doing" was perhaps the product of her own experience with blindness. She was nearly blind in early childhood, though her sight was partially restored some time after her fourteenth year when she entered the Perkins Institution to prepare for work with blind and deaf children. Perhaps it was her prolonged experience with the dependency imposed by blindness that gave her insight into the relationship between dependency and trust. And perhaps it was her own experience that convinced her of the value of independence and a positive self-concept for her pupil, Helen Keller. In any case, Anne Sullivan's extraordinary success demonstrates the power of teachers' perceptions of task, role, pupil needs, and pupil values to determine their functioning as significant/salient others and controllers of pupil environment.

Because teachers' perceptions of task, role, and pupil are so critical to their success, the source of these perceptions—i.e., teachers' own self-concept, values, and attitudes—warrants investigation. The relationship between teacher behavior and pupil self-concept cannot be fully understood until the values and concepts of self that shape teachers' perceptions (which, in turn, determine their classroom behavior) are first identified.

TEACHER SELF-CONCEPT, VALUES, AND BEHAVIOR

> **What counts in education is attitudes expressed in skills. The attitudes that count are known. In fact, teachers are tired of hearing about them again and again at every conference and convention. As one teacher put it: "I already know what a child needs. I know it by heart. He needs to be accepted, respected, liked, and trusted; encouraged, supported, activated, and amused; able to explore, experiment, and achieve. Damn it! He needs too much. All I lack is Solomon's wisdom, Freud's insight, Einstein's knowledge, and Florence Nightingale's dedication."**
>
> *H. Ginott, 1972.* Teacher and child, *p. 38.*

Self-concept, as we have defined it, consists of five psychological constructs of self: Sense of Bodily Self, Self-Identity, Self-Extension, Self-Esteem, and Self-Image. Theoretically, each one of these senses contributes to teachers' perceptions of self and others, and to their values, beliefs, and attitudes. An attempt to identify the specific effect of self-concept on the teacher's perceptions and values logically begins with the behavioral expression of these perceptions and values. Whether we are interested in teacher characteristics, teacher personality, teacher values, attitudes and beliefs, or teacher effectiveness, we must first focus on *teaching behaviors*—as role performances, as formative processes, and as products.

THE TEACHER'S PERFORMING SELF

All teacher behaviors can be viewed as products of the teacher's Performing Self, the active Sense of Self-Extension. The Performing Self is affected by all five senses of self and is a part of the continually developing self. Influenced by past and current psychological experiences, it continues to change and grow within the ongoing behavioral dialogues of the individual.

The Performing Self of a teacher, then, can be described as the five senses of self executing the teacher's role, each sense contributing self-limitations and acquired abilities to shape the teacher's performance. The professional functions of that role range from surrogate parent, to instructor, to authority figure. Sawrey and Telford (1973) include in their description of the teacher's role the following components.

Negative roles   Scapegoat, detective, and disciplinarian;
Authoritarian roles   Parental surrogate, dispenser of knowledge, group leader, model citizen;
Supporting roles   Therapist, friend, and confidant.

Similar lists appearing in the literature include additional functions such as organizing, planning, facilitating, enabling, and record keeping. Superimposed on all of these professional duties, of course, are the roles of salient/significant other and controller of classroom environment. Because the former is assigned and defined by the pupil and the latter inseparably enmeshed in the teaching task, these roles are performed, consciously or unconsciously, by all teachers, regardless of how one analyzes the teacher's specific professional functions.

Considering the responsibility inherent in the role of significant/salient other, in addition to the innumerable professional functions ascribed to the teacher in the literature, one wonders why teachers are not as scarce as spear catchers. The answer, of course, is that teachers define their role not according to textbook or reseach models, but instead according to their own perception of that role. It is the teachers' perceptions and values that determine their success not only as disciplinarians, model citizens, and therapists, but also as significant/salient others.

To function positively in the role of significant or salient other, the teacher must be able to accurately perceive and reflect the developing self, to adequately interpret events, and to supply correct information. And this perceptual ability and the quality of the teacher's performance in the behavioral dialogue are determined by the teacher's self-concept.

Combs (1969), comparing the perceptual styles of individuals rated "effective" and those rated "ineffective" in the "helping" professions (e.g., counselors, nurses, priests, and teachers), observed perceptual differences between the two groups in four major categories:

I. *General Perceptual Organization*

Is the individual more interested in people or things? Does he look at people from the outside, or does he try to see the world as they see it? Does he look for the reasons people behave as they do here and now, or does he try to find historical reasons for behavior?

II. *Perceptions of Other People*

Does he see people as generally able or unable to do things? As friendly or unfriendly? Worthy or unworthy? Dependable or undependable?

III. *Perceptions of Self*

Does he see himself as with people or apart from them? As able or unable? Dependable or undependable? Worthy or unworthy? Wanted or unwanted?

IV. *Perceptions of the Professional Task*

Does he see his job as one of freeing people or controlling them? Does he see his role as one of revealing or concealing? Being involved or uninvolved? Encouraging process or achieving goals?

The perceptual differences emerging in each of these categories reveal a positive/negative dichotomy characterizing the five senses of self and their effect upon perception. The Sense of Bodily Self is reflected in the general attitude of trust (positive) or mistrust (negative), which stems from a positive (safe) or negative (threatened) sense of continuing self. Similarly, the propensity toward inclusion or exclusion of others, toward affiliation or isolation, may result from, respectively, a positive or negative Sense of Self-Identity. These perceptual differences also reflect a positive/negative dichotomy characterizing the senses of Self-Esteem and Self-Extension (Performing Self). Considering the five senses together, a positive or negative image of the Self as Helper emerges.

As one might expect, Combs found that the perceptions of "effective" helpers fell on the positive side of the dichotomy. Teachers identified as effective helpers exhibited consistent and decisive classroom behavior and "positive," "realistic" self-concepts. And, according to Combs, a positive self-concept is a necessary prerequisite to the creation of a supportive classroom environment. This conclusion corroborates an earlier finding by Combs and Soper (1963) that self-confident teachers generally exhibit classroom behavior that fosters positive pupil self-concepts. If we may be allowed to make what may be a tenuous link, effective teachers, as Combs *et al.* have described them, and effective salient others, as we have described them, appear to share a positive perception of self and others which has a positive effect on pupil self-concept.

While the studies of Combs *et al.* suggest that perceptual "set" is associated with teacher effectiveness, research conducted at The University of Texas identified another kind of perceptual limitation that may affect the teacher's performance as a salient other. In an extended series of studies initiated by R. F. Peck, researchers found that the concerns of preservice teachers could be grouped into definable developmental and sequential stages (Borich, Godbout, Peck, Kash, and Poynor 1974). The first stage in the sequence revealed that preservice teachers are primarily concerned with self and self-protection. Later stages in the sequence showed a shift from self-concern to concern for the task of teaching, and finally to concern for pupils. After analyzing the reported concerns and observed behaviors of preservice teachers during their practice teaching, Fuller (1969) concluded that student teachers who were preoccupied with personal concerns and self-protection, or who were worried primarily about their image as achievement-oriented authority figures (concern for task and self-as-performer), did not have sufficient freedom from "self" to allow them to perceive or address the needs and concerns of their pupils. Pre-service teachers with positive self-concepts and "reasonable" self-confidence, however, exhibited a flexibility that allowed them to foster pupil autonomy and accept pupil ideas.

Teachers with positive self-concepts and perceptual sets, whose concerns for pupils are greater than their concerns for self, will function within the teaching role as effective significant or salient others and will use the class-room environment to foster positive self-concepts in those pupils with whom they are not engaged in a behavioral dialogue. A negative perceptual set or self-concept rooted in any of the five senses of self can only limit a teacher's Performing Self, distorting the perception of self, others, and the teaching role (by influencing the structure of the behavioral dialogue), transforming the classroom into a place for teacher rather than pupil reflection.

When teachers structure their roles to serve their own concerns and rein-force their own perceptions and values, this structuring is, of course, carried over to the behavioral dialogue, where it colors the psychological experiences of pupils engaged in that dialogue. The positive or negative reflections that pupils receive are based on the teacher's interpretations and are subject to the teacher's perceptual distortions. Yet the pupils who consider the teacher a significant/salient other—who *value* these reflections—will incorporate them into their developing self-concepts.

Suppose that a teacher's basic psychological state is one of mistrust. We would hypothesize that this teacher is fearful and suspicious in the classroom and in his or her relationships with pupils, parents, and colleagues. But how is this fear manifested in classroom behavior? Assuming that the mistrust stemmed from early experiences with parental significant others, we would expect a fear of all authority figures. To cope with this fear, the teacher might identify with all authority figures and authoritarian roles, adopting and imitat-ing negative and controlling behaviors while at the same time seeking approval from those in command. Or, the teacher might continue to identify with chil-dren, the "victims" of authority, unable or unwilling to assume or perform any authoritarian behavior.

Theoretically, the teacher who adopts the controlling, authoritative model is reinforced by conforming and threatened by nonconforming pupil behavior. Perceived threats to control and authority may, however, provide cause for enlisting the authoritative support system of the school, further gratifying the teacher's need to identify with, and gain the approval of salient others in power. Successful control of pupils' threatening behavior will reinforce the teacher's perception of self as an authority figure and will encourage him or her to continue acquiring and using control and power-based behaviors.

Those pupils for whom the controlling, authoritarian teacher functions as a significant other will find their teacher a source of positive self-reflection only when their behaviors are compliant and compatible with the teacher's interpretation of the pupil role as an indicator of the teacher's own authority. Those pupils who are unwilling to accept this interpretation of their role, or who do not consider the teacher a significant or salient other, will select behavioral options other than compliance. Depending on the value system and self-concept of the individual pupil, the option chosen may be withdrawal, or disruptive, authority-confronting behavior or even intermittent compliance redefined in a way that preserves the integrity of the pupil's self-concept.

Teachers who cope with fear by identifying with their pupils are unlikely to exert control or initiate authoritative behaviors. They enter the classroom seeking acceptance and approval from their pupils at the expense of their leadership role. Theoretically, such teachers are likely to encourage dependency rather than conformity in their pupils and are inclined to interpret the products and performances of the pupils as demonstrations of the pupils' appreciation of them. Dependent pupils, who need role interpretation and direction, easily conform to the authoritarian teacher's demands for compliance. In order to get such direction from the approval-seeking teacher, however, dependent children may abandon, to whatever extent possible, responsibility for their own behavior. And for doing so they are rewarded with the teacher's attention. Reinforced for dependent behavior, they continue to reflect the teacher as accepted, needed, and approved. Through this kind of interaction, dependent pupils often acquire effective manipulative skills by which to maintain dependency in future dialogues.

Pupils who, on the other hand, exhibit fairly autonomous and independent behavior may threaten insecure teachers' self-concepts. In response, insecure teachers may conclude that these pupils cannot be "reached" and therefore warrant very little of their time and attention. Or, they may feel that pupils possess, or at least reflect, some potent authority, derived from influential parents perhaps, in which case the teachers may respond to pupil-initiated behaviors with compliance or avoidance.

Whether teachers influence pupil behavior more than pupils influence teacher behavior is best considered in the context of the behavioral dialogue. The nature of this dialogue—its dimensions and its impact upon the participants—depends on the values of the teacher and pupil. In the hypothetical cases presented, the direction of behavioral influence is determined by the individual who initiates interaction—generally the teacher. The other participants in the behavioral dialogue assume a responsive stance by accepting the initiator's interpretation of their role. The teacher who initiates controlling behavior also defines and limits the responding role of the pupils. Approval-seeking teachers, however, create a responding role for themselves in an apparent, but not actual, reversal of their natural position as initiators of the behavioral dialogue. In either case, it is the teachers who determine the initiating and responding roles in the classroom dialogue.

The teacher's power to interpret and control the classroom dialogue is so complete and pervasive that it is difficult to find any pupil behaviors—except those in defiance of teacher directives—that may be considered autonomous, independent, or initiating. Pupil behavior perceived as positive demonstrates acceptance of the teacher-interpreted pupil role, while that considered negative reflects either overt rejection of the teacher-assigned role, or simply a misunderstanding of that role. A pupil whose report card shows high marks for "initiative" has more than likely had jack-rabbit starts on all the teacher's assignments, added color to the social studies map, and gone to the library when faced with free time. "Shows initiative" rarely contradicts "follows directions well."

It is realistic to assume that in the average classroom, teachers tend toward controlling behaviors under certain conditions and responding behaviors under other conditions. Usually, teachers alter some pupil behaviors and pupils, in turn, alter some teacher behaviors, with neither teachers nor pupils demonstrating a discernible or consistent dominance over or influence on classroom activity. Klein (1971) reports an increase in the number of positive teacher behaviors following the occurrence of positive pupil behavior, a higher incidence of negative teacher behavior in response to negative pupil behavior, indicating that the flux of classroom climate is indeed a two-way action.

Pupils, in fact, may function, collectively and individually, as salient others reflecting an image of the teacher. The teacher may value this image as an aid in monitoring, evaluating, and modifying teaching performance. Usually teachers value a composite of pupil reflections rather than a single image, and thus receive both positive and negative content at the same time. Groups of students or individual students, high-achievers, low-achievers, under-achievers, creative pupils, conforming pupils, males and females, economically advantaged and disadvantaged pupils, student leaders and classroom disruptors can all serve as valued reflectors of the teacher's image, and in that capacity can reinforce or challenge teachers' values and beliefs about themselves and others.

Teachers are, however, in a position to choose among various pupil reflections if they wish. They *can* select as salient others only those pupils whose reflections reinforce and affirm their existing perception of self. Yet there is no reason to assume that teachers' preferences for the reflections of certain pupils or their reciprocal dialogues with those pupils will hurt their performances as significant or salient others in behavioral dialogues with other pupils. In a study of teacher characteristics and pupil perception of self and ideal self, for example, McCallon (1966) found that, although teachers generally selected those pupils whose characteristics closely matched their own as "most desirable to teach," the pupils they designated "least desirable to teach" registered the greatest shift toward congruence between perceived self and ideal self from pretest to posttest. In an attempt to explain these findings,

McCallon suggested that while the teachers may have perceived pupils unlike themselves less favorably, they perhaps perceived them more accurately, and were, therefore, better able to meet their needs.

Although perceptual limitations may prevent full actualization of a teacher's performing potential, they do not necessarily hinder the ability to function in any of the many teaching roles at an *acceptable* level of competence. However, other (self-imposed) limitations on a teacher's performance —limitations which act to decrease the value of some pupil behaviors in favor of others—may seriously diminish or negatively alter the psychological experiences of pupils in the classroom.

TEACHER EXPECTATIONS AND PUPIL PERFORMANCE

Teachers are necessarily concerned with exacting performance and products from pupils in accordance with a planned educational curriculum. They are also concerned with evaluating these products and performances in accordance with goals, standards, and values prescribed by the educational system of which they are a part. Both of these concerns are functions of the teacher's Performing Self, and as such they reflect the teacher's perception of self, the teaching role, and pupils. Through the perceptual filter of the teacher's acquired standards and values, the pupil is assessed and evaluated, and on the basis of this evaluation, expectations are formed by and for both pupil and teacher. These expectations represent a measure of perceptual accuracy and, for the teacher, an investment of self-image. Fulfilled expectations affirm perceptual accuracy; those unfulfilled require reassessment and reevaluation, which may force an alteration in existing concepts of self. When a critical amount of "self" (i.e., identity, esteem, and image) is invested in the perceptual set that underlies the prediction, failure to confirm that prediction is often rationalized by assuming that some other unusual influence is at work. The nonsubstantiating results are viewed as "an exception." Or, when the self-investment is extremely high, the results may be ignored or the entire evaluation devalued or dismissed as unimportant. In other instances, the conditions under which the unexpected results were obtained may be reexamined, and new or previously overlooked evidence may be accepted or devised to account for the error in prediction. All of these adjustments preserve the teacher's illusion of perceptual accuracy and reaffirm his or her concept of self.

Teachers are in a particularly good position to make these adjustments since their behaviors and values are part of the antecedent conditions that determine pupil performance. According to their own values, teachers form hypotheses about learning conditions and pupil performances: *If* certain conditions prevail, *then* certain results will occur. Teachers not only formulate the hypotheses, however; they can also interact with antecedent classroom conditions, influencing and interpreting pupil performance to conform to their expectations. That is, they can act, or perceive, in a manner that confirms their hypotheses. Teachers can limit or expand pupil participation, increase or diminish opportunities for learning, reduce or broaden access to information, restrict or encourage pupil performance, as they see fit. Good (1970) reports, for example, that teachers consistently give high achievers more opportunity to speak in the classroom, and Brophy and Good (1970) report that boys receive more direct teacher questions than do girls and are more often praised for giving correct answers. Boys also appear to have more interactions with the teacher and to receive more criticism as well. Focusing on racial rather than sexual bias, Rubovits and Maehr (1973) demonstrated that black pupils designated as having high IQs received less overall but more negative attention from their student teachers than all other students (grouped by race and IQ designation).

Because teachers are themselves participants in the events, they are clearly in a position to influence the conditions preceding the expected outcomes. When they use that influence to ensure reinforcement of their expectations, they are engaging in a "self-fulfilling prophecy." Such behavior is evidently not rare among teachers. Rist (1970) reports that a kindergarten teacher in a ghetto area placed children in ability groups that reflected their socioeconomic status. Furthermore, high ability pupils were seated closest to the teacher, and low ability children on the periphery of the classroom. The high ability group also received more overall contact and more positive contact with the teacher. This pattern of interaction persisted through the children's early elementary school experience, leading Rist to conclude that the kindergarten teacher's behavior influenced the pupils' achievement, creating not only a self-fulfilling prophecy but also a self-perpetuating prophecy.

Changing the teacher's perception of pupils is a complex process precisely because it does involve the teacher's self-concept. In fact, researchers have successfully altered teacher expectations only when (1) teachers were given biasing information early in the school year, before they had an opportunity to make their own assessments and observations; (2) teachers were relatively inexperienced; and (3) the validity of the biasing information was reinforced by a trusted school official or expert.

These conditions prevailed in a study conducted by Meichenbaum, Bowers, and Ross (1969) who were apparently successful in their efforts to bias teachers and their expectations. They asked four teachers to rate each of fourteen adolescent female offenders enrolled in a special unit of a training school according to expected academic potential, level of appropriate classroom behavior, and amount of teacher attention received prior to the experimental period. The teachers were also asked by a member of the school administration to evaluate on a 7-point scale the intellectual potential of each girl based on previous examinations and classroom behaviors. In rating the subjects, teachers were requested to compare them with other pupils in the training school rather than a "normal" population of ninth grade girls. There was significant agreement among the four teachers' ratings.

Measures of academic performance on objectively and subjectively scored tests were obtained for all of the girls. Teacher–pupil interaction and the girls' total classroom behavior were recorded (by observers, unaware of the purpose or details of the study) before and after the teachers were given biasing information about six of the fourteen students. Classroom observation was undertaken to document changes in teacher and pupil behavior which might demonstrate operation of the bias.

The biasing information was transmitted by the school psychologist, who discussed "potential for blooming" with the teachers and described the success of a "late bloomer" test in identifying subjects whose present performance did not indicate their actual potential. He suggested that present and past student performance might lead teachers to make erroneous estimates of the actual academic potential of "late bloomers." Approaching the subject casually, as a matter of possible interest to the teachers, the school psychologist then named six girls in two classes who had been identified by the test as "potential bloomers." Three of the girls named were students for whom the teachers had previously indicated high expectations, while the remaining three were those for whom they had admitted low expectations. The teachers were initially very surprised at the inclusion of the three low-potential subjects, but after discussing the matter and reconsidering past indications of possible potential, their surprise changed to knowing hindsight, as if they had suspected all along that these three girls had academic promise.

Analysis of the observational data, however, revealed that these teachers altered their behavior toward the subjects differentially. While teachers 1 and 2 did not increase overall interaction with the "late bloomers," they did increase the positive content of their communications with them. (Teacher 2 also increased the amount of positive interaction with *all* pupils who had been rated as having potential.) Teacher 4 did not increase the amount of positive interaction, but did decrease the amount of negative interaction, particularly with the "high-potential" subjects who had previously received high expectancy ratings by the teachers. Teacher 3 significantly decreased positive interaction with all "high-potential" subjects and increased it with the control pupils (who, incidentally, showed significant improvement in academic and classroom behavior on the posttests).

The fact that four teachers reacted diversely to the same biasing information reflects differential valuing of that information. The teachers responded differently because they were biased to different degrees, depending on their own values.

A comparison of the subjects' pre- and posttest scores indicated that teacher expectations significantly influenced the academic and classroom behavior of the "late blooming" subjects (with the exception of Teacher 3's subjects). The greatest gains were achieved by the subjects of Teacher 4, who had decreased the amount of negative interaction with the late bloomers previously rated as having high potential. The teachers who increased the amount of positive interaction, but did not appreciably reduce negative interactions, improved the performances of their subject pupils, but not as significantly as did Teacher 4. In the light of other research on the effect of decreased negative feedback (e.g., Crandall, Good, and Crandall 1964), we can speculate that, to these girls, already labeled as juvenile offenders, the *decrease in negative interaction with an adult was of more value* than adult praise and may have provided an atmosphere of psychological safety in which their Senses of Self-Extension were enhanced and their Performing Selves affirmed. (For we may conclude that it was the girls' performance, not the teachers' grading, that changed, since gains in academic achievement were obtained on the objectively scored tests, but *not* on the subjectively scored examinations.)

The Meichenbaum, Bowers, and Ross study is reminiscent of the classic investigation of Rosenthal and Jacobson (1968) which generated a great deal of research testing the hypothesis that teacher expectations influence pupil performance. In their study, Rosenthal and Jacobson attributed the increased IQ scores of pseudo-late bloomers to the effects of false information on teacher expectations and subsequent pupil performance. Teachers were told that randomly selected pupils in their first through sixth grade classes were "special students" who could be expected to blossom intellectually in the next few months. End-of-year IQ tests showed significant gains for the late bloomers in comparison to other students. Pre- and posttesting were not accompanied, however, by classroom observation.

Claiborn (1969) criticized the interpretations made by Rosenthal and Jacobson on the grounds that their data showed no teacher expectancy effects for two-thirds of the grades in which pupils were designated late bloomers. He further maintained that the conclusions drawn by Rosenthal and Jacobson were based on difference scores uncorrected for known pretest differences and partially attributable to regression effects. According to Claiborn, the gain in IQ scores was caused by the greatly improved performance of first grade subjects on the vocabulary subtest, and thus demonstrated neither a teacher expectancy effect nor an overall increase in pupil IQ.

In his own research, Claiborn tested the hypothesis that teacher expectancy influences pupil gain in IQ scores and also attempted through classroom observation to identify teacher behaviors related to teacher expectations. In addition, he had observers rate as positive, negative, or neutral the effect of the teachers' interaction with "special" pupils.

Claiborn's results did not support the teacher expectancy hypothesis. Nor did they capture significant differences in teacher behavior toward control pupils and those designated "special." Claiborn acknowledged that he had not replicated the conditions of the Rosenthal and Jacobson study: his project began well into the second semester of the school year (after teachers had had an opportunity to develop stable impressions of their pupils); it covered only two months rather than a full school year; and it employed a different method of selecting "special" students. Claiborn minimized the importance of these differences, maintaining that other research has demonstrated that teacher set toward the pupil, timing of the study, and duration of the investigation are not critical factors in testing for expectancy effects.

Claiborn's findings can be questioned on other grounds, however. As evidence of an operating teacher bias, he accepted the mere ability of teachers to recall the names of children designated "special." Thus his study can be considered a test of the teacher expectancy hypothesis only if one accepts his assumption that teacher recall of specific pupil names is sufficient evidence of teacher bias. Unfortunately, this assumption and other weaknesses of the Claiborn research have, in our opinion, obscured his valid criticisms of the Rosenthal and Jacobson study.

The teacher expectancy studies reported thus far have all introduced a *positive* bias—that is, the teacher's expectations have been *raised*. It can be assumed that the pupils involved in these studies were not initially performing at their optimum levels, since results indicated performance gains. The power of elevated expectations to increase pupil performance depends on the discrepancy between pupil performance and pupil ability. Because it is difficult, if not impossible, to determine the size of this discrepancy, it is also difficult to interpret the results of research in which teacher expectations have been *raised*. The teacher expectancy effect might be more reliably assessed if teacher expectations were *lowered* rather than raised. Though this would be an ethically objectionable research procedure, it might better indicate the role of teacher expectations in the classroom.

In lieu of lowering teacher expectations, researchers can, with clear conscience, identify teachers whose expectations are already low and measure the effect of those expectations on pupil performance. Palardy (1969), for example, asked 63 first grade teachers to report their beliefs about the rate at which first grade boys learn to read. Among the 42 teachers who responded to the questionnaire, he identified three groups. Group A consisted of teachers who believed boys learn to read at an equal pace with girls. Teachers in Group B thought boys considerably slower than girls in learning to read, and Group C teachers believed boys to be somewhat slower. For research purposes, Group C was dropped, and comparisons were made between the two extreme groups. A reading pretest administered to all pupils showed no differences among them. On the posttest, however, boys taught by Group B teachers scored significantly lower than girls, while there were no significant differences between the scores of boys and girls taught by Group A teachers. These results suggest that pupil performance can be depressed as well as raised by teacher expectations. Both groups of teachers managed to support their beliefs.

Apparently, the teachers' *expressed* beliefs affected the achievement of their pupils. By making the reading rate of boys an issue—and requiring teachers to commit themselves to a stand on that issue—the investigators perhaps encouraged a teacher expectancy effect. Thus, while bias was not introduced in this study, the mere interaction between investigator and subjects (i.e., teachers) may have cued the latter toward responses that proved the hypothesis being tested.

As we have pointed out, teachers' expectations are rooted in their own self-concepts and values. The teacher must value a change before behavior will be altered to effect that change. It is for this reason that classroom observation plays such an essential role in teacher expectancy research: behavioral data provide our only evidence of valuing—our only evidence that the teacher has internalized a bias that could effect a change in behavior.

However, several of the teacher expectancy studies reviewed, including one cited here (Rosenthal and Jacobson), did not include classroom observation. These studies introduced IQ information as a bias and *assumed* not only that teachers valued high IQs but also that they valued high IQs over other pupil traits and behaviors. It is easy to understand why investigators made this assumption, since research has demonstrated a teacher bias favoring high *achievement*. But IQ and achievement are not the same thing. And however likely it may seem that teachers value high IQ scores, investigators should have demonstrated rather than assumed this by observing actual teaching behavior.

Moreover, it should be recalled that when researchers did successfully demonstrate a teacher bias toward high IQ (Meichenbaum, Bowers, and Ross 1969; Rubovits and Maehr 1971, 1973; Chaikin, Sigler, and Derlega 1974), the following conditions prevailed: (1) Teachers were given biasing information early in the school year; (2) Teachers were relatively inexperienced; and (3) The validity of the biasing information was reinforced by a trusted expert, such as the school psychologist. Only under these conditions have researchers demonstrated a bias favoring high IQ scores that caused teachers to change their behavior toward pupils. This differential teacher behavior, documented through classroom observation in all of these studies examined (except that of Rosenthal and Jacobson) indicates that teachers' demonstrated bias did alter their perception of the pupil. And the behavioral manifestation of this altered perception in turn affected pupil performance.

TEACHER ATTITUDES AND BELIEFS

Teachers' attitudes, whether reflected in skills or in values and beliefs, are all expressed in their behavior toward pupils. That behavioral expression of attitude affects the nature of the psychological experiences of pupils in a learning situation. Differences in the teacher's attitudes toward different pupils account in large measure for variations in the school experience of students in the same classroom. Behaviorally expressed attitudes also account in part for the teacher's differential impact on pupil self-concept.

Because our interest in teacher behavior as an expression of teacher attitudes is confined to the effect of that behavior on pupil self-concept, we have, for the most part, reviewed only those attitude studies illuminating this particular aspect of the teacher–pupil relationship.

There are a number of other books which comprehensively review studies of teacher attitude, among which are *The study of teaching* (Dunkin and Biddle 1974), *Psychological concepts in the classroom* (Coop and White 1974), and *Teacher–student relationships: causes and consequences* (Brophy and Good 1974). These books document the relationship between teacher attitudes and teacher behaviors and, generally, examine the impact of specific behaviors on the pupil's academic performance.

There are, however, two teacher attitude studies that we would like to consider before addressing the behavioral expression of attitudes in the remainder of this book. Both of these studies deal with assumptions we have made about teacher attitudes in interpreting the studies we have reviewed. The first of these, conducted by Silberman (1969), applies to the basic assumption that teacher attitudes are indeed expressed in teacher behaviors, thus becoming a part of the behavioral dialogue as the teacher reflects, interprets, and informs.

Investigating teacher behavior for evidence of teacher attitude toward pupils, Silberman found that:

1. Teachers' attitudes are generally revealed in their actions, regardless of attempts to conceal them or circumstances which might disguise them;

2. Teachers express some attitudes more clearly than others, and pupils are more inclined to accept attitudes of concern and indifference than attitudes of attachment or rejection;

3. Pupils are aware of teacher expressions of attitude toward themselves and others, and these expressions may influence not only a pupil's perception of self, but also his perception of other pupils.

The first of these findings supports our theoretical contention that the behavioral dialogue includes not only communications that are verbal and intended, but also messages that are behavioral and/or "hidden," stemming from the self-concept and value system of the significant/salient other. The second finding lends support to the pivotal role of pupil valuing in the hypothesis that teacher behaviors influence pupil self-concepts. We have theorized that the pupil's value for teacher authority and teacher function elicits a reaction at the first two levels of the internalization process, *receiving* and *responding*. These behavioral reactions would be expected to appear more frequently than the third level of internalization, i.e., *valuing,* since the pupil is selective in valuing teacher behaviors. The pupil's greater inclination to accept teacher attitudes of concern and indifference than rejection and attachment is, in our opinion, reasonably supportive documentation of pupil valuing.

Silberman's third finding appears to support our position that teachers affect pupil self-concept not only through their functioning as significant or salient others but also through their influence on the human and physical environment of the classroom.

The second study we would like to consider here applies to our assumption that the teacher values, beliefs, and attitudes expressed in classroom behavior are generally those of the core culture or middle-class members of this society.

Yee (1969) investigated the attitude patterns that characterize pupil perception of teachers and teacher perception of pupils, using data collected during a two-year study involving a large sample of teachers and pupils from middle-class areas of two large urban centers, one in the southwest and one on the west coast. Results of this study indicate that teachers show different patterns of interaction with middle-class and lower-class pupils. The attitude patterns of middle-class teachers differ a great deal from those of their lower-class pupils, while the attitude patterns of middle-class teachers and middle-class children are compatible. Since teachers are predominantly middle-class, we may assume that public school systems are structured on the value and behavior systems of the middle class and are staffed by individuals who model and enforce these values and behaviors in the classroom.

We have theorized that teachers' values, attitudes, and beliefs are the source of perceptual distortions that affect performance, particularly in the two roles through which they affect a pupil's self-concept development: (1) as a salient or significant other reflecting the developing self of the pupil; and (2) as controller of classroom environment, interpreting the pupil's role in the behavioral dialogue and determining the pupil's psychological experiences. And this theorizing is supported by studies of teacher self-concept, values, attitudes, and beliefs (including those inherent in teacher expectations), which show that teachers are in fact influenced by their self-concept and values, and that they behave differently toward different pupils. Thus, pupils in the same classroom may encounter varying psychological experiences. Those who reinforce the teacher's value system and who give positive reflections of the teacher's Performing Self receive positive reflections of their Performing Selves in return. The two studies cited here offer substantial support for the hypothesis that teacher self-concept determines teacher perception and directly or indirectly affects the teacher's Performing Self.

With the exception of classroom observation studies designed to identify differential teacher behavior toward pupils with specific characteristics, most research to date has investigated teacher self-concept and teacher behavior in relation to measures of teacher effectiveness. Effectiveness in most cases is defined as the ability to produce positive change in pupil academic performance or achievement levels. While continuing to search for teacher behaviors that are effective, we might also identify those that enhance the teacher's performance as significant other and controller of classroom environment. Identification of teacher beliefs and values that impair perception of self and others would help teachers in their performance in these two roles.

The research on teacher behavior reflects one of the most persistent and commonly held beliefs in our society—that teachers can influence the character development of their pupils. For most members of our society, personal memories provide sufficient support for this belief. But teachers should not continue to be charged with such a heavy responsibility if this belief is not founded in fact; and pupils should not continue to be subjected to arbitrary teacher influence if it *is* founded in fact. In spite of the research limitations in this area, we believe that there is substantial evidence that teachers, through their behavior, have a potent impact upon the developing self-concept, and therefore character, of their pupils. This realization carries with it a responsibility to further investigate the teacher–pupil relationship and to implement the knowledge made available through research.

REFERENCES

Branan, J. 1972. Negative human interaction. *Journal of Counseling Psychology* **19** (1): 81–82.

Fuller, F. F., O. H. Bown, and R. F. Peck 1967. *Creating climates for growth.* Austin: The Hogg Foundation for Mental Health, The University of Texas.

Ginott, H. 1972. *Teacher and child.* New York: Macmillan.

TEACHERS AS A RESEARCH POPULATION

Biddle, B. J. 1964. The integration of teacher effectiveness research. In B. J. Biddle and W. J. Ellena (eds.), *Contemporary research on teacher effectiveness.* New York: Holt, Rinehart and Winston.

Borich, G. D. 1977. *The appraisal of teaching: concepts and process.* Reading, Mass.: Addison-Wesley.

Getzels, J. W., and P. W. Jackson 1963. The teacher's personality and characteristics. In N. L. Gage (ed.), *Handbook of research on teaching.* Chicago: Rand McNally.

National Education Association. *Estimates of school statistics.* 1971–1972.

Ornstein, A. C. 1971. Systematizing teacher behavior research. *Phi Delta Kappan* **52** (9): 485–488.

Peterson, W. A. 1964. Age, teacher's role, and the institutional setting. In B. J. Biddle and W. J. Ellena (eds.), *Contemporary research on teacher effectiveness.* New York: Holt, Rinehart and Winston.

Ryans, D. G. 1960. *Characteristics of teachers.* Washington, D.C.: American Council on Education.

THE TEACHER AS SIGNIFICANT OTHER

Keller, H. 1968. *The story of my life.* New York: Lancer Books.

TEACHER SELF-CONCEPT, VALUES, AND BEHAVIOR

Ginott, H. 1972. *Teacher and Child.* New York: Macmillan.

The Teacher's Performing Self

Borich, G. D., R. Godbout, R. F. Peck, M. M. Kash, and L. H. Poynor 1974. *Final report: an evaluation of the personalized model of teacher training.* Austin, Texas: Research and Development Center for Teacher Education.

Combs, A. W. 1969. *Florida studies in the helping professions* (Social Science Monograph No. 37). Gainesville: University of Florida Press.

————, and D. W. Soper 1963. The helping relationship as described by "good" and "poor" teachers. *Journal of Teacher Education* **14:** 64–68.

Fuller, F. F. 1969. Concerns of teachers: a developmental conceptualization. *American Educational Research Journal* **6:** 207–226.

Klein, S. 1971. Student influence on teacher behavior. *American Educational Research Journal* **8:** 403–421.

McCallon, E. L. 1966. Teacher characteristics and their relationship to change in the congruency of children's perception of self and ideal-self. *Journal of Experimental Education* **34:** 84–88.

Sawrey, J. M., and C. W. Telford 1973. *Educational psychology* (4th ed.) Boston: Allyn and Bacon.

Teacher Expectations and Pupil Performance

Brophy, J., and T. Good 1970. Teachers' communication of differential expectations for children's classroom performance: some behavioral data. *Journal of Educational Psychology* **71:** 365–374.

Chaiken, A., E. Sigler, and V. Derlega 1974. Nonverbal mediators of teacher expectancy effects. *Journal of Personality and Social Psychology* **30** (1): 144–149.

Claiborn, W. L. 1969. Expectancy effects in the classroom: a failure to replicate. *Journal of Educational Psychology* **60**: 377–383.

Crandall, V., S. Good, and V. J. Crandall 1964. Reinforcement effects of adult reactions and nonreactions on children's achievement expectations: a replication study. *Child Development* **35** (2): 485–497.

Good, T. 1970. Which pupils do teachers call on? *Elementary School Journal* **70**: 190–198.

Meichenbaum, D. H., K. Bowers, and R. Ross 1969. A behavioral analysis of teacher expectancy effect. *Journal of Personality and Social Psychology* **13** (4): 306–316.

Palardy, J. M. 1969. What teachers believe—what children achieve. *Elementary School Journal* **69** (7): 370–374.

Rist, R. C. 1970. Student social class and teachers' expectations: the self-fulfilling prophecy in ghetto education. *Harvard Educational Review* **40**: 411–451.

Rosenthal, R., and L. Jacobson 1968. *Pygmalion in the classroom: teacher expectations and pupils' intellectual development.* New York: Holt, Rinehart and Winston.

Rubovits, P. C., and M. L. Maehr 1971. Pygmalion analyzed: toward an explanation of the Rosenthal-Jacobson findings. *Journal of Personality and Social Psychology* **19** (2): 197–203.

——— 1973. Pygmalion black and white. *Journal of Personality and Social Psychology* **25** (2): 210–218.

Teacher Attitudes and Beliefs

Brophy, J., and T. Good 1974. *Teacher-student relationships: causes and consequences.* New York: Holt, Rinehart and Winston.

Coop, R. H., and K. White 1974. *Psychological concepts in the classroom.* New York: Harper & Row.

Dunkin, M. J., and B. J. Biddle 1974. *The study of teaching.* New York: Holt, Rinehart and Winston.

Silberman, M. 1969. Behavioral expression of teachers' attitudes toward elementary school students. *Journal of Educational Psychology* **60**: 402–407.

Yee, A. H. 1969. Social interaction in classrooms: implications for the education of disadvantaged pupils. *Urban Education* **4** (3): 203–219.

CHAPTER 3
The Sense of Bodily Self

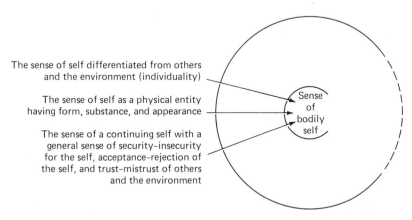

The sense of self differentiated from others and the environment (individuality)

The sense of self as a physical entity having form, substance, and appearance

The sense of a continuing self with a general sense of security-insecurity for the self, acceptance-rejection of the self, and trust-mistrust of others and the environment

Sense of bodily self

Fig. 3.1 The bodily self of the general self-concept.

The Sense of Bodily Self—the awareness of "self" as a physical entity continuing throughout our lives—evolves from the individual's earliest physiological experiences of sensing and recording. Sullivan (1953) views this phenomenon, which he calls "experiencing one's own body," as the first step in the perceptual process of differentiating the bodily self from its environment. It is also the first step toward individuality, and, in turn, self-identity.

In the process of experiencing itself, the body performs the functions of both the significant other and the environment: it provides feedback to the self as well as opportunity for exploration and limitation. The Sense of Bodily Self that emerges from experiencing one's own body forms the physical self-awareness that remains with the individual throughout life, even as the body changes through growth, development, aging, trauma, sickness, and health. As the process of differentiating self from environment continues, the individual begins to interact with significant others and the external environment, thus acquiring additional sources of reflection which contribute to a Sense of Bodily Self. The emerging self now perceives not only personal feelings, but also the feelings of others toward the self. From the early responses of others to the emerging self, the individual forms a basic attitude of trust or mistrust. Individuals who feel they are accepted will trust others and the environment; individuals who sense rejection by others will become mistrusting and fearful (Erikson 1963).

THE SENSE OF PHYSICAL SELF

Would he like you to look younger? (Advertisement)
Don't let bad breath spoil your chances. (Advertisement)
Lose weight, Girls 8 to 21, Camp _____ will help you lose weight (typical girl, 20–45 lbs) this summer. (Advertisement for camp)
Don't let unsightly hair spoil your . . . (Advertisement)
Nature isn't always right, but Tinthair is. (Advertisement)
For that young executive look. (Advertisement)

Our society does not take the body and bodily appearance lightly. Our cultural aspirations for the body beautiful include growing straight and tall, being the "right" weight for height, developing the right muscles, and having the correct skin condition, dental arrangement, looks, hair, and odors (or absence of the latter two if they are deemed unsightly or offensive). We are admonished to have clothes clean beyond the ultimate index—cleaner than clean and whiter than white. And we are assured that appearances *do* count in gaining entry into even the most mundane society. Anyone in our culture with ambition or desire for success knows that making a good first impression starts with the body and its adornments. Considering the predominance of this cultural value, can we expect the teacher to suspend all responses to the physical stimuli of pupil height, shape, size, attractiveness, cleanliness, or personal habits?

Evidence from popular and professional publications indicates that the teacher definitely does react to the physical characteristics of pupils. Furthermore, theory and research from disciplines such as social psychology, child development, and personality theory confirm that the response of others to one's body affects body image, which in turn forms an important part of the self-concept, particularly during adolescence. Unfortunately, most of the literature focusing specifically on teacher response to the physical characteristics of pupils is anecdotal rather than research-based; and relevant research from disciplines other than educational psychology concerns the development or acquisition of self-concept rather than the relationship between teacher behavior and pupil body-concept. Thus, it is within the confines of these research limitations that we are examining the teacher's impact on pupil body image.

A child entering school has already acquired an operating concept of self as a physical entity. The child has had psychological experiences through which reflections of his or her physical form and performances have been transmitted. These reflections have positively or negatively influenced the child's concept of self as a physical being. Yet this concept of physical self is not so firm that it is unaffected by new reflections received in the classroom. Generally, it may be reinforced or altered by new psychological experiences.

Pupils carry with them several physical characteristics that may evoke responses from the teacher and the classroom environment, responses which may influence the formation of self-concept. These characteristics, which may be termed the "givens" of genetics, are: sex, body build, race, physical appearance, physical defects or anomalies, and age.

Teachers' responses, of course, are rooted in their values. The question is: Which teacher values determine the reflections, interpretations, and information they transmit in their role as significant other? And which teacher behaviors are valued by the developing self as reflections, interpretations, and information to incorporate into a sense of self as a physical entity?

TEACHER BEHAVIOR AND THE PHYSICAL ATTRACTIVENESS OF PUPILS

Cultural values create standards and ideals of physical attractiveness. The pervasiveness of these cultural values, and their impact on children's body concepts, is dramatically illustrated in self-reports from racial groups who cannot meet the standards of the core culture (Angelou 1969, pp. 4–5):

> **Wouldn't they be surprised when one day I woke out of my black ugly dream, and my real hair, which was long and blond, would take the place of the kinky mass that Momma wouldn't let me straighten? My light-blue eyes were going to hypnotize them ... because my eyes were so small and squinty. ... Because I was really white and because a cruel fairy stepmother, who was understandably jealous of my beauty, had turned me into a too-big Negro girl, with nappy black hair, broad feet and a space between her teeth that would hold a number-two pencil.**

Pupils in the white core culture may not experience the devastating impact of cultural standards quite as intensely and hopelessly as black American females did before black became beautiful (Grier and Cobbs 1968). But failure to meet standards of physical attractiveness valued by significant others can have an intense and painful effect on the self-concept development of any child. When she was a small girl, Eleanor Roosevelt was called "Granny" by her beautiful socialite mother, who claimed she used the nickname because Eleanor's behavior was so old-fashioned. But tiny Eleanor knew that her physical appearance was a disappointment to her beautiful mother. Many years later she wrote (Lash 1971, p. 46):

> **I knew a child once who adored her father. She was an ugly little thing, keenly conscious of her deficiencies, and her father, the only person who really cared for her, was away much of the time; but he never criticized her or blamed her, instead he wrote her letters and stories, telling her how he dreamed of her growing up and what they**

> would do together in the future, but she must be truthful, loyal, brave, well-educated, or the woman he dreamed of would not be there when the wonderful day came for them to fare forth together. The child was full of fears and because of them lying was easy; she had no intellectual stimulus at that time and yet she made herself as the years went on into a fairly good copy of the picture he had painted.

This paragraph reflects a child's sense of self as a physical entity and also her unqualified acceptance of a significant other, in defiance of real and witnessed events. Eleanor's relationship with her father would have seemed to an observer completely at variance with her perception of the relationship. Yet, however imperfect it may have been in reality, this relationship provided standards to which Eleanor could aspire—standards she sorely needed since she could not meet her mother's ideal of physical attractiveness. In the course of her life, Eleanor Roosevelt was subjected not only to personal, but also national, reflections on her physical unattractiveness.

The word "pretty" seems to be a key reflecting word for female children in the American culture. ("She's so pretty, what a little doll!") For boys the key reflecting words are generally related to physical strength, prowess, and body build. ("My, isn't he strong, what a little man!") While we can speculate that attractive children will have positive body concepts, and unattractive children negative body concepts, we should remain forever aware that these are generalizations, reflecting cultural values rather than the psychological experiences of attractive and unattractive children.

Our cultural values might lead us to assume, for example, that physically attractive children receive more attention from their teachers. Research indicates, however, that this is not always the case. Adams and Cohen (1974) found an interaction between pupil facial attractiveness and the frequency and type of teacher contact with students during the first few days of school. Both kindergarten and fourth grade pupils rated *below* average in facial attractiveness by their teachers received more supportive and neutral contact from these teachers than did pupils rated above average. This interaction was not observed for seventh grade subjects. Because this study employed a small, restricted sample (three females teaching upper middle-class male pupils in a private school setting) and failed to control a number of factors, we, like the investigators, can only speculate from the findings.

Adams suggests that the observed teachers, recognizing our cultural value for attractiveness, may have been giving compensatory attention to the younger children whom they perceived as unattractive. The fact that teachers at the upper grade level did not respond to the facial attractiveness of pupils could indicate a shift in teacher concerns. Teachers of younger pupils may be concerned about the children's first encounter with school, while those at upper grade levels, whose pupils are more experienced, may be concerned primarily about establishing authority and control. As we understand it, teacher concern for self and task (i.e., concern for establishing and maintaining control) can make the teacher less receptive to *pupil* stimuli such as facial attractiveness, or self-consciousness about one's appearance.

Or, viewing the teacher's behavior as a product of perceptual set, rather than concern, we can interpret the findings according to Combs' (1969) "helping" dimensions. Theorizing a difference in the perceptual sets of first and seventh grade teachers, we can assume that the instructors of the younger children, taking a "helping" stance, were characterized by a positive, open perceptual style. This allowed them to see and respond to behavioral cues given by the unattractive pupils—cues unperceived by the seventh grade teachers, who were presumably limited by a more closed, less "helping" perceptual set. The lower grade teachers may have perceived these cues (facial expressions such as lowered eyes, or body language such as muscle rigidity, immobility, posture droop, or withdrawal) as indications of fear or lack of self-confidence. Since pupil behaviors were not observed and recorded, we are merely speculating (based on the supposition that unattractive children are more likely to have negative self-concepts) that such cues were more prevalent among unattractive than attractive students. Perhaps when unattractive children are confronting new situations and new people, their negative feelings of bodily self are intensified in anticipation of more unflattering self-reflections.

In any case, pupil appearance may function primarily as an influence on *pupil* behavior (an influence to which the perceptive, concerned teacher responds), rather than as a direct influence on *teacher* behaviors that indicate a projection of the teacher's value for attractiveness. Eleanor Roosevelt remembers standing at the door of a room with a finger in her mouth waiting for her mother to say in a gentle but indifferent tone, "Come in Granny." A perceptive mother might have responded differently to such behavior.

Unfortunately, there is reason to question the perceptiveness of at least some teachers in regard to pupil body concept. A study by Clifford (1975) indicates that first grade teachers may be unaware of the important role that the sense of the physical self plays in pupil self-concept development and peer relationships. Passport type photographs of first grade pupils previously rated according to High/Low, Male/Female Attractiveness were attached to simulated pupil performance information and distributed to a large population of first grade teachers. On an accompanying "opinion" sheet, teachers were asked to estimate (on the basis of the information and photos supplied) pupil IQ, success in peer relations, degree of parental interest in pupil achievement, level at which the pupil's education would probably terminate, and pupil self-concept. Responses to the questionnaire indicated an "attractiveness" effect on teachers' estimates of pupil IQ, parental interest, and level of future education, with the High Attractiveness pupils eliciting more positive responses. However, teacher estimates of pupil self-concept and success in peer relationships were not characterized by a significant attractiveness effect. Evidently teachers were influenced by appearance when making their own estimates of the pupil, but not when projecting a self- or peer perception of the pupil. It is possible that these teachers believe that appearance plays no part in peer relationships or pupil self-concept. It is also possible that the request to estimate the perception of others produced a generalized judgment, rooted in the belief that most first graders will have reasonably good peer relationships and positive self-concepts.

From this research and a follow-up study relating pupil attractiveness and teacher expectancy effects, Clifford determined that teachers agree only moderately in their judgment of pupil attractiveness. He further concluded that teachers, though initially influenced by first impressions of physical attractiveness, are not necessarily affected by these early impressions in predicting the long-term academic success of pupils. There is evidence in both the Clifford and Adams and Cohen studies that pupil attractiveness may color a teacher's expectations *before* actual pupil performance data are available. We have no way of knowing, however, whether, or to what extent, initial expectations, rather than subsequent perceptions altered in light of the pupil's performance, are reflected in the teacher's behavior. Therefore, we can only speculate about the nature of the behavioral dialogues and psychological experiences of the pupils involved in these studies.

Since the Adams and Cohen research identified a difference in teacher behavior in response to pupil appearance, we can make several assumptions about the pupils' experience at each of the two grade levels studied. First grade pupils considered unattractive were receiving positive reflections and interpretations of themselves. And, viewing the lower overall frequency of controlling behavior among first grade teachers as evidence of their behavior toward attractive as well as unattractive pupils, we can assume that attractive children were also receiving positive reflections and interpretations of themselves. The teacher's behavior, then, communicated to every first grader that he or she was expected to play a positive, participating role in the classroom dialogue. The higher frequency of controlling behavior among seventh grade teachers suggests that the older pupils were given comparatively negative reflections of themselves and assigned a role stressing limited participation and conformity. Of course, we have no way of knowing which pupils, if any, were perceiving, responding to, or valuing these teacher behaviors.

In situations such as these, in which teachers' values for appearance are thought to influence their classroom behavior, we can determine the effect of that behavior on pupil body concept only when there is evidence that the behavior in question directly reflected the pupil's physical appearance. The behaviors exhibited by first grade teachers in the Adams and Cohen study, for example, were more likely to have altered the pupil's perception of acceptability and worth than body self-concept.

When research deals directly with the pupil's value for bodily appearance, however, we can expect changes in the concept of physical self. Cole, Oetting, and Miskimins (1969) investigated the effectiveness of a group treatment program in producing self-concept changes among female adolescents with behavioral problems. The ten-week program, under the direction of appropriate female models, focused on physical appearance and social behavior. Subjects were divided into two treatment groups, one led by professional counselors, the other by lay volunteers. A comparison of pre- and posttests indicated that the self-concepts of girls in both treatment groups changed more positively and consistently than those of girls in the control group, who represented a "normal" female adolescent population.

It is generally believed that adolescent girls, with or without behavior problems, are interested in their appearance. Thus, we can assume that the information transmitted in the behavioral dialogue between models and subjects was *valued* by the latter and therefore could be used to alter their concepts of self. Of the three studies reported here, only this one incorporates all the roles and processes characterizing the behavioral dialogue and the psychological experiences through which self-concept change occurs.

TEACHER BEHAVIOR AND PUPIL HANDICAPS

Children with physical handicaps encounter a variety of responses to their bodies: curiosity, pity, avoidance, ridicule—and with it all, the message that one is different. Helen Keller wrote that she did not remember when she first realized she was different from other people, but she knew it before Anne Sullivan arrived to teach her. She noticed that other people moved their mouths when they wanted something, instead of gesturing as she did; she also noticed that a doll which had been improvised for her had no nose, mouth, ears or eyes. "Curiously enough," she wrote, "the absence of eyes struck me more than all the other defects put together."

The American culture values "overcoming" as opposed to "succumbing to" difficulties and defects. Many parents want their handicapped children to behave "as if" they are not handicapped and encourage them to devote all their physical and emotional energy to "proving" that they are just as capable as other children. Less frequently parents generalize the impact of a handicap in one area to all aspects of physical behavior. In either of these circumstances, the child may be unable to acquire a realistic image of his or her true capabilities.

The same situation may occur in school. Teachers find that handicaps and illness, real or imagined, have definite, though not always predictable, effects in the classroom. The teacher faced with an allergic pupil, for example, may experience internal conflict about how to respond. The teacher who does not "believe" in allergies may refuse to acknowledge or enforce restrictions requested by parents or doctors. On the other hand, the teacher may respond by demonstrating exaggerated compliance with the requests. It is not at all uncommon for a teacher to overreact to a child's handicap in order to satisfy the teacher's own need to project a nurturant image. Neither of these reactions reflects a positive self-image to the child.

Perhaps more important than the interaction between teacher and handicapped child, however, is the response of other pupils to that interaction. The teacher's behavior not only shapes the pupil's reaction toward handicapped students but also defines the nature of physical incapacity in general. Since young children have limited experience with illness and physical disability, their knowledge of these things is gathered in large part from the teacher's reaction to pupils with such problems (e.g., an allergy is, or is not, psychosomatic). Children who perceive that the teacher's attitude toward a handicapped pupil is negative may acquire a fear that they, too, can lose the teacher's approval, and their own self-esteem, through an illness or accident. Children who see handicapped pupils receiving special attention or valuing may imitate illness or trauma in order to obtain similar treatment.

Clearly, the teacher's attitude toward handicapped students has considerable impact. Yet research indicates that teachers may be unaware of their specific behavioral responses to these pupils. Studying a population of preservice teachers training to become physical or special education instructors or physical therapists, Wolfgang and Wolfgang (1968) found a discrepancy between expressed attitudes about various handicaps and actual behavior toward handicapped children. Although the teachers' attitudes were overwhelmingly positive (four times more sympathetic than rejecting statements), their behavior, assessed with social distance measures, varied according to the nature of the child's handicap. In the classroom, teachers placed themselves closer to children with temporary handicaps (e.g., a broken arm or leg) than to children with permanent-uncontrollable handicaps (e.g., amputation, clubfoot), and farthest from pupils with controllable physical problems (e.g., obesity, bad teeth). These teachers were evidently perceiving the handicap rather than the child. Such a perceptual block can blind teachers to behavioral cues which under normal circumstances would guide their responses. Projecting their own feelings into the situation, teachers can misjudge the pupil's needs. The teacher of a badly scarred little girl, for example, referred the child early in the year to a remedial reading class. The remedial reading teacher, who knew that the child had been reading well beyond her grade level the previous year, questioned her and found that she had stopped performing up to her capability because the new teacher never called on her in class. In private conversation, the new teacher explained that she didn't want to "embarrass" the child by calling on her and thus drawing attention to her.

This child was receiving a false impression of her ability, as many handicapped children do. Keeve (1967), studying pupils excused from physical education classes due to previous trauma or past diagnosis of chronic disability, found that several of this group were in reality no longer handicapped. They were instead perpetuating "phantom" handicaps. By continuing to excuse these pupils from physical education classes, Keeve concluded, the school administration was supporting their false body-concepts, and perhaps reinforcing a maladaptive behavioral mechanism that would become an inappropriate response to stress in adulthood. Keeve did acknowledge, however, that the situation was not entirely under the control of school administrators, who in altering policy might have encountered conflict with parents over the presumed handicaps of their children.

Whether real or "phantom," a handicap undoubtedly colors a child's school experience. Unintentionally, teachers and peers can communicate to handicapped children that they are unaccepable. Teachers, for example, may allow a child's grooming, cleanliness, or physical defects to determine the degree and frequency of their contact with that child. Teacher behaviors that tell children they are not nice to be near or to see or to hear (e.g., consistently placing them in the back row of school photographs or performances, and prohibiting them from handling school property) reflect a negative image of those children's bodily selves. We all know, without the benefit of research, that behavior demonstrating that one is nice to be near, nice to see, hear, or touch, carries a message of acceptance and positive value.

TEACHER BEHAVIOR AND PUPIL BODY BUILD

Physique influences the quality of an individual's life by determining the experiences encountered and the self-reflections received. Children's classroom experiences are often dictated by their size or body type. Short pupils spend a great deal of time in front rows; tall pupils fetch supplies from top shelves, hold up maps for all to see, decorate high bulletin boards, and pin up classwork displays; heavy-set girls play the grandmother while tall girls play the mother; small boys and girls play the children; and stocky boys carry or move the equipment. All of these children know how others perceive their bodies. They know the advantages and disadvantages of their size and shape, and may come to rely upon or resent their physical image.

In a study by Walker (1962) teachers were able to predict pupil behaviors associated with physique, particularly for boys. Furthermore, children with certain body types were apparently "channeled" into specific kinds of activities: one male body group was directed toward more physical, gross-motor activities, while one female body group was guided into social behaviors. This "channeling" perhaps warrants further investigation. For example, do parents and teachers consistently stress certain kinds of behavior according to their perception of the child's body type? Does the school experience affect self-concept development differently for pupils with different body types? Is teacher–pupil interaction influenced more by physical characteristics than personality attributes; i.e., is the teacher's interaction with a tall boy dominated by his "tallness"? Which specific teacher behaviors alter or reinforce pupil body concepts? Do pupils alter their appearance in imitation of the teacher? Do pupils base their image of the "ideal" body on particular teachers (i.e., physical education instructors), parents, or other models, such as sports heroes or heroines? Is the teacher's functioning as a physical model related to the age or socioeconomic status of the pupil?

Finally, the teacher's verbal behavior should also be considered in relation to the pupil's bodily self-concept. Teachers who refer to a child's continual clumsiness or lack of coordination, or who express preferences for particular physical characteristics, are undoubtedly affecting pupil body-concept. Although the role of language in self-concept formation will be fully considered in the chapter on self-identity, its influence on body-concept development should not be overlooked.

TEACHER BEHAVIOR AND SEX OF PUPIL

While all of the conditions into which an individual is born affect self-concept development, none is more prescriptive than sex.

Biologically, sex can be viewed as a single, bipolar characteristic combining in each individual degrees of masculinity and femininity. Practically, however, sex is considered an either/or condition: as one of Miss Barrett's pupils in *Up the down staircase* (Kaufman 1964) would say, "It's male or female, there's no two ways about it." Each sex label carries with it a host of value-weighted prescriptions for an individual's behavior and for the attitudes of others toward that individual. Even those behaviors considered appropriate for both sexes are defined and understood in exactly those terms—*appropriate for both sexes.*

Since sex-typing is culturally determined, a society that includes several subcultures may find that sex-appropriate behaviors do not apply to the total population. "Traditional sex roles" in our society describe a male/female dichotomy, with "homemaker, wife, and mother" on the female side, and "wage-earner, father," and, rather incidentally, "husband," on the male side. Accompanying these roles are traditionally assigned personality traits: males are characterized as dominant and aggressive, females as submissive and passive. Subsumed under these global descriptors, however, are behavioral prescriptions dictated by socioeconomic status, age, and subculture membership, which are in fact the more powerful determinants of sex role and sex-appropriate activity. This situation leaves room for confusion. When behavior considered appropriate by one's age or ethnic group is inconsistent with the sex role prescribed by the culture at large, an individual may experience role conflict.

Such conflict often arises in the school, which is, of course, an institutional representation of the traditional values of the dominant middle-class culture. Generation gaps and culture/subculture differences which occur among teachers, pupils, parents, and school administrators often involve the definition of sex roles, attitudes toward sex, and sex-appropriate behavior. Conflicts over sex discrimination in dress and behavior codes, curriculum content, and activity restrictions reflect the less than universal agreement about sex roles and sex-appropriate behavior.

Concern about the school's effect on female self-concept has recently been expressed in charges that curriculum content, through sex stereotyping, discourages females from making cognitive contributions to society. Although these charges have perhaps received more publicity, concern has also been expressed for the self-concept development of boys. Because child rearing and teaching are primarily in the hands of females, it has been suggested that young boys are deprived of male models necessary for proper acquisition of the male role. The school environment is assailed as "feminine"—requiring conforming, submissive, and passive behaviors far more consistent with the traditional female than male role. The assumption is, of course, that male teachers would not exact conforming, submissive behavior from pupils. Clearly, these "feminine" behaviors are more aptly characterized as *pupil* behaviors, considered appropriate (or expedient) in learning situations. In fact, the behaviors criticized as "feminine" in the school setting (conformity, silence, obedience) are demanded by the armed services in order to "make a man out of you" during basic training. Perhaps we are really dealing with bias against women acting as authority figures, a presumed "masculine" prerogative.

The assumption that male and female elementary teachers differ markedly in their treatment of male and female pupils is not supported by the research. In a review of the literature, Lahaderne (1975) reports no significant sex-related differences in teacher perception or treatment of pupils. (If anything, the evidence suggests that women may discriminate somewhat less than men on the basis of pupil sex and socioeconomic status.) Evidently, both male and female teachers respond primarily to the demands of the teaching situation and the social norms impinging upon the school environment. Teacher sex and pupil sex appear to be irrelevant in facing the exigencies of the classroom.

This does not imply, however, that the school experience is the same for male and female pupils. Though few studies address the teacher and classroom effects on pupil self-concept development from the standpoint of pupil sex and school-enforced sex roles, the research reported here supports the widespread assumption that girls are better conditioned than boys for school and are therefore more positively perceived by teachers. In a study by Jackson and Lahaderne (1967), boys received eight to ten times as many prohibitory control messages from the teacher as their female classmates. Furthermore, in criticizing a boy, teachers were more likely to use harsher and angrier tones than when criticizing a girl for the same or equivalent behavior. Good and Brophy (1972) found that teachers nominated twice as many boys as girls for a "Rejection" group. Low-achieving females were more often nominated for teacher "Concern," while low-achieving males were more often nominated for "Rejection." And apparently these differences in teacher behavior do not go unnoticed by the children. Meyer and Thompson (1956) report that pupils perceived teachers expressing more approval of girls and more disapproval of boys.

Studies of reading performance have also focused on differences in teacher behavior related to pupil sex. McNeil (1964) investigated teacher behavior and pupil reading performance using an auto-instruction sequence followed by teacher instruction. After the auto-instruction, the performance of boys was slightly superior to that of girls. However, after the teacher's instructional sequence, the boys' performance lowered significantly, while the girls' performance did not. Pupils reported that during teacher instruction, boys received more negative comments and fewer opportunties to perform, leading McNeil to conclude that teacher behavior is related to pupil performance in beginning reading.

Although Davis and Slobodian (1967) were unable to confirm their hypothesis that female teachers discriminate against boys and favor girls in first grade reading instruction, Palardy (1969) found that male pupils learn to read more slowly than females when the teacher has previously expressed a belief that girls acquire reading skills more rapidly than boys.

There was a time when pupils entered public school buildings through doors marked "Boys" and "Girls." Though the labeled doors are no longer in use, school is still a sex-differentiated experience. Contrary to the opinion that the classroom is the realm of female teachers intent on feminizing the masculine population, research indicates that the public school is a bastion of middle-class values, preserving traditional sex roles, encouraging "sex-appropriate" activities, and utilizing the teacher controlling behaviors valued by middle- and lower-class parents, principals, and school boards. It is possible that this reinforcement of class-related behaviors and roles is adversely affecting pupil learning while at the same time confining the potential of *both* boys and girls.

TEACHER BEHAVIOR AND PUPIL RACE

> **Abollish prejudice. Abollish Miss Freedenburgs interviews they make me sick to my stomache. Like when she ask am I ashame where I live?**
> **Edward Williams, Esq.**

> **When he said the fault dear Brutis is not in our stars meaning we got only ourselfs to blame he wasn't a color person.**
> **Edward Williams, Esq.**

> *Quotations from The Suggestion Box, B. Kaufman 1964,* Up the down staircase, *pp. 175, 246.*

The potent effect of racial attitudes (expressed as behaviors) on the developing self is clear and unmistakable. Racial prejudice—white, black, brown, yellow, and red—is part of our national and personal experience and is a very real factor in the classroom.

One of the most powerful properties of racial prejudice is its ability to permeate every aspect of life and every mode of expression. And as it permeates, it destroys the perception of those who are prejudiced and those who are victims of prejudice. Teachers who have no perceptible racial prejudice are not free from its effects if their pupils are prejudiced or, like Edward Williams, Esq., particularly sensitive to prejudice (whether real or fancied).

> **Teachers too stingy with the marks and unfair in dishing them out.**
> **Questions are too prejudice and tests too hard.**
> **Edward Williams, Esq.**
>
> *B. Kaufman, 1964.* Up the down staircase, *p. 264.*

A study by Rubovits and Maehr (1973) indicates that there may be truth in Edward's charge. These investigators selected pupils, both black and white, from the same ability group and arbitrarily assigned them "gifted" and "nongifted" labels. These pupils were then taught microlessons by student teachers who had been informed of their gifted or nongifted status. Results showed significant differences in teacher behavior on dimensions of race and giftedness. While all pupils received a similar *amount* of teacher attention, the *quality* of teacher attention differed for gifted and nongifted children. Gifted pupils were called on and criticized more often, but the high frequency of criticism came during teacher interaction with the gifted *black* students. Gifted white students were called on, praised, and criticized more often than nongifted white students, and in subsequent interviews with the student teachers, gifted white students were most frequently named as "most liked," "brightest," and "most probable leaders" of their class. Black students were given less attention than were whites, ignored more, praised less, and criticized more by all the teachers. And, interestingly, the gifted black pupils received more negative attention than the nongifted blacks. Since all pupils had been selected from the same ability group, these teacher behaviors were not based on actual pupil performance differences.

> **When you call on me to answer don't call on me when I don't know**
> **what the answer is, it makes me look dumb in front of the class. You**
> **always call on the others when they know what the answer is.**
> **Edward Williams, Esq.**
>
> *B. Kaufman, 1964.* Up the down staircase, *p. 249.*

It is possible that teachers play a more important role in black than white self-concept development. Kleinfeld (1972), investigating the relative influence of parents and teachers on the academic self-concepts of black and white students, collected estimates of pupil ability from parents, teachers, and pupils themselves. The self-estimates of white pupils strongly reflected the ratings given by their parents, while those of black students were closer to teacher assessments of their ability. In fact the self-estimates of black females correlated significantly and positively with teacher rather than parental ratings. Apparently, teachers were functioning as salient others to a greater extent for black than white students—and particularly for black females. In light of this conclusion, Kleinfeld suggests that teachers be trained to help black pupils develop positive estimates of their abilities. St. John's (1971) finding that black pupils demonstrated positive growth when teachers were kind, adaptable, and optimistic (determined by Ryans' Teacher Characteristics Scale) might be profitably employed in such training.

Racial majority or minority status within a single school has also been studied in relation to pupil self-concept. Zirkel and Moses (1971) assessed the self-concepts of black, Puerto Rican, and white elementary pupils, using the Coopersmith Self-Esteem Inventory (Coopersmith 1959). Their results revealed interesting but statistically nonsignificant trends. In general, black students tended to have higher self-concepts than white students. Puerto Rican pupils scored lowest on the Self-Esteem Inventory, and particularly when attending schools with a white majority. Both blacks and whites produced lower self-concept scores when they comprised a majority rather than a minority of the student body.

> **What's the good of it [integration] there still prejudice on the outside, it's in the cards. At lease in my old school it was close to where I live so I could catch up on some extra sleep but got nothing out of it.**
> **Edward Williams, Esq.**
>
> **I complaint all ready about my Midterm mark. What's the use of integration if marks are still low?**
> **Edward Williams, Esq.**

> *B. Kaufman, 1964.* Up the down staircase, *pp. 213, 274.*

The classroom and playground abound with the thrill of victory and the agony of defeat for pupils in the process of self-concept development. The evolution of a sense of physical self is particularly critical during the transition from childhood to young adulthood. Though physical hygiene and the development of psychomotor skills are acknowledged educational goals, the effect of these goals, the school environment, and teacher behavior on the pupil's body-concept is still largely unknown.

THE SENSE OF THE CONTINUING SELF

The sense of continuing self is a very intimate concept of self that persists through time, experience, and bodily changes. It is the conscious awareness of the subjective "I," the possessive "my," and the objective "me," rooted in the individual's basic feeling of security (trust) or fear (mistrust). As the developing self responds to early feedback from significant others and the environment, a child forms a generalized condition or feeling—a sense of security or insecurity, ease or anxiety, competence or dependence, trust or mistrust—which is the sense of continuing self. Lash (1971, p. 56) writes:

> In Eleanor's [Roosevelt] later portrayal of these [early childhood] years she emerges as a child who was full of fears—of the dark, of dogs, horses, snakes, of other children. She was "afraid of being scolded, afraid that other people would not like me." She spoke of a sense of inferiority that was almost overpowering, coupled with an unquenchable craving for praise and affection. She described her mother as the most beautiful woman she ever knew but also as representing cold virtue, severity, and disapproval while her father embodied everything that was warm and joyous in her childhood.

The general feeling characterizing the sense of continuing self is revealed in one's responding and coping behaviors. Whether the individual's coping style is aggressive, passive, attention seeking, approval seeking, withdrawing, independent, or dependent, it is above all persistent. One particular response style is dominant over all others. This stable response pattern, reflecting the general state of self, should not be confused with transitory reactions to immediate and specific stimuli or with atypical behavior related to trauma and provoked by particular circumstances (anxiety-provoking situations).

Well before reaching school age, the child has developed a method of coping with significant others and the environment. The pattern of behavioral responses formed reveals the nature of the child's sense of continuing self, the trust or mistrust the child feels toward others and the environment. Does the teacher (or perhaps we should ask, *can* the teacher) influence this basic sense of bodily self and in any way alter the pupil's general state of trust or mistrust?

TEACHER-CONTROLLED ENVIRONMENT, PUPIL EXPERIENCES AND CONDITIONS

The classroom is a tightly controlled environment adapted to meet the needs of our society. Policymakers, administrators, and classroom teachers use the educational system to realize societal ideals and philosophies. In a democratic and diverse nation like ours, however, opinion on "societal ideals" is rarely unanimous. Stated educational goals function as the circus big top: they encompass a number of "rings" catering to diverse interests and featuring several different acts. And our own goal—to relate the teacher-controlled environment to pupil self-concept development—is a ring in which many individual acts occur.

The school environment provides opportunities for the acquisition of knowledge, beliefs, and skills valued by society. The anticipated product of such opportunities is a useful, contributing, participating citizen. Though the method by which to achieve this goal is the subject of considerable controversy, the pupil is always the product of the system; and the educational process, regardless of specific procedures employed, always involves pupil alteration and change. In other words, it is the pupil who must survive and adapt within the system, whatever the instructional approach.

Entry into the educational system is less likely to be a traumatic and disorienting psychological experience for pupils reared with values and expectations similar to those stressed in school than it is for children who are truly transplanted. Still, continuity from the home to school environment does not automatically protect the pupil from psychological stress or the anxieties inherent in change. While entry into school may be a temporary crisis for some pupils, the continuing process of education may cause chronic anxiety for others.

The child's adjustment to school—or, more specifically, the stable, persistent aspects of that adjustment—can suggest his or her sense of continuing self, and basic state of trust or mistrust. Precise determination of the state of an individual's self-concept is difficult, however, since it involves interpretation of behavior, a process colored by cultural and linguistic factors. And the connection between a given behavior and self-concept is not necessarily direct or predictable. Both general and situation-specific anxiety can be expressed through aggressive, passive, dependent, or withdrawing behaviors. For this reason, the *pattern* of behavior expressed by a child over time is the most reliable index of the child's self-concept. That pattern reflects the nature, and success or failure, of the pupil's efforts to survive psychologically in school.

To achieve professional goals and meet the societal responsibilities placed upon them, teachers must manipulate the classroom to create an environment that encourages not only learning but also socialization and "character development." No teacher teaches only reading, or mathematics, or music, or any other academic subject. Even school districts purportedly returning to the fundamental approach, stressing the "three Rs," are concerned that the classroom environment also promote obedience, honesty, respect for authority, and adherence to societal norms. It is the teacher's obligation to control and manipulate the classroom environment so that pupils may achieve both cognitive and affective objectives.

ENVIRONMENT CONTROL AND PUPIL RESPONSE TO CONFLICT

I come into the world with this against me: that if a man comes to take away what I have and he don't have a fair claim against me, I'll die before I stand quiet as a fence post and let him do it. If I die tryin to defend myself, why, let me go. I'm goin to try, definitely.

Nate Shaw in T. Rosengarten, 1974. All God's dangers, *p. 546.*

The pupil's adaptation to the school environment depends on the state of the pupil's developing self-concept and the nature of the psychological experiences and concomitant reflections of self provided by that environment and the significant others within it. Whether the change from home to school environment ultimately benefits or harms a child, the transition itself is very likely to cause the child some stress.

The child's ability to deal with this stress depends to some extent on his or her "social competence," which is evidently related to the child-rearing behavior of parents. Baumrind (1967) divided preschool children into three groups according to their social competence. Pattern I children, identified as the most mature and competent boys and girls, had parents who were essentially firm, loving, demanding, and understanding. Pattern II children, labeled as discontent, withdrawn, and distrustful (dysphoric and disaffiliative, in Baumrind's terms) had parents who were firm, punitive, and unaffectionate. Pattern III children, described as immature, dependent, lacking in self-control, and tending to withdraw from novel experiences, had mothers who were moderately loving but unable to control their children, and fathers who were ambivalent and lax in performing their parental role.

The parents of Pattern I (mature) children balanced high nurturance with high control. They gave reasons for their actions, encouraged verbal give and take, made high demands, communicated clearly, used power openly in a nonmanipulative way, and exhibited an ability to maintain control without inviting rebellion or passivity from their children. Baumrind noted that restrictiveness and control are not synonymous and that the "interacting effects of restrictiveness and warmth clearly differ from the interacting effects of control and warmth." In Baumrind's interpretation, control interacts with warmth to encourage mature behavior in children, while restrictiveness leads to inhibiting, dependent, and submissive behavior.

Pattern I children presumably had psychological experiences in the home that reflected their unconditional acceptability as individuals, that interpreted children as active, valued participants in the behavioral dialogue, and that provided information helpful in developing internalized, socially acceptable standards of behavior. Pattern II children, on the other hand, most likely had psychological experiences that reflected their unacceptability, interpreted children as passive members of the behavioral dialogue, and informed them that power and control are exercised exclusively and absolutely by adults. Pattern III children were probably reflected as acceptable, but given neither a consistent interpretation of their role nor information from which to develop goal achieving behaviors.

It can be assumed that Pattern I children, armed with social competence, would be least troubled by the transition from home to school. Even these children, however, may encounter difficulty if the school and home environments are very different. Though these children may have a positive image of self and role, they may find that the "socially acceptable" standards of behavior they acquired in the home are, in fact, acceptable only in the society from which they come. The pupil from a low socioeconomic environment, to whom conflict generally represents a physical threat, may find that the physical coping style used so effectively at home is an unacceptable response to disagreement in the middle-class school milieu. A middle-class pupil, who has learned to deal with conflict by using language and ideas rather than physical behaviors, has already acquired the coping style approved in the new environment.

The relationship between socioeconomic status and children's response to conflict in school has been investigated by Berk (1971). Observing nursery school children, Berk classified "conflict environmental force units" (classroom events conflicting with a child's desire or intention) into several categories based on the thing or person obstructing the child. He also categorized pupil response behaviors into four major Modes of Adaptation: (I) Unresponsive–Withdrawing, (II) Dependent–Compliant, (III) Thoughtful–Persistent, (IV) Offensive–Combative.

Berk found significant differences related to the socioeconomic status and sex of pupils. In conflict situations, middle-class children reacted verbally far more often than lower-class children, who more frequently responded with physical attack. But, there was no significant difference between the two SES groups in the ratio of verbal responses to number of conflict units observed. As a group, boys had more "Desire vs. Teacher" encounters and a greater number of conflict situations in general than girls. Contrary to Berk's hypothesis, boys had a higher percentage of Dependent–Compliant adaptations and were *not* more Offensive–Combative than girls.

Children with a high frequency of conflict units had relatively more "Desire vs. Teacher Expectation" encounters than children with low frequencies, for whom more "Desire vs. Ability" conflicts were observed. Also, children in the high-frequency group reacted more openly, and more often employed an Offensive–Combative adaptation. Low-frequency pupils responded more often with Persistent and Withdrawing adaptive modes.

In an earlier study, Wolfson and Jackson (1970), observing three- and four-year-old pupils enrolled in a university-attached nursery school, recorded events which intruded upon the intended behavior of the children. They classified these events into seven categories (later used by Berk) defined according to the child's intent and the source of intrusion. An average of six events per child was recorded every 30 minutes. Seventy-five percent of these events fell into two categories representing the following situations: (1) a child's desire conflicting with another child's desire, and (2) a child's desire conflicting with a teacher demand. Observation of the children outside the school environment revealed that out-of-school events fell into the same two categories (substituting adult for teacher), with only slightly less frequency.

Analysis of these observation data showed that children with a high frequency of conflict incidents in one environment had a high frequency in the other as well. However, even children with low incident records experienced a great many conflict encounters—about 2000 per child, projecting the figures for one school year.

While Wolfson and Jackson did not examine the effect of these encounters on the pupil's developing self-concept, they did suggest that consistent use of certain response styles might contribute to a child's "social reputation" and influence the child's relationships with both peers and teachers.

Although the Wolfson and Jackson research was more limited than the study by Berk (who included socioeconomic status as a variable, observed children in a broader age range, and reported adaptive modes by SES, sex, and age of subjects), the investigators did analyze their data for age and sex differences. They found none in regard to (1) frequency of event, (2) dominant event categories, and (3) the stability of individual encounter frequencies. The dominance of two particular event categories and the large number of conflict encounters reported in Wolfson and Jackson's study were generally confirmed by Berk. However, since both studies employed the same event categories, any weakness in the classification system would have been reproduced in Berk's research.

The large number of conflict events recorded in these studies is perhaps due to the age of the subjects, the nature of the preschool learning experience, and the level of socialization reached by preschool children. We can hypothesize that a regular classroom environment and an older pupil population would yield nowhere near as many conflict events. Still, these studies do suggest a novel way of examining the effects of teacher control and the conflict inherent in the schooling process itself. The categories used (e.g., "pupil desire vs. teacher demand," "pupil desire vs. pupil ability," and "pupil desire vs. another pupil's desire") could be further developed and applied in relating classroom control to affective pupil behaviors. The adaptive response categories could be used as indicators of pupil self-concept. Change in behavioral patterns in reaction to specific conflict events could be interpreted as change in self-concept.

As a source of psychological experiences affecting the development of self-concept, the environmental continuum from home to school is sufficiently recognized but insufficiently researched. The conflict categories devised by Wolfson and Jackson and the response modes used by Berk could provide the basis for comparing the child's home and school environments. Information about the home environment (similar to that obtained by Baumrind) could be related to the child's experience in school. *Patterns* of response in the home and in school could be studied as a key to self-concept.

TEACHER BEHAVIOR AND PUPIL ANXIETY

Anxiety is a response to threat and therefore an indicator of events or conditions that are valued by the individual for the reflections, interpretations and information they provide. Only where values exist can anxiety be aroused.

The relationship between the research reported in this section and pupil self-concept development rests on the theory that aspects of the school environment, particularly demands for academic performance, threaten the self-concepts of children. The impact of the child's reflected academic performance depends on the child's value for academic achievement or approval. Pupils who rely on the school environment or the teacher for affirming self-reflections are, theoretically, under more stress than those who do not. We would expect these pupils to exhibit trait anxiety and to respond with more intensity to threatening cues from the school environment.

Pupils whose self-concepts are relatively positive and less dependent on the reflections supplied by the school environment and the teacher are unlikely to become anxious about school-related problems. Threatening cues from the school environment raise anxiety in these pupils just enough to allow them to deal with the situation. Such limited doses of anxiety can motivate a child toward a better performance. A curvilinear relationship between anxiety and performance has been posited by Malmo (1966), who suggests that a balanced ratio between anxiety level and degree of threat can raise performance. An imbalance between anxiety and threat may lower or completely inhibit performance. When anxiety is so intense that a child is unable to respond, the child's sense of continuing self is totally threatened.

Most of the research dealing with pupil anxiety examines either its effect on learning processes, or its relationship to specific teacher behaviors. Studies focusing on the latter frequently employ Flanders' (1966) constructs of Direct and Indirect teaching in selecting teacher behaviors to relate to pupil anxiety. Direct behaviors are characterized by teacher control and management, teacher dominance, and/or task orientation (e.g., "lecturing," "giving directions," "criticizing or justifying authority"). Indirect behaviors are more likely to be pupil-centered, with an emphasis on discussion, discovery, and democratic decision-making processes (e.g., "accepts pupil feeling," "praises or encourages," "accepts or uses ideas of students," "asks questions"). A ratio of Direct to Indirect behaviors is used in the Flanders' system to indicate which of the two styles is characteristic of the teacher, without reference to subject matter or lesson content.

Research, though inconclusive, suggests that Indirect behaviors are more effective than Direct behaviors in teaching anxious pupils. Duffey and Martin (1973), for example, found that highly insecure, trait-anxious pupils, who were very sensitive to threatening conditions, performed better under Indirect teaching (i.e., less teacher-demand) than pupils with low trait anxiety. (Since they did not measure the anxiety levels aroused by the test conditions, the investigators could not support Malmo's proposition that a curvilinear relationship exists between performance and anxiety.) The Duffey and Martin results are not inconsistent with those of Soar (1968), who found that *both* high- and low-anxious pupils improved under *both* Indirect and Direct teaching styles, though the high-anxious group improved less than the low-anxious under Direct conditions. In a third study employing the Flanders' system, Zimmerman (1970) found that the frequency of teacher controlling behaviors was significantly and positively related to pupil anxiety. Although these three studies differ in design and focus, they all suggest that Indirect may be more effective than Direct teaching for pupils with high anxiety.

Departing from Flanders' constructs, Doyal and Forsyth (1973) investigated the relationship between teacher trait anxiety and pupil test anxiety. Their results suggested that the teacher's manifest anxiety does influence pupil test anxiety, with a particularly significant positive correlation emerging between the anxiety scores of female pupils and their female teachers.

The research cited above offers sufficient evidence that teacher behavior affects pupil anxiety. This being so, it is reasonable to suggest that researchers and teachers examine the many instructional strategies and environmental innovations introduced each year for means to reduce pupil anxiety. New methods, curricula, and organizational strategies are developed ostensibly for one purpose—improving education. Although the ultimate index of improvement is the academic achievement of pupils, these educational innovations may, by altering the classroom environment, also offer opportunities for positive self-concept development. Improving pupil self-concept may not raise mean academic achievement, but it may increase the number of pupils achieving at the mean, or reduce the number of pupils failing, or even the number dropping out of school.

All of our educational strategies should be examined for potential to reduce the stress and anxiety of pupils. By creating supportive and responsive environments, teachers can minimize the negative impact of the school experience by relieving the threat to pupil self-concept, particularly the sense of continuing self. There is every reason to believe that such attempts will be successful, since research efforts to reduce pupil anxiety, though limited, are generally encouraging.

Muller and Madsen (1970), for example, report positive results using desensitization techniques to reduce pupil anxiety in reading and test situations. And Meathenia (1971) describes the success of a program implemented with kindergarten pupils to alleviate recurring fear and anxiety caused by trauma. Although she collected no evaluation data, Meathenia reports that pupils who suffered personal loss and injury in a severe tornado were able to work out their anxiety and fear of storms through physical and verbal expression and exploration of their feelings.

Felker, Stanwyck, and Kay (1973) successfully cultivated self-reward behavior in children to enhance their self-concepts and lower their anxiety. Mean anxiety scores for *both* experimental and control subjects were significantly reduced from pre- to posttest. Felker *et al.* speculate that enthusiasm for the program spread from experimental to control teachers during the treatment period, creating no significant difference in the posttests of their studies.

Team teaching has also been shown to lower anxiety in elementary school children. Schmidt and Gallessich (1971), studying a Mexican-American and Anglo-American population of 160 first graders and 382 sixth graders, report that team teaching, compared with instruction in a self-contained classroom, yielded lower anxiety scores for first grade girls and for Mexican-American pupils at both grade levels. They suggest that the presence of more than one instructor in the team situation increases the pupils' opportunity to obtain teacher approval and at the same time motivates the teachers, under the scrutiny of colleagues, to maintain a more positive relationship with pupils.

While the studies described above suggest methods for creating a classroom environment that is less anxiety-provoking, they do not necessarily help the individual teacher to identify the highly anxious pupil. Anxiety can be described as psychologically holding one's breath in anticipation, or emotionally waiting for the other shoe to fall. Behaviors that reflect anxiety are not confined to nervous jitters, giggling, or nail biting, which are usually recognized by even an insensitive and unperceptive individual. Anxiety related to a threatened sense of continuing self can be manifested by withdrawal and unresponsiveness, dependent behavior, or aggressiveness. Since these behaviors also appear in response to specific stimuli (and therefore sometimes reflect other senses of self), one must identify the *pattern* of behavioral reaction and consider the pupil's *values* before drawing conclusions about the pupil's sense of continuing self.

TEACHER BEHAVIOR AND PUPIL DEPENDENCY

Pupils exhibit varying degrees of dependent behavior in the classroom. Those who require constant reassurance about their performance, who need and want a great deal of teacher supervision and support, are "dependency-prone."

Among the most significant factors influencing dependency in children is control—by the teacher or the parent. Osofsky and O'Connell (1972) report that parents responded to the dependent behaviors of their 5-year-old daughters by increasing verbal and physical interaction with them and displaying more controlling behavior toward them. (Mothers were inclined to encourage the efforts of their children, while fathers more often helped them perform the assigned task.)

Apparently, dependent children learn at home to elicit controlling (dependence-supporting) behaviors—a skill that, according to the research, is transferred to the classroom. Flanders, Anderson, and Amidon (1961) report that the most significant factor in assessing the incidence of dependent behavior within a classroom is the pattern of control used by the teacher. Teachers who exert more control than the "average" instructor exact dependent and compliant behavior from their pupils (or, viewing the matter from another perspective, teachers who *supply* more control than "average" *support* the dependent behavior exhibited by their pupils). Anderson (1960) reports that dependent-prone pupils indicated a preference for less directive teachers than their more independent peers, and that girls preferred less directive teachers than boys did. This might indicate a value for independence among those who are still exhibiting dependent-complying behaviors.

Although the studies cited above indicate that control is one of the most important factors influencing pupil dependence, research investigating methods of dealing with dependent behavior has focused instead on approval (presumably because approval can easily be construed as supporting and reinforcing dependent behavior). Hartup (1958) found that nurturance withdrawal, or a low frequency of approval, was significantly related to faster, more accurate learning for girls and for dependent boys. Relatively independent boys, however, performed better under consistent nurturance. Theoretically, and apparently, dependent children value teacher approval as a reflection of acceptance, conditional though it may be. When they fail to receive it, they try harder. Less dependent children value teacher approval as a positive reflection and interpretation of their competence, which motivates them toward improved performance.

Speer, Briggs, and Gavalas (1969), examining the possibility that lack of approval for competence (initiating behavior) might be more potent in encouraging dependence than approval for dependent behavior, found that dependence and competence are not mutually exclusive. They report that preschool girls had a higher ratio of dependent to competent behaviors, and that boys, in reverse, had a higher ratio of competent to dependent behaviors, suggesting a possible sex difference at this early age. They also found that pupils rewarded for dependence show more dependent than competent behavior, and a higher ratio of dependent to competent behavior than pupils rewarded for competence or not rewarded at all. But the amount of dependent behavior exhibited was not appreciably different among the three reward groups, leading the authors to conclude that simple reinforcement, or approval, of behavior may be overrated as a change agent.

On the basis of our theoretical framework, we would hypothesize that dependent pupils value their teachers as significant or salient others. When teachers are thus valued as a source of approval, and their behaviors communicate approval or disapproval, they foster dependency in the pupil. However, when teachers provide interpretation or information along with reflections of approval or disapproval, they encourage independent pupil behavior. Teachers who function fully in the role of significant or salient others have positive impact on the self-concepts of dependent pupils.

TEACHER BEHAVIOR AND PUPIL AGGRESSION

Aggression, verbal or physical, is the least approved and most heartily disapproved behavioral mode in the classroom. Aggression is highly valued in combat, and therein lies the cue: Aggressive behaviors signal that the aggressor perceives the situation as combat, the other participants in the behavioral dialogue as foes or potential victims, and the eventual outcome of the exchange as necessarily win, lose, or draw. Precisely because aggression is valued in combat, it is deplored in the classroom.

According to middle-class American values, verbal aggression is superior to physical aggression, just as eating with a fork is superior to eating with the fingers. In both cases, behavior is elevated through the use of an acquired tool that eliminates actual physical contact. Our middle-class value system also allows more aggressive behavior in males than females, and less aggression overall than various subcultures within our society. On the basis of culture alone, we can expect differences in the aggressive behaviors of middle- and lower-SES pupils, and of males and females. In addition, since the socialization process involves systematic channeling of self-interest into behavioral forms that consider and accommodate others, we can expect a decrease in aggressive behavior as children become more socialized, a difference to which both age and intelligence contribute.

Pupils who are overtly aggressive, who cannot seem to acquire or value the social limitations on aggressive behavior in the classroom, may be "acting out" frustration. This kind of behavior is directly related to a threatened sense of the continuing self, stemming from a critical deficiency of psychological experiences reflecting the self and interpreting the self's role. The psychological isolation imposed by Helen Keller's physical condition, for example, accounted for many of her seemingly "unprovoked" tantrums (Keller 1968, p. 30).

> Meanwhile the desire to express myself grew. The few signs I used
> became less and less adequate, and my failures to make myself under-
> stood were invariably followed by outbursts of passion. I felt as if
> invisible hands were holding me, and I made frantic efforts to free
> myself. I struggled—not that struggling helped matters, but the spirit
> of resistance was strong within me; I generally broke down in tears and
> physical exhaustion. If my mother happened to be near I crept into
> her arms, too miserable even to remember the cause of the tempest.
> After awhile the need of some means of communication became so
> urgent that these outbursts occurred daily, sometimes hourly.

Helen's need to communicate, to become a social creature, was not met by
the warm acceptance of her mother or the loving indulgence of her father. Both
of these reflections were valued by Helen, but they did not distinguish her role
from that of a well-loved household pet. She acquired no basis for internal self-
control, and therefore when she was "crossed," she responded with anger and
tantrums.

Theoretically, children who receive no guidance, who test limits and find
none, who in the face of parental indulgence or neglect find themselves the sole
occupants of their world, must structure a monologue in place of the missing
behavioral dialogue, by which to interpret events and value reflections of their
impact on the world outside their bodies. That world and those who inhabit it
can only be perceived as sources of self-gratification. In effect, we are describing what Peck, Havighurst *et al.* (1964) in their typology of character development, have termed the Amoral and Expedient type.

Teachers confronted with this kind of behavior face a contest they will not
win, and should not enter. They will be neither significant nor salient others,
and their efforts to alter the pupil's value system within the framework of the
teacher's role and the classroom environment will simply not meet the challenge. However, it is not the teacher's job to diagnose such pupils; the problems
they present are usually severe enough to force the most determined salient
other to seek outside help.

The research reported on aggressive behavior is singularly distinguished
by the fact that it is not generally tied to pupil academic performance. But it
is not usually tied to pupil self-concept either. The value of research on pupil
aggression lies in its relationship to teacher control; and the educational intent
of such research is to increase teacher understanding.

Studies by Hicks (1965), Madsen (1968), and Dubanoski and Parton
(1971) report that aggressive behaviors modeled by adults seem to cue children, particularly boys, to increase their own aggressive behaviors and to extend the limits that ordinarily restrict the use of aggression. Apparently, when
practiced by adults, aggressive behavior is legitimatized in the eyes of children.

Siegal and Kohn (1959) found that adult behavior has two important
effects on the aggressive behavior of children: (1) When an adult is present,

children appear to relinquish responsibility for their behavior to the adult, allowing the adult to mediate their actions by setting and enforcing limits; (2) In the absence of adult supervision, children tend to implement their own limitations on aggressive behavior. (The length of time that children take to put such limitations into effect is a function of social maturation.) While supervision of children is often necessary, the presence of a highly directive, controlling adult can be viewed as a deterrent to the development of self-control, independence, and responsibility. Thus, controlling teachers may be sabotaging their professed goals of establishing order and encouraging responsible behavior.

An apparent developmental difference in the frustration–aggression responses of fourth and sixth grade boys is reported by Cohen (1971). Defining frustration–aggression experiences in terms of punitive, restrictive, and rejection encounters with parents, teachers, and peers, Cohen found a significant, negative correlation between frustration and overt aggression among fourth grade boys. For sixth grade boys, he found only peer-related frustration associated with aggression.

Cohen concluded that fourth grade boys suppress aggressive behavior when frustrated, perhaps because they do not distinguish among frustration experiences; they use only adults as their frame of reference for behavior. Sixth grade boys, on the other hand, appear to differentiate frustration experiences according to their source (i.e., peer or adult), using children as well as adults for standards of behavior and thus freeing themselves somewhat from adult control.

Shantz and Voydanoff (1973) found age differences in the ability of boys to distinguish intentional from accidental provocation of aggressive behavior. Boys aged nine to twelve years differentiated between the two circumstances and responded less aggressively to accidental provocation, while seven-year-olds failed to distinguish the two conditions. Twelve-year-old boys responded less aggressively to intentional verbal than intentional physical provocation, but nine- and seven-year-old boys made no distinction between the two forms. When subjects were asked to recall the circumstances of provocation, they differentiated between intentional and accidental, but not between verbal and physical provocation.

Deur and Parke (1970) report that punishment consistently applied suppressed the strength and persistence of aggressive response in second and third grade boys. Children with a history of inconsistent punishment and reward for aggression gave stronger resistance to consistently applied punishment and withstood for a longer time efforts to extinguish their aggressive behavior.

If, as we have suggested, aggressive behavior creates a win or lose situation, aggressors who are not consistently punished can always hope to win the next time. Occasional "losses" may even strengthen determination to make the next contest a victory.

Methods to reduce the deviant and basically aggressive behavior of problem students have been studied by Stoffer (1970), Glavin, Quay, and Werry (1971), and Quarter and Laxer (1970). Glavin *et al.* report positive academic and behavior changes after two years of an individualized "psycho-educational" program. Stoffer, using warm and empathetic mothers as aides in a three-month program of one-to-one counseling, reports greater success with shy, withdrawn children than with aggressive children, although improvement occurred across groups. Presumably, the "warm" mothers provided the shy, withdrawn children with more self-reflection and interpretation, which produced behavioral and self-concept changes. The aggressive children, however, probably received less initial approval; it is doubtful that the mothers sought to "draw" them out, a procedure that is usually applied immediately to shy and withdrawn children. Aggression elicits disapproval rather than approval. Thus it is difficult for adults to restructure and reinterpret aggressive children's roles, or gain access to their values on the basis of their current behavior. Furthermore, efforts to control such children, which may pose a conflict situation, will be valued as reflections and interpretations only after considerable time and consistent application.

Quarter and Laxer found that a program of small-group counseling, along with seminars in which material on aggression and frustration was indirectly introduced, did not reduce problem behavior in their subjects. They suggest that the treatment may have reinforced a "troublemaker" self-image valued by these junior high school subjects. This is reminiscent of the man who robbed the poorbox after he was befriended by the clergyman. As the good pastor said, "At least he was in church." At least the program provided by these counselors served the subjects' value systems.

Anxious pupils may act aggressively to force an outcome, one way or the other, in order to relieve their anxiety. Dependency-prone pupils may aggressively seek approval from their teachers. Frustrated pupils often behave aggressively, acting out the defeat they are experiencing, and unsocialized children are sometimes aggressive due to ignorance of or indifference to behavioral modes that serve the self while at the same time considering others. Even withdrawn and shy pupils can be described as passively aggressive if their behavior controls the behavior of others. What perceptive, sensitive adult fails to take initiative with shy children, softening the tone of voice, usually to one of intimacy, and more often than not, stooping or bending in an effort to appear less threatening?

The only true reward for aggression is victory. When teachers allow an aggressive child to cast them in the role of foe, victim, or combatant, they join the battle. The function of a significant or salient other is to define the child's role and interpret the behavioral dialogue in light of the child's concerns. By providing a positive reflection that offers support, the teacher can help relieve the anxiety of the anxious pupil. By specifying terms for approval (which the child is able to meet), the teacher can help the aggressive-dependent pupil control aggression and move toward independence. By creating psychological safety for passively aggressive pupils, and by setting and consistently enforcing firm limits for unsocialized children, the teacher can fulfill the role of significant or salient other and have positive impact on pupil self-concept.

THE SENSE OF SELF DIFFERENTIATED FROM OTHERS AND THE ENVIRONMENT

The sense of self differentiated from others and the environment is the basis of individuality and the focus of the Sense of Self-Identity. While individuality is valued in our society, the real psychological struggle is for identity, the need to be not only recognized but also identified and affiliated. For example, it is not enough that we each have our own Social Security number, shared with no one else. Being just a number or, as we usually say, just another number, however unique, does not appeal to us. A number distinguishes us from others but relates us to no one. It does not serve our sense of self-identity.

Few people believe that they stand out in a crowd, but almost everyone has felt lonely in one. The sense of self differentiated from others and the environment is the basic concept on which we predicate the organization of our conscious being, and those who lack this sense of self are in a pathological state.

Charles M. Schulz, originator of the *Peanuts* comic strip and creator of Charlie Brown, the lad with a perpetually flagging self-concept, described the feelings he had about himself as a boy (Schulz 1975):

> When I was small, I believed my face was so bland that people would not recognize me if they saw me someplace other than where they normally did. I was sincerely surprised if I happened to be in the downtown area of St. Paul, Minnesota, shopping with my mother, and we would bump into a fellow student or a teacher, and they recognized me.

To recognize the pupil as an individual is the most and best any teacher can do to enhance a pupil's sense of self differentiated from others and the environment.

TEACHER BEHAVIOR AND THE SENSE OF BODILY SELF

The Sense of Bodily Self with its three basic self-conceptualizations is the core of the General Self-Concept and the foundation for the remaining senses of self. A sense of self differentiated from others and the environment is fundamental to the concept of individuality. A sense of self as a physical entity with form, substance, and appearance is essential to a concept of self-identity. And, a sense of self-continuity that incorporates basic feelings of safety or peril, acceptance or rejection, and trust or mistrust is the foundation of the concept of self as performer and participator.

When we theorize that the Sense of Bodily Self is at the core of every person's self-conceptualizations, we are presuming that each individual is in this respect like every other individual. We are also presuming that the process of self-concept formation (i.e., the internalization of psychological experiences) is the same in all individuals, and therefore that every person's psychological experiences are the product of the interaction between that person's physical and psychological *nature* and physical and psychological *nurture*. But we must look beyond this universality in process and form to specific attributes in the nature and specific events in the nurture of individuals to find those aspects of self-concept that are alike in all individuals, those that are alike among some individuals, and those that are unique to particular individuals.

There is surely a presumption that all people are alike in some respects in the very concept of public, let alone compulsory, education. And there is a further presumption that some individuals are alike in some respects in the ordering and systematizing of grade levels and curricula. The presumption of *individual uniqueness,* however, enters into the concept of public education primarily as an educational philosophy, a philosophy that is constantly confronted with institutional conditions designed to implement the more dominant presumption of similarity among children and to promote a value for conformity.

It is not realistic to view public education as a process conducive to individualization as if it were comparable to gem cutting and polishing. But in a society that professes a value for the individual, neither is it realistic to view public education as an entirely collective process, as indiscriminate in application and as narrowly focused as crushing rocks to produce graded gravel. A public education system that incorporates a value for the individual and focuses on the excellence of the end product is instead akin to "rock tumbling," a process that shapes and polishes while it preserves and highlights the unique nature of each rock, a process in which the product depends upon the interaction of the rocks as well as the power of the machinery.

If public education is to serve society's need to make all of its members alike in some respects (e.g., with regard to values and traditions) and some of its members alike in other respects (e.g., roles required to maintain the society) and at the same time encourage and preserve the uniqueness of the individual, it must acknowledge diversity as well as similarity in the nature and nurture of children.

Although any group of pupils may share similarities, it should be recognized that they are individuals. At the very core of effective nurturance is a value for the individual and an attitude of acceptance toward the physical, social, and psychological characteristics of each pupil. What counts in the development of a positive Sense of the Bodily Self, or of any sense of self, is a value for the individual expressed in an attitude of unconditional acceptance of that individual and concern for his or her physical and psychological safety. Both the value and the attitude are reflected in the perceptual set of the "effective helper" (Combs and Soper 1963; Combs 1969) and in the concerns for task and impact on others shown by competent and nurturant teachers (Fuller 1969).

A teacher who perceives that all pupils are alike in their need for acceptance, safety, and assistance with learning can also recognize that some pupils are like others in their particular needs and concerns without losing sight of each pupil's individuality. Public education is essentially a group process; and the subject of group formation and group experiences is more fully discussed in the Sense of Self-Identity. In relation to pupil individuality and the Sense of Bodily Self, however, it should be noted that group experiences can obscure pupil individuality if the teacher consistently reflects, interprets, informs, and perceives the class as a unit. Whether pupils are working as a group or individually, the uniqueness of the individual is always present in his or her person, performance, and products. Whenever possible, person, performance and products deserve individual recognition, reflection, and interpretation. Unless there is a definite reason for reflecting group membership, the language of the classroom should be individually referenced. For example, "Good morning to each of you," reflects a one-to-one teacher-pupil relationship, while "Good morning, class," reflects group membership. Trivial though it may seem, teacher language can be one of the most effective means of creating psychological safety in the classroom. Instructors who build a permanent "teacher/class" or "teacher/group" structure in the classroom create a psychological barrier between themselves and their pupils and intensify the psychological risk involved in performing or participating as an individual. How much understanding is lost and how many opportunities to participate are passed over by pupils who not only dread exposure to teacher evaluation in that no-man's-land between the "teacher" and the "class" but also fear the isolation that can come from being, or appearing to be, the one person out of step with the drill team.

On the other hand, instructors who establish a teacher/child focus in their classrooms have a bridge rather than a barrier between themselves and their pupils. Yet they are still free to use group processes and reflections purposefully and constructively.

It is not the teacher's recognition of pupil similarities or differences that influences the pupil's Sense of Bodily Self. It is the interjection of teacher values expressed in attitudes and behavior toward pupils that has a critical effect. When pupils perceive that the teacher's response to them is determined by some physical, social, or performance characteristic, they will incorporate that perception into their self-concepts. They will conclude that a condition determines their acceptance and safety, their rejection and peril. Even when the teacher reflects a *positive* value for a particular pupil characteristic, the teacher still introduces a condition, and therefore a self-concern into the teacher–pupil relationship. If pupils feel accepted *regardless* of their characteristics, their sense of safety and trust will free them from the concern for self that otherwise influences the nature of their self-concept and sometimes interferes with their learning. Yet, unconditional acceptance of individuals does not preclude the rejection of certain asocial *behaviors*. Such rejection, in fact, allows pupils to see that it is their behavior (something ostensibly within their control), and not their "self," that is unacceptable.

Applying our self-concept theory to the teacher's classroom behavior, it appears that the pupil's Sense of Bodily Self, and specifically his or her individuality and feeling of safety and trust, can be best nurtured by teachers who:

1. Value and accept all pupils;

2. Reflect this value and acceptance in their language, their lesson plans, and their classroom behavior in general, creating a climate that offers physical and psychological safety to every pupil (see Chapter 5, The Sense of Self-Extension); and

3. Examine their teaching procedures from the pupil's perspective to determine whether grouping truly serves the individual student and not merely the teacher or the system (see Chapter 4, The Sense of Self-Identity).

Pupils who are concerned that they are "different" may allow this concern to shape their self-perception and obscure the value of their own uniqueness. Helen Keller's desire to overcome her "difference" almost subverted her most valuable contribution, the story of her own experience. Anne Sullivan helped her identify with others, but Charles T. Copeland, one of her college professors, reflected her value as an individual (Keller 1968, pp. 312–313):

> ... I never knew what my difficulty was [in writing themes] until you pointed it out to me. When I came to your class last October, I was trying with all my might to be like everyone else, to forget as entirely as possible my limitations and peculiar environment. ...
>
> I have always accepted other people's experiences and observations as a matter of course. It never occurred to me that it might be worth while to make my own observations and describe the experiences peculiarly my own. Henceforth I am resolved to be myself, to live my own life and write my own thoughts when I have any.

94   The Sense of Bodily Self

REFERENCES

Erikson, E. H. 1963. *Childhood and society*. (2nd ed. rev.) New York: Norton.

Sullivan, H. S. 1953. *The interpersonal theory of psychiatry*. New York: Norton.

THE SENSE OF PHYSICAL SELF

Teacher Behavior and the Physical Attractiveness of Pupils

Adams, G. R., and A. S. Cohen 1974. Children's physical and interpersonal characteristics that affect student-teacher interactions. *Journal of Experimental Education* **43** (1): 1–5.

Angelou, M. 1969. *I know why the caged bird sings*. New York: Random House.

Clifford, M. M. 1975. *Physical attractiveness and academic performance*. Paper presented at the annual meeting of the American Educational Research Association, Washington, D.C., March.

Cole, C. W., E. R. Oetting, and R. W. Miskimins 1969. Self-concept therapy for adolescent females. *Journal of Abnormal Psychology* **74** (6): 642–645.

Combs, A. W. 1969. *Florida studies in the helping professions* (Social Science Monograph No. 37). Gainesville: University of Florida Press.

Grier, W. H., and P. M. Cobbs 1968. *Black rage*. New York, N.Y.: Basic Books.

Lash, J. P. 1971. *Eleanor and Franklin*. New York: W. W. Norton.

Teacher Behavior and Pupil Handicaps

Keeve, P. J. 1967. Perpetuating phantom handicaps in school age children. *Exceptional Children* **33** (8): 539–544.

Wolfgang, J., and A. Wolfgang 1968. *Personal space—an unobtrusive measure of attitudes toward the physically handicapped*. Paper presented at the 76th annual meeting of the American Psychological Association, San Francisco.

Teacher Behavior and Pupil Body Build

Walker, R. N. 1962. Body build and behavior in young children: I. Body build and nursery school teachers' ratings. *Society for Research in Child Development* **27** (3), Monograph Serial No. 84.

Teacher Behavior and Sex of Pupil

Davis, O. L., Jr., and J. J. Slobodian 1967. Teacher behavior toward boys and girls during first grade reading instruction. *American Educational Research Journal* **4** (3): 261–269.

Good, T., and J. Brophy 1972. Behavioral expression of teacher attitudes. *Journal of Educational Psychology* **63**: 617–624.

Jackson, P. W., and H. M. Lahaderne 1967. Inequalities of teacher-pupil contacts. *Psychology in the Schools* **4**: 204–208.

Kaufman, B. 1964. *Up the down staircase.* Englewood Cliffs, N.J.: Prentice-Hall.

Lahaderne, H. M. 1975. *The feminized elementary school: an unpromising myth to explain boys' reading problems.* Unpublished expanded version of a paper presented at the annual meeting of the American Educational Research Association, Washington, D.C., March.

Meyer, W. J., and G. G. Thompson 1956. Teacher interaction with boys as contrasted with girls. In Sex differences in the distribution of teacher approval and disapproval among sixth grade children. *Journal of Educational Psychology* **47:** 385–397.

McNeil, J. D. 1964. Programmed instruction versus usual classroom procedures in teaching boys to read. *American Educational Research Journal* **1** (2): 113–120.

Palardy, J. 1969. What teachers believe—what children achieve. *Elementary School Journal* **69:** 370–374.

Teacher Behavior and Pupil Race

Coopersmith, S. 1959. A method for determining types of self-esteem. *Journal of Abnormal and Social Psychology* **59:** 87–94.

Kaufman, B. 1964. *Up the down staircase.* Englewood Cliffs, N.J.: Prentice-Hall.

Kleinfeld, J. 1972. The relative importance of teachers and parents in the formation of Negro and white students' academic self-concept. *Journal of Educational Research* **65** (5): 211–212.

Rubovits, P. E., and M. L. Maehr 1973. Pygmalion black and white. *Journal of Personality and Social Psychology* **25** (2): 210–218.

St. John, N. 1971. Thirty-six teachers: their characteristics, and outcomes for black and white pupils. *American Educational Research Journal* **8** (4): 635–648. (ERIC Document Reproduction Service No. EJ 052 663.)

Zirkel, P. A., and E. G. Moses 1971. Self-concept and ethnic group membership among public school students. *American Educational Research Journal* **8** (2): 241–252.

THE SENSE OF THE CONTINUING SELF

Lash, J. P. 1971. *Eleanor and Franklin.* New York: W. W. Norton.

Environment Control and Pupil Response to Conflict

Baumrind, D. 1967. Child care practices anteceding three patterns of preschool behavior. *Genetic Psychology Monographs* **75:** 43–88.

Berk, L. E. 1971. Effects of variations in the nursery school setting on environmental constraints and children's modes of adaptation. *Child Development* **42:** 839–869.

Rosengarten, T. 1974. *All God's dangers.* New York: Knopf.

Wolfson, B. J., and P. W. Jackson 1970. *Life's little problems: an intensive look at the daily experiences of young children.* (Informal paper). National Laboratory on Early Childhood Education, April. (OEC-3-7-070706-3118.)

Teacher Behavior and Pupil Anxiety

Doyal, G. T., and R. A. Forsyth 1973. Relationship between teacher and student anxiety levels: MAS and TASC. *Psychology in the Schools* **10:** 231–233.

Duffey, J. B., and R. P. Martin 1973. Effects of direct and indirect teacher influence and student trait anxiety on the immediate recall of academic material. *Psychology in the Schools* **10:** 231–233.

Felker, D. W., D. J. Stanwyck, and R. S. Kay 1973. The effects of a teacher program in self-concept enhancement on pupils' self-concept, anxiety, and intellectual achievement responsibility. *Journal of Educational Research* **66** (10): 443–445.

Flanders, N. A. 1966. *Interaction analysis in the classroom, a manual for observers.* Ann Arbor: University of Michigan.

Malmo, R. B. 1966. Studies of anxiety: some clinical origins of the activation concept. In C. D. Spielberger (ed.), *Anxiety and behavior.* New York: Academic Press.

Meathenia, P. S. 1971. An experience with fear in the lives of children. *Childhood Education* **48** (2): 75–79.

Muller, S. D., and C. H. Madsen, Jr. 1970. Group desensitization for anxious children with reading problems. *Psychology in the Schools* **7** (2): 184–189.

Schmidt, L., and J. Gallessich 1971. Adjustment of Anglo-American and Mexican-American pupils in self-contained and team-teaching classrooms. *Journal of Educational Psychology* **62** (4): 328–332.

Soar, R. S. 1968. Optimum teacher-pupil interaction for pupil growth. *Educational Leadership Research Supplement* **26** (3): 275–280.

Zimmerman, B. J. 1970. Relationship between teacher classroom behavior and student school anxiety levels. *Psychology in the Schools* **7** (1): 89–93.

Teacher Behavior and Pupil Dependency

Anderson, J. P. 1960. *Student perceptions of teacher influence.* Unpublished doctoral dissertation, University of Minnesota.

Flanders, N. A., J. P. Anderson, and E. J. Amidon 1961. Measuring dependence proneness in the classroom. *Educational and Psychological Measurement* **21** (3): 575–587.

Hartup, W. W. 1958. Nurturance and nurturance-withdrawal in relation to the dependency behavior of preschool children. *Child Development* **29:** 191–201.

Osofsky, J. D., and E. J. O'Connell 1972. Parent-child interactions: daughters' effects upon mothers' and fathers' behaviors. *Developmental Psychology* **7** (2): 157–168. (ERIC Document Reproduction Service No. EJ 063 949.)

Speer, D. C., P. F. Briggs, and R. Gavalas 1969. Concurrent schedules of social reinforcement and dependency behavior among four-year-old children. *Journal of Experimental Child Psychology* **8** (2): 356–365.

Teacher Behavior and Pupil Aggression

Cohen, S. 1971. An examination of frustration aggression relations in boys during middle childhood. *Journal of Genetic Psychology* **118** (1): 129–140.

Dubanoski, R. A., and D. A. Parton 1971. Imitative aggression in children as a function of observing a human model. *Developmental Psychology* **4** (3): 489.

Deur, J. L., and R. D. Parke 1970. Effects of inconsistent punishment on aggression in children. *Developmental Psychology* **2** (3): 403–411.

Glavin, J. P., H. C. Quay, and J. S. Werry 1971. Behavioral and academic gains of conduct problem children in different classroom settings. *Exceptional Children* **37** (6): 441–446.

Hicks, D. J. 1965. Imitation and retention of film-mediated aggressive peer and adult models. *Journal of Personality and Social Psychology* **2**: 97–100.

Keller, H. 1968. *The story of my life.* New York: Lancer.

Madsen, C. 1968. Nurturance and modeling in preschoolers. *Child Development* **39** (1): 221–236.

Peck, R. F., R. J. Havighurst, R. Cooper, J. Lilienthal, and D. More 1964. *The psychology of character development.* New York: Wiley.

Quarter, J. J., and R. M. Laxer 1970. A structured program of teaching and counseling for conduct problem students in a junior high school. *Journal of Educational Research* **63** (5): 229–231.

Shantz, D. W., and D. A. Voydanoff 1973. Situational effects on retaliatory aggression at three age levels. *Child Development* **44**: 149–153.

Siegal, A. E., and L. G. Kohn 1959. Permissiveness, permission, and aggression: the effect of adult presence or absence on aggression in children's play. *Child Development* **30**: 131–141.

Stoffer, D. L. 1970. Investigation of positive behavioral change as a function of genuineness, nonpossessive warmth, and empathetic understanding. *Journal of Educational Research* **63** (5): 225–228.

THE SENSE OF SELF DIFFERENTIATED FROM OTHERS AND THE ENVIRONMENT

Schulz, Charles 1975. *Peanuts jubilee, my life and art with Charlie Brown and others.* New York: Holt, Rinehart and Winston.

TEACHER BEHAVIOR AND THE SENSE OF BODILY SELF

Combs, A. W. 1969. *Florida studies in the helping professions* (Social Science Monograph No. 37). Gainesville: University of Florida Press.

———, and D. W. Soper 1963. The helping relationship as described by "good" and "poor" teachers. *Journal of Teacher Education* **14**: 64–68.

Fuller, F. F. 1969. Concerns of teachers: a developmental conceptualization. *American Educational Research Journal* **6**: 207–226.

Keller, H. 1968. *The story of my life.* New York: Lancer.

CHAPTER 4
The Sense of Self-Identity

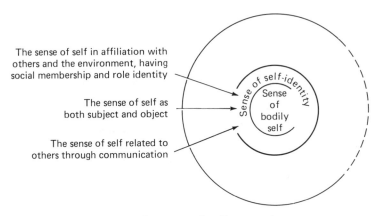

The sense of self in affiliation with
others and the environment, having
social membership and role identity

The sense of self as
both subject and object

The sense of self related to
others through communication

Sense of self-identity

Sense of bodily self

Fig. 4.1 Self-identity of the general self-concept.

The psychological construct of "Self-Identity" represents the sense of self *in relation* to significant/salient others and the environment—a sense of self built upon the reflections and responses supplied by these external sources. From the outset, the infant's impact initiates the behavioral dialogue, prompting significant others to assume their responding and interpreting roles:

"The baby's crying, he must be hungry."
"I just fed him, he's probably wet."
"I just changed him, maybe it's gas."
"I don't think so, I think he just needs a little exercise, he sounds tired to me."
"Please be quiet, the baby's sleeping."

Significant others respond to the developing self according to their own explanations of the self's physiological state, physical movements, and vocalizations. It is the significant others' *interpretations* of the baby's behavior that determine the reflection of self transmitted. And these interpretations are colored by the self-concepts of the attending significant others and by their perceptions of their relationship with the new arrival.

In the preceding chapter we described how the infant experiences a sense of self, forming a Sense of Bodily Self—of physical entity, self-continuity, and individuality—by differentiating the sensed self from others and the environment. Each day the infant experiences a flow of varying sensations, marked by repetitions in the biological cycle—e.g., hunger, rest, hunger, rest. These form the infant's first psychological experiences. To these experiences are added the interpretations and responses of significant others, thus creating a behavioral dialogue that extends beyond the senses of a bodily self to encompass the external environment. The repetition of physical sensations and human responses provides the basis for the formation of cognitive constructs and, eventually, behavioral schema developed through the cognitive processes of association, differentiation, generalization and internalization.

As the child acquires a symbolic system of communication, the feelings about self can be cognitively identified, organized, and conceptualized to form a sense of self-in-relation-to-others, of self as a social being with a social role. Having differentiated a self from others and the environment, the child now seeks to affiliate with others and gradually gains *identity* as part of an emerging concept of self-in-relation-to-others. As language is acquired, the child expands the categories and concepts available for further defining relationships and interpreting behavior.

THE SENSE OF SELF IN AFFILIATION WITH OTHERS AND THE ENVIRONMENT—HAVING SOCIAL MEMBERSHIP AND ROLE IDENTITY

The first communication of relationship to the infant is, as Erikson describes it, a message of acceptance or rejection, of friendliness or hostility (Erikson 1959). If that initial message persists, it produces in the child an internalized attitude "set" toward the objectified self and toward others and the environment. An attitude of trust or mistrust colors the child's interpretation of all succeeding psychological experiences from which self-concept derives. However, this is not intended to imply that the initial attitude set is unalterable. Life offers many opportunities for attitude change. The development of one's sense of self-in-relation-to-others—the formation of one's sense of identity—is a fluctuating process, characterized at times by expanding association, at times by disaffiliation. Encountering new psychological experiences, the individual can reinterpret events and change attitudes toward the self and others.

THE EFFECT OF THE SIGNIFICANT OTHER'S SELF-CONCERNS ON THE CHILD'S FORMATION OF SELF-IDENTITY

> I ask all her friends to encourage her to tell them of her doings, and
> to manifest as much curiosity and pleasure in her little adventures as

they possibly can. This gratifies the child's love of approbation and keeps up her interest in things. This is the basis of real intercourse. . . . The impulse to tell is the important thing. I supply a word here and there, sometimes a sentence, and suggest something which she has omitted or forgotten.

Anne Sullivan in Helen Keller 1968, The story of my life, *pp. 378– 379.*

The role of the significant other in the development of self-identity is difficult to overemphasize. It is the significant other who nurtures or inhibits the child's "impulse to tell," and the dialogue between the two gives the child an opportunity to define the self in relation to others. However, because the nature of the behavioral dialogue is in large part determined by the self-concept and values of the significant other, it can become distorted if he or she is preoccupied with self-concerns. The predominance of such self-concerns (grounded perhaps in fear of responsibility, incompetence, or inadequacy) can in fact reduce the behavioral dialogue to a monologue delivered by the significant other. The absence of a dialogue, or the intrusion of the significant other's self-concerns into the images reflected to the developing self, can affect the child's sense of self-identity in various ways.

If the significant other, absorbed in self-concerns, creates a primarily monological relationship with the developing self, keeping interaction to a minimum and providing few psychological experiences, the developing self may in turn limit interactions with others and the environment, further reducing the opportunity to obtain positive self-reflections. If, in addition, the few reflections supplied by the significant other are negative, the developing self will perceive relationships with others and the environment as essentially negative.

When significant others are excessively concerned about their own adequacy and perceive their relationship with a developing self as a test of competence, they will reflect a child as a product or extension of themselves, acceptable only when the child's behaviors affirm the significant other's capability. Or, in order to ensure that they are seen as completely adequate and totally responsible, significant others may anticipate and carry out both sides of the behavioral dialogue. And in so doing, they may obscure the image of the developing self, negating both the process and product of identity formation.

In the classroom environment, it is the teacher, of course, who functions as significant or salient other. And, in turn, it is the teacher's self-concept and concerns which shape the behavioral dialogue and influence the pupils' sense of self-identity.

Teachers who feel personally or professionally inadequate, or who dislike teaching, for example, may allow these feelings to color the classroom dialogue. They may be overly controlling, authoritarian, and defensively hostile toward their pupils. Or, they may be excessively and inappropriately nondirective, easily diverted from teaching tasks and indifferent to pupil performance and products. The point is that extreme feelings, or self-concerns, will produce extreme behavior of one type or another. We might look for verbal hostility toward pupils or unmerited praise and flattery; we might also anticipate low acceptance of pupil ideas or the reverse—unguided pupil leadership. A high frequency of convergent questioning (when divergent queries would be more appropriate) or an unstructured effort to pool pupil ignorance might also occur. And, finally, we might expect extreme patterns in the teacher's use of social and spatial distance.

Teachers who view pupils as an extension of themselves or proof of their adequacy have an equally negative effect on the classroom dialogue. They may, for example, ignore slow and/or passive pupils or offer them excessive assistance in order to maintain the appearance of learning progress.

In any case, teachers' self-concerns affect their definition of the pupil role and, in so doing, confine or expand the pupil's opportunity to establish a sense of identity in the classroom. Research suggests, in fact, that certain, pronounced interpretations of the pupil role are associated to some extent with the extremes in teacher behavior described above. Dobson, Goldenberg, and Elson (1972), in an attempt to determine whether the teacher's ideology of pupil control is expressed in classroom behavior, identified from a large group of elementary school teachers in a southern suburban area extremely "custodial" (i.e., very controlling) and extremely "humanistic" (i.e., very non-directive) instructors. The two groups were then observed on the Flanders Interaction Analysis Scale (Flanders 1966).

Significant differences were found in the verbal behavior of custodial and humanistic teachers. While there was no significant difference between the two groups in the proportion of indirect to total teacher statements, the humanistic teachers accepted and developed pupil ideas significantly more than did the custodial teachers. Similarly, the proportion of direct to total teacher statements was essentially the same for both groups, but custodial teachers lectured significantly more than did humanistic teachers. There was no significant difference between groups on the dimension of total pupil talk, but the amount of pupil-initiated talk was significantly higher in humanistic classrooms. The investigators conclude that the teachers' pupil control ideology is expressed in their classroom behavior and that humanistic instructors employ a significantly greater number (though not a higher proportion) of indirect teaching behaviors than do custodial instructors.

While the Dobson, Goldenberg, and Elson research supports our contention that the teacher's interpretation of the pupil role influences the classroom dialogue, the subjects observed in this study probably did not demonstrate the behavioral extremes we previously described. Such pronounced behavior is more likely to occur among first-year teachers or instructors in private schools which specifically endorse one or the other of these two ideologies of pupil control.

We have illustrated how the self-concerns of significant others (parents and teachers) can distort or diminish the behavioral dialogue and the child's role. When such distortion is extreme, the child's reaction may also be extreme. The child who experiences repeated rejection, frustration, and non-recognition will not establish a concept of self affiliated with others and the environment. The extreme consequence of a failure to organize a self or to identify with others is infantile or childhood autism, a condition reflecting a serious disruption in the process of "self" conceptualization, whether the cause of the condition is psychological, physiological, or both. Accordingly, autism is often treated by establishing a behavioral dialogue in which therapists, functioning as constant and consistent significant others, first provide remedial psychological experiences through which the child can *differentiate* self from others and the environment to acquire a sense of individuality, and then supply additional experiences through which the child can develop a sense of self-*in-relation*-to-others and the environment (Lovaas, Koegel, Simmons, and Long 1973).

It was precisely this sort of remedial dialogue that Anne Sullivan established with Helen Keller. Her primary concern in doing so was to facilitate communication with Helen. However, the nature of the dialogue initiated by Miss Sullivan (her perception of the pupil role and the value of communication) indicates that she was also deeply concerned about her pupil. Helen's report of her learning experience reflects not only the cognitive, but also the affective elements of Anne Sullivan's view of communication and the developing self in the pupil role (Keller 1968, p. 46).

> ... If I did not know the words and idioms necessary to express my thoughts, she supplied them, even suggesting conversation when I was unable to keep up my end of the dialogue.
> ... The little hearing child learns these from constant repetition and imitation. The conversation he hears in his home stimulates his mind and suggests topics and calls forth the spontaneous expression of his own thoughts. This natural exchange of ideas is denied to the deaf child. My teacher, realizing this, determined to supply the kinds of stimulus I lacked. This she did by repeating to me as far as possible, verbatim, what she heard, and by showing me how I could take part in the conversation. But it was a long time before I ventured to take the initiative, and still longer before I could find something appropriate to say at the right time.

TEACHER BEHAVIOR, PUPIL ETHNICITY, AND SOCIOECONOMIC STATUS

As a society, we picture ourselves as people who love and care for children. Childhood should be happy and carefree; each child should have a good start in life, so we say. Our ideals for children are admirable; the realities of childhood, however, often fall short of these ideals.

The forces we have marshalled to improve the lives of our children are generally unleashed in the classroom. We depend on education to elevate the lower socioeconomic classes, to introduce ethnic minorities to the American way of life, to correct racial attitudes and destroy racial prejudice, and to compensate for the bad start that some children get in life. But we have discovered, of course, that education is not removed from society, but is instead part and parcel of the system it hopes to improve.

It is our society that produces the pupils, the teachers, the conditions into which they were born, the conditions under which they teach and learn, and the environment in which they encounter psychological experiences necessary for self-concept development.

> **The beautiful buildings sat on a moderate hill in the white residential district, some sixty blocks from the Negro neighborhood. For the first semester, I was one of three Black students in the school, and in that rarefied atmosphere I came to love my people more. Mornings as the streetcar traversed my ghetto I experienced a mixture of dread and trauma. I knew that all too soon we would be out of my familiar setting, and Blacks who were on the streetcar when I got on would all be gone and I alone would face the forty blocks of neat streets, smooth lawns, white houses and rich children.**

M. Angelou, 1969. I know why the caged bird sings, *pp. 208–209.*

It is fortunate that our educational system does afford some opportunity for children to withdraw from the greater society into the smaller world of the classroom, an environment that attempts to preserve societal standards and encourages youthful idealism. Schools can plan experiential learning in democratic processes and opportunities for positive self-concept development. However, implementation of these plans, and realization of a better learning environment in general, rests in great part with the teacher. Do teacher values and behaviors reflect the ideals of a democratic society with respect to pupil race, ethnicity, and socioeconomic status? What impact do these values and behaviors have on the pupil's effort to establish identity?

Anecdotal, but powerful, evidence of the intrusion of teacher values—values incompatible with democratic ideals—into the teaching situation can be found in the interaction of Anne Sullivan and Helen Keller. Miss Sullivan's racial attitudes (though firmly rooted in the cultural values of the time and therefore not as *obviously* inconsistent with societal ideals as they would be today), illustrate the power of inadvertent expressions of teacher belief to affect the pupil's perception. Miss Sullivan's racial beliefs crept into the behavioral dialogue, captured Helen's curiosity, and apparently shaped her perceptions, though in an unexpected way. The excerpts below, taken from different sections of Miss Sullivan's letters, convey one of Helen's psychological experiences which resulted in concept formation. Describing the extent of her interaction with Helen, Miss Sullivan reports (Keller 1968, p. 370):

> She sleeps with me now. Mrs. Keller wanted to get a nurse for her; but I concluded I'd rather be her nurse than look after a *stupid, lazy negress*. Besides, I like to have Helen depend on me for everything, and I find it much easier to teach her things at odd moments than at set times. (April 3, 1887) (Emphasis added.)

A few months later Miss Sullivan (Keller 1968, pp. 396–397) notes that Helen has an interest in color:

> "What colour is think?" was one of the restful questions she asked, as we swung to and fro in the hammock. I told her that when we are happy our thoughts are bright, and when we are naughty they are sad. Quick as a flash she said, "My think is white, Viney's think is black." You see she had an idea that the colour of our thoughts matched that of our skin. I couldn't help laughing, for at that very moment Viney was shouting at the top of her voice:
> "I long to sit on dem jasper walls
> And see dem sinners stumble and fall!" (September 18, 1887)

And the following month, Miss Sullivan (Keller 1968, p. 402) reports Helen's association of color with social position:

> On being told that she was white and that one of the servants was black, she concluded that all who occupied a similar menial position were of the same hue; *and whenever I asked her the colour of a servant she would say "black."* When asked the colour of someone whose occupation she did not know she seemed bewildered, and finally said "blue." (October, 1887.) (Emphasis added.)

Of course, it is possible that Helen had what Miss Sullivan terms a "reminiscent impression of light and sound," having had both sight and hearing until she was 19 months old. Perhaps she was able to relate color to previous experience. Still, we cannot help wondering about the extent to which she was influenced by Miss Sullivan's remarks to form culturally determined concepts of color. In fact, it seems very likely that Miss Sullivan transmitted cultural values to Helen, causing her to associate color with position in life. Yet Helen's interpretation of these values—the idea that "the colour of our thoughts matched that of our skin"—though amusing to Miss Sullivan, reflects a rather clear understanding of the black perception. Helen would have perhaps understood James Weldon Johnson, who in *The Autobiography of an Ex-Colored Man* (1965, p. 403) writes:

> **And this is the dwarfing, warping, distorting influence which operates upon each and every coloured man in the United States. He is forced to take his outlook on all things, not from the viewpoint of a citizen, or a man, or even a human being, but from the viewpoint of a *coloured* man. It is wonderful to me that the race has progressed so broadly as it has, since most of its thought and all of its activity must run through the narrow neck of this one funnel.**

This perspective, apparently perceived on some level by Helen, eluded Miss Sullivan, who had not only more access to, but also less escape from, predominant cultural values.

Thus, while their effect is not always predictable, the teacher's values and behaviors concerning pupil ethnicity and socioeconomic status can influence the child's sense of self-in-relation-to-others. Their impact is documented, though somewhat tangentially, by the teacher behavior research. The studies reported in this section are united more by theory than purpose. None have directly addressed the relationship between teacher behavior and the self-concept development of pupils from the standpoint of pupil race, ethnicity, or socioeconomic status. Several studies, however, do examine the role of the teacher as a reflector, focusing specifically on teacher perception and expectations related to pupil ethnicity and socioeconomic status. Other studies report children's perception of and, in some some cases, response to teacher behaviors that project an image of the pupil.

Children arriving in the classroom have self-concepts developed in the home. The teaching behaviors they have experienced are those of their mothers and other significant models in the home environment. The classroom teacher, then, is faced with a group of pupils whose previous learning experiences differ. And each of the several learning styles brought to the classroom incorporates values and beliefs already internalized by the pupil. At the same time, of course, the entering pupils are confronted with a teacher who also has certain values and beliefs and who has developed a definite teaching style.

Steward and Steward (1973), examining maternal teaching in a sample representing seven ethnic groups, videotaped mothers instructing their three-year-old sons and coded the interaction according to total time, input, and pacing, and the mother's alertness, the teaching format used, the child's response, and the mother's feedback. Results indicated that ethnicity was the single best predictor of (1) the child's response and (2) the mother's teaching style. Steward and Steward comment that the children observed had experienced different home learning environments which perhaps produced different skills and expectations which would in turn be carried with these children into the classroom. It is unfortunate for pupils from minority ethnic groups that the skills prized in the home environment are not always those valued in the classroom, a situation which creates a break in the home to school continuum.

While ethnicity is related to maternal teaching behavior, pupil SES is apparently associated with the classroom teacher's behavior. Rist (1970), in an observational and longitudinal study of a black kindergarten teacher and her 30 black pupils, found that "permanent" seating assignments made on the eighth day of school coincided with the social class of the students. The teacher grouped the children at three tables, explaining that they were seated according to their ability to "learn." The occupants of Table I were from families with higher incomes, higher education levels, fewer children, and both parents in the home. These children were better dressed, neater and cleaner than those at Tables II and III. They conversed and interacted more easily with the teacher in what the investigator calls "Standard American English" than children at the other two tables, who spoke in a dialect. In short, children at Table I possessed middle-class characteristics similar to those of the teacher. As the school year progressed, they interacted considerably more frequently with the teacher and received more positive responses and privileges from her. The teacher presented lessons directly to Table I and described children at Tables II and III as "not having any idea what was going on in the classroom." While some children from Tables II and III scored higher on an end-of-year IQ test than some children at Table I, when the pupils moved on to the first grade, they retained the "ability" grouping assigned them on the eighth day of their kindergarten experience. This ability grouping, reinforced in first grade by performance records, accompanied the pupils into second grade. Rist concludes from observation of teacher-pupil interaction that the children's learning experiences reinforced the original "ability" grouping, producing a "self-fulfilling prophecy." While this study focused on only one teacher and her pupils, and is thus an inadequate basis for generalization, educators and researchers can speculate about the factors operating and examine them further.

Mazer (1971) found that pupil socioeconomic status is also related to teacher expectations of pupil performance. After giving teachers from various backgrounds and instructional situations photographs of pupils with accompanying descriptions of pupil socioeconomic status, Mazer asked them to estimate each student's performance on a 5-point scale covering 12 variables. The photographs (of male and female, black and white pupils) were switched among the SES descriptions. Results indicated that the socioeconomic status of the pupil, rather than sex or race, differentiated the performance predictions. Teacher background and experience did not affect the estimates in any measurable way.

Pupil socioeconomic status is apparently related to pupil self-concept as well as teacher behavior. Trowbridge (1972), attempting to identify self-concept differences between middle- and lower-class children, found that lower-SES pupils had higher self-concept scores in general than middle-SES students and tended to feel more confident, and more able to take care of themselves, make up their own minds, and make worthwhile contributions. The lower-class children reported that they were generally happy and unworried. Middle-class pupils reported ability to adjust to new things, to understand themselves, and to accept scolding without being easily upset. On home-referenced items (except "feeling pushed"), middle-class children were more positive than lower-class children. On peer-referenced scales, the lower-SES pupils rated themselves higher on individualistic indices, while the middle-class children showed more social characteristics. On school-referenced items, middle-class pupils reported that they were not doing their best, while their lower-SES peers perceived themselves in a relatively positive light within the school context. Discussing these findings, Trowbridge suggests that low-SES pupils may have lower aspirations than do middle-class children and therefore derive more satisfaction from their performance. Furthermore, they may not blame themselves for bad school experiences. Middle-class pupils, on the other hand, performing up to their capacity but faced with teacher exhortations to improve, may report themselves as underachieving in order to preserve their self-concepts. As the author comments, under such circumstances it is safer for pupils to claim that they aren't doing their best.

The studies cited above suggest two potential sources of teacher-pupil conflict: (1) the values and beliefs of both teacher and pupil with regard to ethnicity and socioeconomic status, which may directly affect their perceptions of each other; and (2) learning and teaching styles, which are largely determined by background and values. These studies illustrate the interpretation problems we encounter when we attempt to measure and compare the self-concepts of pupils from different social backgrounds. The finding that pupils from lower socioeconomic groups registered higher self-concepts than those considered culturally "advantaged" is typical of the kind of situation-specific self-construct assessment that requires a theoretical framework for proper interpretation of results. It is quite possible for a pupil to report a positive self-concept on an instrument measuring General Self-Concept, while at the same time scoring low on items reflecting the academic self-concept, a particular aspect of self which may or may not alter the character of the General Self-Concept.

The relative strength of the various aspects of self-concept depends to some extent on the congruence between home and societal values. The process of establishing a sense of identity, for example, is intricately tied to cultural values, since the individual is expected to define himself or herself in relation to people or things *within* the culture. Cultural values permeate the search for identity, though they reach the child only after filtering through the interpretations of significant others in the home environment. If cultural values pass through this filter more or less intact, the continuum from home to school will be smooth and unbroken. The values, concepts, and behaviors acquired in the familial setting will be compatible with those defined and institutionalized by the dominant culture.

However, when the home and school environments are significantly different, children may lack the skills which facilitate classroom adjustment. Having developed concepts, values, and behaviors apart from the core culture, such children are apt to be classified, along with a variety of other pupils, as "deficient" or "disadvantaged." Broad labels such as these do not recognize their specific problem or distinguish them from pupils with limited conceptual ability, insufficient experience in organizing cognitive constructs, or any of a number of difficulties. For all of these pupils, the label "deficient" or "disadvantaged" reflects the self in the school environment and serves as a psychological experience from which the concept of self-in-relation-to-others, or self-identity, is partially derived. For this reason, teachers should tailor their functions as a significant other to the individual pupil's background, in order to accommodate changes in the continuum from home to school and to address the child's specific needs. And teachers should be particularly aware of their importance as a significant or salient other to pupils whose parents are unconcerned about values and behaviors related to academic achievement.

Because our schools do in fact reflect middle-class values and goals, teachers who feel that middle-class pupils have more academic potential than lower-class children are no doubt dealing with a perceived reality. But, however accurate or inaccurate it may be, this perception generates teacher behavior; and it is the *behavior* that must be examined for its effect on the self-concept development of all potential learners. Behavior which the teacher considers "innocent" or well intentioned may be devastating to the child seeking identity.

Maya Angelou, for example, was abruptly confronted with her identity in the eyes of the dominant white culture while listening to a well-meaning speaker at her graduation from grammar school. The small black community of which she was a part was assembled to hear two white speakers on this great occasion. One of the speakers noted first the academic improvements being made in the white schools and then the remarkable athletes coming out of the black schools. As Maya understood it, he was telling black children that their heroes should be black athletes. The white kids were going to have "a chance to become Galileos and Madame Curies and Edisons and Gauguins, and our boys (the girls weren't even in on it) would try to be Jesse Owenses and Joe Louises." She asked herself why their future, and hers, was thus ordained. And the years spent in pursuit of an education seemed somehow wasted (Angelou 1969, pp. 176–177):

> **Graduation, the hush-hush magic time of frills and gifts and congratulations and diplomas, was finished for me before my name was called. The accomplishment was nothing. The meticulous maps, drawn in three colors of ink, learning and spelling decasyllabic words, memorizing the whole of** *The Rape of Lucrece*—**it was for nothing. Donleavy had exposed us. We were maids and farmers, handymen and washerwomen, and anything higher that we aspired to was farcical and presumptuous.**
>
> **He finished, and since there was no need to give any more than the most perfunctory thank-you's, he nodded to the men on stage, and the tall white man who was never introduced joined him at the door. They left with the attitude that now they were off to something really important.**

THE SENSE OF SELF AS BOTH SUBJECT AND OBJECT

St. Augustine was apparently determined to record his passage from paganism to Christianity from its very beginnings. In order to do so, he observed the behavior of infants and reported what he observed as his own infant experience. Through this mental exercise he conceptualized both the Sense of Bodily Self (the process of differentiating self from others) and the emerging Sense of Self-Identity (the awareness of self-as-object and self-as-subject) (St. Augustine 1955, p. 35):

> **Then, little by little, I realized where I was and wished to tell my wishes to those who might satisfy them, but I could not! For my wants were inside me, and they were outside, and they could not by any power of theirs come into my soul. And so I would fling my arms and legs about and cry, making the few and feeble gestures that I could, though indeed the signs were not much like what I inwardly desired and when I was not satisfied—either from not being understood or because what I got was not good for me—I grew indignant that my elders were not subject to me and that those on whom I actually had no claim did not wait on me as slaves—and I avenged myself on them by crying. That infants are like this, I have myself been able to learn by watching them; and they, though they knew me not, have shown me better what I was like than my own nurses who knew me.**

Had St. Augustine observed the interaction between the infants and their nurses, he would have realized how his own nurse had come to interpret his behaviors and know his infant self.

The cognitive constructs formed by the developing self are determined by behaviors occurring on both sides of the behavioral dialogue—those of the infant and those of others in relation to the infant. When parents interpret the baby's behavior as a cue for food, rest, cleansing, or fondling and attention, they are, in a sense, participating on both sides of the behavioral dialogue. Their interpretations and subsequent reactions, when constant and consistent, strengthen the association made between stimulus and response and reinforce the behaviors of both baby and parents. For example, if parents initially interpret a certain infant behavior as a sign that the baby needs rest, the child will learn to use this cue to communicate the need for rest.

By responding to the infant's cues, parents demonstrate that the child is a stimulus for their behavior; and through this reflection the child experiences personal impact upon others and the environment. Through the response of others to the child's presence and behavior, then, a sense of self-as-object, a sense of self-as-subject, as initiator and as a performer is acquired.

Helen Keller (p. 21) writes:

> **My hands felt every object and observed every motion, and in this way I learned to know many things. Soon I felt the need of some communication with others and began to make crude signs. A shake of the head meant "No" and a nod, "Yes," a pull meant "Come" and a push, "Go." Was it bread that I wanted? Then I would imitate the acts of cutting the slices and buttering them. If I wanted my mother to make ice cream for dinner I made the sign for working the freezer and shivered, indicating cold. My mother, moreover, succeeded in making me understand a good deal. I always knew when she wished me to bring her something, and I would run upstairs or anywhere else she indicated. Indeed, I owe to her loving wisdom all that was bright and good in my long night.**

TEACHER BEHAVIOR AND PUPIL SELF-AWARENESS

The research on pupil self-awareness falls into two categories. The first focuses on "differentiation," a dimension generally related to the pupil's concept of self-in-relation-to-others (though specific definitions of the term vary from investigator to investigator). The second reports the evaluation of theory-based programs stressing pupil self-awareness. Neither of these research categories relates children's self-awareness to specific teacher behaviors. Though the program evaluations tell us curricular emphases and objectives, they do not tell us exactly what teachers do—or how their behavior changes from "old" to "new" program implementation.

The research does, however, identify circumstances and teacher traits apparently associated with pupil self-awareness, and from this information we can infer which teacher behaviors are likely to facilitate the pupil's attempt to establish a sense of identity.

Minuchin (1971), for example, studying black, "disadvantaged" children in an urban Head Start Program, found that pupils exhibiting more exploratory behavior also demonstrated a greater degree of "self-differentiation" (that is, a sense of identity in relation to others and the environment). They also showed stronger expectations of support, coherence, and facilitation from their environment, and greater conceptual mastery than less exploratory children.

Differentiation has also been linked to familial background. Defining the construct more fully, Dyk and Witkin (1965) suggest that differentiation is composed of three sets of behaviors. The first set, *Articulation of Experience,* includes perception, thinking, analyzing, and structuring (assessed through analysis of children's test responses and reports of real-life experience). The second set, *Differentiation of the Self,* includes the child's concept of physical self as a body having discrete parts, yet functioning as an integrated whole, the sense of separate identity manifested in expressed attitudes, judgments, and perceptions maintained without external support, and the child's ability to define and execute a task without seeking further guidance or explanation. The third set of differentiating behaviors, *Structured, Specialized Defenses,* are those demonstrating the degree to which impulses and diffused reactions are moderated and channeled into specific, socialized responses.

Using pairs composed of mothers and their 10-year-old-sons, Dyk and Witkin found that children whose mothers behaved in ways thought to foster differentiation did in fact show a higher level of differentiation in all three areas. Children's self-differentiation ratings correlated with those of their mothers, lending support to the assumption that family background is linked to children's responses on psychological dimensions measuring the development of self-identity.

The behaviors described by Dyk and Witkin as differentiation stem from trust in others and the environment—or a positive sense of continuing self—which, as we have previously theorized, gives the child access to psychological experiences that build or reinforce a positive self-concept. Considering the findings of both Dyk and Witkin and Minuchin, it appears that teachers should try first of all to establish a trusting relationship with the child who exhibits little exploratory behavior or a low level of differentiation. Second, teachers should attempt to extend the child's feeling of trust beyond relationships with the teacher to the general environment, both physical and social, by providing experiences from which the child can receive positive self-reflections. If the child responds with increased exploration and participation, the teacher can assume a change in self-concept and readiness for further development of differentiating behavior.

Further prescriptions for teacher behavior that encourages pupil self-awareness can be derived, though more tentatively, from the evaluation of theory-based programs implemented in a variety of school situations. The Human Development Program (Bessell and Palomares 1973, rev.), for example, founded on Horney's (1950) theory of personality development, concentrates on three pupil objectives: *awareness*, defined as "knowing what your thoughts, feelings and actions really are;" *mastery*, "knowing what your abilities are and how to use them;" and *social-interaction*, "knowing other people." The Human Development Supplementary Guide (1972) reports five minor evaluation studies of the curriculum at kindergarten, first, fourth, fifth grade, and remedial high school levels. Though detailed explanations of the evaluation studies are not provided, the report lists the variables assessed, among which were: language, comprehension, awareness, interpersonal relations, peer relations, and affective performance (the ability to verbalize feelings). In all five evaluations, pre- and posttesting and control group comparisons indicate that the program produced positive change on the variables measured, regardless of grade level or differences in program implementation.

The success of a program like this (which emphasizes "knowing yourself and others"), considered in combination with the pupil awareness research, suggests several behavioral recommendations for teachers. First, teachers should be sensitive to the fact that pupils enter the classroom with varying levels of concept formation and different organizational schema for goal-directed behavior. Furthermore, they should realize that poorly developed conceptual skills, differentiation, or self-awareness can stem from limited ability, lack of opportunity, *or* cultural differences. If cultural differences account for the child's problems in school, the teacher must remember that any program designed to alleviate these problems will necessarily reflect the values and concepts of the dominant culture (since its objective will be to socialize the culturally different child—to bring him or her into the mainstream). This being so, the remedial program may fail to provide the pupil from a different culture with the means by which to relate his or her previous experiences and existing concepts to the curriculum presented.

Finally, in order to help children with limited associative processes, concept development, or differentiation take the initial steps toward improvement, teachers should consider reducing classroom stimuli and simply providing psychological experiences that are constant, consistent, and manageable. Because the process of objectifying the self and identifying the self-in-relation-to-others can be a threatening experience, (Winter, Griffith, and Kalb 1968; Brehm and Cohen 1962; and Erikson 1959), the circumstances under which such self-confrontation occurs should always ensure the individual's psychological safety (Miles, 1959), a requirement that is not fulfilled by the teacher's good intent alone.

TEACHER BEHAVIOR AND PUPIL ACCEPTANCE OF OTHERS

> The unquestioning acceptance by my peers had dislodged the familiar insecurity. Odd that the homeless children, the silt of war frenzy, could initiate me into the brotherhood of man. After hunting down unbroken bottles and selling them with a white girl from Missouri, a Mexican girl from Los Angeles and a Black girl from Oklahoma, I was never again to sense myself so solidly outside the pale of the human race. The lack of criticism evidenced by our ad hoc community influenced me, and set a tone of tolerance for my life.
>
> *Maya Angelou, 1969.* I know why the caged bird sings, *p. 247.*

The pupil entering the classroom has an operating sense of self-identity which is manifested in his or her classroom behavior. If the child's concept of self-in-relation-to-others has produced a very small reference group "like me" and a very large reference group "unlike me" (with value judgments applied to the two categories), the child may find the school environment and school experiences traumatizing. The school milieu already contains distinct reference groups, defined according to age and sex. In the course of the pupil's school days, other reference groups evolve by administrative design or by chance. Because it encourages the development of individual and group identity, the school environment offers many opportunities for negative and positive self-concept change.

Measuring such change, however, is a complex process. Causal circumstances and events are difficult to identify and describe. For example, the argument that ability grouping produces an identifiable "dummy" group and lowers the self-concepts of its members is countered by the contention that pupils know who's dumb and who's smart anyway. But how do children know who is dumb and who is smart unless pupil behaviors have been interpreted and communicated by the teacher? As classroom communicator and interpreter, the teacher can change pupils' concepts of self-identity and their acceptance of others as "like" or "unlike," banishing the value judgments normally accompanying these classifications.

Confirmation of the teacher's effect on the pupil's acceptance of others is abundant in the literature. First of all, research indicates that the concepts of self and others, "we" and "they," are learned. In a study of international scope, Lambert and Klineberg (1969) investigated the manner in which children acquire their views of "foreign" people. Their findings suggest that children first develop a stereotyped concept of their own group, using broad generalizations about their society as a comparative base for differentiating other groups. It is not until the age of ten that children begin to form stereotypes about foreign people, and, in general, ten-year-olds are more inquisitive about and friendly toward foreigners than are six- and fourteen-year-olds.

Variations in children's attitudes from nation to nation indicate that the methods parents and educators use in teaching children to differentiate their own group from others are culturally determined.

While this study provides fairly clear evidence that the distinction between "us" and "them" is learned, other research indicates that acceptance of "them" can also be taught. Research efforts to reduce pupil intolerance and encourage intergroup understanding document the teacher's (or school's) influence on pupil attitudes.

In a study by Griggs and Bonney (1970), fourth and fifth grade children were placed for one semester in a program designed to teach acceptance of behavior through "causal understanding." The hypotheses tested were: (1) Pupils trained with causal understanding will be more accepting of others; (2) they will reduce the discrepancy between self-ideal and self; and (3) they will show improved mental health scores. The first hypothesis was confirmed: pupils trained in causal understanding were significantly more accepting of others. On the remaining hypotheses, predicted but nonsignificant differences emerged between experimental and control groups. The authors suggest that a more thorough and long-term integration of program materials throughout the school curriculum might bring about more conclusive and positive results.

Teaching was also shown to alter the racial attitudes of second and sixth grade children in a study by Katz (1973). Children who had received high prejudice scores on two racial attitude measures were randomly assigned to one of three training conditions: Group I learned distinctive names for photographs of children of different races; Group II viewed pairs of photographs, judging the faces in each pair as same or different; and Group III observed faces without labels. A comparison of pre- and posttests indicated that the children who were taught to differentiate other-group faces showed the greatest reduction in prejudice. Furthermore, Katz found an interaction between children's age and experimenter's race: treatment effects were significant when younger children were tested by a black experimenter and when older children were tested by a white experimenter. He suggested that younger children, accustomed to white teachers, were made more aware of racial issues by the presence of a black experimenter.

In another study involving racial attitudes, St. John (1971) found that teachers rated high on fairness (i.e., those judged "racially fair," "generally fair," and "systematic") contributed to improved overall pupil conduct and greater friendliness from white pupils toward other-race classmates.

Heil and Washburne (1962), investigating the effect of teacher type on pupil type, found that orderly, self-controlling teachers helped all pupil types ("conformers," "opposers," "waverers," and "strivers,") to develop more positive feelings, to perceive authority figures as accepting, to reduce anxiety, and to display more friendliness toward their classmates. These effects were particularly significant among the more negative and hostile students ("opposers").

Blau and Rafferty (1970), focusing on a specific teaching technique rather than teacher personality, used reinforcement strategies to change the friendship status of children engaged in cooperative tasks. They successfully demonstrated that friendship can be developed from bases other than proximity or personality characteristics and similarities, leading them to suggest that reinforcement techniques might prove helpful in classes where minority pupils have peer-acceptance difficulties.

A similar method was used by Lilly (1971) who paired pupils with low sociometric status or low achievement with popular peers and other students to test the effect of such pairing on social acceptance. While results indicated that the less popular pupils achieved a significant, *immediate* gain in acceptance, the effect did not endure over a six-week period.

Children who are not accepted by their peers are often the ones who express hostility toward others or who exhibit deviant behavior in the classroom. Hostile or antisocial behavior, generally rooted in pupils' previous relationships, represents a coping style acquired in past behavioral dialogues. While teachers cannot change previous psychological experiences or control the child's home environment, there is some evidence that they can provide an alternative interpretation of these psychological events and a classroom environment communicating a positive pupil role.

Glavin, Quay, and Werry (1971), for example, report the successful use of positive reinforcement techniques with problem children placed in a special two-year program, the first portion of which emphasized positive behavior change and the second, increased academic achievement. Their findings indicate that, while both parts of the program met their particular objectives, the portion emphasizing achievement produced significant change in pupil conduct as well as academic performance. The authors suggest that since the purpose of remedial instruction is to allow pupils to function in a regular classroom, programs emphasizing both academic and behavioral improvement deserve further attention. Such programs may be effective because they allow pupils to perceive behavior change not as fulfillment of an adult-assigned role, but rather as a means to gain a new role with increased impact.

Further success in altering pupil behavior is provided by Stoffer (1970), who reports the outcome of a program designed to improve behavior by increasing the amount of attention given to pupils. "Problem" students from grades one through six were paired with adult female volunteers, who gave them individual help over a period of time. "Helper" characteristics and pupil perceptions of the relationship were measured, and results indicated that "nonpossessive warmth" and "accurate empathy" in the volunteers were associated with a positive view of the relationship and positive behavioral change in the students.

Several other programs designed for classroom use suggest additional methods for helping children deal with their hostile feelings and resolve their personal and school-related conflicts. In a review of program innovations which focused on teacher–student relationships and therapeutic group dynamics, Crist (1972) evaluated several of these techniques. Role-playing, sociodrama, and simulation games, for example, reportedly increased pupils' insight into their interpersonal relationships, reduced their prejudices, and improved their communication with teachers. *The most frequently reported positive effect of these three techniques, however, was an increase in "teacher insight into pupils."*

The methods mentioned above are only a few of many techniques by which the classroom environment can be altered to facilitate the child's attempts to establish identity. For the pupil whose home environment has not supplied the means to identify self in relation to the dominant culture, these techniques offer ways to acquire new roles without painful confrontation. The realization that "play" is actually essential work of the developing self has legitimatized methods such as simulation and role playing. Unfortunately, it is difficult to assess the effectiveness of these methods since programs implementing them have relied, with only a few exceptions, on subjective rather than objective evaluation.

The DUSO (Developing Understanding of Self and Others) Guidance Program, for example, was evaluated with four subtests of the *California Test of Personality* (Koval and Hales 1972). This program uses guided group experiences, role playing, and other techniques to help children develop adequate self-concepts, identify personal strengths, and accept self-limitations. Responses to the CAT subtests, obtained at the end of a ten-week experimental period, indicated that pupils who participated in DUSO felt more capable of independent achievement, more self-directing, and more accepted by others than did students in the control group.

Programs like DUSO, which offer the pupil an opportunity to objectively view self and self-in-relation-to-others through examination of concepts and values underlying behavior, have good theoretical, if not empirical, support. First, the materials and techniques used in these school-adapted programs are generally coordinated with developmental theories to ensure that they are appropriate for the intended age group. In addition, educators and researchers for the most part view these innovations favorably. Bettleheim (1972), for example, gives theoretical support to the use of games by supplying guidance and purpose. Gilpatrick (1969) suggests the picture book as a tool to help children identify with others while developing broader and more useful concepts of self and others. And Mende and Kauffman (1971) advocate the use of videotaped sessions in which program participants have the opportunity to view themselves and their interactive behavior in an attempt to increase self-awareness, self-control, and socialization.

In this particular area of affective research we are again caught in the position of presuming to "know" more than we can "show." We can produce far more evidence of our faith in developmental theories than the truth of these theories. There is as yet no research proving that simulated or structured experiences expressly designed to objectify the self and allow examination of self-in-relation-to-others actually facilitate the development of self-identity apart from the immediate program environment. While the lack of such evidence does not invalidate this approach, it does leave us with no basis from which to propose the use of these techniques to facilitate the development of self-awareness and self-identity. And, of course, we cannot claim the superiority of any particular technique, materials, or program in producing desired results. If we are to establish a basis for decision making, a great deal of research and evaluation is yet to be done.

THE SENSE OF SELF AS RELATED TO OTHERS BY COMMUNICATION

The initial mode of communication, which endures throughout life, is concrete, experienced, and observable physical behavior. The actions experienced and observed in the behavioral dialogue gradually form patterns that both participants can interpret and predict. These patterns are the basis of communication. Behavioral categories and role concepts mutual to the developing self and the significant other characterize the dialogue between them.

However, significant others initially interpret, predict, and communicate all behavior according to their own culturally referenced role concepts. Thus, the image reflected to the developing self contains a cultural element interpreted by significant others and further modified by the child's own perception. The behaviors experienced and interpreted in the behavioral dialogue are grouped according to their functions in role concept formation. Children can establish their own identities in relation to their roles and identify others according to their concept of others' roles.

Children acquire language through the same relationships and under the same conditions in which they develop self-identity. In theory, language behavior is assumed to be a parallel and interacting product of both physiological and psychological development.

> ... I remember this, and I have since observed how I learned to speak. My elders did not teach me words by rote, as they taught me my letters afterward. But I myself, when I was unable to communicate all I wished to say to whomever I wished by means of whimperings and grunts and various gestures of my limbs (which I used to reinforce my demands), I myself repeated the sounds already stored in my memory

by the mind which thou, O my God, hadst given me. When they called some thing by name and pointed it out while they spoke, I saw it and realized that the thing they wished to indicate was called by the name they then uttered. And what they meant was made plain by the gestures of their bodies, by a kind of natural language, common to all nations, which expresses itself through changes of countenance, glances of the eye, gestures and intonations which indicate a disposition and attitude —either to seek or to possess, to reject or to avoid. So it was that by frequently hearing words, in different phrases, I gradually identified the objects which the words stood for and, having formed my mouth to repeat these signs, I was thereby able to express my will. Thus I exchanged with those about me the verbal signs by which we express our wishes and advanced deeper into the stormy fellowship of human life, depending all the while upon the authority of my parents and the behest of my elders.

St. Augustine, 1955. Augustine: confessions and enchiridion, *p. 38.*

When the developing self accepts significant others' interpretations of his or her behavior, events within the behavioral dialogue become mutually understood by all participants. This understanding was the essential element in Anne Sullivan's method of teaching Helen Keller.

I, little ignorant I, found myself explaining to the wisemen of the East and the West such simple things as these: If you give a child something sweet, and he wags his tongue and smacks his lips and looks pleased, he has a very definite sensation; and if, every time he has this experience, he hears the word *sweet*, or has it spelled into his hand, he will quickly adopt this arbitrary sign for his sensation. Likewise, if you put a bit of lemon on his tongue, he puckers up his lips and tries to spit it out; and after he has had this experience a few times, if you offer him a lemon, he shuts his mouth and makes faces, clearly indicating that he remembers the unpleasant sensation. You label it *sour*, and he adopts your symbol. If you called these sensations respectively *black* and *white*, he would have adopted them as readily; but he would mean by *black* and *white* the same things that he means by *sweet* and *sour*. In the same way the child learns from many experiences to differentiate his feelings and we name them for him—*good, bad, gentle, rough, happy, sad*. It is not the word, but the capacity to experience the sensation that counts in his education.

Anne Sullivan in Helen Keller, 1968. The story of my life, *p. 416.*

These shared experiences form the foundation of a communication system, a system of sounds and motor behaviors that provides a basis for more complex, symbolic communication (though body language, the first means of transmitting knowledge and feeling, remains an effective mode of communication throughout life).

The physiological condition of the developing self dictates his or her physical and intellectual ability to receive and process the experiences essential to the acquisition of language behavior. The cultural background of significant others and the social environment determine the content and frequency of these experiences.

Until the child acquires language, the primary function of the significant other in the behavioral dialogue is interpretation. The significant other interprets the child's behaviors and associates them, as they occur, with things, experiences, and words. Interpretations that are constant and consistent can be differentiated, associated, classified, and organized into a conceptual framework for the acquisition of language behaviors understood by the participants in the behavioral dialogue and others in their social environment.

The significant other's performance as an interpreter is subject to the same influences that affect his or her performance as a reflector. However, such interpretations become the child's initial reality, regardless. Children must accept their significant other's definitions of their behaviors, roles, relationships, and environment until they can discriminate, test, and judge on their own.

The reality projected to the developing self is continually tested through the processing of additional psychological experiences. Interpretations and associated behaviors that are repeatedly reinforced by positive attention or absence of negative attention stimulate concept formation and initiate goal-directed or need-satisfying activity. The concepts and responses that characterize and identify social groups and individuals are established through consistent interpretation and reinforcement of particular behaviors in combination with environmental opportunities and limitations. This process is clearly illustrated by the interaction of Helen Keller and Anne Sullivan:

> Helen was lying on the floor, kicking and screaming and trying to pull my chair from under me. She kept this up for half an hour, then she got up to see what I was doing. I let her see that I was eating, but I did not let her put her hand in the plate. She pinched me, and I slapped her every time she did it. Then she went all around the table to see who was there, and finding no one but me, she seemed bewildered. After a few minutes she came back to her place and began to eat her breakfast with her fingers. I gave her a spoon, which she threw on the floor. I forced her out of the chair and made her pick it up. Finally I succeeded in getting her back in her chair again, and held the spoon in her hand, compelling her to take up the food with it and put it in her mouth. In a few minutes she yielded and finished her breakfast peaceably. Then we had another tussle over folding her napkin. When she had finished, she threw it on the floor and screamed all over again. It

was another hour before I succeeded in getting her napkin folded. Then I let her out into the warm sunshine and went up to my room and threw myself on the bed exhausted. I had a good cry and felt better.

Anne Sullivan in Helen Keller, 1968. The story of my life, *pp. 359–360.*

LANGUAGE BEHAVIOR AND SELF-IDENTITY

The communicating behavior of a group is one of its most identifying characteristics. Symbolic language behavior reflects the group's social organization, expressing its concepts, values, and role definitions. Similarly, the individual's language behavior indicates his or her group membership and the status of his or her physiological and psychological development in relation to the group or groups.

The link between language and identity is beautifully illustrated in Maya Angelou's description of her father. The passage below, which recounts their first meeting, reflects not only the child's newfound identity as a daughter, but also the identity she ascribed to her father on the basis of his speech.

His voice rang like a metal dipper hitting a bucket and he spoke English. Proper English, like the school principal, and even better. Our father sprinkled *ers* and *errers* in his sentences as liberally as he gave out his twisted-mouth smiles. I was so proud of him it was hard to wait for the gossip to get around that he was in town. Wouldn't the kids be surprised at how handsome our daddy was? And that he loved us enough to come down to Stamps to visit? Everyone could tell from the way he talked and from the car and clothes that he was rich and maybe had a castle out in California. (I later learned that he had been a doorman at Santa Monica's plush Breakers Hotel). Then the possibility of being compared with him occurred to me, and I didn't want anyone to see him. Maybe he wasn't my real father. Bailey was his son, true enough, but I was an orphan that they picked up to provide Bailey with company.

Maya Angelou, 1969. I know why the caged bird sings, *pp. 53–54.*

In the past four decades the relationship between language and group identity (specifically, socioeconomic and ethnic group membership) has been under increasing investigation. Grier and Cobbs (1968), for example, suggest that the black patois, or "jive" talk, performs two functions for those who speak it:

In our view, speech patterns, or accents, announce to the world an essential quality of the speaker's identity. He is telling all who will listen who he is, and stating that this aspect of his identity forms an essential

> element of his character structure . . . and the "jive" language and the "hip" language, while presented in a way that whites look upon simply as a quaint ethnic peculiarity, is used as a secret language to communicate the hostility of blacks for whites, and great delight is taken by blacks when whites are confounded by the language.

W. H. Grier and P. M. Cobbs, 1968. Black rage, *pp. 100, 105.*

Other sociolinguists and sociologists, notably Bernstein (1961), have formulated theories relating social factors to language use and have tested the hypothesized relationships.

The studies documenting significant linguistic differences between social, economic, or ethnic groups emphasize the predominance of middle-class values in public education. The differences identified in these studies were initially interpreted in terms of deficits and disadvantages, signaling the need for remedial programs to enable "culturally deprived" children to enter school on a par with their middle-class peers. More recent approaches to preparatory and individualized instruction, however, acknowledge cultural and linguistic differences as simply that—differences. And the current trend is to complement rather than supplant the heritage and language of minority groups with the culture and language of the middle-class majority.

> I noticed that the children frequently said that they were bad at their friends, or their parents, or some teacher who angered them. They insisted upon describing a certain type of anger as "being bad at," and I kept telling them that it was wrong because "to be bad at" someone doesn't exist in English. And in a way I was "right"; it didn't exist, nor did the concept it was trying to express exist in English as I spoke and wrote it. But the children did mean "to be bad at," and meant something very specific by it. "To be bad" is a way of defying authority and expressing anger at the same time, as indicating one's own strength and independence. The use of "bad" here is ironical and often admiring. One child explained to me that down South a "bad nigger" was one who was strong enough and brave enough to be defiant of the white man's demands no matter how much everyone else gave in. Only later did I discover Bessie Smith in J. C. Johnson's "Black Mountain Blues," using "bad" in the same way as the kids.

Herbert Kohl, 1967. 36 children, *p. 36.*

Regardless of children's backgrounds, when they reach school age, their Sense of Self-Identity is an interfusion of the Sense of Bodily Self, the self differentiated from others, and the self-in-relation-to-others in their experienced environment, which is generally the home. They have developed concepts and goal-directed behaviors which allow them to function within this milieu and have assumed some responsibility for interpreting the events in their ongoing behavioral dialogues. They enter school with a repertoire of social behaviors acquired in the home, behaviors which must now be tried and tested in a new environment. If these behaviors pass the test—if the behaviors are as functional in the classroom as they are at home—a child can almost effortlessly assume membership in the new group, thereby enhancing his or her sense of self-identity and the feeling of belonging. If, however, the existing repertoire of behaviors proves inappropriate in the new environment, the child may reject that environment and intensify the concepts and behaviors that reinforce membership and a sense of belonging in the familial surroundings in an attempt to preserve the existing sense of self-identity. Pupils who experience only marginal membership in the school community may meet their need for identity and group affiliation by creating small groups within the larger environment and/or engaging in behaviors that are the reverse of the standards and values of the dominant group. By practicing "deviant" behavior, these pupils establish a distinct self- or group-identity.

As significant others and controllers of the classroom environment, teachers are most opportunely positioned to assist each pupil in maintaining and establishing a sense of self-identity in the school situation. Yet teachers, however well positioned, are not always well prepared to interpret the behavioral dialogue for pupils who have grown up in environments dissimilar from their own. When teachers are only partially prepared, when they can assess pupils but cannot provide those who vary from the norm with appropriate experiences and interpretations, they may end up simply labeling pupils and stopping at that—a gesture that helps neither teachers nor pupils. Labeling may, in fact, cause pupils to devalue their membership in the school community.

> **. . . I braced myself, and defying all precedent as well as my own misgivings, I performed the unforgivable act of showing the children what their reading and IQ scores were according to the record cards. I also taught a lesson on the definition of IQ and of achievement scores. The children were angry and shocked; no one had ever come right out and told them they were failing. It was always put so nicely and evasively that the children never knew where they stood. After seeing the IQ scores—only two of which were above 100, the majority being in the 80 to 90 range—and the reading scores, which with few exceptions were below grade level, the children were furious. I asked them what they wanted to do about it, and sadly they threw back at me:**
>
> **"Mr. Kohl, what can we do about it?"**
>
> *Herbert Kohl, 1967. 36 children, p. 176.*

If, of course, teachers can answer that question—if they can go beyond labeling—they can have positive impact on pupils' self-concepts by helping to make their roles as members of the school community a more profitable and valuable experience. How a teacher goes about this is, unfortunately, not as clear as one would hope. Studies focusing on the impact of teacher behavior are chiefly concerned with those behaviors that relate to pupil cognitive achievement and only peripherally with those that appear to influence pupil self-concept.

However, there are studies examining cultural and language differences in the school environment which suggest inferences regarding instructional approach or classroom environment and pupil self-concept, particularly the sense of self-identity. Instructional programs employing a bilingual/bicultural approach, for example, have been the subject of several investigations. Fisher (1974), evaluating a first grade bilingual/bicultural program stressing individual attention and freedom, found significant differences between experimental and control subjects on measures of self-concept, self-description, and stimulus-seeking activity. Apparently, the program significantly enhanced the self-concepts of Anglo and Chicano girls, but not Anglo or Chicano boys. In fact, it seemed to lower the self-concepts of Anglo boys while having no significant effect on those of Chicano boys. Self-description measures showed a reduction in negative feelings among the experimental Chicano subjects, but not among the Chicano controls. Chicano pupils in the program, unlike their control counterparts, also felt themselves to be important members of their class. Stimulus-seeking behaviors increased among the girls in the program, but not among the boys, a finding which led Fisher to suggest that such behavior is perhaps related to self-concept and thus changes only as self-concept changes.

Effects of this bilingual/bicultural program at the first grade level apparently include a general increase in self-concept for Chicano subjects and a general decrease for Anglo subjects (with a statistically significant decline among Anglo boys). This finding, along with other program-related sex differences favoring female subjects, leads to the conclusion that the bilingual/bicultural approach adversely affected Anglo male participants—a conclusion which raises several interesting questions. Was this effect, for example, unique to this particular program? Perhaps the content of the program, which included presentation of minority language and culture to all pupils, failed to offer males, particularly Anglo males, opportunity for positive self-identification. In this same vein, it may be possible that Anglo boys were exhibiting the effects of alienation and irrelevance usually hypothesized for members of minority groups who have been forced into nonsupportive core-culture environments.

Mixed results are also reported (Harris and Stockton 1973) for bilingual instruction in integrated (Chicano and Anglo) fourth and fifth grade physical education classes. Formal data revealed a significant difference only on a measure of Spanish vocabulary. However, the authors felt that other, informal evidence (pupils appearing less hesitant, and in some cases, eager to identify themselves as Chicanos) demonstrated significant success for the bilingual approach.

More definite and positive support for inclusion of minority culture in the curriculum is provided by Lefley (1974), who compared two groups of American Indian pupils, one of which was involved in a special program which presented Miccosukee and Anglo cultures and Mikasuka and English languages. Using instruments especially suited to the subjects and their background, Lefley found three significant changes in the culture program group: (1) they reduced distance between present self and ideal self; (2) they demonstrated increased valuing of Indian symbols/stimuli; and (3) their ethnic and personal self-perceptions were more highly correlated. There were no sex differences in program effects related to increased self-concept scores. Lefley suggests that the self-concept improvement may reflect greater satisfaction with self through renewed appreciation of Indian identity, an interpretation consistent with the informal observation of Harris and Stockton that Chicano pupils were more willing to be identified as Chicanos after the bilingual program began. These studies indicate that minority group members appear to gain in self-concept when programs relating minority culture and language to the learning environment are offered in the school setting. Lefley speculates that the negative results obtained in other studies of ethnic programs may stem from failure to take a multidimensional approach to self-concept and to use culturally appropriate instruments.

Focusing on the child's perception of classroom climate, rather than the instructional program, Kleinfeld (1973) found that Indian and Eskimo pupils who had a negative view of their integrated classroom and feared ridicule or rejection were rated low in verbal participation. And it can be hypothesized that verbal participation is indirectly related to self-concept since it is, according to Ahlbrand and Hudgins (1970), directly and positively associated with the number of peer nominations pupils receive for good scholarship, leadership, and popularity. Ahlbrand and Hudgins do not explain this finding, suggesting instead that further research is needed to determine if participation creates a social visibility producing a large number of peer nominations, or whether high status among peers encourages the pupil to participate more vocally and frequently.

Although teachers are the controllers of the classroom environment, they function in that role only as it is defined by the larger society. And the conflicts and problems of that larger society permeate the classroom door. As more and more minorities seek to exercise influence over the policy decisions of local school boards, and as schools become involved in the problem-solving efforts of the national community, the teacher's job as leader of the mini-society of the classroom becomes more demanding. Recognition of individual rights sometimes conflicts with custom and curriculum at the classroom level, creating not only philosophical but also personal problems for many administrators and teachers.

The acquisition of self-identity is a continuing process for teachers as well as pupils. How the school environment reflects the individual, defines the pupil role, and interprets pupil behaviors is a very real part of a very personal process. To acquire self-identity, one must relate to a reference group; and to acquire identity in school, one must feel that one has a place in that environment.

> **English would be much better off with more teachers like you that take an interest in their pupils instead of teaching just because they have to due to circumstances. Well ever since you elected me judge, I, for one will never forget you as long as I live. You made me feel I'm real.**
>
> **The reason I like your English is you teach English which can be used in my life to make me somebody. You have arranged your English so that it seems more interesting and it doesn't seem like English though it is. You make likable things I don't like like reading. You teach perfectly and steadily, not too fast or too slow. And you always have time to listen to our side of the book. Can I have you again?**

Jose Rodriguez in B. Kaufman, 1964. Up the down staircase, *pp. 180, 276.*

The classroom does function as a reference group for the child, and it is difficult, but not impossible, for teachers to make that reference group one which reflects its members positively, allowing all to participate in the behavioral dialogue. To achieve such an environment, teachers should ensure that concepts learned in the classroom—such as same/different, inclusive/exclusive—are *not* associated with value judgments—such as good/bad, superior/inferior. To help pupils make this distinction, many teachers need well researched and evaluated culture-oriented programs and training for their proper implementation.

TEACHERS' INTERPRETATIVE AND LANGUAGE BEHAVIORS AND PUPIL IMITATIVE BEHAVIOR

Teachers help pupils acquire concepts and behaviors appropriate to the learning environment, and specifically to the classroom. They define the roles of both parties in the classroom behavioral dialogue and, by interpreting diverse behaviors of many pupils, guide the formation of a functional, shared language that becomes characteristic of this small society.

In a study examining the teacher-imitating behavior of white, "advantaged" and black, "disadvantaged" pupils at the fourth grade level, Portuges and Feshback (1972) found that advantaged children in general, and the girls in particular, imitated the behavior of positive and reinforcing teachers significantly more than the disadvantaged pupils did. Among "advantaged" boys, measures of pupil dependency were positively related to imitative behavior. Advantaged boys were also the only group to demonstrate a relationship between imitative behaviors and preference for a positive, reinforcing teacher. Disadvantaged boys were least imitative of both positive and negative teacher models, and disadvantaged girls did not discriminate between model types.

In a similar study, Friedman (1973) found that first grade pupils in an integrated class imitated the verbal behavior of highly reinforcing teachers. Though pupils who received little reinforcement showed significantly more imitative behavior than those who were frequently reinforced, they did not discriminate between high- and low-reinforcing teachers. Friedman suggests that the frequently reinforced pupils were able to exercise more control over when and how they gained reinforcement, while other, more anxious pupils identified with the teacher and imitated her verbal behavior in an effort to reduce their classroom anxiety. It might also be theorized that the infrequently reinforced pupils, having not yet attained a positive sense of self-identity, were reflecting a limited interpretation of their role and a need for an effective significant other.

The interaction of imitative behavior, dependency, and preference reported in these studies may indicate the level of self-concept development among the pupils assessed and the influence of the teacher as a significant other. Because the imitative behavior of a considerable proportion of the pupils did not vary with the model's reinforcing behavior, it can be assumed that pupils were responding not simply to reinforcement, but also to other teacher characteristics and to their own needs.

For dependent white boys, who imitated and preferred the positive reinforcement model, teachers may function fully as significant others, providing needed self-reflection and prescribed role behaviors; but, perhaps for dependent black girls, neither of the models presented adequately fulfilled the role of the significant other. And the imitative behavior of the black, "disadvantaged" pupils may have been affected by the content of the lesson (a discussion of Africa, using a map and pictures of African animals). This subject may have inhibited black third and fourth graders—who are not ignorant of the association between "blacks" and "Africa." Though the animal pictures and map used in the lesson were certainly innocuous, they may have evoked the stronger, and perhaps embarrassing, image of "savages" inhabiting native villages in Tarzan films.

In a third study, indirectly related to pupil imitative behavior, Herrmann (1972) reports a significant correlation between teacher approval and peer-ascribed pupil status—but not between teacher disapproval and pupil status—in an upper elementary sample. The relationship between teacher approval and three pupil status variables, acceptance, competence, and power, was higher for girls than for boys. While acceptance and competence appeared to have a similar base for both sexes, the power variable evidently stemmed from different sources in boys and girls. The power item "fight" was highly correlated with total power for boys, but not for girls; the power item "nice" correlated highly with total power for girls, but only slightly for boys. It appears that girls acquire influence over others by being "nice," while boys obtain power by fighting. Herrmann suggests that these findings can perhaps be explained by the socioeconomic status of the sample, which he describes as suburban, white, and midway between true middle class and lower class (with fathers in skilled or semiskilled occupations).

It is easy to understand why teacher approval correlated with competence, acceptance, and "niceness"; the fact that teacher disapproval did not relate to low status on these variables is somewhat more difficult to comprehend. We can speculate, however, that the absence of a correlation in the latter case reflects the teacher's ability to interpret pupil roles and behaviors according to community norms, reinforcing those behaviors that are socially approved for girls and boys in that particular socioeconomic group.

DIRECT AND INDIRECT TEACHER BEHAVIOR AND LANGUAGE BEHAVIOR OF PUPILS

The importance of the teacher's role as significant other declines as the pupil grows older and more mature. However, one particular function of the significant other—helping pupils understand, express, and interpret their feelings —continues undiminished.

Children's early language behaviors are generally self-referent and self-serving. They communicate what they want and feel and discuss matters that interest them. But when they enter the school, their language behaviors are curtailed and controlled for other purposes.

> There was the same difficulty throughout the school. In every classroom I saw sentences on the blackboard, which evidently had been written to illustrate some grammatical rule, or for the purpose of using words that had previously been taught in the same, or in some other connection. This sort of thing may be necessary in some stages of education; but it isn't the way to acquire language. *Nothing, I think, crushes the child's impulse to talk naturally more effectually than these blackboard exercises.* The schoolroom is not the place to teach any young child language, least of all the deaf child. He must be kept as unconscious as the hearing child of the fact that he is learning words, *and he should be allowed to prattle on his fingers, or with his pencil, in monosyllables if he chooses, until such time as his growing intelligence demands the sentence.* Language should not be associated

in his mind with endless hours in school, with puzzling questions in grammar, or with anything that is an enemy to joy. But I must not get into the habit of criticizing other people's methods too severely. I may be as far from the straight road as they.

Anne Sullivan in Helen Keller, 1968. The story of my life, *p. 418.*

It is difficult for pupils to find the self-reflection necessary for development of identity when they are simply responding to the teacher's demands. It is also difficult to differentiate the self from others in the limited and focused world of convergent answers and repeated phrases. While there are extremes (and teachers who exercise too little control fail to provide guidance just as those who practice excessive control limit the behavioral dialogue), it can be assumed that indirect teachers, teachers who allow considerable pupil talk, are more likely than their direct colleagues to encourage the expression and interpretation of feelings. And when students express their feelings, they create opportunity for self-concept change.

In fact, according to a study by Anandam, Davis, and Poppen (1971), freedom to verbalize feelings can improve not only pupil self-concept but the entire classroom climate. Third grade pupils were divided into two groups, the first of which was given the opportunity to express feelings and were reinforced by the teacher for doing so. The second group was exposed to a more intensive program of interpersonal skill development involving both teacher and peer reinforcement. Measures of self-concept, social dependency, and "individuation" (differentiating the self from others) showed a non-significant difference in favor of Group II. However, indices of classroom climate revealed significant differences between Groups I and II indicating that two very different environments had evolved during the course of the programs. The teacher of Group I reinforced verbalization of feeling but gradually limited such expression to a particular time of the day. Group II, on the other hand, pursued its more intensive program with enthusiastic support from both teacher and pupils. At the end of the two programs, Group II had increased pupil involvement in the lesson, teacher-pupil interaction, and pupil-pupil interaction, and had decreased the amount of individual desk work significantly more than Group I. These findings dispelled earlier doubts that third grade pupils were capable of verbally expressing their feelings and supported the contention that teachers can create the kind of classroom environment they want.

Creating opportunities for children to express their feelings in the classroom is presumed to be an effective way to help them develop more positive and realistic self-concepts. Sharing feelings helps one identify the self in relation to others, and examining negative feelings presumably helps one remove blocks to cognitive and affective processes.

Two particular expressive techniques, storytelling and creative dramatics, were investigated by Amato, Ziegler, and Emans (1973) as methods for improving children's interest in reading and reading achievement. Although neither technique affected the reading variables, self-concept and creativity measures taken during the investigation indicated that storytelling may have had a positive effect on pupils' self-image and empathy. Furthermore, story-telling rather than creative dramatics appeared to influence creativity. In a similar study (Carlton and Moore 1966), however, "self-directive dramatization of stories," when compared with traditional methods of teaching reading, produced significant improvement in both reading achievement and self-concept among predominantly black, culturally different elementary school children. In both of these studies, the more effective of the two techniques used emphasized the role of the pupil rather than the teacher in selecting and interpreting the reading material.

TEACHER BEHAVIOR AND THE SENSE OF SELF-IDENTITY

While the limited, sometimes peripheral, and admittedly scattered evidence supplied by the studies cited in this chapter does not offer a clear path of teacher behaviors known to positively affect the pupil's sense of self-identity, it does provide some signposts to guide teachers.

The essential self-conceptualizations within the Sense of Self-Identity involve the individual's perception of self as affiliated with others and the environment, as both recipient and initiator of impact, and as linked with others through communication. The Sense of Self-Identity comprises the individual's uniqueness as well as his or her similarity to some or all others. The values that the individual assigns to these differences and similarities between perceived self and others influence the Sense of Self-Extension, the Sense of Self-Esteem, and the Sense of Self-Image.

Pupils are constantly sorted and grouped according to their similarities and differences, and even similarities within differences. The criterion for similarity then becomes an identity reference not only for the group, but for the individuals within the group. And the identity of the group in turn becomes the basis on which administrators and teachers determine the kinds of roles and experiences group members will have in the behavioral dialogue of the classroom and school. Identity-references, classroom experiences, and role interpretations each have the potential to reflect a positive or negative value for the pupil's particular similarities and differences, and are important avenues of teacher impact on the pupil concepts of self-identity.

If this impact is to be positive, teachers must be aware of the social and physical phenomena that give rise to differences in pupil development, ability, experience, and value systems as well as the social standards and personal biases that determine the value assigned to these differences. If all the standards applied and all the positive values awarded in the classroom are derived from the white, middle-class, English-speaking segment of our society, being different from this segment in regard to color, socioeconomic status, language, values, or goals can become the sole basis of one's identity in the school environment.

Once again we return to the value for the individual and the attitude of unconditional acceptance which we considered essential to positive impact on the Sense of Bodily Self. Teachers with this value and attitude who have developed assessment skills and a knowledge of the social and physical influences on pupil nurture can help pupils who have limited ability, limited concept development due to the nature of their previous experiences, and/or concepts, values, and behaviors that differ from those of the dominant culture. To accept pupils is to acknowledge differences. To value individual pupils is to recognize and respect the differences and similarities among them. While it is important that differences be recognized and respected because they exist, it is even more important that additional differences *not be created* by the imposition of identity references that reflect the society's or the teacher's negative evaluation of particular group or individual characteristics.

Often the differences that most concern teachers are those related to the capacity for, motivation for, and rate of learning. In very broad terms, the teacher's function can be described as helping pupils acquire similar identities, behaviors, knowledge, and values—within a specified period of time. The most common approach to this task, an approach that on the surface accommodates pupil differences, is to group children by ability and performance.

When pupil groups are created, so are pupil identities, pupil roles, and pupil values. It is important that teachers be aware of the identity reference inherent in each experience of group membership. Moreover, pupils need to have a positive identity as a student and class member, to acquire the prescribed knowledge and learning behaviors, and to value themselves, their performances and products. Teachers who face their pupils with lists of rules and behaviors, consistently referring to what will be tolerated in "my class" reflect a negative value for pupil identity, a conforming and dependent role for pupils, and a preference for teacher rather than pupil goals. Teachers who refer positively to pupil status and activity, who establish rules and goals as expressions of pupil responsibility and autonomy as well as learning, encourage a positive sense of self-identity, a sense of relationship to the teacher and the class, and a sense of common goals.

It is important to remember that differences in ability and rate of learning are related primarily to one's identity as a pupil. They are significant not at home but at school. Differences in language, social behavior, values, concepts, experiences, or ability represent breaks in the continuum from home to school.

Such breaks affect not only the pupil's academic performance, but also the pupil's sense of safety. And if the difference is interpreted and reflected as a negative characteristic, the pupil may reject the school environment and its values or acquire a negative sense of self-identity in that environment and a dependency on the authoritative interpretations of the teacher.

Most teachers are aware that differences are assessed not merely for labeling but for instruction. And most teachers realize that differences must be treated by providing additional experiences, additional time, and adjusted learning goals. An awareness of the child's sense of self-identity, however, should lead teachers away from the practice of grouping pupils when the identity associated with group membership will be perceived as a negative reflection and interpretation of the child. Defining the group according to specific task goals rather than the ability or performance of its members accommodates the teacher and, with pupil achievement of short-term goals, provides a positive reflection of the child's identity as a student. Teachers can use individual performance assessment to identify pupil learning needs and form temporary *task* groups to meet those needs on a collective basis or they can use self-paced modules for individual instruction. By referring to the *task,* regardless of whether pupils are working in groups or individually, teachers can avoid giving identity-references based on pupil learning characteristics. In some instances, teachers can plan experiences that will be beneficial to the entire class, yet particularly helpful to special groups within the class. And when pupils need continued guidance in performing assignments, teachers can employ cross-group or pupil tutoring.

Teachers can make positive contributions to a pupil's sense of self-identity, particularly his or her identity as a student, by:

1. Increasing their knowledge of the social and physical phenomena responsible for pupil differences;

2. Becoming aware of personal biases that influence their acceptance and valuation of pupil differences;

3. Improving their assessment skills and their use of grouping and identity-referencing as a basis for treating pupil differences (see Chapter 6, Sense of Self-Esteem);

4. Creating an accepting and safe environment for pupils, particularly those who are different in obvious ways from other children, a climate that encourages communication and a sense of relationship to others (see Chapter 5, The Sense of Self-Extension).

We can think of nothing that expresses the relationship between ability (or opportunity) to communicate and the sense of self-in-relation-to-others as dramatically as the following experience of Helen Keller.

... In the still, dark world in which I lived there was no strong sentiment or tenderness. I felt my teacher sweep the fragments to one side of the hearth, and I had a sense of satisfaction that the cause of my discomfort was removed. She brought me my hat, and I knew I was going out into the warm sunshine. This thought, if a wordless sensation may be called a thought, made me hop and skip with pleasure.

We walked down the path to the well-house, attracted by the fragrance of the honeysuckle with which it was covered. Someone was drawing water and my teacher placed my hand under the spout. As the cool stream gushed over one hand she spelled into the other the word water, first slowly, then rapidly. I stood still, my whole attention fixed upon the motions of her fingers. Suddenly I felt a misty consciousness as of something forgotten—a thrill of returning thought; and somehow the mystery of language was revealed to me. I knew then that "w–a–t–e–r" meant the wonderful cool something that was flowing over my hand. That living word awakened my soul, gave it light, hope, joy, set it free! There were barriers still, it is true, but barriers that could in time be swept away.

I left the well-house eager to learn. Everything had a name, and each name gave birth to a new thought. As we returned to the house every object which I touched seemed to quiver with life. That was because I saw everything with the strange, new sight that had come to me. On entering the door, I remembered the doll I had broken. I felt my way to the hearth and picked up the pieces. I tried vainly to put them together. Then my eyes filled with tears; for I realized what I had done, and for the first time I felt repentance and sorrow.

Helen Keller, 1968. The story of my life, *pp. 36–37.*

REFERENCES

THE SENSE OF SELF IN AFFILIATION WITH OTHERS AND THE ENVIRONMENT—HAVING SOCIAL MEMBERSHIP AND ROLE IDENTITY

Erikson, E. 1959. Identity and the life cycle. *Psychological Issues* **1** (1): 1–171.

The Effect of Significant Others' Self-Concerns on Self-Identity Formation

Dobson, R., R. Goldenberg, and B. Elson 1972. Pupil control ideology and teacher influence in the classroom. *Journal of Educational Research* **66** (2): 77–80. (ERIC Document Reproduction Service No. EJ 064 242.)

Flanders, N. A. 1966. *Interactional analysis in the classroom, a manual for observers.* Ann Arbor: University of Michigan.

Keller, H. 1968. *The story of my life.* New York: Lancer.

Lovaas, O., R. Koegel, J. Simmons, and J. Long 1973. Some generalization and follow-up measures on autistic children in behavior therapy. *Journal of Applied Behavior Analysis* **6** (1): 131–166.

Teacher Behavior, Pupil Ethnicity, and Socioeconomic Status

Angelou, M. 1969. *I know why the caged bird sings.* New York: Random House.

Johnson, J. W. 1965. *Autobiography of an ex-colored man* in *Three Negro Classics.* New York: Avon.

Keller, H. 1968. *The story of my life.* New York: Lancer.

Mazer, G. E. 1971. Effects of social-class stereotyping on teacher expectation. *Psychology in the Schools* **8** (4): 373–378. (ERIC Document Reproduction Service No. EJ 048 011.)

Rist, R. C. 1970. Student social class and teachers' expectations: the self-fulfilling prophecy in ghetto education. *Harvard Educational Review* **40**: 411–451.

Steward, M., and D. Steward 1973. The observation of Anglo-, Mexican- and Chinese-American mothers teaching their sons. *Child Development* **44**: 329–337.

Trowbridge, N. 1972. *Self-concept and socio-economic status in elementary school children. American Educational Research Journal* **9** (4): 525–537.

THE SENSE OF SELF AS BOTH SUBJECT AND OBJECT

Keller, H. 1968. *The story of my life.* New York: Lancer.

St. Augustine 1955. *Augustine: Confessions and enchiridion,* Vol. VII. Albert Cook Outler (ed.). Philadelphia: Westminster Press.

Teacher Behavior and Pupil Self-Awareness

Bessell, H., and U. Palomares 1973. *The human development program, revised.* El Cajon, Calif.: The Human Development Training Institute.

————. 1972. *The human development supplementary guide.* El Cajon, Calif.: The Human Development Training Institute.

Brehm, J. W., and A. R. Cohen 1962. *Explorations in cognitive dissonance.* New York: Wiley.

Dyk, R. B., and H. A. Witkin 1965. Family experiences related to the development of differentiation in children. *Child Development* **36**: 21–55.

Erikson, E. 1959. Identity and the life cycle. *Psychological Issues* **1** (1): 1–171.

Horney, K. 1950. *Neurosis and human growth.* New York: Norton.

Miles, M. B. 1959. *Learning to work in groups: a program guide for educational leaders.* New York: Horace Mann-Lincoln Institute of School Experimentation, Teachers College, Columbia University.

Minuchin, P. 1971. Correlates of curiosity and exploratory behavior in preschool disadvantaged children. *Child Development* **42** (3): 939–950.

Winter, S., J. Griffith, and D. Kalb 1968. Capacity for self-direction. *Journal of Consulting and Clinical Psychology* **32** (1): 35–41.

Teacher Behavior and Pupil Acceptance of Others

Angelou, M. 1969. *I know why the caged bird sings*. New York: Random House.

Bettleheim, B. 1972. Play and education. *School Review* **81** (1): 1–13. (ERIC Document Reproduction Service No. EJ 070 386.)

Blau, B., and J. Rafferty 1970. Changes in friendship status as a function of re-inforcement. *Child Development* **41** (1): 113–121.

Crist, J. 1972. *Group dynamics and the teacher-student relationship: a review of recent innovations* (R&D Memo. No. 81). Stanford, Calif.: Stanford Center for Research and Development in Teaching, Stanford University, January.

Gilpatrick, N. 1969. Power of picture book to change child's self-image. *Elementary English* **46** (5): 570–574. (ERIC Document Reproduction Service No. EJ 005 596.)

Glavin, J. P., H. C. Quay, and J. S. Werry 1971. Behavioral and academic gains of conduct problem children in different classroom settings. *Exceptional Children* **37** (6): 441–446.

Griggs, J. W., and M. E. Bonney 1970. Relationship between "causal" orientation and acceptance of others, "self-ideal self" congruency and mental health changes for fourth and fifth grade children. *Journal of Educational Research* **63** (10): 471–477.

Heil, L. M., and C. Washburne 1962. Brooklyn College research in teacher effectiveness. *Journal of Educational Research* **55**: 347–351.

Katz, P. A. 1973. Stimulus predifferentiation and modification of children's racial attitudes. *Child Development* **44** (2): 232–237. (ERIC Document Reproduction Service No. EJ 077 332.)

Koval, C. B., and L. W. Hales 1972. The effects of the DUSO Guidance Program on the self-concepts of primary school children. *Child Study Journal* **2** (2): 57–61.

Lambert, W. E., and O. Klineberg 1969. The development of children's views of foreign peoples. *Childhood Education* **45** (5): 247–253.

Lilly, M. S. 1971. Improving social acceptance of low sociometric status, low achieving students. *Exceptional Children* **39**: 341–347.

Mende, R. H., and J. M. Kauffman 1971. Effects of videotape replays on behavior of culturally different young children. *Perceptual and Motor Skills* **33** (2): 670. (ERIC Document Reproduction Service No. EJ 045 464.)

St. John, N. 1971. Thirty-six teachers: their characteristics and outcomes for black and white pupils. *American Educational Research Journal* **8** (4): 635–647. (ERIC Document Reproduction Service No. EJ 052 663.)

Stoffer, D. L. 1970. Investigation of positive behavioral change as a function of genuineness, nonpossessive warmth, and empathetic understanding. *Journal of Educational Research* **63** (5): 225–228.

THE SENSE OF SELF AS RELATED TO OTHERS BY COMMUNICATION

Keller, H. 1968. *The story of my life*. New York: Lancer.

St. Augustine 1955. *Augustine: confessions and enchiridion*, Vol. VII. Albert Cook Outler (ed.). Philadelphia: Westminster Press.

Language Behavior and Self-Identity

Ahlbrand, W. P., Jr., and B. B. Hudgins 1970. Verbal participation and peer status. *Psychology in the Schools* **1**: 247–249.

Angelou, M. 1969. *I know why the caged bird sings*. New York: Random House.

Bernstein, B. 1961. Social class and linguistic development: a theory of social learning. In A. H. Halsey, J. Floud, and C. A. Anderson (eds.), *Education, economy, and society*. New York: Free Press.

Fisher, R. I. 1974. Study of nonintellectual attributes of children in first grade bilingual-bicultural program. *Journal of Educational Research*. **69**: 323–328.

Grier, W. H., and P. M. Cobbs 1968. *Black rage*. New York: Basic Books.

Harris, M. B., and S. J. Stockton 1973. A comparison of bilingual and monolingual physical education instruction with elementary school students. *Journal of Educational Research* **67** (2): 53–56.

Kaufman, B. 1964. *Up the down staircase*. Englewood Cliffs, N. J.: Prentice-Hall.

Kleinfeld, J. S. 1973. Classroom climate and the verbal participation of Indian and Eskimo students in integrated classrooms. *Journal of Educational Research* **67** (2): 51–52.

Kohl, H. 1967. *36 children*. New York: The New American Library.

Lefley, H. 1974. Effects of a cultural heritage program on the self-concept of Miccosukee Indian children. *Journal of Educational Research* **67** (10): 462–466.

Teachers' Interpretive and Language Behaviors and Pupil Imitative Behavior

Friedman, P. 1973. Student imitation of a teacher's verbal style as a function of natural classroom reinforcement. *Journal of Educational Psychology* **64** (3): 267–273. (ERIC Document Reproduction Service No. EJ 078 963.)

Herrmann, R. W. 1972. Classroom status and teacher approval and disapproval: study of children's perceptions. *Journal of Experimental Education* **41**: 32–39.

Portuges, S. H., and N. D. Feshback 1972. The influence of sex and socioethnic factors upon imitation of teachers by elementary school children. *Child Development* **43** (3): 981–989. (ERIC Document Reproduction Service No. EJ 962 923.)

Direct and Indirect Teacher Behavior and Language Behavior of Pupils

Amato, A., E. Ziegler, and R. Emans 1973. The effectiveness of creative dramatics and storytelling in a library setting. *Journal of Educational Research* **67** (4): 161–162.

Anandam, K., M. Davis, and W. Poppen 1971. Feelings—to fear or to free? *Elementary School Guidance and Counseling* **5** (3): 181–189.

Carlton, L., and R. H. Moore 1966. Effects of self-directive dramatization on reading achievement and self-concept of culturally disadvantaged children. *Reading Teacher* **20:** 125–130.

Keller, H. 1968. *The story of my life.* New York: Lancer.

TEACHER BEHAVIOR AND THE SENSE OF SELF-IDENTITY

Keller, H. 1968. *The story of my life.* New York: Lancer.

CHAPTER 5
The Sense of Self-Extension

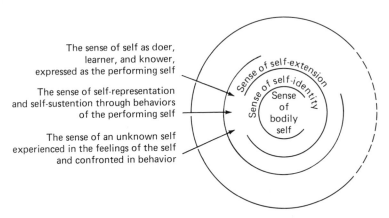

The sense of self as doer, learner, and knower, expressed as the performing self

The sense of self-representation and self-sustention through behaviors of the performing self

The sense of an unknown self experienced in the feelings of the self and confronted in behavior

Sense of self-extension

Sense of self-identity

Sense of bodily self

Fig. 5.1 Self-extension of the general self-concept.

The Sense of Self-Extension, like the Sense of Bodily Self, links a concrete, observable element to a psychological abstraction. The individual's *manifest* behavior—his or her Performing Self—and the psychological and cognitive concepts that produce these visible behaviors together comprise the Sense of Self-Extension. The psychological element of this sense of self coordinates the other aspects of self-concept which motivate, moderate, and inform concrete behavioral performances. Through the Sense of Self-Extension, the concepts of self are not only coordinated, but also arranged and orchestrated to produce behavioral performances that feature the self's most highly valued attributes. Consequently, the Performing Self exhibits repeated, characteristic patterns of valued behavior.

The behavior of the Performing Self can be observed, described, and classified by others. However, what others see is not necessarily part of the Sense of Self-Extension. It encompasses only the self's interpretation of motives, purposes, intent, and impact—and occasionally an awareness of an "unknown" self whose behaviors are sometimes pleasantly surprising ("I didn't know I could do that!"), sometimes perplexing ("I don't know what made me do that."), and sometimes totally alien to the concept of self ("I can't control myself; I just don't seem to have any will-power; I can't trust myself.").

In other words, the Sense of Self-Extension includes the individual's motive and performance, but not another's objective view of that performance.

This being so, the behavior of the Performing Self may be motivated by feelings very different from those inferred by observers, a situation clearly illustrated in Eleanor Roosevelt's account of her behavior, its motivation, and its perceived effect.

> **Looking back I see that I was always afraid of something: of the dark, of displeasing people, of failure. Anything I accomplished had to be done across a barrier of fear. I remember an incident when I was about thirteen. Pussie (a maternal aunt) was ill with a bad sore throat and she liked me to do things for her which made me very proud. One night she called me. Everything was dark, and I groped my way to her room. She asked if I would go to the basement and get some ice from the icebox. That meant three flights of stairs; the last one would mean closing the door at the foot of the stairs and being alone in the basement, making my way in pitch-black darkness to that icebox in the back yard! My knees were trembling, but as between the fear of going and the fear of not being allowed to minister to Pussie when she was ill, and thereby losing an opportunity to be important, I had no choice. I went and returned with the ice,** *demonstrating again the fact that children value above everything else the opportunity to be really useful to those around them.* **(Emphasis added.)**

> *Eleanor Roosevelt 1961.* Autobiography of Eleanor Roosevelt, *p. 12.*

To Eleanor, the choice lay between fear of the dark and fear of losing the privilege of ministering to her aunt. What might have appeared to another as a simple midnight errand performed by a child unafraid of the dark was in fact a critical assignment, fulfilled only because Eleanor's opportunity to serve, to "be important," was hanging in the balance. Behavior that one might have interpreted as complying and conforming, and from which one might have inferred respect for authority and need for approval, was valued by Eleanor as a means to acquire a positive reflection of self. Losing the opportunity to minister, to serve, to help, would have been disastrous to her Self-Image, Self-Esteem, Self-Identity, and Bodily Self. (Since physical appearance had, in Eleanor's case, been ruled out early in life—". . . I was made to feel so conscious of the fact that nothing about me would attract attention or would bring me admiration"—she derived even the senses of individuality and self-continuance, usually associated with the Bodily Self, from her serving role.)

Eleanor needed not only to serve, but to serve *well,* to do a good job. Because she fully accepted her role as servant to others (and adopted others' standards of behavior), she valued her accomplishments in that capacity. She acquired knowledge and skills to enhance her performance, and, achieving continued success and approval, gained self-confidence and a measure of independence.

> Mlle. Souvestre taught me also on these journeys that the way to make
> young people responsible is to throw real responsibility on them.
> She was an old lady and I was sixteen. The packing and unpacking for
> both of us was up to me, once we were on the road. I looked up
> trains, got the tickets, made all the detailed arrangements necessary
> for comfortable traveling. Though I was to lose some of my self-
> confidence and ability to look after myself in the early days of my
> marriage, it came back to me later more easily because of these trips
> with Mlle. Souvestre.

Eleanor Roosevelt, 1961. Autobiography of Eleanor Roosevelt, *p. 31.*

Through these attending behaviors, Eleanor represented herself and sustained her existing concepts of self. The "ministering" role, defined by Aunt
Pussie, was reproduced in Eleanor's behavioral dialogue with Mlle. Souvestre
and again in her relationship with her mother-in-law, Sara Delano Roosevelt.
In each of these relationships, she performed the serving role, defined and
interpreted by the salient other, and thereby gained approval. However, because Mlle. Souvestre, the educator, had expanded the role to include approval
for some independent behaviors, Eleanor began to value independence and
intrinsic reward. This complicated her later relationship with her mother-in-
law, who dominated the behavioral dialogue with Eleanor, allowing her only
minimal participation and no independence whatsoever. This extremely limited
role, in which everything was done *for* Eleanor, offered so little opportunity
for approval through "serving" others that the attending behaviors she had
practiced all her life suddenly provided neither self-representation nor self-
sustention.

> ... instead of taking an interest in these houses, one of which I was
> to live in, I left everything to my mother-in-law and my husband.
> I was growing dependent on my mother-in-law, requiring her help on
> almost every subject, and never thought of asking for anything that
> I thought would not meet with her approval. ... I remember that a
> few weeks after we moved into the new house on East 65th Street
> [Note: owned and built by her mother-in-law] I sat in front of my
> dressing table and wept, and when my bewildered young husband
> asked me what on earth was the matter with me, I said I did not like
> to live in a house which was not in any way mine, one that I had
> done nothing about and which did not represent the way I wanted
> to live. Being an eminently reasonable person, he thought I was quite
> mad and told me so gently .... I pulled myself together and realized
> that I was acting like a little fool, but there was a good deal of truth
> in what I had said, for I was not developing any individual taste
> or initiative. I was simply absorbing the personalities of those about
> me and letting their tastes and interests dominate me.

Eleanor Roosevelt 1961. Autobiography of Eleanor Roosevelt, *p. 61.*

Although her early behavior suggests a helping perceptual set, the fact that Eleanor (by the time she moved into the house on 65th Street) had not learned to run her household, cook, or attend to her children suggests that she was, until midlife, motivated by a concern for self rather than task or others. And when in later years, after achieving independence, she did develop a helping perceptual set, she expressed her concern for task and others through enhancement of her original "serving" role.

The serving behaviors that Eleanor acquired and valued were not modeled by the significant and salient others surrounding her. She took on these behaviors because, by her own admission, she had not the prerequisite beauty, talent, charm, or control of money to adopt the female roles modeled by her significant and salient others. To assume that Eleanor had a full range of alternatives, that she was free to simply imitate modeled behavior, ignores the fact that the significant or salient other's central function is to reflect and interpret the developing self. It was from the reflections of her "self" and the interpretations of her behavior supplied by significant others and the environment that Eleanor Roosevelt formed her Sense of Self-Extension, her concept of an appropriate and feasible way to gain approval and acceptance. The role of the server, the "minister," became her behavioral mode of self-representation, a role that fulfilled her need to be needed and allowed her to express her Sense of Bodily Self, Self-Identity, Self-Esteem, and Self-Image. The compliance, the dependence on others, and the acceptance of rigid, external standards persisted as self-sustaining behavior until she was middle-aged.

After her seventy-fifth birthday, Eleanor Roosevelt (1961, p. 411) wrote the following description of herself:

> In the beginning, because I felt, as only a young girl can feel it, all the pain of being an ugly duckling, I was not only timid, I was afraid. Afraid of almost everything, I think: of mice, of the dark, of imaginary dangers, of my own inadequacy. My chief objective, as a girl, was to do my duty. This had been drilled into me as far back as I could remember. Not my duty as I saw it, but my duty as laid down for me by other people. It never occurred to me to revolt. Anyhow, my one overwhelming need in those days was to be approved, to be loved, and I did whatever was required of me, hoping it would bring me nearer to the approval and love I so much wanted. . . .
>
> As a young woman, my sense of duty remained as strict and rigid as it had been when I was a girl, but it had changed focus . . . I was timid, still afraid of doing something wrong, of making mistakes, of not living up to the standards required by my mother-in-law, of failing to do what was expected of me. . . .
>
> It was not until I reached middle age that I had the courage to develop interests of my own, outside of my duties to my family.

Through Eleanor Roosevelt's experience, we can see how the individual assumes a self-sustaining behavioral mode based on the reflections of self received from significant others and the environment. Eleanor Roosevelt's "serving" behaviors stemmed primarily from a desire for approval, not a desire to serve. And by adopting these behaviors, she did in fact gain approval and, in turn, broaden the psychological experiences available to her. As she matured, she used her serving behaviors as a means to implement her own interests and contribute to others rather than to obtain approval.

Two of the most important factors in the development of the Sense of Self-Extension are the Sense of Bodily Self and the Sense of Self-Identity. These influence the child's perception of his or her impact on others and the environment and therefore affect the child's choice of behavior. They determine the developing self's perception of the safety and risk—the consequences —of every event in the child's behavioral dialogue. And the perception of safety or danger, physical and psychological, influences the extent and level of participation and performance. Through participation in the dialogue and exploration of the environment, the child gains self-knowledge, knowledge of others, additional psychological experiences, and, consequently, more opportunity to learn alternative behavior that will help satisfy needs and achieve goals.

THE SENSE OF SELF AS DOER, LEARNER, AND KNOWER THROUGH THE PERFORMING SELF

> I had never known my daddy to do nothin that profited him much and he eventually drifted me off to Mr. Knowland in 1904. Well, that ruint me to an extent because I learnt to see further under the white man than ever I seed before; I was trusted more. Mr. Knowland weren't home more than half of the time. Hit the road and leave me there with two other hired boys like myself, colored boys, and if anything needed to be done that he wanted done, he'd leave it in my hands. And that stuck me up and made me think a lot of myself. Things went absolutely straight under my administration. Just anything Mr. Knowland put me at I could do it and did do it. That year Mr. Knowland made twenty-five bales of cotton and corn to walk on. Well, that put my britches on, put me in the lights of what I could do. Mr. Knowland done trusted me and I found out what was in me—it was just revealed to me in the work I done. I begin to feel like I was becomin part of a man.

Nate Shaw in T. Rosengarten 1974. All God's dangers, *p. 52.*

Theoretically, the objective of the Performing Self is to achieve a positive self-reflection from significant others and the environment. Along with the response to the developing self's physical presence, the self begins to experience a reaction to his or her behavior, which becomes the basis of communication. When behavior becomes mutually understood, it also becomes a source of approval or disapproval. As we have mentioned, the Sense of Bodily Self and the Sense of Self-Identity, characterized respectively by feelings of acceptance or rejection and inclusion or exclusion, influence the Sense of Self-Extension by determining the extent of performance and participation in the behavioral dialogue. When performance, at any level, has a positive impact, it increases the value of the performance, modifies the subsequent estimate of risk, and increases anticipation of reward for the behavior performed. When a behavior has negative (or less positive than expected) impact, it will be performed less often and at greater estimated risk in the future.

The developing self's efforts to acquire skills and to explore and test the environment comprise the Performing Self, whose behaviors can be observed and judged by others. Both the behaviors and products of the Performing Self are consistently subjected to evaluation by the significant other, who reflects their impact to the developing self. It is the Performing Selves of pupils and teachers that constantly interact in the classroom and that furnish data for the study of teacher behavior and pupil academic performance.

In acquiring the behaviors and skills that gain acceptance and approval from others, the developing self learns the standards by which performance and products are judged, standards which affect Self-Esteem and Self-Image. Behaviors acquired and performed initially for approval and acceptance can eventually become valued as a self-rewarding source of autonomy and independence. And, when they become valued as an expression of self-direction, or as a representation of the self, they are no longer performed for the approval of others, although they no doubt continue to be approved.

From early experiences in the behavioral dialogue, children learn that they can change the responses of others and alter their circumstances through their behavior. They learn that they can meet some of their needs directly by performing certain behaviors and others indirectly through the effect of their behaviors on others and the environment. They learn that there are rules for behavior, rules over which they have no control. They experience approval for compliance and disapproval for noncompliance. They learn that certain behaviors are allowed and others prohibited because of their age, sex, or family and social environment. They associate conditions and circumstances (i.e., "a time and place") with varying consequences of the same behavior. They learn that their own bodies sometimes enable and sometimes limit their performances.

From the perceived consistent effects of their behaviors, children form their behavioral schemas. They are initially motivated to acquire certain behaviors by their value for acceptance and approval from significant others. However, once children perceive that they can use acquired behaviors to control the responses of others or to achieve independence, they shift their value structure: they begin to prize autonomy over approval. Behaviors and skills that serve the senses of self are valued. Those that do not directly contribute to self-concept formation may be acquired, but only as responses, and therefore cannot be considered behavioral clues to the existing self-concept.

Children's values, then, play an important part in determining the behavior of their Performing Selves. However, two other factors are also critical to the concept of self as doer, learner, and knower: (1) the adequacy of the significant other as an interpreter, informer, and reflector; and (2) the nature of the cultural and familial environments.

THE SIGNIFICANT OTHER AND THE PERFORMING SELF

The parental pride that accompanies the behavioral progress of a warmly received and accepted infant is usually conveyed in a series of bulletins announcing the baby's latest performance: "Joey turned over by himself today," "He's beginning to respond with smiles, and I'm sure it's not just gas," "He's sitting up by himself now," "He took his first steps today," etc. These announcements continue until the baby arrives at the point where parental control and behavioral progress meet. At this point, the child must be "trained" and controlled, and, consequently, the traits and practices of significant others begin to have considerable impact on the development of the child's Sense of Self-Extension, particulary the concept of self as Performer.

The effect of parental traits and practices on the behavior of preschool children is reported by Baumrind (1966, 1967, 1971, 1972) and Baumrind and Black (1967). In Baumrind's 1967 study, three pupil behavior patterns were identified and related to parental traits and practices. From these findings we can (1) infer a relationship between the behavior patterns identified and the children's self-concepts, and (2) hypothesize the behavioral dialogues that occurred between the parents and children studied.

The behaviors of Pattern I children were described as appropriately mature: independent but social, self-reliant, explorative, realistic, competent, affiliative, and content. Parents of these children exercised strong and consistent guidance, but respected the independent decisions of the child. They were directive, but they accompanied directions with reasons. They demanded a good deal of their children, but were supportive and nurturant, loving, conscientious, and self-assured in their role as parents.

We can infer from these behavioral descriptions that Pattern I children had initially experienced unconditional acceptance and thus had developed a sense of trust and safety (independent, explorative behaviors), indicating a positive Sense of Bodily Self. They had participated fully in the behavioral dialogue and had formed a sense of self related to others and a sense of self as communicator (social, realistic, affiliative), indicating a positive Sense of Self-Identity. In the process of acquiring prescribed behaviors (training), they had received approval and eventually come to value the learned behavior as a source of independence and autonomy (self-reliant, competent), indicating a positive Sense of Self-Extension. They had also experienced a positive reflection of self, first as stimulus and then as performer, and had thereby acquired standards and values for their performances (realistic, competent, social), suggesting a positive Sense of Self-Esteem. Finally, they had satisfied their needs and achieved their goals through the direct impact of their behavior or through its indirect effect on others (content), evidence of a Positive Sense of Self-Image, past, present, and future.

The parents of these children exhibited behavior characteristic of perfectly functioning significant others. They had given their children positive self-reflections. They had allowed their children an active role in the behavioral dialogue. They had provided a consistent interpretation of their children's behaviors, thus establishing clear understanding and communication. They had supplemented their directions with interpretation and information so that their children could begin to construct schema for approved behaviors and self-direction. They had attended to both approved and disapproved behaviors, allowing their children to develop a more "mature" behavioral style.

Pattern II children were less secure, more apprehensive, and more likely to become hostile or regressive under stress than were Pattern I subjects. Furthermore, their behavior was more conforming, less autonomous and less social. The parents of these children were less nurturant and less involved with their children than Pattern I parents. They were firm, using power freely, offering no explanation of their orders, and encouraging no disagreement. Mothers tended to use fright as a controlling device and to exhibit less sympathy toward and less approval of their children.

Theoretically, Pattern II children had experienced conditional acceptance in the initial behavioral dialogue and had thus developed a sense of mistrust and fear for self-continuance (less secure, hostile, regressive under stress). From their behavior we can infer a weak Sense of Bodily Self with an inadequately developed sense of individuality. In fact, we can theorize that all concepts of self were inadequate in these children. Their participation in the behavioral dialogue had been limited primarily to compliant behavior, which their parents had approved (while at the same time excessively censuring noncompliance). Because these children had been provided little interpretation and information about their behavior, their learning had been limited to associative processes. They had remained dependent upon moment-to-moment rather than systematic interpretation, a conditon which inhibits the development of behavioral schema. The association between power and conformity, theoretically, had inhibited these children's perception of standards and caused them to value conforming behavior primarily as a means to disarm the threat to self-continuance rather than as a method of obtaining approval or autonomy. Their parents' use of power and fright as controlling behaviors, in the absence of other experiences and dialogues, had led Pattern II children to value power and threat as means of protecting the Sense of Bodily Self and acquiring Self-Identity and Self-Esteem (by imitating the role or identifying with those who practiced it).

Children in the Pattern III group were described as immature and dependent, compared with Pattern I and II subjects. They showed less self-control and self-reliance than children in the other two groups. Their parents were less demanding, and much less controlling than Pattern I and II parents. They also babied their children more. The fathers in this group were lax disciplinarians, and the mothers used love in a more manipulative manner than did mothers of children in the first two groups.

Since Pattern III children were simply described as more immature than the other children, we have no specific behaviors or characteristics from which to infer the Sense of Bodily Self. However, since their parents were described as "babying" and undemanding, it seems likely that the role they had assigned their children was that of a dependent baby. In turn, it is also likely that the self-reflections and interpretations these children received had failed to give them a realistic concept of themselves, their behavior, or their environment, all of which would lead us to expect a weak Sense of Self-Identity and a low level of social and communicative behavior among Pattern III children. Apparently the behavior of these children had been poorly interpreted by significant others. And, without parental demand, control, or reinforcement, these children had no way of assessing the impact of their behavior.

Groups II and III offer almost opposite patterns of parental behavior, both of which, however, if projected to their logical extremes, severely limit development of the child's Sense of Self-Extension. For example, parents (like those in Pattern II) who fail to affirm appropriate behavior, while at the same time attending to inappropriate behavior (without explaining *why* it is inappropriate), only provide the children with information about how they should *not* behave. Given no information about how they *should* behave or *why* they should restrain themselves in certain situations, children have difficulty determining which behaviors are approved, and are therefore apt to conclude that any action which does not provoke a response (i.e., which is unseen or ignored) is approved.

On the other hand, if parents (like those in Pattern III) fail to differentiate the child's behaviors with regard to appropriateness and impact, they provide little cognitive information from which a child can interpret those behaviors and in turn develop a goal-oriented behavioral schema. Under these circumstances, behavior can become neither the source of approval (and eventually independence and autonomy) nor the basis of communication.

Furthermore, any effort on the child's part to acquire independent behavior (by imitating the behavior of peers or incorporating the reflections, interpretations, and information supplied by salient others) may cause withdrawal of the mother's love and a negative reflection of self. To maintain a positive relationship with the significant other, then, the child's Sense of Self-Extension may confine the Performing Self to dependent behavior and allow the acquisition of only those skills that ensure continued acceptance by and approval of the mother, thereby sacrificing autonomy for continued security.

Somewhere between these extremes, however, lies a course of parental behavior that encourages positive development of the child's Performing Self. The sense of self as doer, learner, and knower is acquired from psychological events in the behavioral dialogue that transmit positive reflections of the developing self and realistic, consistent interpretations of the self's behavior. Typically, these reflections and interpretations are valued first as a means of gaining approval and subsequently as a method of achieving independence and autonomy.

The traits and practices of significant and salient others directly influence the development of the child's Performing Self. A less immediate influence, often working indirectly through significant others, is the network of cultural values.

CULTURAL VALUES AND THE PERFORMING SELF

The influence of cultural values on the formation of the Sense of Self-Extension is most obvious, of course, when most acutely felt. Nate Shaw, for example, experienced the impact of cultural values in reflections of himself as doer, learner, and knower:

> It's stamped in me, in my mind, the way I been treated, the way I have seed other colored people treated—couldn't never go by what you think or say, had to come up to the white man's orders. "You aint got sense enough to know this, you aint got sense enough to know that, you aint got sense enough to know nothin—just let me tell you how to do what I want you to do." Well, that's disrecognizin me, and then he slippin around to see that I doin like he say do, and if I don't he don't think it's on account of I got my own way of doin, but he calls it ignorant and disobeyin his orders. Just disrecognized, discounted in every walk of life. "Just do what I say, like I tell you. Don't boot me." Showin me plain he aint got no confidence in me. That's the way they worked it, and there's niggers in this country believed that shit. The only way you could gain any influence—he puts you out there, come along after a while and look over what you done—"O, it's done nice, it's done to suit me." Then he'll—some of em will do it—he'll give you praises, thisaway he'll give it: "O, Nate, you is better than I thought,

you all right." And so on. Pleased at it, didn't know I could do it. I've studied and studied these white men close. And I've studied em up to many and many a thing that surprises me.

Nate Shaw in T. Rosengarten 1974. All God's dangers, *p. 109.*

Although these experiences were, as Nate says, "stamped" in his mind, they were not stamped in his concept of self as doer, learner, and knower. He perceived himself differently from the way the white man saw him: "I always—not boastin or braggin—but I always was a apt little kid, and I was willin." It was not self-reflections from others but reflections of his direct impact on the environment that formed Nate's concept of his Performing Self: It was "just revealed to me in the work I done." However, the cultural values expressed in the attitudes and behavior of others influenced Nate's performance, if not his self-concept. These cultural values alerted Nate "never to go by what you think" but to simply "come up to the white man's orders." Nate was somewhat unusual since he, unlike others, was able to discount the image of himself reflected by white men, and thereby maintain a positive self-concept. He could not, however, keep cultural values from influencing his *behavior.*

Cultural beliefs regarding sex, like those regarding race, can reach the developing self through significant or salient others and affect behavior and self-concept. Sex differences in academic achievement, for example, can be explained in terms of cultural values. From the beginning, culturally determined sex roles defining what little girls and boys are made of ("sugar and spice and everything nice," and "snips and snails and puppy dog tails," respectively) influence the significant other's interpretations of the developing self's part in the behavioral dialogue.

In some social milieus, females learn from the behavior of significant and salient others that success in the female role depends on one's ability to please others. They may also gather that the best way to please others is by meeting cultural standards of physical attractiveness. Failure to meet these standards requires the acquisition of behaviors and skills that enable one to please by serving and accommodating others.

Feminism notwithstanding, physical attractiveness remains a powerful determinant of success in the female role. For women, being judged according to cultural standards of beauty is a "pass–fail" situation, similar to that experienced by blacks, in which the impact of self upon others is decided in large part by a physical attribute over which the individual has little or no control. And, since the sense of physical self is an aspect of the concept of Bodily Self, females who value appearance as the basis for self-approval will form a concept of Bodily Self that is highly dependent on reflections of physical attractiveness. And because it is at the "core" of self-concepts, the Sense of Bodily Self—its positive or negative nature—affects the Senses of Self-Identity, Self-Esteem, and Self-Image.

But even more important is the effect of this cultural valuing of physical attractiveness on the Sense of Self-Extension. Though we are told that beauty is only skin deep, as a cultural value its impact on self-concept is far from shallow. First, it defines the self as an object, rather than a doer, learner, or knower. Second, as the prime requirement for approval in the female role, it demotes all other attributes and behaviors to a secondary, compensatory level. Accordingly, success in the female role depends on an interpretation of the self as either an inactive stimulus or a response to others (defined by their particular needs and values)—or both. For females who have internalized these interpretations of the approved female role, the task is to enhance one's physical attributes and acquire pleasing, serving behaviors. In spite of a multimillion dollar beauty industry and a proliferation of cosmetic products unmatched by any other culture, efforts to enhance physical attractiveness are not always successful. Therefore, the most reliable, tried-and-true method of gaining approval as a female is to acquire and exhibit behaviors that please others. In the school environment, academic achievement may be viewed as a means of pleasing others, particularly the teacher.

If this theorizing does, indeed, reflect reality, we would expect females to show higher levels of academic achievement as a pleasing response in the pupil role, defined by the source of approval in the classroom, i.e., the teacher. We would also expect academic achievement to lose its value as a means of gaining approval when the valued source of approval shifts from teacher to peer group, particularly peers of the opposite sex. Academic achievement might even become negatively valued as females learn that it is not necessarily approved by these new salient others. Continued high academic achievement might reflect a compensatory behavior, or simply undisguiseable intelligence.

In other instances, when the female role has been interpreted to include a concept of self as doer, learner, and knower (rather than merely server), cultural values intrude by limiting the occupations considered appropriate for women. Occupationally, the emphasis is again on serving roles, i.e., nurse, stewardess, waitress, clerk, secretary, and assistant whatever.

With the exception of wife and mother, the approved female occupation most commonly modeled is that of the school teacher. From early childhood girls observe this female role. In doing so, they see that this role requires a mastery of academic knowledge and the acquisition of specific behaviors and skills. Like the roles of housewife and mother, the teacher's job demonstrates a clear relationship between acquired knowledge and role performance. This relationship between function and knowledge is not nearly as obvious for other occupational roles, male or female. Whether this demonstrated and observed relationship influences girls toward higher academic achievement than boys in the early years is open to speculation, but it may be a contributing factor.

Cultural values determine the sex role interpretations transmitted to boys as well as those conveyed to girls. Theoretically, these value interpretations influence boys' motivation toward academic achievement. In a culture where the approved male role stresses physically active, risk-taking, explorative, and dominating behavior, motivation toward academic achievement may be somewhat lacking in boys during the early years. Early experiences may communicate to boys that success and acceptance in future male roles is related primarily to the performance of physical behaviors and the acquisition of motor rather than cognitive skills.

Regardless of socioeconomic class, boys are generally exposed to a wider variety of future role options than girls. But the relationship between the acquired knowledge and performance of these roles, as we have already noted, is rarely clear. When, in adolescent years, occupational choice becomes a more immediate concern, the connection between academic knowledge and role performance is more systematically and clearly communicated.

The prime cultural dictate for success in the male role is superior performance, physical and intellectual. Although physical size and attractiveness are culturally valued and often facilitate success, they are not the primary determinants of one's impact on others. Yet, if a boy has internalized a value for physical size, his stature will influence his Sense of Bodily Self and his acquisition of performing behaviors. Among boys, academic achievement is sometimes an alternative to physical prowess as a means of gaining approval, particularly in the years before occupational choice is made. The cultural press for success and the understood relationship between academic achievement and social and economic advancement provide males, as they mature, with increased motivation for academic performance. Conditions, more than cultural values, limit opportunities for white males.

In our society females and minority group members are currently finding expanded occupational options and increased opportunity, evidence that the cultural values influencing sex-role interpretations and concepts of self as doer, learner, and knower are changing. These changes will most likely be reflected in the research, producing findings which depart from those obtained in the past with regard to sex- and race-related differences in academic achievement.

It takes no gift of prophecy to foresee that the public school classroom will be the major arena in which the conflict between traditional and new cultural values will take place. Teachers will be faced with pupils from families representing both value positions; they may find that their own values conflict with those of the community they serve. At the core of this conflict between traditional and "reformed" interpretations of sex and minority roles is the concept of the self as doer, learner, and knower, a concept which directly influences the behavior and performance of each individual.

TEACHER BEHAVIOR AND PUPIL PERFORMANCE

Theoretically, the objective of the Performing Self is to gain approval and a positive reflection of self from significant/salient others and the environment through the impact of the self's performance. In the school situation, the child's teacher and fellow pupils are significant/salient others, and, along with the applied standards for performance, products, and participation, they reflect the child's Performing Self. The effort and energy that the child expends as a performer, producer, and participator will be determined by the Sense of Self-Extension and an estimation of the risk, threat, or chance for affirmation involved in each classroom task. Theoretically, then, conditions that maximize psychological safety and the possibility of experiencing a positive self-reflection will raise the level of performance, production, and participation in the classroom.

There are many obstacles impeding the teacher who would like to create an environment that benefits all the Performing Selves in the classroom. As prime reflector and evaluator, the teacher is short of time, eyes, ears, and responses. Although progress has been made in individualizing the academic work presented to pupils, the problem of individualizing the relationship between teacher and pupil on the teacher's side remains. A large part of that problem involves the teacher's orientation toward pupils. In a study by Kranz (1972), the six problems most commonly reported by teachers all involved attitude toward pupils: (1) teacher expectation of instant improvement in pupil performance; (2) eagerness to direct the child along a prescribed educational route rather than a child-paced route; (3) difficulty in tolerating silence and nonverbal periods; (4) difficulty focusing on the child's feelings; (5) confusion between therapist and teacher roles; and (6) reluctance to accept some children as they present themselves in the classroom situation. Although these problems have the potential to limit pupil performance, each is highly amenable to change.

There is ample evidence in the research that the teacher's limited resources are being expended in a way that benefits primarily the high-achieving pupils. Academic achievers receive more positive reflections and more positive attention from their teachers than other pupils. Silberman (1969), Good and Brophy (1972), Nash (1972) and Chaikin, Sigler, and Derlega (1974) are only a few of the many who report observable differences in the teacher's behavior toward high and low achieving pupils. Aspy and Roebuck (1972) report that the teacher's positive regard for pupils correlates positively and significantly with pupil cognitive achievement. And, since academic achievement is considered the main objective of education, and a positive reflection of the *teacher*'s Performing Self, it would be both unusual and undesirable for teachers to withhold approval for high academic performance.

As far as self-concept development is concerned, the problem is not teacher approval for academic achievement, but the kind of pupil behavior reinforced and the kind of pupil reflection communicated by that approval. If teacher approval is related only to the pupil product, "academic achievement," then pupils who value approval may be reinforced for behavior that is merely expedient, since the end will justify the means. Pupils who value approval, but haven't the ability or the means to produce a valued product, may see no point in performing—the anticipated results are too low and the estimated risk too high. Pupils who achieve because they value their own performances and products may also value teacher approval for the confirmation of their work inherent in that approval. Of course, if teacher approval reflects reinforcement of the teacher's perception of the child as an achiever, rather than a true evaluation of the child's performance, it conveys an unrealistic image of the Performing Self.

Teacher approval, then, can have negative as well as positive impact on pupil self-concept. However, teacher disapproval, particularly disrespect for pupils as performing, participating, and producing individuals, has an even more powerful effect on the child's Performing Self. Not surprisingly, ignoring, avoiding, rejecting, and criticizing behavior that communicates disapproval or disrespect has been positively correlated with negative teacher attitudes concerning pupil achievement, socioeconomic status, sex, and race.

Other teacher behaviors communicating disapproval, whether intended or not, include arbitrary use of authority, inconsistent application of standards, rules, punishments, and rewards, or any behavior that structures the classroom dialogue to serve the Performing Self of the teacher rather than the Performing Selves of pupils.

Because some of these behaviors are related to teaching skills and experience, they can be changed with training to benefit the pupil's Performing Self. Tardiff (1971) reports that teachers trained to increase the clarity of their presentations, to keep their questions logically related, and to respond to pupils in a positive manner, encouraging further contributions and higher levels of cognitive activity, increased pupil participation and critical thinking significantly more than control teachers. They also reduced the frequency of teacher directives and trivial pupil responses. Both clarity and logic raise the level of pupil understanding, which in turn reduces the risk involved in making class contributions. A clear, logical, and accepting teacher, then, creates an atmosphere that frees rather than inhibits the child's Performing Self.

Another aspect of the teacher's verbal style known to discourage pupil performance (but amenable to change) is unwarranted interruption of pupil activity. Farnham-Diggory and Ramsey (1971) found that children whose classroom activity had been constantly interrupted showed significantly less task persistence than control subjects whose work had not been arbitrarily interrupted. Presumably, the teacher's ability to give clear directions and to correctly assess the time required to complete an assigned task—skills that can be learned—reduces the need to interrupt (and inadvertently communicate disrespect for) pupil performance.

As one might expect, the use of praise and the absence of blame in the classroom also have a positive effect on pupil performance. Brown, Payne, Lankewich, and Cornell (1970) report that pupils in classrooms where praise is given often and criticism or blame given rarely initiate considerably more responses than those in classrooms where these practices are reversed. It is not surprising that pupil participation is inhibited when personal risk is high.

There are many instructional methods and practices that convey respect and consideration for the pupil as a performing individual. The simple, but time-consuming procedure of including personal feedback and evaluative comments on returned test papers (Page, 1958) was found to significantly improve the subsequent test performance of pupils, particularly those with poor achievement records. In addition, this practice improves pupils' ability to evaluate their own performances, reflects the teacher's perception of the pupils as individuals, and recognizes pupils as performers who can make use of information given to them. The teacher's willingness to devote considerable time to writing personal comments also communicates that pupils are valued as individuals.

For teachers with too many pupils and too little time, instructional methods that allow pupils to see themselves positively reflected by sources other than the teacher are helpful in communicating positive regard for pupils as individual performers. Cross-peer tutoring, for example, has been shown to help a broad range of pupils increase their classroom participation and achievement levels (Fleming 1969; Mohan 1971).

Achievement can also be increased—at least for some students—by employing a pupil-directed, rather than a teacher-directed, instructional approach. White and Howard (1970) report that seventh-grade boys classified as "externally controlled" raised their achievement levels significantly more under a pupil-directed instructional system that allowed them to participate in lesson planning. The achievement of "internally controlled" boys was affected by neither the pupil-directed nor the teacher-directed approach. Because other studies have produced opposite findings with "externally controlled" pupils, it appears that instructional approach may interact with subject matter, making certain content (i.e., science and math) more compatible with pupil-centering techniques.

We have theorized that the teacher's functioning as significant/salient other and controller of the classroom environment influences not only the child's self-perception but classmates' perception of the child as well. We have also theorized that the objective of the individual's Performing Self is to obtain a positive reflection from the impact of the self's performance on the environment and significant/salient others. In a study that offers some support to our theorizing, Epperson (1963) investigated the hypotheses that (1) pupils seek to control their environment and to influence others in order to be seen by their peers as capable performers in the academic and social arenas of the school and that (2) pupils who fail to achieve control and influence become alienated from their peers and teachers. Epperson identified two forms of alienation—Isolation (a low value for behaviors highly valued by teachers and peers) and Powerlessness (perceived inability to influence rewards by behavior)—which he assessed on measures of peer-exclusion and actualization.

Pupils who were excluded by their teachers also showed isolation from their teachers. However, *actual* exclusion by classmates was not related to *feelings* of exclusion by peers. These findings led Epperson to speculate that classroom "deviates" were excluded by teachers but not by peers. (While excluded pupils were sure of their status with the teacher, and thus reported alienation from the teacher, they were unsure of their status among peers and therefore reported less alienation from them.) Pupils were seen by their peers as having both academic and social power or academic power without social power, but never as having social power without academic power. (Epperson suggests that pupils are made more aware of each other's academic than social performance in the school situation.) Pupils who saw themselves unable to influence either their social or academic rewards registered low actualization of their potential.

Because all pupils are expected to perform, participate, and produce in the classroom, the teacher has considerable opportunity to reinterpret the roles they have previously assumed and to alter or reinforce their perception of the impact of their behavior. In this context, it is less important how the teacher rates the performance of each pupil than how he or she interprets that performance to the child.

The impact of success or failure on self-concept is determined by the value system of the pupil, not by the teacher's values and not by an external standard. The assumption that all pupils are deeply affected by academic failure is usually made by those who value education. Pupils may acquire negative self-concepts from academic failure not because they failed to achieve, but because they failed to please a significant/salient other and, in turn, failed to be approved. When academic achievement is valued neither as a means of obtaining approval nor as a means of acquiring autonomy and independence, success or failure in academic tasks has little or no effect on the pupil's self-concept.

THE SENSE OF SELF-REPRESENTATION AND
SELF-SUSTENTION IN THE PERFORMING SELF

> I've joked with white people, in a nice way. I've had to play dumb
> sometimes—I knowed not to go too far and let them know what I
> knowed, because they taken exception of it too quick. I had to humble
> down and play shut-mouthed in many cases to get along. I've done it
> all—they didn't know what it was all about, it's just a plain fact. I've
> played dumb—maybe a heap of times I knowed just how come they
> done such and such a trick, but I could go to em a heap of times
> for a favor and get it. I could go to em, even the heavy-pocketed white
> man, if I couldn't get what I wanted out of one, I could get it out the
> other one. They'd have dealins with you, furnish you what you needed
> to make a crop, but you had to come under their rulins. They'd give
> you a good name if you was obedient to em, acted nice when you met
> em and didn't question em bout what they said they had against you.
> You begin to cry about your rights and the mistreatin of you and
> they'd murder you.

Nate Shaw in T. Rosengarten 1974. All God's dangers, *p. 545.*

The quotation above provides a fairly clear picture of the Nate Shaw
that observers saw—the Performing Self of Nate Shaw—seeking a favor from
the white landowners in his community: A black man, hat-in-hand, with
slumping shoulders, grinning mouth, and cast-down eyes, speaking defer-
entially in a heavy dialect, who said little and ignored slurs, insults, and false
accusations hurled his way. He appeared unable to understand that the terms
offered to him were unfair and continued to display an affable, agreeable,
slow-witted reaction, finally thanking the white man profusely for the note
of credit given him. Then he left, still bowing and scraping.

Were these behaviors of Nate Shaw, the self-described competent
farmer who cares for and respects himself? They were, indeed, because Nate
knew what kind of behavior the circumstances required. Under these conditions, Nate had to "play dumb" and "shut-mouthed" in order to "get along."
His actions were prompted by his appraisal of risk and reward and the behavior required to avoid one and gain the other. These actions did not reflect
his opinion of himself or even his actual opinion of the white man. His individuality, his belief in his own autonomy, were obscured by the role he had to
assume, a role dictated by the white man's need to exert power over Nate and
all others in Nate's circumstances. If it were not for Nate's self-reporting, we
would never have known that even in these circumstances he reinforced his
concept of self as one who is able to affect the behavior of others and his
environment.

It is not difficult to perceive the element of danger, the threat to self-
continuance, and the need for acceptance by others in Nate's contacts with

the white landowners. All the power, all the control over acceptance, approval, and reward were on one side of this dialogue. As Nate reports, "They'd give you a good name if you was obedient to em, acted nice when you met em and didn't question em bout what they said they had against you."

Nate's circumstances and behavior illustrate the role that power plays in interpersonal relationships. The assessment of power positions is the function of the Sense of Self-Extension, and the self-representing or self-sustaining behaviors of the Performing Self are based on this assessment.

The developing self enters the behavioral dialogue dependent and powerless. Whatever power the self acquires is ascribed or released to the self by significant or salient others. If children are unconditionally accepted and approved at the outset, and if their significant others view power as responsibility, not merely authority, children will form a positive concept of Bodily Self and Self-Identity. As they acquire prescribed behaviors and skills, and the concomitant approval of significant others, they will learn to control their impact and to assume responsibility for their actions. Conditional approval and acceptance by significant others produces only conditional control over and responsibility for behavior. And rejection in the initial behavioral dialogue produces a negative sense of Bodily Self and Self-Identity: though children may win occasional, conditional approval, control over the impact of their behavior remains with the significant other who retains the *power* to approve.

This theorizing is supported by research relating parental behavior to locus of control in children (Joe 1971; Katkovsky, Crandall, and Good 1967). Findings suggest that "self-controlled" children—those with an *internal* locus of control—have parents (significant others) who accept their children, administer discipline in a consistent manner, and encourage early independent behavior, while "other-controlled" children—those with an *external* locus of control—have mothers who are highly authoritarian, hostile-rejecting, or overly protective, with a tendency to use affective punishment or withdrawal of privileges as a method of discipline.

Along with locus of control, experience and maturation also influence the child's assessment of the conditions and power involved in interpersonal events. Therefore, it is difficult to determine from a single behavioral event the child's locus of control.

Frightened, dependent, conforming, externally controlled Eleanor Roosevelt, for example, tromped unescorted through Europe as an adolescent, exhibiting what most would consider courageous and independent behavior. Nate Shaw, who served twelve years in prison because he wouldn't "go nobody's way against my own self," bowed, scraped, and "humbled down" to play dumb and shut-mouthed. Yet the behavior of both of these individuals was consistent with his or her locus of control. Mlle. Souvestre told Eleanor to "Take your Baedeker and go see it," and Eleanor, because she wanted her teacher's approval, did so. Her behavior was self-representing and characteristic of her locus of control. Similarly, Nate Shaw, who "always knowed to give the white man his time of day or else he's ready to knock me in the head," behaved in a self-sustaining manner in accordance with his perception of the power positions in the relationship. Nate intentionally manipulated his role to obtain financing and to ensure his safety.

TEACHER BEHAVIOR AND PUPIL AUTONOMY

Autonomy is acquired and increased through the mastery of behaviors and skills that reduce individuals' dependence on others and enable them to achieve their desires and goals on their own. These acquired skills are first interpreted and then reinforced by significant others and the environment as approved behavior. The extent of children's autonomous behavior is determined by three things: the role assigned them in the behavioral dialogue; the degree to which this role fosters the acquisition of concepts and values for goal-directed behavior; and opportunity to use the skills acquired. Physical limitations interact with psychological experiences to determine the amount of autonomy developing selves can achieve in their particular circumstances.

The behavioral dialogue that children encounter in the classroom is very similar to the child–parent dialogue in which they acquired early self-concepts and behavioral constructs. In the classroom children continue to learn behaviors prescribed for them, and they are still dependent upon a significant other's interpretation, information, and reflections of approval. They exercise only as much autonomy as their teacher is willing to grant them.

Even when teachers are willing to promote a fair measure of independence and autonomy in pupils, they may have difficulty doing so. They must first correctly assess each pupil's Performing Self in order to tailor the child's role to his or her own particular capacity for self-direction, self-control, self-criticism, and independence. The externally controlled child, for example, must first be assured of acceptance and approval before the child can assume autonomous behavior. A study by Flanders, Morrison, and Brode (1968) indicates that children showing the greatest decline during the school year in positive attitude toward teachers and schoolwork were those with an external locus of control and those with teachers who gave little praise and encouragement. This decline occurred regardless of pupil IQ, grades, or socioeconomic status. These findings suggest that the externally controlled child in particular should be accepted and approved early in the school year, if independent behavior is ever to be achieved. But whatever the status of the child's Performing Self, the teacher must not only assess it, but also continue to equip it with additional skills and behaviors so that the capacity for independence and autonomy can expand.

After assessing the child's Performing Self, teachers must examine their own Performing Selves in order to determine which of their behaviors encourage independence in pupils. In a study of parental behavior and adolescent autonomy, Elder (1963) found that parents who were democratic, who explained their directives, and who created opportunities for autonomous behavior while supplying reasonable guidance and control fostered appropriate independence in their children. Furthermore, these parents modeled independent behaviors for their children to imitate and emulate. All of these behaviors can be practiced by the classroom teacher without additional materials, equipment, or space. For example, the simple procedure of allowing children free time for independent activity as a reward for completing assignments and reducing disruptive behavior not only increases work accomplished and decreases classroom disruptions (Wilson and Williams 1973), but also gives children an opportunity to experience some autonomy.

Teachers can help pupils acquire a positive Sense of Self-Extension by fostering self-directing, self-controlling, and self-evaluating behavior that increases pupil independence and autonomy. To be self-directing, the pupil must know what to do, how to do it, and what constitutes successful completion. To be self-controlling, the pupil must know which behaviors are appropriate and goal-directed and which are inappropriate and unproductive. To be self-evaluative, the pupil must know which behaviors relate to a successful performance or product. When teachers rate a pupil "able to work with a minimum of supervision," they imply that the child exhibits autonomous and independent behavior, appropriate to his or her age or grade level.

There has been some controversy about the relative effectiveness of open and traditional (self-contained) classrooms in promoting independent, self-directed behavior. A study comparing the effects of open and traditional environments on the self-concepts, specifically, the feelings of Autonomy, Interpersonal Adequacy, and Academic Adequacy, of fourth-, fifth-, and sixth-grade pupils revealed no significant differences between the two instructional settings (Ruedi and West, 1973). Though comparisons generally favored the open environment, Academic Adequacy measures for the sixth-grade subjects were higher in traditional classrooms. Pupils in open classrooms, however, had more positive attitudes about school and teachers. Ruedi and West note that this study was limited by a small sample and the use of a single criterion, self-concept. Unfortunately, it is further limited by the investigators' failure to assess and compare the conditions, role interpretations, educational objectives, and opportunities for autonomous behavior in the two situations.

Teacher behavior has also been investigated in relation to the development or reinforcement of conformity and dependence in pupils. Findings indicate that competence and dependence are not mutually exclusive behaviors (Speer, Briggs, and Gavalas 1969). Children can be both dependent and competent. But failing to approve competence is perhaps more likely to encourage dependence than is rewarding dependent behavior.

Furthermore, general studies of conformity in children indicate a strong developmental shift in the source providing the standards to which one conforms—from parents, to peers, to ideals. The teacher as a significant or salient other must have the ability to relate children's conforming behavior to their developmental level and to help them move from dependence toward emotional maturity and independent, autonomous behavior.

At this point, we would like to emphasize that promotion of autonomy and competence does not automatically expunge conforming and dependent activity from the roster of goal-achieving behaviors. Conforming or dependent behavior can lay the foundation for mastery of skills or assumption of roles that eventually give rise to competence and autonomy, thereby enhancing self-esteem and the Sense of Self-Extension. Unfortunately, however, teachers too often tend to accommodate pupil dependence (for example, by altering teaching styles) rather than to promote emotional maturity by setting gradual, realistic, and individual goals through which the dependent pupil can acquire autonomous, independent behavior.

TEACHER BEHAVIOR AND PUPIL MOTIVATION

> **Anyhow, my one overwhelming need in those days was to be approved, to be loved, and I did whatever was required of me, hoping it would bring me nearer to the approval and love I so much wanted.**
>
> **I could cheerfully lie any time to escape a scolding, whereas if I had known that I would simply be put to bed or be spanked I probably would have told the truth. This habit of lying stayed with me for years. My mother did not understand that a child may lie from fear; I myself never understood it until I reached the age when I realized that there was nothing to fear.**
>
> *Eleanor Roosevelt 1961*. Autobiography of Eleanor Roosevelt, *pp. 7, 412.*

Motivation is either intrinsic (in which case the source of reward is internal) or extrinsic (in which case the source of reward is external). Either type, however, is rooted in the value system of the individual. If one has a positive value for acceptance and approval, one will have a negative value for rejection and disapproval. While rejection and disapproval inhibit both externally and internally controlled children, they more profoundly affect the motivation of the former, who are highly dependent on the approval of significant others. For those who experience rejection or live in a state of conditional approval, fear of failure further inhibits motivation.

Children who are secure, who are sure of acceptance and approval, may experience failure and disapproval, and the experience may influence their subsequent behavior; but it will not represent a psychological threat to their sense of self-continuance because basic acceptance is not contingent upon approved behavior. But when acceptance, or approval, or success is linked to a specific behavior, the individual will be motivated toward that behavior, whether the source of reward is intrinsic or extrinsic.

Children's early experiences in the home affect their later motivation and adjustment to school. Teevan and McGhee (1972) found that adolescent boys with a high fear of failure had mothers who expected them to show independence and achievement very early in life, yet who responded to their children's independent and achieving behaviors in a neutral rather than a highly rewarding manner. Boys with a low fear of failure had undemanding mothers who did not expect early performance of independent and achieving behaviors.

Teevan and McGhee conclude that while a mother's early expectation of independent and achieving behavior may cause her child to be motivated by fear of failure, it does not affect the child's value for achievement. The reinforcement pattern practiced by the mother influences the nature of motivation, not the value for achieving and independent behavior. Therefore, while the value for achievement may remain positive, achievement motivation will be based on fear of failure if the reinforcement pattern is neutral or punitive.

Maternal response patterns have also been related to children's emotional adjustment. Murray, Seagull, and Geisinger (1969) found that mothers of well-adjusted boys reacted to poor performance with scolding and yelling, the content of which was related to their sons' behavior. Mothers of maladjusted boys used restriction and deprivation—practices which communicated disapproval of their sons' behavior, but in no way helped to identify more effective or appropriate behavior.

A child entering the classroom brings along a value system and a concept of the relationship between the child's performance and the response of others. Initially, each child perceives the classroom dialogue and the roles of those participating in it according to previous experiences, and motivation stems from the values the child has acquired in the home. On the basis of theory, we can hypothesize several perceptual patterns with concomitant motivating values.

Pattern I pupils have an internal locus of control and perceive the teacher as a salient other whose function is to provide information and interpretation. They value the acquisition of skills and behaviors as a means of reinforcing their internal locus of control, and they value their performances and products as an expression of independence and autonomy.

Pattern II pupils have an internal locus of control derived from interaction with the environment or from interaction with significant others who gave undifferentiated and unqualified approval to all of their behaviors. These pupils do not perceive the teacher as a significant or salient other with the power to designate roles or dispense approval contingent upon performance. Their behavior is motivated by a perceived threat to self-continuance and a need to sustain their concept of self as controller and judge of their own worth. The acquisition of academic skills and behaviors is unrelated to the values of Pattern II children.

Pattern III pupils have an external locus of control and perceive the teacher as a significant or salient other who functions as the source of approval or disapproval. They recognize the teacher's power to designate and interpret roles and view the pupil's power in terms of ability to fulfill assigned roles and thereby gain approval. Acquisition of academic skills and behaviors is a means of exercising the power to please.

For Pattern I and III pupils, teacher approval and recognition of performance is an intrinsic reward. For Pattern II pupils, teacher approval is valued only when it reinforces the child's concept of his or her ability to control. To motivate Pattern II children toward academic performance the teacher must (1) interpret academic performance as a means of expressing self-value or (2) offer extrinsic rewards for achievement related to the pupil's existing value system.

These hypothetical patterns of pupil perception and motivation find some support in the research. Goldberg (1968) investigated the hypothesis that pupil attitude affects pupil perception, causing different students to respond differently to the same teacher behaviors (specifically those associated with "authoritarianism" or "nonauthoritarianism"). After assessing pupil flexibility, compulsivity, and attitude toward authority, Goldberg found that compulsivity was statistically related to pupil perception of teacher authoritarianism. Pupils scoring high in compulsivity perceived their teachers as less authoritarian, while pupils scoring low in compulsivity perceived them as more authoritarian. Also, compulsive pupils reported doing less work, and noncompulsive pupils more work, under nonauthoritarian teachers.

Though these findings indicate perceptual differences in pupils according to their compulsivity, it is difficult to determine, without an objective measure of the teacher's actual behavior on an authoritarian/nonauthoritarian dimension, whether these differences actually reflect perception and not reality: it is possible that pupils with different characteristics actually received different treatment from teachers.

White and Aaron (1967) found differences in pupil perception of and reaction to four kinds of motivating cues (achievement, affiliation, orderliness, and test and feedback) given by teachers. These differences were associated with pupil sex, achievement status (underachieving, achieving, overachieving), and anxiety. Across achievement groups, girls were more perceptive than boys of all motivating cues except those emphasizing scholastic achievement. While the teachers' cues elevated anxiety in all achievement and sex groups, girls indicated more debilitating (fear of failure) anxiety than boys did.

White and Aaron suggest that girls may have registered a lower perception of scholastic achievement cues because they are already motivated toward academic achievement as a conforming response and therefore need no additional cues in that direction. Their higher perception of test and feedback cues perhaps stems from a tendency to view the teacher as an evaluative and reinforcing agent, dispensing extrinsic rewards and punishment. (Girls were more sensitive than boys to test announcements, immediate feedback, and correction by the teacher.) Perhaps because they have weaker intrinsic motives for academic achievement, girls require more extrinsic rewards from their teacher and therefore are more perceptive of teacher feedback. Boys, on the other hand, are more perceptive of cues involving learning and academic performance, presumably because their achievement motivation is more intrinsic.

The failure of boys to respond to orderliness cues was, in White and Aaron's opinion, related to the fact that males in our culture are encouraged in independent and divergent behavior and therefore do not readily respond to conforming and controlling cues.

Although the perceptual differences reported above relate to only two pupil variables, sex and compulsivity, they do support the theory that (1) pupils interpret teacher behavior according to their perception of the significant or salient other's function, (2) pupils are motivated to perform according to their own values and their interpretation of their role in the classroom dialogue, and (3) role definitions and performances, as well as investigators' interpretations of these performances, are influenced by pervasive cultural values.

Pupils' behavior and values reflect their perception of their own power and purpose. St. Augustine, as a boy, had a full roster of unapproved behaviors to sustain his youthful self-esteem and values. We can derive some comfort from the fact that values and behaviors quite obviously change with positive experiences and opportunities.

> **For in thy eyes what was more infamous than I was already, since I displeased even my own kind and deceived, with endless lies, my tutor, my masters and parents—all from a love of play, a craving for frivolous spectacles, a stage-struck restlessness to imitate what I saw in these shows? I pilfered from my parents' cellar and table, sometimes driven by gluttony, sometimes just to have something to give to other boys in exchange for their baubles, which they prepared to sell even though they liked them as well as I. Moreover, in this kind of play, I often sought dishonest victories, being myself conquered by the vain desire for pre-eminence. And what was I so unwilling to endure, and**

what was it that I censured so violently when I caught anyone, except the very things I did to others? And, when I was myself detected and censured, I preferred to quarrel rather than to yield.

St. Augustine 1955. Augustine: confessions and enchiridion, *pp. 48–49.*

PUPIL RESPONSE TO
SPECIFIC MOTIVATIONAL AND
INCENTIVE TECHNIQUES

The construct of Self-Extension involves the behavior and extrinsic motivation used by significant others to help the developing self acquire values, standards, and behaviors that bind individuals to the value systems of their societies. Intrinsic and extrinsic motivation interact to produce performance, but the relationship between values, motivation, and performance is less apparent.

Clifford (1972) compared the effects of reward-competition and game-competition on the performance, interest, and learning retention of fifth grade pupils. Both the control and experimental classes engaged in a vocabulary learning task, the former on a noncompetitive basis. The experimental subjects competed either for a reward or advancement in a game. In the reward condition, the vocabulary scores of "relatively homogeneous students" were compared daily, and high scorers were rewarded with candy. The scores of subjects in the game treatment were rank ordered (with markers) on a large board. Black tabs were attached to the markers of the two highest scoring players, who then had the option of choosing another vocabulary word, which, if defined correctly, earned another black tab. The object of the game was to get as many tabs as possible.

Comparisons between the experimental and control groups indicated that interest was significantly higher in the former, but neither performance nor retention was apparently affected by the introduction of competition. Furthermore, there was no significant difference in the effect of the experimental conditions on interest, performance, and retention. A very low positive correlation emerged between the three academic variables and pupil sex, and relatively high correlations between performance and pupil IQ and between retention and pupil IQ. Interest, however, was negatively related to IQ.

Reviewing his data in terms of motivational theory, Clifford hypothesizes that: (1) intrinsic motivation becomes increasingly important as task complexity increases; (2) extrinsic motivation becomes decreasingly important as task complexity increases; and (3) extrinsic motivation becomes increasingly important as intrinsic motivation becomes decreasingly important. He concludes that intrinsic rather than extrinsic motivation should be emphasized in the classroom environment, where students encounter tasks requiring problem solving.

Clifford's study rests on the assumption that candy represents extrinsic motivation and black tabs represent intrinsic motivation to pupils—an assumption stemming, of course, from his own value system. One wonders whether pupils who value performances as a reflection of their autonomy and independence would consider candy better recognition of good performance than black tabs. And would pupils who value performance as a means of gaining approval consider black tabs better symbols of approval than candy?

These questions could have been at least partially answered had the motivating techniques been related in some way to pupil values. Simply requesting volunteers for the game and reward conditions and allowing students to have their vocabulary scores included in the teacher's evaluation for grades might have given some basis to the assumption that candy and black tabs create intrinsic–extrinsic motivating conditions.

We can support Clifford's revised hypotheses, with the following qualifications: (1) pupils must value the rewards given for acquiring and performing difficult behavior; (2) the assessment of reward value or psychological risk influences motivation for performing difficult behavior; and (3) when the behavior required is not valued by the pupils, it must be reinterpreted so that it does appeal to their value system. In other words, children will not be motivated unless the motivating force relates to their values. This contention is supported by the following studies.

Wasik (1970), for example, reports success using a free-choice activity period as a reward to second graders for increasing appropriate behavior. Comparing the effect of social rewards (grades) and material rewards (crayons) on the spelling scores of black fourth graders from low socioeconomic backgrounds, Benowitz and Busse (1970) found the latter an effective motivator. The pupil who achieved the least under social-reward conditions made the greatest gain when given a material reward. Cartwright (1970), testing elementary school students, without regard to SES, under high-preference and low-preference reward conditions, found no significant performance difference related to reward condition. He notes that pupils tended to perform in accordance with their established achievement patterns. Several of the subjects refused to accept the low-preference reward given them. Perhaps the experimenter's interpretation of "preference" differed somewhat from that of the pupils. Children situationally "compelled" to choose between two exhibited "rewards" may oblige, but may actually value neither reward.

On the premise that the traditional learning situation operates against achievement motivation, pupil initiative, and pupil responsibility, Alschuler (1969) restructured the learning process in several classrooms (with the help of the teachers) to emphasize "achievement-oriented" rather than "power-oriented" games. He restructured a typing class after three weeks of school, when both this class and a control group were achieving at the same average level. Pupils in the restructured class helped set performance goals and, with the teacher's assistance, established the grades to be given for various typing speeds. Each of these pupils recorded his or her own progress and determined the length and difficulty of the daily test. In the control class, tests were chosen by the teacher and administered in the traditional fashion. At the end of the third quarter, achievement in the restructured class was 54 percent higher than that in the control class, with the lowest typing speed in the restructured class equaling the highest speed in the control class.

In a second "restructuring" study, Alschuler used fifth grade mathematics classes. Work done by the experimental subjects was compared with their previous year's achievement (under the same teacher but in the "power" oriented setting) and with work done by another fifth grade class being taught in the traditional style by a "very competent and kind teacher." In the restructured classroom, students made commitments to produce a certain number of correct answers for each chapter of the standard textbook used in all fifth grade classes at that school. The contracts required the pupils to pay a fee for all revised due dates and to deduct a certain percentage of their "government" money for each incorrect answer. Pupils also deposited a fee for material and franchise. The fee earned by pupils on contract was directly proportional to the goals they set: the higher they bid and produced, the more they earned. Pupils were in charge of their own assignments, obtaining help when they needed it and working through the book at their own pace. At the end of the year, students in this restructured class showed a gain of 2.85 years on the Stanford Achievement Test, while pupils in the traditional class showed a corresponding gain of 0.36.

The teachers of the restructured class commented that pupils who had previously shown no interest in math had begun taking their books home voluntarily. Many had begun to assess their abilities more optimistically and to perform up to their own standards. The teacher also reported that very few deadlines were missed, and the pupils reported that they liked mathematics much better than they had before.

Reviewing the restructuring efforts, Alschuler notes that some pupils prefer a power-structured classroom. For these pupils, he suggests training designed to inculcate a value for achievement rather than power motivation. His studies of restructuring represent sound use of pupil perception and values and illustrate the teacher's role in moving pupils toward independent behavior.

Teachers spend a good deal of time presenting behaviors and skills for pupil mastery. They spend additional time eliciting a performance that demonstrates extent of mastery and then evaluating the quality of that performance. Every phase of this procedure presents problems for teachers and for pupils. Yet the entire process can be eased—performance can be motivated—if the teacher relates the behavior or skill to be mastered to the pupil's particular values.

TEACHER FEEDBACK TO THE PERFORMING SELF

By responding to pupils and providing feedback on their work, the teacher can give a positive reflection of the impact of pupil performance. Positive responses and relevant feedback help pupils acquire motivation, goal-directed behaviors, and eventually performance mastery.

Christensen (1960) investigated the effect of teacher warmth as an affective motivating factor, teacher permissiveness–directiveness as a guidance factor, and pupil affect-need as a response modifier. After obtaining measures of warmth and permissiveness from fourth grade teachers, he classified instructors with the most extreme scores into four groups: High Permissiveness–High Warmth; High Warmth–Low Permissiveness; Low Warmth–High Permissiveness; and Low Warmth–Low Permissiveness. Pupils were divided into High and Low Affect-Need groups according to their scores on an instrument assessing affect-need. Pre- and posttest scores on a standardized test indicated that gain in vocabulary and arithmetic achievement was significantly greater for pupils of high-warmth teachers. No other significant relationships or interactions were found. Christensen concludes that these findings support the theory that affective response (warmth) is more important than permissiveness to growth in achievement.

A simple but effective study reported by Page (1958) indicates that teacher comments on returned test papers influence subsequent pupil performance. High school teachers gave regularly scheduled objective tests in their own subject area (i.e., math, English, social studies, etc.) and corrected them in the usual way, assigning letter grades according to their own standards. Test papers were then rank ordered and randomly assigned to one of three categories, "No Comment," "Free Comment," or "Special Comment." The "No Comment" group received only letter grades; "Free Comment" papers were given remarks made at the teacher's discretion and inspiration; and "Special Comment" papers received notes devised by the investigator and intended to support and apply to the work done and the grade given. The papers were returned to the pupils without drawing attention to teacher comment or its absence. Thus the students remained unaware of the experiment in which they were involved. Scores from the next objective test taken by these pupils were then used as the basis for measuring change in pupil performance.

Results showed that the "Free Comment" group made the most improvement on the next test; the "Special Comment" group was second, and the "No Comment" group improved least, indicating that teacher remarks on returned test papers had a beneficial effect on subsequent pupil performance. While no significant or conclusive differences in comment-effect appeared by grade level, there were indications that pupils in higher grades were more responsive than those at the lowest (seventh) grade level. Although teachers had predicted (through numerical rankings) that higher achieving pupils would be more responsive to their comments, "F" pupils actually showed the greatest improvement.

The effect of teacher praise and criticism on pupil-initiated responses was studied in relation to teacher and pupil race by Brown, Payne, Lankewich, and Cornell (1970). Hypothesizing that teachers of one race instructing pupils of another race might be inclined to inhibit their critical behavior and increase their praise in classroom interaction, the investigators observed white teachers with black pupils, black teachers with white pupils, white teachers with white pupils, and black teachers with black pupils—all in upper elementary grades. Observers recorded the pupil-initiated responses occurring in a taped, 20-minute discussion period. Pupils who raised their hands in response to teacher questions and pupils who tried to respond without raising their hands were considered to have initiated responses. Second responses to repeated questions were not counted; nor were "forced" responses (those made at the demand of the teacher). The discussions were analyzed and placed in four "praise" and three "criticism" categories.

Results indicated that teachers of one race facing pupils of another, the "mixed" classrooms, used significantly more praise in classroom interaction than teachers instructing pupils of the same race. However, group differences in the teacher's use of criticism were not statistically significant, though there was a trend toward less criticism in classrooms where teacher and pupil race differed. In addition, pupils in "mixed" classrooms where praise was used initiated significantly more responses than those in racially homogeneous classrooms.

Although it cannot be conclusively stated that the racial factor inhibits teachers' critical behaviors, it is possible that a racial difference between pupils and their teacher does enhance praise and pupil-initiated responses. However, in a study we mentioned previously, Rubovits and Maehr (1973) report that in a classroom of racially mixed pupils, black children received more criticism, less attention, and less praise from their white teachers than did their white counterparts, suggesting that race may interact differently with praise and criticism in classrooms containing an *integrated pupil* population.

Teacher feedback gives pupils a reflection of their Performing Selves and an evaluation of their products. Since all teachers give feedback, it seems one of the most obvious avenues by which to initiate positive changes in the reflections, interpretations, and information transmitted to pupils. A positive reflection is not necessarily blanket approval, but it does communicate recognition of and respect for the pupil as an individual whose performances are taken seriously.

Spaulding (1964) found that the level of self-esteem in fourth and sixth grade pupils was positively related to teacher behaviors categorized as "socially integrative"; i.e., behaviors that demonstrate a calm and accepting interactive style, a concern for divergency (encouraging individuality), attention to task, and task-appropriate procedures. These are the behaviors that characterize an effective significant other; one who provides the developing self with positive reflections, realistic interpretations, and accurate information, all of which help the child acquire skills and behaviors that serve his or her Sense of Self-Extension and the other concepts of self.

THE SENSE OF THE UNKNOWN SELF

The sense of the unknown self involves positive and negative discoveries in the behavior of the Performing Self. Positive discoveries generally involve talents and special gifts revealed in achievements or in the reflections of others. Moss Hart, for example, describes the discovery of his dramatic talents:

> **Had I had the wit to perceive it, there was already a hint that I was a dramatist; even then I could dramatize a story and hold an audience, and when I inadvertently stumbled on this gift, I used it the way other boys use a good pitching arm or a long reach in basketball. It gave me the only standing I was ever to have in the tough and ruthless world of boys of my own age, and I wielded the tiny sense of power it gave me hungrily and shrewdly.**
>
> **. . . I would stop at the most exciting part of a story by Jack London or Frank Norris or Bret Harte, and without warning tell them that that was as far as I had gone in the book and it would have to be continued the following evening. It was not true, of course; but I had to make certain of my newfound power and position, and with a sense of drama that I did not know I possessed, I spun out the long summer evenings until school began again in the fall.**
>
> *Moss Hart 1960.* Act one, *pp. 28–29, 31.*

Negative discoveries, on the other hand, involve the revelation of a self that performs in opposition to one's standards and values. Such discoveries are dramatically demonstrated by the experience of alcoholics.

> **Long since I had come to believe I was insane because I did so many things I didn't want to do. I didn't want to neglect my children. I loved them, I think, as much as any parent. But I did neglect them. I didn't want to get into fights, but I did get into fights. I didn't want to get arrested, but I did get arrested. I didn't want to jeopardize the lives of innocent people by driving an automobile while intoxicated, but I did. I quite naturally came to the conclusion that I must be insane.**
>
> Alcoholics Anonymous, *1955, p. 199.*

> ... I wasn't entirely immoral; I wasn't bad; I wasn't vicious. It was
> such a feeling of relief that I wanted to know more about it and with
> that, I think for the first time, came the realization that there was
> something horribly, horribly wrong with me. Up to that time, I was
> so completely baffled by my behavior that I had never really stopped
> to think at all.

Alcoholics Anonymous, *1955, p. 351.*

For some pupils, the unknown self is the one to which others respond.
These pupils may see no relationship between the response of others to their
behavior and their own perception of that behavior. They may lack a conceptual framework by which to associate behavior with goals, or they may be
locked into behavior that was successful in an earlier situation, unable to
perceive that circumstances have changed. In either case, failure to achieve
an anticipated impact or the incursion of unanticipated, negative impact may
initiate a sense of self-distrust, a feeling that the self is really unknown—a
source of unpredictable and unavoidable consequences.

TEACHER BEHAVIOR AND PUPIL CREATIVITY

The most highly valued characteristic of the Performing Self is "creativity."
The label "creative" implies a direct and recognized relationship between the
Performing Self and a valued process or product. It imputes a quality of
uniqueness and originality to a contribution made by the Performing Self, or
at least suggests the potential to make such a contribution. The label may
also reflect a particularly new or fresh approach, an open attitude, new associations, new concepts, or restructuring of concepts. Creativity appears to be
a dimension quite independent of the cognitive abilities generally measured
by achievement and IQ tests. It may be viewed as a "depth" dimension,
related to, but independent of, the "height" and "breadth" dimensions measured by IQ and achievement tests.

Creativity can also be considered distinct from talent and giftedness, two
other exceptional characteristics of the Performing Self, though a combination
of talent, giftedness, and creativity is usually highly valued and rewarded by
the benefitting culture.

If creativity is viewed as an additional cognitive dimension, one would
expect it, like intelligence, to appear in varying degrees in the general population, represented as a "low–high" continuum rather than as a simple "absent–
present" dichotomy. Such a concept does not preclude the interpretation of
creativity as a set of behaviors or products any more than the concept of
intelligence as a cognitive dimension prevents certain behaviors or products
from being categorized as unintelligent or highly intelligent. The idea of crea-

tivity as a separate cognitive domain achieved prominence when it was advocated by J. P. Guilford in his presidential address to the American Psychological Association in 1950 (Getzels and Dillon 1973). Since that time, a great many psychologists have attempted to identify, define, and measure factors comprising creativity. A review of their efforts, and of creativity theory and research in general, appears in the *Second Handbook of Research on Teaching* (Getzels and Dillon 1973).

One of the creativity components that has been identified and extensively researched is divergent thinking, a cognitive process involving the production of additional information from given information, with an emphasis on variety and quality. This process includes an ability to adapt and modify information and requires a facile and flexible intellect. The opposite of divergent thinking, convergent thinking, is the cognitive process by which information is used to derive a single best answer or correct response. Divergent thinking is generally associated with creativity and convergent thinking with achievement orientation. Although these categories are often used to indicate a style of or preference for cognitive behaviors, they are not mutually exclusive.

The possibility that development of and preference for one or the other of these two modes of thinking stems from environmental influences has been suggested by various researchers (Eisenman and Schussel 1970; Getzels and Jackson 1961, 1962). Considering the theoretical importance of the significant other and the environment, it seems logical that the cognitive behavior acquired by a child would reflect his or her psychological experiences as clearly as his or her acquired social behavior does.

When the significant other confines the developing self to an accepting, unquestioning, passive role and approves only conforming and compliant responses, the behaviors practiced most often and reflected most positively will be those categorized as convergent. If, on the other hand, experiences in the behavioral dialogue affirm questioning and explorative behavior and reward nonconforming as well as conforming responses, the child will exercise both convergent and divergent cognitive processes. When products of creative behavior are acknowledged and approved by significant others and the environment, creativity becomes a source of positive self-identity and a means of acquiring self-esteem. The positive impact perceived encourages the child's divergent thinking and reinforces creative behavior.

The relationship between cultural environment and the role of significant others in promoting creativity in children was investigated by Torrance (1969), who hypothesized that cultural values determine the level, direction, and focus of creative behavior. Studying data collected from a large population of elementary school children and their teachers, representing 11 cultures or subcultures, Torrance concluded that culture motivates creativity in two ways: (1) by encouraging behavior that facilitates creative functioning and discouraging that which does not, and (2) by making careers in creative arts and sciences available to members of the culture.

The effect of environment on teacher behavior was the subject of a study by Walker (1969), who investigated high school "climate" in relation to teacher authoritarianism and rationality. He hypothesized that teachers in schools having climates favorable to creativity would score lower on measures of authority and higher on measures of rationality than teachers at traditional schools. Results indicated that teachers from schools designated "creative" did score significantly lower on authoritarianism than those at traditional schools; however, there were no significant group differences in rationality scores. Since pupil creativity was not measured, we can conclude only that a "creative" high school climate is associated with comparatively less teacher authoritarianism.

Pupil creativity, however, has been related to pupil perception of teacher behavior. Anderson, White, and Stevens (1969), investigating pupils and teachers from grades 9 through 12, found that teacher behavior seen as knowledgeable and democratic was positively related, while that perceived as "friendly, cheerful, and admired" was negatively related, to pupil creativity. The three negatively correlated variables can be interpreted as behaviors valued by dependent, approval-seeking, and conforming pupils for whom creative activity is risky, while knowledge and democratic behavior in teachers would be valued by pupils who have an internal locus of control.

Pupil creativity has also been investigated in relation to pupil achievement (Merz and Rutherford 1972). Fifth grade pupils were administered four achievement subtests and four creative tasks. In addition, teacher judgments of each pupil's performance in several academic areas were obtained. Thus three separate factors—achievement, creativity, and teacher judgment—were measured. Findings indicated that teacher judgments and scholastic achievement were more clearly related to each other than to pupil creativity. However, low positive relationships emerged between achievement test scores and creativity task performance, and better teacher judgments and creativity task scores.

Merz and Rutherford conclude that pupils who perform well on achievement tests are probably more favorably judged by their teachers than pupils who perform poorly, and that teachers perceive creative pupils as more able than less creative pupils. Teachers in this study, however, reported a preference for teaching highly intelligent, achieving pupils rather than average pupils and average rather than creative pupils.

Additional information regarding pupil creativity emerged from a study investigating the effectiveness of convergent and divergent (direct and indirect) teaching modes in achieving concrete and abstract learning objectives (Soar 1968). Hypothesizing that optimal levels of direct and indirect teaching behavior could be identified through measures of pupil anxiety and creativity, Soar found that creative behavior in both high-anxious and low-anxious pupils increased with teacher indirectness, although the rate of increase was steeper for low-anxious pupils.

Soar concludes that this study, though limited by a restricted sample (third through sixth graders), clearly indicates that concrete material, such as spelling, number facts, foreign language vocabulary, should be highly structured and taught in a direct style, while abstract material, dealing with concepts and creativity should be less structured and presented in an indirect manner. He comments that an effective teacher is one who can shift teaching modes to accommodate the subject matter. One weakness of progressive education, Soar claims, is its failure to recognize the need for direct teaching of concrete objectives. The broad concept of educational permissiveness which encourages the teacher warmth essential to pupil growth may at the same time exclude an equally essential teacher behavior—directness.

The effect of training specifically designed to promote creative thinking has been investigated by Bachtold and Werner (1970). Fifth and sixth grade pupils with a mean IQ of 139 were given eight months of creativity training, including instruction in Guilford's five mental operations. Their creative abilities and vocational goals were assessed before and after training.

Results (which should be interpreted cautiously due to small sample size) indicate that training did improve creativity scores. Fluency and flexibility of response were significantly improved on tests of evaluative thinking but not on tests of divergent thinking. This lack of improvement (and in the case of fluency, decline) in divergent thinking can perhaps be explained by the students' approach to the tests. It is likely that the gifted students in this sample had gained some insight into the creative ability tests to be administered. They may have, in fact, spent as much time "evaluating" the divergent as the evaluative thinking tasks. That is, the process of test taking may have become more convergent than divergent.

Findings also showed that boys had higher pre- and posttest scores on tasks requiring divergent thinking, while girls had higher pre- and posttest scores on tasks requiring evaluative thinking. Bachtold and Werner note that no other studies report an advantage for girls on evaluative thinking tasks, although many report the superiority of boys on divergent thinking tests. They suggest that these differences may be due to sex-role expectations. The vocational choices recorded by pupils in this study showed evidence of sex typing: gifted girls chose service occupations of considerably lower professional status than those selected by gifted boys. Choices made by boys shifted over the eight-month period toward occupations requiring more education and preparation, but girls' choices changed little. Perhaps this stability is related to Torrance's finding that culture promotes creativity by providing career opportunities in creative arts and sciences. If girls perceive that society offers them fewer options for creative careers, their vocational choices are unlikely to be affected by creativity training.

Two other programs, purporting to develop creative ability in pupils were compared by Shively, Feldhusen, and Treffinger (1972). Fifth grade teachers were given a battery of creativity tests and divided into high- and low-divergent thinking groups. Their pupils were also given a pretest of creative ability. Teachers and pupils were then randomly assigned to one of four treatment groups differing by creativity program offered and discussion approach employed. Results indicated that both program groups made significant gains on posttests of creative ability, though one appeared to produce more consistent gains than the other across all variables measured. Groups in which the teacher did not lead discussion attained higher posttest scores than those characterized by teacher-led discussion. Pupils taught by highly creative teachers using the more effective program scored significantly higher on verbal originality and somewhat higher on fluency and flexibility. The investigators note, however, that program differences may be related to the fact that the less effective approach was used neither in its entirety nor according to its designer's exact specifications. Furthermore, it is possible that differences were minimal between "discussion" and "no-discussion" teachers, since teacher activity was not measured or monitored.

Teacher behavior that fosters creativity appears to be that which minimizes the directing and criticizing functions of the teacher. Cultural values influence divergent production and creative behavior by encouraging or discouraging certain activities, sometimes depending upon the sex of the performer. Creative behavior seems as closely linked to intelligence as to the positive effects of (1) acceptance and approval of task-directed but nonconforming behavior, (2) acceptance of pupil ideas and exploration, (3) a basic attitude of trust that allows risk taking, and (4) freedom within cultural sex roles.

TEACHER BEHAVIOR AND PUPIL BEHAVIOR MODIFICATION

Pupils who engage in disruptive behavior, who will not perform the tasks prescribed by the educational system, and teachers who cannot cope with this behavior, have been the major subjects of research on classroom behavior modification. Behavior modification is intended to change specific behaviors of the Performing Self. The focus is on manifestation of, rather than reason for, the disruptive or objectionable behavior. To change a target behavior, the response to or reflection of it is altered *when* and *where* the behavior occurs. In some cases, an aversive or punishing response is given in order to extinguish or decrease the incidence of the target behavior. In other cases, appropriate behavior is positively reflected and rewarded in order to increase its incidence. A reward for good behavior is sometimes combined with an ignoring or neutral response to undesirable behavior.

The cognitive process involved in behavior modification is primarily associative: objectionable behavior is associated with noxious or ineffective consequences, and appropriate behavior is associated with reward and effective consequences. Initially, the locus of control in a behavior modification program is external. The external control functions as the significant other, monitoring the behavior and administering the reward or punishment. Eventually, however, such a program offers a restructured behavioral dialogue in which the significant other or modifying agent provides an objectively determined constancy and consistency and a clear interpretation of the target behavior which is communicated through rewarding and unrewarding responses.

The reward system used as an incentive for behavioral change must appeal to the values of the child, just as the significant other's approval and the child's positive impact on the environment are valued in the initial, natural behavioral dialogue. To function as an incentive, the reward system must retain its value until the child has adopted a new schema of goal-directed behavior and changed his or her self-concept. If rewards are no longer valued or if they are withdrawn before the child begins to value the revised behavior itself, the target behavior may be only briefly modified or only temporarily extinguished.

The child's dependency on the reward dispenser replicates the earlier dependency on significant others. The responsibility of the modifying agent, like that of the significant other, is to move the child toward self-monitoring and self-rewarding behavior by helping the child to acquire internalized standards of conduct and performance. Thus, while dependence is initially desirable, it can, if it continues, promote unrealistic expectations. The child's motivation must eventually switch from external reward to internal satisfaction. Though behavior modification focuses on the manifestation, *not* the psychological origin of objectionable behavior, it must alter the subject's previous perception of the target behavior and its impact before that behavior can be extinguished or modified.

Although behavior modification programs employ several very common training procedures, the application of these procedures in a controlled, systematic manner requires time and specific skills. The teachers involved in the research reported here participated in behavior modification programs under the supervision or direction of trained professionals or had themselves been trained in the necessary skills.

Scott, Burton, and Yarrow (1967) report the application of a behavior modification program in a natural setting. The program was intended to change the interacting behaviors of a four-year-old boy who was aggressive and antisocial in his preschool environment. Analysis of the problem indicated that the child's unacceptable behavior received more consistent attention from his teacher and peers than did his acceptable behavior. Under a program of positive reinforcement from an adult for good behavior, the child's acceptable behavior increased while his undesirable behavior decreased. When former conditions were briefly reestablished, the child's unacceptable behavior rose toward previous levels.

To assess the influence of uncontrolled peer reinforcement, classroom interaction was recorded. Observation data indicated that during one particular treatment period, boys in the class initiated more interaction than usual with the subject and received stronger positive responses from him. At the same time, girls reacted to the subject's negative behavior with increased intensity. The investigators conclude that the increased positive interaction with male peers accounted for a continuing rise in the subject's acceptable behavior observed during this period (when positive reinforcement from the adult experimenter had been withdrawn), and the negative interaction with his female classmates accounted for a simultaneous increase in the subject's negative behavior.

The peer interaction recorded in this study makes it clear that conditions present in a natural setting may alter principles of operant conditioning which are unaffected in the laboratory. This is particularly true if a program of behavior modification continues over an extended period of time. In the natural setting, over an extended period of time, use of a single reinforcer may not always be effective or appropriate. In addition, the modifying agent must recognize the many sources and combinations of reinforcers over which he or she has no control.

Behavior modification in natural settings must also address the problem of alternative behavior. In this particular study, increased peer interaction exposed the subject's lack of social skills; and there is some danger in calling attention to such a behavioral shortcoming without offering the child help in overcoming it (i.e., help in learning appropriate social skills). Furthermore, modification of an interacting social behavior depends on changing not only the target behavior, but also the established, habitual responses of others toward the subject.

Another successful behavior modification program carried out in a natural classroom setting involved an 11-year-old boy whose behavior had been reported by his teachers as disruptive, aggressive, and unmanageable (Coleman 1973). He walked about and in and out of his classrooms at his pleasure, and when he was sent to a punishing room for detention, he left that room with equal aplomb.

Three target behaviors were identified for the behavior modification program. The desired behavior was defined as "working"—engaging in task-achieving activity in both math and reading. The two undesirable target behaviors were "talking aloud" and "out-of-seat," under specified conditions. After baseline behaviors were tabulated and the subject introduced to the procedure, a reinforcement schedule was instituted. At stated intervals, the child was awarded points for positive behavior. The points gained were redeemable for prizes worth approximately fifty cents each. After a few sessions, the point value was set at two cents each, and an account of earned point value was sent home to the subject's parents each Friday. This earned point value replaced the subject's previous allowance of $1.25 a week (supplemented with small amounts as needed). The parents took the subject shopping on Friday nights, allowing him to spend what he wished of his reward.

As the program progressed through various stages, reward intervals were extended and points were deducted for negative behavior. In the final phase, the teacher prepared a report on the subject's behavior and sent it to the parents at the end of each week. The subject's allowance was contingent upon his behavior that week. A good week was worth $7.50, an average week $5.00, and a poor week $1.25. The average cost of the program (in allowance paid) was $6.37 a week—an indication that the subject maintained substantial improvement over his previous behavior.

The intent of the final reinforcement condition was to continue the fading strategy in order to return the subject to the pre-experimental intervention status, except that he would be receiving a contingently earned allowance. To maintain the child's good behavior, however, the teacher apparently had to continue sending home weekly reports and the parents had to continue budgeting what is a fairly hefty allowance for an 11-year-old child. (Let us hope he had no siblings who caught on to the profit system.) Yet, to many parents and teachers, eternal vigilance, weekly reporting, and a big allowance are a small price to pay for freedom from class disruptions and the alteration of behavior that could jeopardize the future of a child. The technique used in this study, however, raises a question about the associations and expectations inherent in a program of monetary reward and the role they will play in the child's future. Without additional program phases to revise the child's behavioral constructs and assist him in acquiring internalized standards and values, the subject's perception of his Performing Self and his impact upon others and the environment will, in our opinion, remain distorted, unrealistic, and expensive.

A less complex procedure for controlling classroom behavior is reported by Broden, Hall, and Mitts (1971). Two junior high students, a girl with poor study habits and a boy who engaged in disruptive talking, were selected as experimental subjects. The girl had expressed to the school counselor a wish to improve in her history class. When discussing the problem failed to produce improvement, the counselor consulted the investigators who initiated a system which required the subject to record her "studying" behavior whenever she "thought of it" during her history class. The counselor accepted the subject's self-reports and praised her for the number of plus marks indicating studying behavior. In all, the program phases included a baseline period, self-recording, self-recording with praise from teacher and counselor, praise from the teacher only, and a return to baseline conditions in which increased teacher attention was withdrawn.

Results indicated that the subject's study behavior increased to 88 percent of class time under self-recording and praise conditions, and dropped to 77 percent under the praise-only condition, where it stabilized for the remaining experimental periods. The investigator noted that teacher attention increased with the subject's improved performance. Also, the frequency of self-reporting decreased markedly from the second to the third phase, declining from an average of 12, to 2.3 marks per session.

In the second experiment, the teacher rather than the pupil requested help. The subject's math teacher wanted to reduce the child's disruptive talking. After the baseline observation period, a self-recording program was instituted by the teacher. The subject was instructed to record for half of each class period every instance in which he talked without permission. Results indicated that the subject's disruptive behavior did decline during that portion of the period when he recorded his talking, but not during the unrecorded portions. The record showed a decrease below the baseline rate, followed by an increase above the baseline rate after the return to preintervention conditions. In the last phase of the experiment, the subject's disruptive behavior declined for the first half of the class period, and increased over the baseline rate in the last half. Unlike the procedures used with the female student previously discussed, this subject received no reinforcement, praise, or additional attention from the teacher, the counselors, or the investigators.

In comparing the reponses of the female and male subjects in this study, it should be recalled that the former requested help, while the latter was referred for help. Furthermore, the self-recording process differed for the two students: the female subject was asked to record positive target behavior, while the male subject was asked to record negative target behavior. The process of self-recording may have served different functions for these subjects. In order to record, the female subject had to produce the positive target behavior, while the male subject, who may have perceived the fun of recording as his only reward, had to produce negative behavior in order to participate in the project. Yet in neither case did the self-recorded incidence of target behavior correlate with the observer-recorded incidence of target behavior.

Another successful behavior modification project is reported by Duncan (1969). Senior high school pupils, enrolled in a psychology class were taught the principles of behavior modification in three simplified steps. They voluntarily participated in a program of self-help intended to eliminate undesirable target behaviors such as eating between meals, swearing, face touching, nail biting, knuckle cracking, and sarcasm.

Pupils helped each other record baseline activity and define target behavior. Locally available instruments such as tally sheets, golf score devices, and knitting stitch counters were used to tabulate behavior "emission." And, since most subjects wanted to decelerate or extinguish target behavior, consequences were devised employing joke shocker packs, boxing gloves, and surgical masks. Three groups were formed, two of which met with the investigator and one of which met with a graduate student on a regular, contingency basis (e.g., six days of recorded data were required for admittance to the second meeting). During the meetings the subjects presented their projects. No formal lectures were given. Out of 55 subjects involved in the project, 33 reported successful behavior modification. A follow-up of randomly selected subjects generally indicated a sustained level of success, although one subject had returned to swearing (but only in the fraternity house).

Four first grade teachers, seeking a program that would decrease disruptive behavior, increase academic productivity, and accommodate differences in pupil ability were involved, along with their pupils, in a behavior modification project conducted in an open classroom situation (Wilson and Williams 1973). Each teacher was asked to designate her "worst" behavior problem so that program efficiency could be evaluated. Four male students were thus designated and selected as targets for observation. The classes were then divided into groups of 9 to 12 pupils each to form units for the morning instruction in language arts.

A task requiring students to copy a sentence from the blackboard was selected for daily reinforcement procedures. Free play was made contingent upon pupil deportment and work completion during performance of this task. Misconduct was punished by taking free time from the entire group, even if only one child misbehaved. Results indicated an increase in task-related behavior and a reduction in disruptive behavior. After the study ended, the team of teachers involved organized the entire morning's activity around the group contingency program, and the following year they continued to make extensive use of group-contingent free time as a classroom management technique. While this approach was clearly successful in meeting its objectives, the group punishment provision hardly demonstrates respect for individuality and good behavior.

Another study focusing on classroom management employed the Premack Principle (1959), which states that high frequency behaviors are potential reinforcers of low frequency behaviors (Andrews 1970, 1971). The subjects of the study were low-performing, "culturally deprived" seventh grade students who displayed severe behavior problems in their first morning class, but only mild disruption in their afternoon class. A brief analysis of classroom conditions revealed that in the afternoon students were allowed to interact with tutors and to watch television, activities which they genuinely enjoyed.

In discussion with the subjects, 12 undesirable behaviors were identified and defined. A contract was then made between the pupils and the teacher: if no more than three of the identified behaviors occurred during the morning hour, pupils would be allowed tutor contact and television time in the afternoon. The pupils accepted the contract and on the first day of its implementation achieved the criterion. This level of performance was maintained for the remainder of the monitored four-week period. The teacher reported that disruptions met with strong peer disapproval and objectionable behaviors were unlikely to be repeated by the offending student for the rest of the morning hour.

Based on these findings, the experimenter suggests that teachers can minimize unacceptable activities by using them as rewards for acceptable behavior. For example, pupils who talk too much or read comic books during class can be rewarded with time to talk or read comics if they display appropriate behavior during class time.

Orme and Purnell (1968) report the application of behavior modification in a classroom described as "out-of-control." The participating school served a large urban ghetto and was strongly oriented toward experimental and innovative programs addressing the needs of its pupil population. School discipline had been decentralized, and all teachers were expected to handle the problems arising in their own classrooms. The particular class studied—a combined third and fourth grade containing pupils from 9 to 13 years old—was known throughout the school for its noisy, truant, physically aggressive, abusive, destructive, and disruptive behavior, a reputation that was verified by baseline observation. Responsible for this group was one black teacher with six years experience. He was assisted in the mornings by one white, female teaching intern with no previous experience.

At the request of the intern teacher, Orme and Purnell obtained permission from the school principal to institute a six-week study incorporating behavior modification procedures in order to increase classroom control and learning activity. The room was first divided into two sections, A and B, so that total milieu control could be established in one room (B). The intent was to arrange conditions so that desirable behavior change could be produced in Room B and then transferred to Room A. The first objective was to establish effective teacher control, by altering the physical organization of the classroom and instituting a token reinforcement program.

Room B was rearranged so that the teacher had command of the door. Desks and other equipment were placed to give the teacher greater mobility and control over a larger portion of the room. Extraneous fixtures and furniture were removed to decrease the environmental stimulus and make the room more attractive. A store was set up for redeeming reinforcement tokens. The store contained not only the usual rewards (i.e., confections and toys), but also instructional prizes such as books, art lessons (from a professional artist), model airplanes, ships, and science packages, field trips, and other items that would expand educational opportunities and allow pupils to work on a project of their own choice for part of the school day.

When pupils were exposed to Room B and introduced to the point system, the desired target behaviors were defined. At the beginning of the program, each pupil was given 25 free points—enough to buy a small prize, with some left over to be used toward the next purchase. After exposure to Room B, pupils were taken to Room A, where they were told that only half of the class members could be in Room B at a time. For this reason, the points earned in Room A would give them access to Room B, but only points earned in Room B could be converted into prizes.

The pupils then defined the Room A behaviors that would earn points for access to Room B. The behaviors they listed were almost identical to those rewarded with prize points in Room B. In addition, they decided that the two high point earners in Room B, the total milieu room, would be allowed to remain in Room B another day. The seven highest point earners in Room A were to be allowed in Room B the next day.

Meanwhile, the intern teacher was trained to develop skills that would enable her to produce pupil behavior that could be positively reinforced and to prevent disruptive behavior. Both teachers were given assistance in establishing behavioral objectives for their lessons. Curriculum materials were selected and evaluated according to their educational and control potential. (The latter was determined by opportunity for pupil participation, role play, choral reading, competitive format, etc.)

Both teachers showed the effects of training in increased reinforcement rates for pupil responses. There were indications that the intern teacher may have temporarily reduced the reinforcement power of praise by overapplication during one phase of the treatment. However, reinforcement procedures did substantially increase positive pupil behavior and reduce disruption in both Rooms A and B for both teachers.

The contingencies used in this program apparently allowed the pupil to perceive the impact of his Performing Self on the environment. By focusing on behaviors within the pupil's control and standards within his or her reach, the program gave the pupil an opportunity to experience positive impact by attaining a rewarded position (a place in Room B) and earning concrete and valued prizes. The prizes not only appealed to the pupil's values, but also reflected a value for education. They allowed students to experience not only the pleasure of material rewards, but also the satisfaction of competence and achievement, thus moving them from extrinsic to intrinsic motivation for academic behavior. It is questionable, however, whether a six-week program is long enough to allow pupils to become bored with easily obtained prizes and begin to develop a value for delayed rewards that are difficult to achieve.

There is no question that the teaching-learning situation is greatly enhanced when pupils can control their own behavior and direct it toward the academic task. Yet behavior modification should be undertaken not merely to make the classroom manageable, but also to change the pupil's perception of his or her impact on the environment. This would not only enhance the pupil's concept of self but would also reduce the need for controlling behavior on the teacher's part. Self-control should be a primary objective in an educational system charged with preparing individuals to live in a free, democratic society in which they will be expected to obey laws, not individuals.

TEACHER BEHAVIOR AND THE SENSE OF SELF-EXTENSION

The two concerns most characteristic of the teaching profession are concern for pupil academic performance and concern for pupil control. And there is no question that any teaching-learning situation would be greatly enhanced if all pupils demonstrated appropriate classroom behaviors and directed their energies toward learning tasks. But until the unlikely day that such circumstances prevail, teachers will remain concerned about student performance and classroom management.

These two concerns can arise from a preoccupation with self—the teacher's need to establish personal psychological safety, using the power and authority of the teacher role to define, limit, and control pupil participation and performance. Or they can arise from a professional concern for task, characterized by a desire to be seen as an "excellent" teacher whose knowledge of the tricks of the trade is recognized, approved, and rewarded by superiors and colleagues. Or, they can be motivated by a sense of responsibility for providing the best educational experience possible for all pupils. Yet, regardless of their origin, teacher concerns about pupil performance and control are invariably linked to the Sense of Self-Extension in teachers as well as pupils. The Performing Self of the pupil is, after all, the clearest reflection of the Performing Self of the teacher. The teacher's concern for pupil academic performance is directly related to the pupil's concept of self as doer, learner, and knower. And the teacher's concern for control is directly related to the pupil's sense of self-sustention (preserving and serving the self), self-representation (revealing the self), and sense of an unknown self as the pupil is confronted with performance demands that he or she cannot reference to past experiences and responses. Therefore, all teachers, regardless of their motivation, should benefit from an understanding of the pupil's Sense of Self-Extension. Whether pupils will benefit equally depends on the teacher's General Self-Concept expressed through his or her Performing Self.

To understand the role of the pupil's Sense of Self-Extension in his or her academic performance and classroom behavior, teachers should consider the following:

1. It is the pupil's perception of the situation and the pupil's system of values that motivates his or her behavior. Teacher's should remember that while they may be significant or salient others to some pupils, to others they are neither. Here it is important to remember the role of the environment (and the teacher's power to shape it) as an alternate as well as complementary source of pupil reflection, interpretation, and information.

2. When teachers are valued as significant or salient others, their acceptance or rejection of the pupil, their interpretation of the pupil's role in the classroom behavioral dialogue, and the guidance and information they provide influence the pupil's estimation of his or her psychological safety, the perception of the conditions for approval, the impact of acquired skills and behaviors, independence and autonomy, and the relevance of his or her experiences to the pupil's existing system of values. We can hypothesize that pupils who experience a sharp break in the continuum from home to school may be forced to either accept the teacher as a salient other or to reject the new environment. Those who choose the first of these alternatives may become dependent upon and value the teacher primarily as an interpreter and guide in the new environment. For these children psychological safety depends upon a clear definition of the pupil role, a clear understanding of the behavior that will gain acceptance and approval, and a reliable, authoritative source of reflection, interpretation, and information. The teacher placed in this role can either maintain his or her control and perpetuate the pupil's dependence, or instead provide circumstances and conditions that will move the pupil toward independence and autonomy through the mastery of skills and behaviors needed in the new environment.

3. Within the classroom dialogue, the teacher has the power of approval over the Performing Selves of pupils. Thus, pupils may perceive learning as an approval-gaining, self-sustaining behavior unless or until they are helped to see it as a means of increasing their independence, autonomy, and control of their own environment. To encourage the latter perception and to provide conditions that foster goal-oriented, self-directed, and self-controlled pupil behavior, the teacher must make specific preparations. First, using his or her interpretive and informative functions, the teacher must relate prescribed skills and behaviors not only to approval but also to independence and autonomy or other appropriate, positive values such as individuality, identity, esteem, and image. Second, through positive pupil reflection and manipulation of the classroom environment, the teacher should provide the kind of feedback that allows pupils to realistically perceive their progress and to test their impact in a protected arena. This is the essence of "relevance" in the pursuit of cognitive objectives. Finally, the teacher, as the source of power in the classroom, should be prepared to share an appropriate amount of that power with pupils, thereby moving them away from teacher authority, external control, and extrinsic reward, toward internalized standards, an internal locus of control, and intrinsic reward. Teachers who have been observed providing these interpretations and experiences are described in the literature as "flexible," "democratic," "indirect," "pupil-centered," "accepting of pupil ideas," "nonauthoritarian," and "nurturant."

The purpose of public education is to prepare children to function as productive, participating citizens in a society governed by laws that reflect the value and rights of the individual. The teacher's concern for pupil performance and pupil control should be specifically directed toward each pupil's attainment of this goal. As educators we all share a concern for pupil academic performance and pupil control. Yet the feelings motivating this concern differ from teacher to teacher, and these differences are evident in teacher behaviors and their effect on the pupil self-concept.

REFERENCES

Roosevelt, E. 1961. *The autobiography of Eleanor Roosevelt.* New York: Harper & Row.

THE SENSE OF SELF AS DOER, LEARNER, AND KNOWER THROUGH THE PERFORMING SELF

Rosengarten, T. 1974. *All God's dangers.* New York: Knopf.

The Significant Other and the Performing Self

Baumrind, D. 1972. An exploratory study of socialization effects on black children: some black-white comparisons. *Child Development* **43** (1): 261–267. (ERIC Document Reproduction Service No. EJ 055 656.)

———. 1967. Child care practices anteceding three patterns of preschool behavior. *Genetic Psychology Monographs* **75**: 43–88.

———. 1966. Effects of authoritative parental control on child behavior. *Child Development* **37** (4): 887–907.

———. 1971. Harmonious parents and their preschool children. *Developmental Psychology* **4** (1): 99–102.

———, and A. E. Black 1967. Socialization practices associated with dimensions of competence in preschool boys and girls. *Child Development* **38** (2): 291–327.

Cultural Values and the Performing Self

Rosengarten, T. 1974. *All God's dangers.* New York: Knopf.

Teacher Behavior and Pupil Performance

Aspy, D., and F. Roebuck 1972. An investigation of the relationship between student levels of cognitive functioning and teacher's classroom behavior. *Journal of Educational Research* **65** (8): 365–368.

Brown, W., L. Payne, C. Lankewich, and L. Cornell 1970. Praise, criticism, and race. *Elementary School Journal* **70** (7): 373–377.

Chaiken, A., E. Sigler, and V. Derlega 1974. Nonverbal mediators of teacher expectancy effects. *Journal of Personality and Social Psychology* **30** (1): 144–149.

Epperson, D. C. 1963. Some interpersonal and performance correlates of classroom alienation. *School Review* **71:** 360–376.

Farnham-Diggory, S., and B. Ramsey 1971. Play persistence: some effects of interruption, social reinforcement, and defective toys. *Developmental Psychology* **4** (2): 297–298.

Fleming, J. C. 1969. Pupil tutors and tutees learn together. *Today's Education* **58** (7): 22–24.

Good, T., and J. Brophy 1972. Behavioral expression of teacher attitudes. *Journal of Educational Psychology* **63:** 617–624.

Kranz, P. L. 1972. Teachers as play therapists: an experiment in learning. *Childhood Education* **49** (2): 73–74. (ERIC Document Reproduction Service No. EJ 065 565.)

Mohan, M. 1971. Peer tutoring as a technique for teaching the unmotivated. *Child Study Journal* **1** (4): 217–225.

Nash, R. 1972. Measuring teacher attitudes. *Educational Research* **14** (2): 141–146. (ERIC Document Reproduction Service No. EJ 054 027.)

Page, E. 1958. Teacher comments and student performance: a seventy-four classroom experiment in school motivation. *Journal of Educational Psychology* **49:** 173–181.

Silberman, M. 1969. Behavioral expression of teachers' attitudes toward elementary school students. *Journal of Educational Psychology* **60:** 402–407.

Tardiff, R. 1971. *Modification of the verbal behavior of teachers: its impact on the verbal behavior of pupils.* Washington, D.C.: Educational Resources Information Center, Office of Education, U.S. Department of Health, Education and Welfare, 1971. (ERIC Document Reproduction Service No. ED 065 457.)

White, K., and J. Howard 1970. The relationship of achievement responsibility to instructional treatments. *Journal of Experimental Education* **39** (2): 78–82.

THE SENSE OF SELF-REPRESENTATION AND
SELF-SUSTENTION IN THE PERFORMING SELF

Joe, V. C. 1971. Review of the internal-external control construct as a personality variable. *Psychological Reports* **28** (2): 619–640.

Katkovsky, W., V. C. Crandall, and S. Good 1967. Parental antecedents of children's beliefs in internal–external control of reinforcements in intellectual achievement situations. *Child Development* **38:** 765–776.

Rosengarten, T. 1974. *All God's dangers.* New York: Knopf.

Teacher Behavior and Pupil Autonomy

Elder, G. H., Jr. 1963. Parental power legitimation and its effect on the adolescent. *Sociometry* **26:** 50–65.

Flanders, N. A., B. Morrison, and E. Brode 1968. Changes in pupil attitudes during the school year. *Journal of Educational Psychology* **59:** 334–338.

Ruedi, J., and C. K. West 1973. Pupil self-concept in an "open" school and in a "traditional" school. *Psychology in the Schools* **10** (1): 48–53. (ERIC Document Reproduction Service No. EJ 073 730.)

Speer, D. C., P. F. Briggs, and R. Gavalas 1969. Concurrent schedules of social reinforcement and dependency behavior among four-year-old children. *Journal of Experimental Child Psychology* **8** (2): 356–365.

Wilson, S. H., and R. L. Williams 1973. The effects of group contingencies on first graders' academic and social behaviors. *Journal of School Psychology* **11** (2): 110–117. (ERIC Document Reproduction Service No. EJ 078 947.)

Teacher Behavior and Pupil Motivation

Goldberg, J. 1968. Influence of pupils' attitudes on perception of teachers' behaviors and on consequent school work; California F Scale, Flexibility Scale, and Compulsivity Scale. *Journal of Educational Psychology* **59:** 1–5.

Murray, E. J., A. Seagull, and D. Geisinger 1969. Motivational patterns in the families of adjusted and maladjusted boys. *Journal of Consulting and Clinical Psychology* **33** (3): 337–342. (ERIC Document Reproduction Service No. EJ 005 148.)

Roosevelt, E. 1961. *The autobiography of Eleanor Roosevelt.* New York: Harper & Row.

St. Augustine. 1955. *Augustine: confessions and enchiridion,* Vol. VII. Albert Cook Outler (ed.). Philadelphia: Westminster Press.

Teevan, R. C., and P. McGhee 1972. Childhood development of fear of failure motivation. *Journal of Personality and Social Psychology* **21** (3): 345–348.

White, W., and R. Aaron 1967. Teachers' motivation cues and anxiety in relation to achievement levels in secondary school mathematics. *Journal of Educational Research* **61:** 6–9.

Pupil Response to Specific Motivational and Incentive Techniques

Alschuler, A. S. 1969. The effects of classroom structure on achievement motivation and academic performance. *Educational Technology* **9** (8): 19–24. (ERIC Document Reproduction Service No. EJ 008 096.)

Benowitz, M. L., and T. V. Busse 1970. Material incentives and the learning of spelling words in a typical school situation. *Journal of Educational Psychology* **61** (1): 24–26.

Cartwright, C. A. 1970. Efficacy of preferential incentives with elementary school children. *Journal of Educational Psychology* **61** (2): 152–158.

Clifford, M. M. 1972. Competition as a motivational technique in the classroom. *American Educational Research Journal* **9** (1): 123–137.

Wasik, B. H. 1970. The application of Premack's generalization on reinforcement to the management of classroom behavior. *Journal of Experimental Child Psychology* **10:** 33–43.

Teacher Feedback to the Performing Self

Brown, W., L. Payne, C. Lankewich, and L. Cornell 1970. Praise, criticism, and race. *Elementary School Journal* **70** (7): 373–377.

Christensen, C. M. 1970. Relationships between pupil achievement, pupil affect-need, teacher warmth, and teacher permissiveness. *Journal of Educational Psychology* **41** (3): 169–174.

Page, E. 1958. Teacher comments and student performance: a seventy-four classroom experiment in school motivation. *Journal of Educational Psychology* **49:** 173–181.

Rubovits, P., and M. Maehr 1973. Pygmalion black and white. *Journal of Personality and Social Psychology* **25** (2): 210–218. (ERIC Document Reproduction Service No. EJ 080 591.)

Spaulding, R. L. 1964. Achievement, creativity, and self-concept correlates of teacher-pupil transactions in elementary schools. In C. B. Stendler (ed.), *Readings in child behavior and development* (rev. ed.). New York: Harcourt, Brace and World.

THE SENSE OF THE UNKNOWN SELF

Alcoholics Anonymous World Services 1955. *Alcoholics Anonymous.* New York.

Hart, Moss 1960. *Act one, an autobiography.* New York: Random House.

Teacher Behavior and Pupil Creativity

Anderson, H. E., Jr., W. White, and J. Stevens 1969. Student creativity, intelligence, achievement, and teacher classroom behavior. *Journal of Social Psychology* **78:** 99–107. (ERIC Document Reproduction Service No. EJ 005 574.)

Bachtold, L. M., and E. E. Werner 1970. An evaluation of teaching creative skills to gifted students in grades 5 and 6. *Journal of Educational Research* **63** (6): 253–256.

Eisenman, R., and N. Schussel 1970. Creativity, birth order, and preference for symmetry. *Journal of Consulting and Clinical Psychology* **34:** 275–280.

Getzels, J., and J. Dillon, 1973. Giftedness and the education of the gifted. In R. M. W. Travers (ed.), *Second handbook of research on teaching*. Chicago: Rand McNally.

————, and P. Jackson 1962. *Creativity and intelligence: explorations with gifted students*. New York: Wiley.

————, and P. Jackson 1961. Family environment and cognitive style: a study of the sources of highly intelligent and of highly creative adolescents. *American Sociological Review* **26**: 351–359.

Merz, W. R., and B. M. Rutherford 1972. Differential teacher regard for creative students and achieving students. *California Journal of Educational Research* **23** (2): 83–90. (ERIC Document Reproduction Service No. EJ 055 478.)

Shively, J., J. Feldhusen, and D. Treffinger 1972. Developing creativity and related attitudes. *Journal of Experimental Education* **41**: 63–69.

Soar, R. 1968. Optimum teacher-pupil interaction for pupil growth. *Educational Leadership Research Supplement* **26** (3): 275–280.

Torrance, E. P. 1969. What is honored: comparative studies of creative achievement and motivation. *Journal of Creative Behavior* **3** (3): 149–154. (ERIC Document Reproduction Service No. EJ 008 855.)

Walker, W. J. 1969. Teacher personality in creative school environments. *Journal of Educational Research* **62** (6): 243–246. (ERIC Document Reproduction Service No. EJ 001 436.)

Teacher Behavior and Pupil Behavior Modification

Andrews, H. B., Jr. 1970–1971. The systematic use of the Premack principle in modifying classroom behaviors. *Child Study Journal* **1** (2): 74–79.

Broden, M., R. V. Hall, and B. Mitts 1971. The effect of self-recording on the classroom behavior of two eighth grade students. *Journal of Applied Behavior Analysis* **4**: 191–199.

Coleman, R. G. 1973. A procedure for fading from experimenter-school-based to parent-home-based control of classroom behavior. *Journal of School Psychology* **11** (1): 71–79. (ERIC Document Reproduction Service No. EJ 078 949.)

Duncan, A. D. 1969. Self-application of behavior modification techniques. *Adolescence* **4** (16): 541–556.

Orme, M. E., and R. F. Purnell 1968. *Behavior modification and transfer in an out-of-control classroom* (Monograph No. 5). Cambridge, Mass.: Center for Research and Development on Educational Differences, Harvard University.

Premack, D. 1959. Toward empirical behavior laws. *Psychological Review* **66**: 219–233.

Scott, P., R. Burton and M. Yarrow 1967. Social reinforcement under natural conditions. *Child Development* **38** (1): 53–63.

Wilson, S. H., and R. L. Williams 1973. The effects of group contingencies on first graders' academic and social behavior. *Journal of School Psychology* **11** (2): 110–117. (ERIC Document Reproduction Service No. EJ 078 947.)

CHAPTER 6

The Sense of Self-Esteem

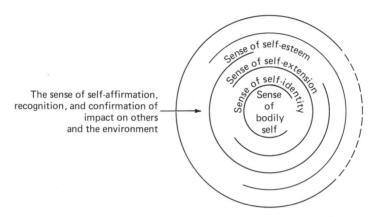

The sense of self-affirmation, recognition, and confirmation of impact on others and the environment

Fig. 6.1 Self-esteem of the general self-concept.

What was wrong? How could I explain I could never ask Mr. Sutcliffe to help me get a hamburger? I folded the letter and put it back in my pocket.

"What's wrong with you?" Ronnie kept asking.

How could I explain: my millionaires were the real rulers of Louisville. But I did not want to be considered "their" boy even in the eyes of those who hated me. I had earned my Gold Medal without their permission. It should mean something without their permission. I wanted that medallion to mean that I owned myself. And to call, seemed to me, to be exchanging one Owner for the Other. And suppose they did come to my rescue? Then I could come and go in the "white only" places, but other blacks couldn't. Then what would I be?

I moved closer to the door, keeping my eyes on The Owner. I felt a peculiar, miserable pain in my head and stomach. The pain that comes from punches you take without hitting back.

... I held the medallion just far enough out so that it wouldn't tangle in the bridge structure, and threw it into the black water of the Ohio. I watched it drag the red, white and blue ribbon down to the bottom behind it....

How could I put the answer together? I wasn't sure of all the reasons. The Olympic medal had been the most precious thing that had ever come to me. I worshiped it. It was proof of performance,

status, a symbol of belonging, of being a part of a team, a country, a world. It was my way of redeeming myself with my teachers and schoolmates at Central High, of letting them know that although I had not won scholastic victories, there was something inside me capable of victory.

Muhammad Ali 1975. The greatest: Muhammad Ali, *pp. 68–76.*

Self-Esteem is the psychological construct representing the verdict rendered from value judgments made by the other senses of self: the senses of Bodily Self, Self-Identity, Self-Extension, and Self-Image. The sense of Self-Esteem, also called the sense of Self-Value or Self-Worth, is the sum of all valued affirmation experienced in the behavioral dialogue. Through the psychological experience of recognition, the self receives confirmation of its existence and impact, to which the psychological experience of affirmation adds a positive quality. If the individual experiences little affirmation, he or she is more likely to develop a negative Sense of Self-Esteem.

Like all senses of self, the concept of Self-Esteem is rooted in the initial acceptance or rejection communicated to the developing self by significant others. If they are accepted, children acquire a sense of worth and value. If rejected, they develop a sense of worthlessness. The earliest events in the behavioral dialogue ("the self experiencing the self") provide the sensations of hunger, pain, discomfort, satiation, ease, and comfort—stimuli from which the senses of self begin to emerge. The feelings *of* the self become the foundation for feelings *about* the self, as the concept of the objective self, the self as stimulus, develops.

In the process of acquiring a Sense of Self-Identity, children accept interpretations made by significant others; and in the process of developing a Sense of Self-Esteem, they indiscriminantly accept the values, standards, and judgments implicit in the significant others' interpretations. Through these interpretations children learn that certain behaviors are valued by others.

Most of the early behaviors prized by significant others are "how to" behaviors that reflect personal, social, and cultural values. As the developing self acquires or imitates these behaviors, the reception and reflection of the child's performance provide recognition and affirmation, from which he or she derives Self-Identity and Self-Esteem. Children enter school, then, with a sense of Self-Esteem derived from their experiences in the home and, unrelated to their new situation, a sense of Self-Esteem that is open and vulnerable to the new environment. This vulnerability makes children particularly susceptible to the teacher's influence as significant other and controller of the classroom environment.

Both the significant other and the environment function in the development of self-esteem as they function in the development of the other senses of self. The child achieves self-esteem by acquiring behaviors and skills that have impact on significant others and the environment. As we have previously noted, these two sources of influence need not function in concert in order for the Performing Self to acquire positive self-esteem; even when they offer alternative or opposing psychological experiences, the child may emerge with a positive self-concept. One source, for example, may counterbalance the other. The child who is rejected by significant others may find that the environment offers his or her Performing Self the opportunity to master behaviors and skills that have positive impact on others and thus generate positive self-esteem.

> **My daddy had nothing goin to learn me but plow a old mule or old horse, chop cotton, hard labor—cut cross-ties, split rails, and all. My daddy would do a little of everything and I had to go, too. But turn the business over in my hands like Mr. Knowland done, he never would do it. And I caught on like fire to whatever Mr. Knowland put me up to. Well, Mr. Knowland wanted me back in 1905 but my daddy wouldn't let him have me. I went on and stayed where my daddy put me; took me back to work for him so he could go on his way. . . .**
>
> **I knowed I had never done nothin that was any value to me before I worked for that man, nothin but go day, come night, God send Sunday. I'd get a thing today and eat it up and I didn't know where anything was comin from tomorrow. I didn't like that old way no more.**
>
> *Nate Shaw in T. Rosengarten 1974.* All God's dangers, the life of Nate Shaw, *pp. 52–53.*

Children born into extreme poverty and deprivation may turn to the environment for positive reflection of self. If their births are unwelcome events, they may be negatively reflected and interpreted by significant others. But the need to survive and mature forces them to interact with their surroundings, where they quickly acquire behaviors and skills from which they can derive a positive self-image and self-esteem. On the most basic level, for example, they may succeed in finding shelter and food. They may learn to dress and care for themselves. Their explorations and assaults upon the environment may be judged by their peers, with whom they may cooperate or compete in achieving further impact upon and mastery of their world. The values they have acquired from battling the environment require very little interpretation, and the standards exacted by their environment are within a child's reach. According to the standards and values of their own self-reflecting society, these children are not "disadvantaged" or "underprivileged." They are able to perform, to compete, to achieve, to behave independently, and to acquire status. Self-rewards reinforce their behavior and reflections of a positive impact on the environment as recognition and confirmation of their presence and performance can enhance the sense of self-esteem.

On the other hand, the child who is accepted and welcomed into the family, who is given security and material advantages, may find the environment a source of prolonged dependence, frustration, and hostility. Though significant others may reflect and interpret the child in a positive way, environmental demands (the "how to" behaviors from which the Performing Self derives a sense of self-esteem) can be very complicated. In this environment, eating may require tools and precise rituals; dressing may involve matching, selecting, buttoning, tying, distinguishing right and wrong, back and front sides. In addition, the child's performance may be subject to the constant judgment and appraisal of significant others. Investigation and exploration of the environment may be restricted and supervised, and many interesting or exciting moments may be interrupted. A daily agenda may be imposed upon the child by significant others. In this sheltered, structured environment, the period during which a child learns to meet basic needs is prolonged, and dependence is extended. Thus the child may experience a sense of inadequacy and a negative reflection of the impact of the Performing Self on the environment, both of which contribute to low self-esteem. This phenomenon is documented by studies finding self-esteem higher in culturally "disadvantaged" than culturally "advantaged" children (Soares and Soares 1969).

Regardless of the child's background, however, the teacher is in a position to recognize and affirm, and to foster the feelings of worth and value which are essential to self-esteem. As controller of the classroom environment, the teacher can create a reasonably safe arena that allows the child to experience positive impact and constructive, productive self-evaluation. Of all the self-constructs affected by the classroom behavioral dialogue, pupil self-esteem is most dependent upon the teacher's value judgments and interpretations and most amenable to positive teacher influence.

> **I did not know that my grandmother and my aunts had written about me before I arrived, so I felt that I was starting a new life, free from all my former sins. This was the first time in my life that my fears left me. If I lived up to the rules and told the truth, there was nothing to fear. . . .**
>
> **I was beginning to make a place for myself in the school, and before long Mlle. Souvestre made me sit opposite her at table. The girl who occupied this place received her nod at the end of the meal and gave the signal, by rising, for the rest of the girls to rise and leave the dining room. . . .**

Eleanor Roosevelt 1961. Autobiography of Eleanor Roosevelt, *pp. 24 and 26.*

THE SENSE OF AFFIRMATION, RECOGNITION, AND CONFIRMATION OF IMPACT

TEACHER BEHAVIOR AND PUPIL SELF-EVALUATION

> ... I liked mathematics best, and next to mathematics I liked history. Having no one with whom to compare myself, I did not know for a long time whether I was better or worse than other boys, but I remember once hearing my Uncle Rollo saying goodbye to Jowett, the Master of Balliol, at the front door, and remarking: "Yes, he's getting on very well indeed," and I knew, though how I cannot tell, that he was speaking of my work. As soon as I realized that I was intelligent, I determined to achieve something of intellectual importance if it should be at all possible, and throughout my youth I let nothing whatever stand in the way of this ambition.

Bertrand Russell 1967. The autobiography of Bertrand Russell, *p. 39.*

Self-esteem can be acquired through a process of self-evaluation, during which children judge the effect of their impact according to their values and standards. Self-evaluation begins long before children reach the classroom, and the high or low self-esteem that becomes apparent in the school environment generally originates in previous psychological experiences. The new environment, however, offers new psychological experiences which ultimately will affect the individual's self-esteem. Pupils who have successfully negotiated their first five years may encounter problems in school if their previous experience has not equipped them with the concepts, values, and behavioral schema necessary for success in the classroom.

The most dominant value operating in the educational system is the value for academic achievement. In the daily classroom dialogue teachers interpret this value to the pupils. They apply academic standards to pupils' assessed achievement potential and to their daily efforts and products. The image of self and the measure of successful impact reflected to each child are permeated with values and standards for academic behavior.

The possibility of acquiring self-esteem in the classroom depends on pupils' ability to relate to the value system operating within it and the teacher's ability to offer experiences that help pupils recognize and affirm themselves as achievers. When achievement is defined in academic terms, it is difficult for pupils to evaluate their performance positively unless they accept the value judgments of the teacher. In order to be reflected as achievers, it is necessary to perform at specified levels of mastery.

There will be pupils, of course, who have low potential for academic achievement. They may compensate for this by valuing the approval given for arduous and continuous effort. There are also pupils who can achieve but whose values conflict with the use of academic performance as a means of gaining self-esteem. Pupils who must abandon their previously successful modes of affecting the environment may suffer a reversal of self-esteem in the new situation. And pupils who have rarely been reflected as achievers may, in spite of their potential, be unable to risk the continual evaluation and judgment constantly operating in the classroom.

High achievers—pupils whose high potential is realized in performance, or whose performance exceeds their potential—are rewarded by the classroom value system. Low achievers, regardless of potential or effort, are either unrewarded or rewarded for behavior other than academic achievement. The underachiever is usually most disconcerting to teachers and often the subject of research examining the relationship between academic performance and self-esteem.

If academic achievement is to serve as a source of self-esteem, it must first be valued; and to acquire this value the pupil must be recognized and affirmed as an achiever who has positive impact on significant others and the environment. This may require that the pupil be given (1) psychological experiences which offer a new basis for self-evaluation, (2) a clear understanding of the values and standards by which to judge performance, and (3) the skills necessary for evaluating his or her own work.

> **At the age of eleven, I began Euclid, with my brother as my tutor. This was one of the great events of my life, as dazzling as first love. I had not imagined that there was anything so delicious in the world. After I had learned the fifth proposition, my brother told me that it was generally considered difficult, but I had found no difficulty whatever. This was the first time it had dawned upon me that I might have some intelligence.**
>
> *Bertrand Russell 1967.* The autobiography of Bertrand Russell, *p. 37.*

Recognition of the self as an achiever may involve nothing more than the opportunity to express one's feelings and to examine one's performance in the presence of attentive and supportive others. If the child can perform under the guidance of well understood standards and clear, evaluative but nonjudgmental feedback—conditions, which according to the research are close to ideal—he or she is likely to feel recognized and affirmed as an achiever. Studies indicate that self-evaluation can enhance self-esteem if it is undertaken in a supportive environment in which the child is given a good measure of attention and constructive feedback.

Stimpson and Pedersen (1970), for example, hypothesizing that failure in school, conflict in the family, and poor peer relationships contribute to underachievement, found a significant and positive increase in the self-esteem of underachieving high school boys following three weeks of survival training designed to encourage self-evaluation and exploration of parental and peer relationships.

Similarly, Ludwig and Maehr (1967) found positive self-concept change among junior high school students given supportive feedback on their performance of physical tasks. Subjects executed a series of physical maneuvers in the presence of a physical development expert who gave each child's performance a positive or negative evaluation. Comparison of pre- and posttests revealed that children rated positively by the expert increased their self-esteem, preference for physical activity, and estimates of their own physical adequacy. Children evaluated negatively showed a decline on the same three variables. Ludwig and Maehr conclude that these findings support their hypotheses that self-concept change (1) is a function of the reaction of significant others and (2) is reflected by change in preferences.

Various educational and vocational counseling programs have also been effective in raising pupil self-estimates. In a study by Catron (1966), for example, high school students interested in college and career guidance reported more positive self-evaluations after participating in fourteen small-group counseling sessions. The process of discussing their problems and concerns apparently allowed students first to identify with the group, thereby attaining a sense of membership, identity, and security, and then, at the end of the counseling sessions, to leave the security of the group with a more positive sense of self-differentiated-from-others.

A similar program of seminars was effective in helping underachievers with above-average intelligence to improve their academic performance (Freeman and Craig 1967). Participating pupils obtained higher grades than did control students and a greater number continued their education after high school. According to the authors, the discussion groups were intended to help pupils gain a positive concept of their self-worth and to help them find satisfaction in purposeful and meaningful activities by airing their problems and grievances in a nonjudgmental, nonevaluative atmosphere.

High achievers have also been the subject of efforts to improve pupil self-evaluation. Werblo and Torrance (1966) investigated the effectiveness of an historical research technique in improving the accuracy of self-estimates reported by high achieving pupils with above-average intelligence who showed a tendency to undervalue their abilities. Subjects were taught historical research procedures and then given practice in collecting, interpreting, and evaluating data and making projections. After this experience, pupils demonstrated greater accuracy in evaluating their reading speed, vocabulary, and curiosity.

The element common to all evaluation programs that have successfully increased pupil self-esteem is the provision of feedback under conditions that are nonjudgmental, and that focus attention on the pupil, his or her conditions, concerns, and abilities.

TEACHER EVALUATION OF PUPILS AND
PUPIL SELF-EVALUATION

> As far as marks, you can either better yourself or become lower. Marks can be fair or unfair depending on how the student answers questions from the teacher and whether or not the teacher asks the questions a student can answer.
>
> Harry A. Kagan
> (The Students Choice)

> The passing mark should be "50" and not "65." Personally I don't care but I worry about my "parents."
>
> Chas. H. Robbins

> 1. On the pro side marks are good to the teacher. In showing how much the pupil listens to her.
> 2. On the con side marks are bad to the pupil. If he doesn't do so good on a test.
>
> Teenager

B. Kaufman 1964. Up the down staircase, *p. 263.*

Students generally consider the teacher's role as an evaluator only in light of her or his "grading" function; they often characterize teachers as "hard" or "easy" graders. (They also comment more frequently on the biases they feel teachers show rather than on the criteria teachers use in grading.) Most research on the teacher's role as an evaluator, however, focuses not on grading but on the accuracy of teacher assessments of pupil potential in relation to pupil performance on standardized achievement tests.

Willis (1972), for example, in an attempt to identify the criteria most commonly used by teachers to assess pupil academic potential found that "attention to the teacher," "level of maturity as assessed by the teacher," "self-confidence," and "ability to work without supervision" were most highly correlated with accurate estimates of pupil performance.

From the Willis data, Brophy and Good (1972) conclude that the impressive accuracy teachers demonstrated in assessing pupil academic potential was due to the use of relevant (that is, reliable and appropriate) criteria. Initial assessments, made before teachers had access to pupil information or time to observe and interact with the children, were strongly related to the four criteria (attending, maturity, confidence, and independent work) identified by Willis. However, teacher assessments made later in the study included pupil personality characteristics, not necessarily related to academic achievement, as evaluative criteria. As the school year progressed and their earlier assessments were reinforced, teachers also showed a tendency to perceive their successful pupils more positively and their unsuccessful pupils more negatively.

Gordon and Wood (1963) investigated the congruence between pupil self-ratings and pupil ratings made by teachers on a school-related self-perception scale. Teacher and pupil predictions of standard achievement test performances were also compared. Teacher-pupil agreement on the self-perception instrument was positively correlated with pupil accuracy in estimating achievement test scores, although the number of pupils whose estimates were accurate was very small. The direction of error (i.e., toward over-estimating or underestimating) was the same for pupils and teachers on both predictions. Teachers were more accurate than pupils in estimating test performance, but they were not very successful in predicting pupil self-perceptions or ability estimates.

Gordon and Wood commented that an "overreaction" was apparently operating: when a teacher overestimated some pupils, those pupils also over-estimated themselves, but to a greater extent. Teacher-pupil differences appeared to be related to perceptual distortion, in the same direction for both teacher and pupil.

Investigating the effect of teacher expectations on pupil academic performance, Meichenbaum, Bowers, and Ross (1969) found gains on teacher-scored objective tests, but not on teacher-scored subjective tests. In other words, if the investigators had not used objective tests to assess academic change, they would not have found a positive and significant correlation between pupil performance and observed changes in teacher behavior.

These studies, considered together, suggest that experience and the use of appropriate evaluative criteria are two important factors contributing to teacher accuracy in assessing pupil academic potential, particularly when referenced to specific learning tasks measured on objective and/or standardized tests. On the other hand, score predictions made by the pupils themselves must be referenced to their past academic performances and their perceived academic rank in the classroom—criteria which are products of teacher evaluation. It seems likely that pupils who significantly over- or under-estimate their performances may be reflecting the teacher's evaluation of their work as it was experienced day-to-day.

Assessing and evaluating pupil products and performances is one of the teachers'. major functions. Successful execution of this function contributes appreciably to teachers' professional standing and self-esteem. But even more important, it determines in large part how well teachers perform as significant others, and, in turn, how they affect pupil self-esteem. Assessments of pupil behavior and level of maturation serve as effective predictors of pupil performance. These criteria should be useful to the significant other, not as an image to reflect to the pupil, but as an indication of the pupil's state upon entering the teacher–student behavioral dialogue. The evaluative function of assessment is the determination of the pupil's academic and psychological needs.

Teachers who answer pupil attention with teacher attention, and pupil indifference with teacher indifference, or who reflect pupil self-confidence by placing confidence only in confident pupils, are not functioning adequately as significant others. Nor are teachers who reinforce and perpetuate immature behavior by reflecting the child's lack of maturity and inability to work without supervision.

Ohlsen (1965), reporting a study (Lister and Ohlsen 1962) in which test interpretations were shown to improve pupil self-understanding, offers teachers six suggestions for giving feedback to pupils: (1) Let pupils know that you know something about them and that you want to understand them better; acquaint pupils with school resources that will help them understand themselves, their peers, and their environment; (2) Tell pupils about sources of information and give them an opportunity to react to what they learn; (3) Use only resources that you are qualified to use; (4) Respect pupil self-perception and encourage pupils to assess themselves by helping them identify and work through their feelings and problems; (5) Be sensitive to cues indicating that a pupil does not understand or refuses to accept your feedback; (6) Watch your own subjectivity and try not to let it influence your interpretation of objective data.

There is no disguising the fact that academic achievement is the prime goal and most valued behavior in the classroom. To maintain or enhance pupil self-esteem, the teacher's evaluative skills should be directed toward diagnosis and interpretation rather than prognosis. The teacher's ability to estimate academic potential should be used to help pupils set realistic goals and to determine the skills and information they need to attain these goals. Pupil self-esteem can then be derived from the positive experience of progress and achievement valued by significant others.

TEACHER BEHAVIOR AS A MODEL FOR PUPIL SELF-CRITICISM AND SELF-REWARD

"Wait a minute!" I caught at his arm. "Just a minute. I know things haven't been going too well, but we're doing better now and we have the whole summer booked up! So why would you want to leave me now?"

Suddenly his face got red and he leaned across the table and said very tensely, "I'll tell you why. Because of you, that's why! We don't want to spend the rest of our lives out here in these sticks and, Lawrence, that's where you're gonna be for the rest of your life! You're never gonna make it in the big time! Let me tell you something ..." he gestured angrily, "you still bounce around like you're playing at a barn dance ... and you can't even speak English! So if

you want to know the real reason we're leaving, it's *you*. *You're* the one who's holding us all back!"

Lawrence Welk 1971. Wunnerful, wunnerful! The autobiography of Lawrence Welk, *p. 134.*

Most pupils (and people in general) think of evaluation as synonymous with "test" or "criticism." Accordingly, most pupils consider "self-evaluation" the same as "self-criticism," unaware that the former is accompanied by "self-reward." Because the term is thus misunderstood, pupils who stand to gain most from constructive self-evaluation are most inclined to fear and avoid it. Pupils entering school may need help in acquiring the concepts and behaviors necessary for maintaining self-esteem in the new environment. Ignorant of what to do or how to do it, confused about the basis of "right" and "wrong" decisions, pupils may keep their interaction to a minimum, thereby losing opportunities to gain self-esteem from successful social experiences. Pupils who continue to interact regardless of their "improper" and "unacceptable" behavior, are often forced to pay the toll in reduced self-esteem.

I felt sick, numb, almost paralyzed with shock, and I couldn't get those blunt words out of my mind "You're never gonna make it in the big time . . . you can't even speak English. You're the one who's holding us all back!" And from farther back in my memory I could hear my father's voice saying clearly, "You'll never be a success in the music business, and you'll be back here begging for a good meal one of these days." Suddenly I swallowed hard and rolled over in bed and buried my face deep, deep into the pillow. But I couldn't get those words out of my head. I think it was the lowest moment of my lifetime.

Lawrence Welk 1971. Wunnerful, wunnerful! The autobiography of Lawrence Welk, *p. 136.*

There is a distinct difference between self-reward and self-indulgence: the former is contingent upon a performance standard. As a technique of acquiring and reinforcing desirable behaviors, self-reward is effective only when the standard is realistic and understood. Examining performance in relation to a standard is evaluative, and determining how to bring that performance up to standard is productive, positive and formative self-criticism. However, because pupils often associate self-criticism with "blame," most teachers must reinterpret it in a positive light before pupils can appreciate the self-esteem attendant upon directing and evaluating—i.e., taking responsibility for—one's own performance. Although the problems involved in teaching positive self-criticism have been only lightly touched in the research, the studies reported in this section may encourage teachers to attempt to impart the skills of self-reward and self-criticism in their classrooms. Teachers who do so, however, should consider self-evaluation not a static judgment but a formative process through which pupils can acquire concepts and behaviors that will enhance self-esteem.

In a study by Liebert and Ora (1968) elementary school children were taught either by direct methods or modeling procedures to reward themselves with tokens (redeemable for prizes in a high-reward group, nonredeemable in a low-reward group) when their performance in a bowling game met a specified standard. Control subjects were given only a demonstration of how to play the game, with no information about reward standards.

Results supported the authors' hypotheses that (1) pupils trained either directly or by modeling procedures would adhere to the reward standards significantly more often than the control group and that (2) such adherence would be further influenced by the value of the reward. Children in the high-incentive (redeemable token) group rewarded themselves significantly more often for substandard performances than did children in the low-incentive group.

This led the authors to suggest that predictions of individual behavior made under conditions in which individuals monitor their own behavior according to standards prescribed by society must take into account the value of the reward given for meeting the standards. Highly moral people who encounter situations in which they are overwhelmed by temptation may temporarily reduce their moral standards to obtain a reward.

In an extension of this study, Liebert, Hanratty, and Hill (1969) examined the effectiveness of oral communication in helping pupils acquire and internalize standards. They found that subjects who had been given the "strongest" explanation of the reward standard (an explanation stressing merit and approval) were significantly more inclined to apply the rules for self-rewarding in the absence of observers. The authors suggest that this finding illustrates the effectiveness of verbal communication in helping children adopt self-imposed standards.

Focusing on self-criticism rather than self-reward, Herbert, Gelfand, and Hartmann (1969) investigated the effects of modeling on the self-evaluative behavior of pupils. According to their scores on several self-concept measures, subjects were divided into high and low self-esteem groups and assigned to a modeling or control condition. Each pupil assigned to the modeling situation watched an individual of his or her own sex play a bowling game. The model relinquished a token for each score of 0 or 5, and criticized his or her own performance aloud. Control pupils were simply instructed on how to play the game. Scoring was done by the experimenter so that all players made identical scores on a preset sequence of points. Results indicated that pupils in the modeling condition did imitate the model by relinquishing tokens for low scores and criticizing their own performances at a statistically significant level. The measures of self-esteem failed to differentiate the groups according to their token-relinquishing behavior, and no significant relationship was found between the self-criticism and self-esteem.

Also examining the effect of modeling on self-criticism, Thelen (1970) divided subjects into four groups: one control group, and three experimental groups who watched a model sort cards under timed conditions. At planned intervals, the model intentionally failed to complete the task in the prescribed time, on which occasions the model made "self-blaming" comments. In response to these comments, the experimenter gave: (1) positive remarks ("Oh, you're doing fine); (2) no reaction; or (3) negative remarks (agreement with the model's self-blaming statements). Each of the three experimental groups saw one of these response conditions. Subjects then sorted cards under the same conditions in which their models had worked. Results showed significant differences among the four groups in the frequency of self-blame responses. The three experimental groups made significantly more self-blame responses than the controls.

In a follow-up study, subjects were asked to play the game again, but two of the model conditions (positive and negative) were not repeated. The "No Response" group and the controls were actually performing under the same conditions provided for them in the first test. Results showed no overall differences in the number of self-blame comments made across treatment groups. However, two of the experimental groups, "No Response" and "Negative Response," made significantly more self-blame comments than the control group. The three experimental groups maintained their previous ranking on frequency of self-blame comments: the "Negative Response" group was first, followed by the "No Response" group and then by the "Positive Response" group. As we have already noted, however, differences between the treatment groups did not attain significance in the follow-up study.

These studies, and another discussed below from which similar results can be extrapolated (Grusec and Ezrin 1972), indicate that pupils do imitate specific behaviors as a result of both modeling and verbalizing procedures. From our perspective, however, they demonstrate even more dramatically the potential for abuse inherent in techniques designed to teach self-criticism. If we consider the Grusec and Ezrin study in terms of the behavioral dialogue rather than the investigators' interpretation, this potential for abuse becomes apparent.

Grusec and Ezrin (1972) prepared an experimental treatment for kindergarten and first grade pupils to test the effects of different punishing behaviors on the development of "self-criticism." The children played a game requiring them to negotiate a toy bulldozer through a series of toy trees enclosed in a box and occasionally altered in position by the experimenter. They could not see the trees. When a child hit a tree, a buzzer rang, signifying that he or she was a "bumper," "the worst thing you can be in this game" (pp. 1278–1279). The game was played under four treatment conditions: (1) "High Warmth," in which the experimenter established rapport with subjects; (2) "Low Warmth," in which the experimenter remained aloof from subjects; (3) "High Value," in which subjects were allowed to exchange the tokens obtained in the game for a prize; and (4) "Low Value," in which subjects were not allowed to redeem tokens. Under the High and Low Warmth conditions, a child's errors were punished by "Withdrawal of Love." (The experimenter expressed unhappiness with the child's play and continued to do so until the child admitted that she or he was a "bumper.") Under the High and Low Value conditions, mistakes were punished by "Withdrawal of Material Reward." (The experimenter took several tokens from the children, repeatedly asking them to explain the loss of tokens until they admitted they were "bumpers.") Subjects were either regularly reinforced for their self-criticism (i.e., rewarded for admitting they were "bumpers") or regularly given no response and instructed to proceed with the game. After successful trials, the experimenter praised the subject's performance.

As a final condition, all subjects were left to finish the game in the absence of the experimenter, who went next door to observe them through a one-way mirror, operating the buzzer by an extension wire. After four or five more trials, the experimenter returned and ended the game by giving prizes to all the subjects.

Results of this study indicated that all subjects who had been reinforced for their "self-criticism" increased this behavior with each trial and continued it in the "absence" of the observer. The difference between the behavior of reinforced and nonreinforced subjects was statistically significant.

This study, and to a lesser extent those of Herbert *et al.* and Thelen, treat self-criticism not as a positive, formative process, but as an inculcation or assumption of guilt. The subjects had no way to relate performance to consequence: identical efforts often achieved opposite results. In addition, the children were unable to evaluate or improve their performance: they could not stop "hitting too many trees." And they were provided no reasonable basis for assuming responsibility for their behavior. Yet these subjects were coerced into accepting a label and exhibiting a behavior according to a "significant other's" (i.e., the experimenter's) interpretation of their role and performance. Reinforcement was used as a method of underscoring that interpretation.

These experimenters had only brief and one-dimensional relationships with the subjects. Yet they exercised considerable power. Teachers, who have a stronger, longer association with pupils, must be alert to the power inherent in their role and its possible misuse.

Teachers can diffuse at least some of that power by sharing with pupils their role as positive reinforcer in the classroom. Research evidence indicates that pupils can be taught to assume part of this function through programs that foster self-rewarding and through a specific technique called "self-talk."

In a study by Felker and Stanwyck (1971), fourth grade pupils in a middle-class, predominantly white school were asked to perform an academic task and then to complete a general measure of self-concept and to engage in "self-talk." This technique required the children to identify statements that they might make to themselves after performing an academic task. Each statement thus identified was coded for its positive content. Pupils who scored higher on the global self-concept measure also scored higher on positive self-talk. However, the relationship between actual performance on the academic task and self-concept scores was not measured. The investigators feel that pupils can be trained to use positive self-talk as a self-reinforcing behavior, but suggest that additional study is needed to understand the relationship between self-talk and self-concept development.

In a related study, Felker, Stanwyck, and Kay (1973) report the implementation of a program in which elementary teachers from predominantly black schools were trained to model appropriate behavior, to help pupils develop adequate bases for judging their own behavior, and to help pupils adopt self-rewarding behavior. A comparison of pre- and posttest measures indicated that pupil self-concept was enhanced and pupil anxiety reduced in the experimental classes. According to the investigators, the findings were confounded by an enthusiastic exchange of ideas between program participants and nonparticipants—a situation which produced a less than ideal control group. They felt that the program was actually more effective than the measures indicated.

Further study is required before we can fully understand the question of self-evaluation in the classroom. Hopefully, such research is forthcoming since the classroom, the gymnasium, and the school playground are logical places to implement programs that teach children to evaluate, criticize, and reward their own behavior and products as a means of improving performance and enhancing self-esteem.

TEACHER BEHAVIOR AND PUPIL STATUS RELATED TO SELF-ESTEEM

The students, however, were shockingly backward. Bailey and I did arithmetic at a mature level because of our work in the Store, and we read well because in Stamps there wasn't anything else to do. We were moved up a grade because our teachers thought that we country children would make our classmates feel inferior—and we did. Bailey would not refrain from remarking on our classmates' lack of knowl-

edge. At lunchtime in the large gray concrete playground, he would stand in the center of a crowd of big boys and ask, "Who was Napoleon Bonaparte?" "How many feet make a mile?" It was in-fighting, Bailey style.

Maya Angelou 1969. I know why the caged bird sings, *p. 61.*

As a source of interpersonal comparison and rank-ordering, the school environment is without rival in our society. Pupils are constantly made aware of their standing with teachers and peers through daily feedback concerning the impact of their Performing Selves on the academic and social systems of the school. Some positions attained in school remain fairly stable; others fluctuate. Although it is usually assumed that any high standing contributes to pupils' sense of self-esteem and their broader self-concept, the interaction between status and self-esteem requires careful interpretation. Prestige enhances self-esteem only when the status is desired and the reference group or standard is valued. Low economic or academic status does not necessarily predict low self-esteem, and social status may be so narrowly defined that it encompasses only peer values.

. . . Yet I made myself out worse than I was, in order that I might not go lacking for praise. And when in anything I had not sinned as the worst ones in the group, I would still say that I had done what I had not done, in order not to appear contemptible because I was more innocent than they; and not to drop in their esteem because I was more chaste.

St. Augustine 1955. Augustine: confessions and enchiridion, *p. 53.*

It is the business of the educational system to inculcate values for academic achievement and the social status it presumably brings. When pupils acquire the values but not the status, their self-esteem may suffer. As a practical matter, then, it is best not to develop a value for status, if status cannot be achieved. If high status can be achieved or ascribed, however, it is psychologically safe to acquire the value or standard to which it is referenced.

Pupils who enter school with a fully developed value for education and social position are, theoretically, equipped with the motivation to achieve. We would expect family values, then, to be associated with pupil achievement, status, and school-related self-esteem, and research indicates that this is indeed the case. Webster (1965) found a significant, positive relationship between maternal support of academic behavior exhibited by children during the years from age six to ten and the physical and intellectual self-esteem reported by these children as high school students. This correlation was somewhat higher for girls than boys. The relationship between maternal behavior and future aspirations, however, was significant only for boys, a finding which the investigator explained in terms of cultural expectation that girls will become wives and mothers. If we recall the theoretical effect of cultural values on the sense of self as doer and knower (Self-Extension), we can hypothesize that adolescent girls value their academic status for the immediate self-esteem it brings in an environment where intellectual performance is highly approved; boys, on the other hand, value academic achievement as a preliminary to future success and esteem. As more girls with average rather than above-average intelligence go on to college, females may begin to invest value and self-esteem in early academic achievement for their futures as well.

Considering the relationship between values, achievement, and status, the success of several attempts to enhance pupil status through direct program intervention is somewhat surprising. Halpin, Halpin, and Hartley (1972) report the effect of guidance programs on the status of second grade pupils. On the basis of sociometric testing, pupils in two of four treatment groups were reseated according to their reported preferences; seating was unchanged in the other two treatment groups. Guidance activities were given to one of the reseated groups and to one of the unchanged groups. Pupils in both of these groups showed significantly more status gain than those in the control group. The effect of reseating could not be determined since teachers felt compelled to change the seating again during the course of the study due to excessive student talking. Results were further confounded by uncontrolled counselor and guidance activity variables. The findings, however, do demonstrate the positive effect of guidance activities in changing the status of second grade pupils as measured on preference–rejection dimensions.

In a similar study by Blain and Ramirez (1968), sociometric rank was altered by increased interaction and reinforcement. Children raised their rankings of peers previously designated as social "isolates" after having the opportunity to interact with them. However, pupil awareness of the isolates (measured by the number of associations made with their names) increased only when interaction with them was reinforced by the experimenter.

Both of these studies suggest that teachers can introduce activities, such as reseating, regrouping, and reinterpreting social behavior, to increase the status and self-esteem of otherwise socially isolated pupils.

Finney and Van Dalsem (1969) found that gifted but underachieving sophomores and juniors registered significant and positive change on measures of personality and psychosocial characteristics following a program of group counseling. Pupils showed improvement on measures of social poise and independent thought and action, but not on measures of social conformity. The investigators emphasize that these changes were brought about under conditions similar to those prevailing in the average high school. They caution, however, that *long-term* counseling is imperative for effecting lasting change in high school age students.

Though teacher intervention has been successful in altering pupil status, teacher assumptions about classroom status structures can be erroneous. In a study by Ahlbrand and Reynolds (1972), a classroom that contained fourth , fifth , and sixth graders (ability grouped across grade levels) was used to examine the effects of such a grade and age mixture upon sociometric nominations made by the pupils. Both older and younger pupils gave considerably more positive nominations to the older children for leadership, scholarship, and popularity. The authors report that the teachers in this situation had felt that the younger pupils resented the older pupils. But analysis of the sociometric data proved this assumption to be erroneous.

The interesting interplay of values with performance and standards with achievement is in constant view of teachers in every classroom. The practice of ascribing status to a pupil by making him or her "feel important" has long been used by teachers who are sensitive to the status needs of children. Buswell (1953) found a positive relationship between the social structure of the classroom and the academic success of pupils. He reports that, in general, pupils who were successful in their school work were also successful in their social relationships. Buswell notes that at the kindergarten level, before pupils were aware of academic ranking, future achievers were not chosen in social relationships any more frequently than future nonachievers. From the first grade on, however, after academic ranking had become obvious, achievers were also the social favorites. The author suggests that in view of the relationship between pupil IQ and academic achievement (and the relative stability of IQ level), it is up to the teacher to improve pupil performance on an individualized basis through his or her power to control, in some measure, the opportunities available to the pupil for achievement and acceptance. By the same token, teachers can improve the social status of pupils by introducing additional criteria for acceptability.

TEACHER BEHAVIOR AND PUPIL SELF-CONFIDENCE

> **In the school itself I was disappointed to find that I was not the most brilliant or even nearly the most brilliant student. The white kids had better vocabularies than I and, what was more appalling, less fear in the classrooms. They never hesitated to hold up their hands in response to a teacher's question; even when they were wrong they were wrong aggressively, while I had to be certain about all my facts before I dared to call attention to myself.**
>
> *Maya Angelou 1969.* I know why the caged bird sings, *p. 209.*

The term "self-confidence," like the term "anxiety," can be used to describe a generalized behavioral trait or a psychological state with a specific reference. Confidence in the self is based upon valuing the self. Although self-valuing can derive from any one or more of the five psychological self-constructs, its offshoot, self-confidence, is observable to others only through the behavior of the Performing Self. As a source of Self-Esteem, however, self-confidence is a product of self-perception, not objective observation. Self-confidence develops only when one perceives one's relationships and performances in a positive light—when one accepts and values one's behavior and considers it successful.

All of the psychological self-constructs can stimulate self-confidence. The Bodily Self can provide self-confidence through physical attributes, mental processes, talents, aptitudes, sex, race, or any other physiologically based characteristic that is perceived by the self as valuable.

> ... I supposed that somewhere in the university there were really clever people whom I had not yet met, and whom I should at once recognize as my intellectual superiors, but during my second year, I discovered that I already knew all the cleverest people in the university. This was a disappointment to me, but at the same time gave me increased self-confidence.

Bertrand Russell 1967. The autobiography of Bertrand Russell, *p. 85.*

Other self-constructs can generate self-confidence through family and group identity or affiliation, through ascribed or acquired esteem and status, or through the competency and positive impact of one's performance. The confidence stemming from any one of these self-concepts can be inferred from the coping style that characterizes the Performing Self (i.e., interpersonal trust or mistrust, risk taking or safety seeking, participation or withdrawal, independence or dependence).

When we infer self-confidence, however, either from behavior or from self-report, we must exercise caution in doing so. The evidence from which we judge self-confidence is subject to all the obfuscations that plague other self-represented or self-reported data, and our interpretation is vulnerable to all the problems that typically complicate any attempt to objectively measure the products of self-perception. Such measures rely on the subject's self-report or an observer's explanation of the discrepancy between the subject's potential and performance. In either case, the difficult task of interpretation introduces the biases of subjectivity.

Interpretation requires judgment, and judgment requires criteria. As Miller (1970) and Bronfenbrenner (1970) have pointed out in their critiques of an impressive research study reported by Siegelman, Block, Block, and von der Lippe (1970), experimenters can be blind to cultural, epochal, and methodological biases that reduce the assumed generalizability of their findings.

In the study reported by Siegelman *et al.,* data were analyzed for parental practices common to the homes of subjects judged to have "optimal psychological adjustment in adulthood." The criterion for "optimal adjustment" was based on an absolute ideal drawn from a consensus of professional judges, and the data were generated from ratings made by professionals on items selected by professionals. Results indicated that well-adjusted subjects came from healthy, democratic, value-oriented homes with nonneurotic parents, and cognitively competent mothers. Evaluating this study in light of the adjustment criterion and data collection procedures used, Miller found a bias in favor of the middle class and, more precisely, in favor of the middle-class bureaucracy. Miller cautions against defining the individual according to an absolute ideal unrelated to the individual's sex, generation, epoch, and culture, and in a similar critique of the Siegelman study, Bronfenbrenner warns against equating clinical judgments with objective reality.

The critical contributions of both Miller and Bronfenbrenner should be heeded by all researchers investigating self-concept development, particularly those examining the influence of teacher behavior and school environment on pupil self-concept formation. Comparing the effects of Authoritarian-Rejecting black parents and Authoritarian-Rejecting white parents, Baumrind (1972) found that while black parents were considered authoritarian by white norms, their daughters were the most self-assertive and independent girls in the study. Baumrind suggests that the "authoritarian syndrome" produced different effects in white and black girls because black girls perceived the parental behavior not as rejecting, but as nurturant and caring. In addition to being independent, black girls were "domineering" with peers and "resistive" with adults, and were therefore considered to have little "social responsibility." Yet the mothers (or mother models) of these black girls were described as having an "equalitarian relationship" with the fathers and an active role in decision making in their own social milieu. According to Baumrind, these factors constitute crucial differences between the white authoritarian and black authoritarian homes. This being so, one would expect that the "domineering," "resistive" behavior of these preschool black girls might have been interpreted as an indication of self-confidence, not social irresponsibility, in another social milieu. Thus, even when one is aware of cultural differences among subjects, value judgments can influence the interpretation of data.

The problem of interpretation is further illustrated in a study by Landry, Schilson, and Pardew (1974). Children of military personnel, representing various ethnic groups, were exposed to an 11-week program designed to enhance the physical, intellectual, emotional, and social aspects of self. Participants completed a variety of individually administered self-concept measures. In addition, teachers rated the pupils, creating a profile for each child referenced to specific dimensions: (1) awareness of self; (2) self-confidence indicated by response to new and challenging situations; (3) interpersonal comprehension measured by the child's understanding of his or her impact on others; (4) sensitivity to others, (5) coping ability; and (6) tolerance, indicated by the child's ability to accept individual differences.

Results indicated that the experimental subjects showed significant gains on self-concept scales of sociability, sharing, concept of self-as-subject, total self-concept, and fear (i.e., they reported a reduction in fear). On the teacher-rated dimensions, the control group changed significantly only in regard to self-awareness, while the experimental group made significant changes in self-awareness, self-confidence, and sensitivity to others.

The authors conclude that the gains made by the experimental group were attributable to the guidance program. They also report their own subjective observation that the experimental subjects showed increasing and deepening responses and expressions of feeling, more commitment to each other, and an improvement in listening skills through the rules invoked for discussions. And, according to the investigators, these children also appeared to develop an understanding of cause and effect relationships. However, teachers, while indicating gains for the experimental subjects from pre- to postratings, did not see significant differences in the behavior of control and experimental groups.

Did the children actually become less afraid of things and people as a result of the guidance program, or did they merely *learn* that things and people should not be feared, and therefore *report* less fear? Did they learn to share or did they learn that sharing is approved by adults? Were they able to more accurately perceive each others' feelings or did they learn that they should report greater consideration of others' feelings? Several of the variables included in this study would benefit from more objective measurement—measurement that would permit more of the data to be generated from "objective reality" rather than clinical or professional interpretation.

Bishop and Beckman (1971), reporting a study far more limited in scope, found that the age of subjects and the ambiguity of assigned tasks contributed to the degree of conforming and confident behavior exhibited by children. Lower middle-class, male and female pupils from four ethnic groups were asked to judge the length of a line. They did so under peer pressure to make their estimates conform to the group's estimate. The pupils' confidence in their own judgment (in their ability to estimate the length of a line) varied with task ambiguity and increased with grade level and experience.

If the conforming behavior of these students had been motivated by need for social approval, it would not have varied with the ambiguity of the task, but would have remained stable. This suggests that assessment of self-confidence would be more interpretable if it were based on a comparison of task performance achieved with and without the application of social pressure. Such comparison would permit the identification of differences in confidence and conformity.

Efforts to help children acquire self-confidence in the classroom appear to be successful, at least at the self-report level. There is serious question, however, whether the values and self-concepts written into test items actually represent the values and self-concepts of the pupil populations studied. Theoretically, if we could assess what children want to achieve, measure their self-confidence using their own estimate of their ability and performance, and provide information and experiences directed toward their goals, we might successfully enhance the children's self-confidence.

The Performing Self is the self-construct most often observed by teachers in the classroom, but it is not necessarily the best index of pupil needs. Children's *real* needs are dictated by their values and concerns, not by an objective measure of performance. Teachers who address the "needs" of pupils without regard for their concerns are in fact responding to their own concerns, and they may, with the pupils' help, enhance their own self-confidence. To build self-confidence in *pupils,* teachers must help them succeed in areas where they are concerned about succeeding and offer them psychological experiences containing both affect and information geared to improve their self-esteem.

TEACHER BEHAVIOR AND PUPIL COOPERATION AND COMPETITION

> **Competition has always been an aspect in my life. I hate to lose and I love to win. Competition has been involved in me since grammar school. It gives a person a goal. It makes you push yourself to be better. Some people are satisfied with placing second or third in life. I don't. I want to be the best at it and I don't want to be overtaken.**
>
> **You noticed the American flag on my lapel, which I wore every day for a year now. I got four stickers all over my car. I think America is the greatest country in the history of the world. One of the reasons? Free enterprise. You can go to your heart's content in life. You can set your goals anywhere you want to set 'em in America. This is all part of the American spirit, to compete, to be better, to be number one. To go as far as you can. If the next man can't go that far, don't stop and wait for him. Life will pass you up.**
>
> *Ralph Werner—Department Store Salesman*
> *From S. Terkel 1974.* Working, *p. 456.*

The teacher's purpose in encouraging cooperative or competitive behavior in the classroom should be to facilitate pupil learning and to provide experiences that reflect the pupil's positive impact upon the environment. Teachers should recognize, however, that ability to cooperate or compete, like ability to achieve academically, varies from pupil to pupil. They should further recognize that cooperative and competitive techniques have affective consequences, intended or not. Pupils who constantly experience failure may have to settle for the self-esteem derived from being a "good loser." But the classroom should be able to offer them alternatives to failure.

> **I think it's a reflection of the North American way of life. This is one of the ways you are somebody—you beat somebody. You're better than they are. Somebody has to be less than you in order for you to be somebody. I don't know if that's right any more. I don't have that drive any more.**
>
> *Eric Nesterenko—Hockey Player*
> *From S. Terkel 1974.* Working, *p. 385.*

Teachers' positions as controllers of the classroom environment allow them to use competitive and cooperative situations in order to achieve affective objectives. In general, research tends to support the belief that we are a competitive society. If, for any reason, teachers would like to increase competitiveness among pupils, they can do so by offering limited performance rewards.

Nelson and Madsen (1969) found that four-year-olds responded to cues for cooperative and competitive behavior in accordance with a reward schema. However, cooperative behavior emerged only when it was the *sole* method of obtaining the group reward. The initial behavior in both reward situations was competitive, and in the limited reward situation (where only one of a pair could receive the reward) competitive behavior was sustained. The subjects were of mixed racial and socioeconomic backgrounds, but there were no significant behavioral differences between Caucasians and blacks, or between middle- and low-income groups.

Some subjects appeared to want to cooperate, but this produced a dominant-submissive rather than a cooperative pattern of behavior: instead of taking turns for the rewards, one child in the pair earned a greater share. The investigators suggest that the subjects did not have a concept of mutual assistance that would allow them to share the rewards in the limited reward situation, though they were able to cooperate for a group reward. However, it also appeared that a tendency to focus on the mechanics of the task and the immediate reward affected the pupils' ability to see alternative ways to gain rewards.

Richmond and Weiner (1973) found significant differences in the competitive–cooperative behavior of first and second grade pupils according to reward condition, ethnicity, and age. Pupils were placed in one of two reward conditions: cooperative (in which both subjects in a pair could receive a prize on every trial) and competitive (in which only one child in a pair could win a prize).

The investigators report that pairs of black children were more cooperative and less competitive than pairs of whites, and that racially mixed pairs were less cooperative than black pairs and less competitive than white pairs. Second graders were more competitive than first graders, but no significant sex differences were found.

These studies and others (Harvey *et al.* 1968) indicate that a limited reward can stimulate competition among children. This being so, we can infer that teachers may, through dictatorial, controlling, and punitive behavior toward pupils, create a situation in which they become a source of limited rewards, thereby increasing competitiveness among pupils who strive for the rare reward of teacher approval. The occurrence of this situation in a culture that is already highly competitive underscores the need to directly teach cooperative behavior to students. Research indicates that this can be done through task-structuring, pupil teaming, or rewarding cooperative behavior.

Based upon previous observations of the group behavior of five-year-olds, Torrance (1971) devised two structuring procedures in order to study their effects on children's cooperative and planning behavior. One procedure structured the task, and the other structured the group. In the first procedure, pupils were randomly assigned to groups of six, and those in the experimental sections were each instructed to draw and color a castle, and then, with their group, to select one or a composite to serve as the model for a castle to be built from blocks. (Castle selection required the aid of an observer in some groups.) Control subjects were simply instructed to plan and build a dream castle as a group. The behavior of all group members was observed and recorded on five dimensions: (1) planning, (2) cooperation, (3) verbal aggressiveness, (4) physical aggressiveness, and (5) withdrawal.

Results indicated that the task-structuring procedures had significantly increased the amount of planning and cooperating behavior and reduced the amount of aggressive behavior. Withdrawing behavior was unaffected.

In Torrance's second procedure, pupils were similarly assigned to groups and observed. In this case, however, a group leader was designated in each experimental group, and members were instructed to help their "captain" build a football stadium. Control pupils were merely told to cooperate in building a football stadium, without designated leadership.

Results indicated that the designation of a leader produced more planning behavior, but also more physical aggressiveness and less cooperation in experimental than control groups. Torrance comments that structuring the task rather than the group appeared to be a more effective way to increase cooperative behavior, at least among five-year-olds. He adds, incidentally, that castles produced by the experimental groups were judged to be more elaborate and original than those produced by the control groups.

It is possible that the designation of a leader introduced an element of status reward and reduced group reward (and reinforcement) by ascribing task achievement to a single individual. If the leader were selected arbitrarily, it is also possible that the group task may have been subverted by the competitive efforts of individuals to attain leadership or "depose the king." These possibilities, considered in conjunction with difficulties in castle selection observed in Torrance's first procedure, lead us to conclude that whenever there was room for competitive behavior, it did in fact emerge. Still, the effectiveness of task structuring (even without the use of contingency rewards) in achieving cooperative behavior is well demonstrated by the Torrance study.

Another method shown effective in producing cooperative behavior among pupils is team learning. Maurer (1968) reports that team learning was highly effective (and enthusiastically supported by teachers) in junior and senior high schools. According to his report, pupil teaming produced stimulation, motivation, involvement, and self-discipline, as well as cooperation among pupils. Yet Maurer suggests limited application of this technique since it requires considerable maturity and responsibility on the pupils' part. It is our feeling, however, that any tendency among pupils to socialize or fritter away the time in pleasant companionship, or to become overly dependent on their team partners, could be counteracted by appropriate task structuring.

In addition to rewarding, reinforcing, task-structuring, and pupil teaming, a technique described as "I/We" orientation can be used to influence the cooperative behavior of pupils. To measure the cooperative and competitive behavior of four- and five-year-old Anglo- and Mexican-Americans and seven- to nine-year-old Anglos, Mexican-Americans, and Mexicans, Kagan and Madsen (1971) paired subjects according to ethnicity and tested them in two situations. In the first situation, cooperative play earned a reward for both members of a pair, in the second, play was structured so that no one could gain a reward. The behavioral patterns observed were similar to those found in the Richmond and Weiner study reported earlier in this section. Among the seven- to nine-year-old subjects, Mexicans were most cooperative, and Anglo-Americans least cooperative. The four- to five-year-olds exhibited more cooperative behavior than the seven- to nine-year olds.

Results indicated that an orientation (given prior to testing) stressing a "we" attitude increased cooperative behavior, while an "I" orientation increased competitive behavior among older subjects. Preschool children, who showed the most cooperative behavior, did not appear to be influenced by either orientation. When a neutral orientation was given and subjects were allowed to create a reward situation according to their preference, Mexican and Mexican-American subjects structured the task much as they had following the "we" orientation, while Anglo-Americans performed much as they had after the "I" orientation.

The investigators suggest that developmental differences accounted for the more cooperative behavior of younger children and that cultural differences accounted for the varying responses characterizing the older group.

Another investigation studying cultural and developmental influences on cooperative and competitive behavior is reported by McClintock and Nuttin (1969). Flemish and American boys of above-average IQ from second, fourth, and sixth grade levels, were paired and divided into two treatment groups to play a game. In one treatment condition (Single Display), each boy was shown his own score but not his partner's score; in the other condition (Double Display), each boy was shown both his and his partner's scores. The game offered three ways to make points: (1) by maximizing individual gain score; (2) by maximizing the joint or team score; or (3) by maximizing relative gain scores (winning as much—or losing as little—as possible, relative to the other player in the pair).

The pattern of choices made indicated that knowledge of one's own and one's partner's scores increased competitive rather than cooperative behavior. This is consistent with the investigators' expectation that performance comparison encourages competition. Significant cultural differences appeared in younger but not older age groups, leading McClintock and Nuttin to conclude that in both cultural milieus children are taught to compare and compete for gains.

Factors promoting cooperation, rather than competition in the classroom, were uncovered in a study by Calonico and Calonico (1972). They hypothesized that the classroom contains two unrelated systems: internal and external. The internal system consists of the sentiments held and expressed by pupils while the external system is the formal structure imposed by educational administrators (i.e., the age grouping, work conformity output demands, task requirements, and extracurricular organizations). The internal system is characterized by the individual pupil's feeling for other pupils, and the friendly, helping, and imitative activities in which students voluntarily engage. This student-ordered society exists independent of, but within, the external system.

Examination of the classroom in terms of these two systems substantiated three hypotheses that Calonico and Calonico consider important: (1) More frequent interaction results in stronger sentiments of friendship between the interactors (also supported by data reported by Blain and Ramirez 1968); (2) people express their affection, or dislike, for each other in activities beyond those provided by the external system; and (3) people who rank high in a group engage in activities that conform to the norms of that group.

Calonico and Calonico suggest that the teacher behaviors which foster pupil cooperation and learning are those that: (1) encourage friendliness and interaction among pupils; (2) take the internal structure of the classroom into consideration, (3) promote positive sentiments in the group, and (4) permit helping relationships, including "copying" when it is used as a learning aid and not a cheating aid.

In another study of classroom climate, Anderson (1970) found that its effects vary with pupil ability, at least among females. Using a sample randomly selected from grades 10, 11, and 12 in the United States and Canada, Anderson divided subjects by sex and classified them according to four learning criteria related to academic subject content. Among the results of this study was the finding that a competitive classroom atmosphere facilitated learning in high-ability females, while a cooperative climate fostered learning in low-ability females.

Cooperation and competition play particularly important roles in the acquisition and maintenance of self-esteem. Through successful competition (that is, through a favorable comparison of one's behavior and performance with that of others), the individual's impact is clearly demonstrated—by "winning." Lack of impact, or "losing," though often less obvious, especially in close outcomes, is usually more keenly felt. The old adage that we learn through our failures probably stems from the common practice of examining our performances for clues explaining those failures. (Winning is usually accepted without a second glance.) But when failure is near complete and near constant, its explanation generally lies outside of the individual's performance—in conditions involving missing knowledge and/or unmastered skills. These conditions prohibit winning, and without a hope of winning it is useless to compete. The classroom is sometimes the scene of forced competition. The competitors have not entered the race voluntarily; they have been drafted. The ever-present bell-shaped curve, representing the normal distribution, peals constant victory for some pupils and knells constant failure for others.

Yet it should not be assumed that cooperation is the automatic or complete solution to the "evils" of competition. Cooperation suits all pupils no more than competition does. To cooperate requires, if not confidence, at least sufficient self-esteem to consider one's contribution worthy. For pupils with low self-esteem, demands for even small contributions can appear too risky. Pupils who have little esteem for their academic competence may need to fully master tasks before performing them with a group. They should be encouraged to cooperate in other, nonacademic areas of classroom life so that their contributions can be perceived positively. Even if some pupils' achievements rest merely on their unique physical characteristics (i.e., if they can take care of the bulletin board because they are tall or wash out paste jars because they have small hands), they can view their achievements as worthwhile contributions to the group.

TEACHER BEHAVIOR AND THE SENSE OF SELF-ESTEEM

In the introduction to this chapter we described the Sense of Self-Esteem as the total of the individual's self-affirming experiences (i.e., experiences that define the self such as performances and products done in accordance with the individual's acquired system of values). When children enter school, they may or may not have acquired a value for academic achievement. The behaviors and skills that have served as a source of self-esteem in their familial setting may or may not serve them in the new social setting. A pupil's Sense of Bodily Self (sex, physical characteristics, and motor abilities) and Sense of Self-Identity (ethnic group, language, and status within the family) may continue to provide positive self-esteem in the new situation; but it is equally possible that these senses may cease to function in this manner or, worse, may become a source of negative psychological experiences that not only fail to affirm, but actually damage, the pupil's sense of self-esteem. And, of course, there is also the possibility that some children entering the school situation may have had so few self-affirming experiences that they have failed to derive positive self-esteem from *any* source.

Regardless of the state of the child's self-esteem upon entering the school, the teacher can, as significant or salient other and controller of the classroom environment, provide psychological experiences from which each pupil can derive a positive sense of self-esteem. Pupils whose demeanor indicates low self-esteem, or self-esteem rooted in behaviors and skills that are inappropriate in the new situation, require a behavioral dialogue structured to provide them new interpretations and reflections of their Performing Selves.

Theoretically, then, the teacher's first objective in structuring a behavioral dialogue should be to provide experiences through which the developing self can be reflected, recognized, and affirmed as an achiever who has positive impact on significant others and the environment. The demonstrated ability of experienced teachers to assess and evaluate the academic potential of their pupils should be used as a diagnostic tool for planning cognitive *and* affective objectives for each pupil.

The second goal of the teacher in creating a behavioral dialogue is to help pupils acquire and internalize a value for academic achievement as a source of self-esteem and to acquire the evaluative skills needed to assess their Performing Selves.

Research suggests that teachers who clearly communicate and interpret the standards employed in evaluating pupil performance are most effective in encouraging pupils to voluntarily apply standards to their own work. Pupils who learn to apply appropriate standards to their performances and products not only increase the accuracy of their self-evaluation, but also experience independent judgment from which they can derive positive self-esteem.

The research also appears to underscore the teacher's considerable influence as a model and as an interpreter of standards. As a model, the teacher can demonstrate the proper use of self-criticism and self-reward. As an interpreter of performance standards, however, the teacher can inadvertently communicate biases that limit pupils' self-evaluative abilities or reinforce behaviors detrimental to pupil self-esteem. Thus, it is extremely important that the use of pupil self-criticism be accompanied by a clear understanding, on the pupils' part, of the relationship between performance and products, an understanding that will allow pupils to identify those elements of their performance that require correction or alteration. Unless this relationship is clear to each pupil, the positive effects of self-criticism and self-evaluation will be obscured by a sense of guilt or replaced by a reduction in self-esteem caused by a negative perception of the impact of the Performing Self.

As a repository and interpreter of the values and standards permeating the learning situation, teachers can influence the status of individual pupils or groups of pupils. Teachers are in a position to impose a status system on the classroom that reflects and reinforces their own status hierarchy, with its attendant effects on pupil self-esteem. By valuing the products and performances of individual pupils and positively interpreting or directing pupil interaction, teachers can shape the psychological experiences of children in the classroom. By utilizing methods such as cross-age tutoring, group work, and activities fostering positive social interaction, teachers can increase the sources of positive impact and affirmation available to pupils in the classroom.

The teacher who wishes to help pupils develop a positive Sense of Self-Esteem in the classroom environment should:

1. Recognize and affirm the value of each pupil;

2. Keep in mind that the fundamental basis for acquiring self-esteem in the classroom is the reflection of self as an achiever;

3. Help pupils learn to value the assessment of their performance and products by establishing a clear, positive relationship between evaluative processes and achievement;

4. Model the proper use of self-criticism and self-reward;

5. Clearly communicate and interpret the standards used for evaluating performances and products in the classroom;

6. Help pupils acquire and allow them to use evaluative skills;

7. Make individual improvement the value underlying competitive activity in the classroom; and

8. Associate teacher praise and criticism with specific elements of pupil performance, reinforcing the positive aspects and providing a basis for improving negative aspects of the pupil's work.

> **I discourage competition in the classroom. The only one I accept is the student's competition with himself. He has to compete against where he is, against where he wants to be, and against where he has been. I think every kid understands that. They don't have to prove anything to me. Each kid has to prove to himself that he's worthwhile. There's no cheating here. There's no reason for it.**

... If you con someone into learning, you really believe they're not capable of it. So we're straightforward. Our learning materials are very hard.

Pat Zimmerman—*Alternative School Teacher, S. Terkel 1974. Working, p. 490.*

REFERENCES

Ali, M. 1975. *The greatest: Muhammad Ali.* With Richard Durham. New York: Random House.

Roosevelt, E. 1961. *Autobiography of Eleanor Roosevelt.* New York: Harper & Row.

Rosengarten, T. 1974. *All God's dangers.* New York: Knopf.

Soares, A. T., and L. M. Soares 1969. Self-perceptions of culturally disadvantaged children. *American Educational Research Journal* **6:** 31–45.

THE SENSE OF AFFIRMATION, RECOGNITION, AND CONFIRMATION OF IMPACT

Teacher Behavior and Pupil Self-Evaluation

Catron, D. W. 1966. Educational-vocational group counseling: the effects of perception of self and others. *Journal of Counseling Psychology* **13:** 202–207.

Freeman, W., and A. Craig 1967. Discussion courses spur bright underachievers. *National Association of Secondary School Principals Bulletin* **51** (320): 22–35.

Ludwig, D., and M. Maehr 1967. Changes in self-concept and stated behavioral preferences. *Child Development* **38** (2): 453–468.

Russell, B. 1967. *The autobiography of Bertrand Russell.* Boston: Little, Brown.

Stimpson, D. V., and D. M. Pedersen 1970. Effects of a survival training experience upon evaluation of self and others for underachieving high school students. *Perceptual and Motor Skills* **31** (1): 337–338.

Werblo, D., and E. P. Torrance 1966. Experiences in historical research and changes in self-evaluations of gifted children. *Exceptional Children* **33:** 137–141.

Teacher Evaluation of Pupils and Pupil Self-Evaluation

Brophy, J., and T. Good 1972. *Teacher-student relationships: causes and consequences.* New York: Holt, Rinehart and Winston.

Gordon, I., and P. Wood 1973. Relationship between pupil self-evaluation, teacher evaluation of the pupil, and scholastic achievement. *Journal of Educational Research* **56** (8): 440–443.

Kaufman, B. 1964. *Up the down staircase.* Englewood Cliffs, N.J.: Prentice-Hall.

Lister, J., and M. Ohlsen 1962. *The effects of orientation to testing on motivation for and outcomes of test interpretation* (Cooperative Research Project No. 1344). Urbana: College of Education, University of Illinois.

Meichenbaum, D. H., K. Bowers, and R. Ross 1969. A behavioral analysis of teacher expectancy effect. *Journal of Personality and Social Psychology* **13** (4): 306–316.

Ohlsen, M. 1965. Increasing youth's self-understanding. *Educational Leadership* **22:** 239–241.

Willis, S. 1972. Formation of teacher's expectations of students' academic performance. Cited in J. Brophy and T. Good, *Teacher-student relationships: causes and consequences.* New York: Holt, Rinehart and Winston, p. 183.

Teacher Behavior as a Model for Pupil Self-Criticism and Self-Reward

Felker, D. W., and D. J. Stanwyck 1971. General self-concept and specific self-evaluation after an academic task. *Psychological Reports* **29** (1): 60–62.

————, D. J. Stanwyck, and R. Kay 1973. The effects of a teacher program in self-concept enhancement on pupils' self-concept, anxiety, and intellectual achievement responsibility. *Journal of Educational Research* **66** (10): 443–445.

Grusec, J. E., and S. A. Ezrin 1972. Techniques of punishment and the development of self-criticism. *Child Development* **43** (4): 1273–1288. (ERIC Document Reproduction Service No. EJ 067 151.)

Herbert, E. S., D. Gelfand, and D. Hartmann 1969. Imitation and self-esteem as determinants of self-critical behavior. *Child Development* **40** (2): 421–430. (ERIC Document Reproduction Service No. EJ 005 958.)

Liebert, R. M., M. Hanratty, and J. Hill 1969. Effects of rule structure and training method on the adoption of a self-imposed standard. *Child Development* **40** (1): 93–101. (ERIC Document Reproduction Service No. EJ 003 058.)

Liebert, R. M., and J. P. Ora, Jr. 1968. Children's adoption of self-reward patterns: incentive level and method of transmission. *Child Development* **39:** 527–536.

Thelen, M. H. 1970. Long-term retention of verbal imitation. *Developmental Psychology* **3** (1): 29–31.

Welk, L. 1971. *Wunnerful, wunnerful! The autobiography of Lawrence Welk,* with Bernice McGeehan. Englewood Cliffs, N.J.: Prentice-Hall.

Teacher Behavior and Pupil Status Related to Self-Esteem

Ahlbrand, W. P., Jr., and J. A. Reynolds 1972. Some social effects of cross-grade grouping. *Elementary School Journal* **72** (6): 327–332. (ERIC Document Reproduction Service No. EJ 055 107.)

Angelou, M. 1969. *I know why the caged bird sings.* New York: Random House.

Blain, M. J., and M. Ramirez 1968. Increasing sociometric rank, meaningfulness, and discriminability of children's names through reinforcement and interaction. *Child Development* **39** (3): 949–955.

Buswell, M. 1953. The relationship between the social structure of the classroom and the academic success of the pupils. *Journal of Experimental Education* **22:** 37–52.

Finney, B. C., and E. Van Dalsem 1969. Group counseling for gifted underachieving high school students. *Journal of Counseling Psychology* **16** (1): 89–94. (ERIC Document Reproduction Service No. EJ 002 049.)

Halpin, G., G. M. Halpin, and D. Hartley 1972. The effects of classroom guidance programs on sociometric status of second grade pupils. *Elementary School Guidance and Counseling* **6** (4): 227–231. (ERIC Document Reproduction Service No. EJ 958 297.)

St. Augustine. 1935. *Augustine: confessions and enchiridion,* Vol. VII. Albert Cook Outler (ed.). Philadelphia: Westminster Press, 1955.

Webster, S. W. 1965. Some correlates of reported academically supportive behaviors of Negro mothers toward their children. *Journal of Negro Education* **34:** 114–120.

Teacher Behavior and Pupil Self-Confidence

Angelou, M. 1969. *I know why the caged bird sings.* New York: Random House.

Baumrind, D. 1972. An exploratory study of socialization effects on black children: some black-white comparisons. *Child Development* **43** (1): 261–267. (ERIC Document Reproduction Service No. EJ 055 656.)

Bishop, B., and L. Beckman 1971. Developmental conformity. *Developmental Psychology* **5** (3): 536.

Bronfenbrenner, U. 1970. Some reflections on "antecedents of optimal psychological adjustment." *Journal of Counseling and Clinical Psychology* **35** (3): 296–297.

Landry, R. G., E. Schilson, and E. Pardew 1974. Self-concept enhancement in a preschool program. *Journal of Experimental Education* **42** (4): 39–43.

Miller, D. R. 1970. Optimal psychological adjustment: a relativistic interpretation. *Journal of Counseling and Clinical Psychology* **35** (3): 290–295.

Russell, B. 1967. *The autobiography of Bertrand Russell.* Boston: Little, Brown.

Siegelman, E., J. Block, J. Block, and A. von der Lippe 1970. Antecedents of optimal psychological adjustment. *Journal of Consulting and Clinical Psychology* **35** (3): 283–297.

Teacher Behavior and Pupil Cooperation and Competition

Anderson, G. J. 1970. Effects of classroom social climate on individual learning. *American Educational Research Journal* **7** (2): 135–152.

Calonico, J. M., and B. A. Calonico 1972. Classroom interaction: a sociological approach. *Journal of Educational Research* **66** (4): 165–168.

Harvey, O. J., M. Prather, J. B. White, and J. K. Hoffmeister 1968. Teacher's beliefs, classroom atmosphere, and student behavior. *American Educational Research Journal* **5** (2): 151–166.

Kagan, S., and M. C. Madsen 1971. Cooperation and competition of Mexican, Mexican-American, and Anglo-American children of two ages under four instructional sets. *Developmental Psychology* **5** (1): 32–39.

Maurer, D. C. 1968. Team learning: how did you work number five? *Today's Education* **57**: 63–64.

McClintock, C. G., and J. M. Nuttin, Jr. 1969. Development of competitive game behavior in children across two cultures. *Journal of Experimental Social Psychology* **5** (2): 203–218. (ERIC Document Reproduction Service No. EJ 003 430.)

Nelson, L., and M. C. Madsen 1969. Cooperation and competition in four-year-olds as a function of reward contingency and subculture. *Developmental Psychology* **1** (4): 340–344.

Richmond, B., and G. Weiner 1973. Cooperation and competition among young children as a function of ethnic grouping, grade, sex, and reward condition. *Journal of Educational Psychology* **64** (3): 329–334. (ERIC Document Reproduction Service No., EJ 078 965.)

Terkel, S. 1974. *Working.* New York: Pantheon.

Torrance, E. P. 1971. "Structure" can improve the group behavior of five-year-old children. *Elementary School Journal* **72** (2): 102–106. (ERIC Document Reproduction Service No. EJ 049 937.)

TEACHER BEHAVIOR AND THE SENSE OF SELF-ESTEEM

Terkel, S. 1974. *Working.* New York: Pantheon.

CHAPTER 7
The Sense of Self-Image

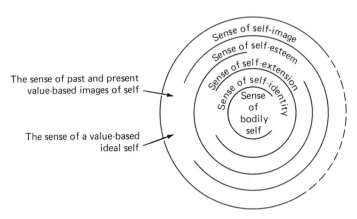

The sense of past and present value-based images of self

The sense of a value-based ideal self

Sense of self-image
Sense of self-esteem
Sense of self-extension
Sense of self-identity
Sense of bodily self

Fig. 7.1 Self-image of the general self-concept.

The Sense of Self-Image is the psychological construct representing perceptions of self formed from the *dominant values* (including standards, beliefs, and goals) of and for the self. All self-images, past, present, or future-oriented, reflect the value system of the individual and the circumstances and conditions he or she has experienced. Since value, circumstances, and conditions are all subject to change, so is the Self-Image. The Sense of Self-Image can be likened to an album of self-portraits, sometimes candid, sometimes posed. Those that are candid are more objective and insightful; those that are posed are more suggestive and ideal. Some are detailed, some are enlarged, and all are close-ups.

This does not mean, however, that there are no persistent features characterizing the many images of self. When values persist, images persist. And when a particular hierarchy of values persists, the Sense of Self-Image orchestrates from that hierarchy a dominant theme, or leitmotif, which characterizes the behavior or life style of the individual.

Nate Shaw, for example, maintained throughout his life, in a variety of circumstances, an image of himself as an intelligent, autonomous, and honorable man:

> I was a game peacock, uneducated boy that I was, and I had many
> things in my mind that was pointin to my advancement regardless of

223

education. I'd been here long enough. I'd been trusted by people and I never had had no trouble and everybody seemed to think well of me.

Nate Shaw in T. Rosengarten 1974. All God's dangers, *p. 83.*

Nate's value for independence and his image of self as a competent man pervade his autobiography. Yet, however clear and persistent Nate's self-image may seem, we must remember that it is inferred from our knowledge of his Senses of Bodily Self, Self-Identity, Self-Extension, and Self-Esteem. Of all the Senses of Self comprising the General Self-Concept, Self-Image has the most idiosyncratic content. We cannot hypothesize the essence of this construct of self unless we know the content of the other self-constructs.

Nor can we hypothesize, analyze, interpret, or describe the Self-Image of another without assuming a culturally biased philosophical stance. Self-Image is most commonly described as "positive," "negative," "realistic," or "unrealistic"—terms rooted in a cultural base. A positive self-image, for example, is one which, in the observer's view, reflects the presence of culturally approved attitudes and beliefs about the "self." And a realistic self-image is a view of self that coincides with culturally dictated and uniformly accepted standards or behavioral conventions—a view of self congruent with "society's" perception of the particular individual in question. Theoretically, in order for children to acquire a positive perception of self, significant others within the behavioral dialogue must provide them with acceptance and positive reflection. In order to acquire a realistic construct of self and therefore a realistic Self-Image, children must receive accurate and complete feedback from significant others and the environment, which enables them to associate their attributes and behaviors with their consequent impact.

The formation of a realistic Self-Image also requires a knowledge of culturally defined and approved roles as well as the acquisition of societal standards and values. Therefore, any attempt to measure or interpret self-image must take into account the cultural influences acting upon the target individual or population. Data produced without regard to cultural milieu may identify differences related to cultural values and psychological experiences rather than positive, negative, realistic, or unrealistic dimensions of self-concept, particularly the value-based sense of self-image.

What is "known" about an individual's self-image is usually learned by assessing and interpreting his or her performance and products. From these two sources of information, the individual's particular characteristics and beliefs about self are inferred. This process is, of course, two steps removed from the real, operating self-image of the individual—first by the intrusion of the observer's *subjectivity*, which amplifies, diminishes, or filters out certain characteristics and behaviors, and second by the observer's *objectivity,* which allows him or her to see the performance and the product but not the observed individual's perception and interpretation of that performance and product. In assessing behavior, the observer may come to know something that is unknown to the performer. This knowledge, however, cannot become a part of the performer's Self-Image until it is known to the performer too. And knowing something is not simply a matter of hearing it: the information must also be accepted and valued.

How one wishes to be seen determines the hierarchical value system of the Self-Image, which incorporates standards for Bodily Self, Self-Identity, Self-Esteem, and Self-Extension to form an internalized model of an Ideal Self. The Ideal Self may be realistic or unrealistic in relation to objective standards used to estimate the individual's potential for achieving the ideal. The young Maya Angelou's (1969) ideal physical self, with long blond hair and light blue eyes, was totally unrealistic for a little black girl "with nappy black hair, broad feet and a space between her teeth that would hold a number two pencil." Eleanor Roosevelt's Ideal Self, defined by her father's request that she be "truthful, loyal, brave, and well educated," was more realistic. Eleanor made herself "as the years went on into a fairly good copy of the picture he had painted."

Eleanor Roosevelt, in fact, succinctly illustrates the power of the significant other in establishing values and standards for individuals who perceive themselves as only conditionally accepted and approved.

> **I had a bad habit of biting my nails. In short order that was noticed by Mlle. Samaia, who set out to cure me. It seemed a hopeless task, but one day I was rereading some letters of my father's, which I always carried with me, and I came across one in which he spoke of making the most of one's personal appearance, and from that day forward my nails were allowed to grow.**
>
> *Eleanor Roosevelt 1961.* Autobiography of Eleanor Roosevelt, *p. 24.*

The Ideal Self is revealed in the Performing Self when the individual wishes to be "seen as" a person possessing certain prized characteristics and attributes. Wishing to be "seen as" demands an audience and, like any staged performance, often requires behavioral exaggeration to ensure that the viewers don't miss the point. The child's concept of social roles, manifest in the imitation of mother, father, or baby, or the child's concept of social stereotypes (such as cowboy, Indian, or fireman), manifest in play behavior, emphasizes the importance of social environment in the formation of the Ideal Self. During adolescence, a similar kind of role play can be observed as teenagers "try on" different behaviors and appearances selected from the environment and valued for their perceived effect.

In some instances, the Ideal Self may arise from perceived inadequacies of the self, and striving toward that Ideal Self may be a compensatory behavior that exacts a high toll in energy. Such striving may force a narrow focus on one aspect of self-concept development, to the detriment of other facets of self.

Helen Keller's editor, John A. Macy, observed that Helen had all her life "been trying to be 'like other people.' " And Helen Keller herself left no doubt that, at least in one respect, Macy's insight into her self-image was correct (Keller 1968, p. 171). In her letters, Helen wrote:

> ... Oh, Carrie, how I should like to speak like other people! I should be willing to work night and day if it could only be accomplished. Think what a joy it would be to all of my friends to hear me speak naturally! !
>
> *Helen Keller 1968.* The story of my life, *p. 262.*

And later:

> ... You know it has long been my ambition to go to Radcliffe, and receive a degree, as many other girls have done; but Dean Irwin of Radcliffe ... showed me how very foolish it would be for me to pursue a four years' course of study at Radcliffe, simply to be like other girls, when I might better be cultivating whatever ability I had for writing. ... I found it hard, very hard, to give up the idea of going to college; it had been in my mind ever since I was a little girl. ...
>
> *Helen Keller 1968.* The story of my life, *p. 296.*

The desire to be "seen as" can also represent an acknowledgment of social standards and values present in the environmental milieu. For Muhammad Ali, boxing was the way to prove that "there was something inside of me capable of victory," in his social circumstances, the way from the back door to the top of the world. His Ideal Self demanded that he be "seen as" the heavyweight champion.

> ... I have gotten there just in time to hear the announcer crying out above the noise, "And still the Heavyweight Champion of the World, Rocky Marciano!"
>
> A cold chill shoots through my bones. I have never heard anything that affected me like those words: "Heavyweight Champion of the World." *All* the world? And from that day on I want to hear that said about me.
>
> *Muhammad Ali 1975.* The greatest, Muhammad Ali, *p. 50.*

The Ideal Self can also take the "wish to be" (rather than to be "seen as") form, in which case it generally prompts the assumption of a cultural role or vocational choice, stereotyped functions of which encapsulate the prized values and standards. Fulfillment of the wish "to be" a doctor, lawyer, teacher, or mother requires not only an image of self in the role but also the ability and opportunity to perform the role. "Wish to be" ideals are often unrealistic and unrealizable in the face of environmental circumstances. Cultural values dictating sex, race, and socioeconomic roles sometimes stand obdurately in the path of achievement. Or, the values of significant others create similar obstacles.

The opposition of Lawrence Welk's father to his son's decision to become a musician was in one sense an obstacle to the fulfillment of that ambition, since it promoted guilt, and in another sense, it was an incentive to succeed.

> ... "A traveling musician ... no ... that's not the life for you, Lawrence. ... Stay on the farm. You can always make a living here. If you leave home and try the music business you'll be back here begging for a meal in six months' time!"
>
> I would never have contradicted my father, but I knew I would starve before I would ever do that.
>
> Lawrence Welk 1971. Wunnerful, wunnerful!, p. 47.

The significant other's role is to supply the developing self with valid information that facilitates the formation of adequate and accurate perceptions and values of and for the self. When these perceptions and values are ordered to form a Self-Image, they will provide a basis for realistic goals and ideals and positive standards for self and society.

THE SENSE OF PAST AND PRESENT VALUE-BASED IMAGES OF SELF

> Polonius: This above all—to thine own self be true,
>   And it must follow, as the night the day,
>   Thou canst not then be false to any man.
>
> Hamlet, I:iii, William Shakespeare.

Although, as we have stated, Self-Image has of all the five Senses of Self the most idiosyncratic content, there are several general image patterns that we can identify by hypothesizing particular values and circumstances. At the top of the hierarchy of positive values are concepts of self incorporating the traits and attributes from which the individual has received or expects to receive the most positive or self-affirming recognition. And at the top of the hierarchy of negative values are concepts of self incorporating traits and attributes from which the individual has received or expects to receive the most negative or adverse recognition. The Sense of Self-Extension operates with these two systems to derive from conditions and circumstances reflections of self that are most congruent and least dissonant with the existing image of self.

The man who perceives that his most valuable image is that of the physically powerful male or performing athlete may perpetuate this impression whenever possible. If this self-image rests on a triumphant experience in the past (such as a 95-yard kickoff return to score the winning touchdown in a football game) it may trap and limit the individual: he may spend a major part of his life trying to maintain the image and recreate the circumstances. In the same way, a woman whose greatest affirmation and impact on the environment has stemmed from youthful beauty may find the task of maintaining her image and replicating her impact an equally consuming focus of life. Since athletic prowess and youthful beauty have a tendency to diminish, so do the experiences of affirmation predicated on these valued attributes.

The admonition of Shakespeare's Polonius to be true "to thine own self" is particularly difficult when, at least theoretically and empirically, there are so many opportunities in our daily experience to change our perceptions of "self." The potential for self-image change is always present when a variety of experiences incorporate different values and standards.

The most comprehensive and accurate view of another's operating self-image is gained through lengthy observation of and close association with the subject under a great variety of circumstances. Concern for such extensive knowledge of an individual's self-image, however, is generally reserved for intimate personal or therapist/patient relationships. Here we are more concerned about the role Self-Image plays as the source of perception in the teacher/pupil relationship under specific classroom circumstances.

Though the verbal and physical behavior of individuals is generally considered the most reliable indicator of Self-Image in everyday circumstances, self-report instruments designed to tap attitude and belief systems and projective techniques requiring professional interpretation have been developed to aid researchers in organizing verbal avenues to Self-Image. Without the use of several sources of data, however, it is difficult to tell whether subjects are reporting their actual beliefs and attitudes, or what they think their beliefs and attitudes should be (which offers insight into their perception of social values). Both of these response sets are related to Self-Image, but when they are used interchangeably, they confuse data collection and interpretation.

In an experimental situation, pretest measures of self-image taken to establish a benchmark could well produce a social desirability (i.e., "I ought to think or be") response from both control and experimental subjects. If the experimental group were then given a treatment that encouraged and approved free expression of feelings and perceptions, subsequent comparison of the two groups on posttest measures might well indicate a "loss" of positive self-image among experimental subjects. Rather than reflecting failure of the treatment, such group differences might simply suggest more honest, self-referent reporting by experimental subjects. This would, in fact, be quite likely if the treatment period was long enough to produce the security required for honest self-reporting, but too short to allow subjects sufficient time to resolve their exposed feelings.

Program effects can be misinterpreted in the opposite direction when the treatment gives subjects increased awareness of valued responses and greater familiarity with specialized vocabularies. This is particularly apt to occur in programs with affective objectives requiring that everyone understand and use specific terminology. Self-reports may improve with or without real change in self-perception. This is especially true when test items are not referenced to the subject's cultural background. When, for example, high scores on independence and competence are equated with a "positive" self-concept, middle-class children may appear to have less "positive" self-images than their lower-class counterparts, who, according to the standards of their culture, may have achieved a good deal of competence and independence. However, when test items deal with complex verbal behaviors, the self-image of middle-class children may appear quite positive in comparison to that of the lower-class subjects.

It is unlikely that middle-class children will be placed in an environment where values, standards, constructs, and behaviors are totally discontinuous with those they have thus far experienced. The probability that lower-class children will experience such discontinuity is much higher. Differences in cultural values and standards are not generally known or considered by a developing self; they are psychologically experienced only when one is confronted with them. Such confrontations have the potential for altering the self-image of the individual. The schooling experience has the potential to change how children see themselves, how they think others see them, and how they would like to be seen.

TEACHER BEHAVIOR AND PUPIL SELF-IMAGE

The teacher behaviors outlined in a study by Staines (1958) represent an almost ideal model of the teacher's role as a significant or salient other who performs the functions of reflecting, interpreting, and informing in the behavioral dialogue of the classroom.

On the premise that self-concepts are learned structures derived from interaction with others and the environment, Staines formed two hypotheses relating the role of the teacher to the self-image of the pupil. The first of these stated that teachers could be distinguished according to their use of pupil self-referencing comments. The second hypothesis stated that change in academic performance and in pupil self-image could be achieved through teaching.

To test the first hypothesis, two pairs of teachers, one at the junior high level and the other at the primary level, were observed, and their comments were recorded for positive, negative, neutral, or ambiguous effect on the Known Self, Other Self, and Ideal Self of pupils. (The effect of specific verbal behaviors was determined by three professional judges.) The categories that most clearly differentiated individual teachers and teacher pairs were: comments on pupil performance, status, values, and wants, and comments pertaining to classroom management. Primary teachers were further differentiated by their comments regarding pupil physique, pupil traits, and pupil self-orientation. Units of each teacher's commenting behavior were analyzed, and the content was related to the following core dimensions of self: salience (a measure of self-consciousness); differentiation (the degree to which self-concepts have been developed and defined by the self); potency (self-adequacy); integrity (self-predictability); insight (the relationship of self-concept to reality); and self-acceptance and rejection (the congruence between the perceived and ideal self). Profiles constructed from scores on these dimensions produced diverse descriptions of teacher styles, suggesting that teachers differ in their effect on pupil self-concept.

In testing his second hypothesis (that teachers can teach toward both academic and pupil self-image change), Staines used only the two junior level classrooms. He described the experimental teacher as having a teaching style and an attitude toward pupils that would have positive impact on pupil self-concept. This teacher, on the basis of several self-construct measures, set self-image improvement goals for each pupil. The teacher also used instructional methods and curricula that provided the events through which pupils could be helped to achieve these affective goals—an illustration of the teacher's assessment expertise being used as a diagnostic and therapeutic tool.

Goals for the Other Self included giving pupils the opportunity to see themselves as purposeful, discriminating individuals, responsible for monitoring and evaluating their own task achievement. Objectives for the Ideal Self were aimed at helping pupils acquire realistic and appropriate aspirations and, for the Known Self, at encouraging pupils toward self-acceptance by recognizing their successes. The teacher's role was to affirm each pupil as a worthy, achieving class member and to attend to each child's status needs. In addition to planning instructional methods, the teacher also evaluated pupil performance and products, giving detailed, constructive feedback that avoided the use of single words such as "good" or "wrong." This process was intended to provide cognitive content from which each pupil could acquire the concepts and behaviors necessary to achieve his or her goals.

Results of this study indicated a highly significant difference between experimental and control subjects on the two self dimensions, differentiation and certainty. According to Staines, these differences represent a gain in "psychological security" among experimental pupils. They might also be interpreted as indicating a move toward less distorted, more realistic self-perception, since experimental pupils were able to assess themselves in less extreme terms and to describe the "boundaries" of self with more certainty. However, as much as we would like to, we cannot wholeheartedly accept either or both of these interpretations without considering the results of this study in relation to other research findings.

The pivotal dimensions in the Staines study, Differentiation and Certainty, were also the source of differences found between experimental and control subjects in an investigation by Chadwick (1966), in which experimental teachers had been trained to use positive commenting behavior in their interaction with teenage pupils. This would seem to confirm the relationship between the teacher's positive commenting and pupil Differentiation and Certainty. Considering this in conjunction with Gordon and Wood's (1963) finding that teachers' distorted perceptions of pupils were reflected, though more broadly, in pupil self-reports, it may well be that teachers who intentionally use positive commenting tend to refrain from making negative or exaggerated pupil-referenced remarks. Since the experimental pupils in both the Staines and Chadwick studies shifted toward more moderate self-assessments, we can infer that they were receiving more accurate and positive self-reflections in the comments of their teachers. Or, alternatively, we can infer that these pupils were simply reflecting the verbal patterns modeled by their teachers. If the experimental teachers in the Staines and Chadwick studies became more aware during training of their effect on pupil self-concept, they may have used, interpreted, and defined self-concept terminology in daily classroom interaction more frequently than control teachers. The Certainty dimension may reflect pupil awareness of terms and definitions used by the teacher rather than change in self-perception, self-image, or psychological security and thus may demonstrate a cognitive rather than an affective gain, or perhaps both.

In Chadwick's study, the affective variables of greatest importance were acceptance, moral values, and physical appearance—concerns typically associated with teenagers. The significance of these variables provides insight into the primary values and, in turn, the operating Sense of Self-Image of pupils in this sample. Improvement on these dimensions, that is, increased friendships and social activity, as well as greater measured congruence between perceived self and ideal self, could be viewed as a reflection of positive change in pupil self-image since these variables were directly related to the value systems of these teenage subjects.

Griggs and Bonney (1970), hypothesizing that knowledge of the causes of behavior would make pupils more accepting of or friendly toward one another and would help them achieve a greater congruence between their perceived and ideal selves, administered a program of behavioral dynamics to fourth and fifth graders. Program materials consisted of paperback booklets used in conjunction with discussion, role play, and story completion techniques. After four months, results indicated that pupils in the experimental groups had made significant gains on "friendship." Measures of congruence between ideal and perceived image reached significance in only one of the two experimental groups, although scores for the other experimental subjects were in the correct direction, and according to the authors probably would have reached significance if the program had continued for a longer period of time.

The teacher's role as a source of information about behaviors, values, and personal relationships is important to pupils. Therefore, teachers and researchers should address and investigate the actual concerns of pupils, concerns that reflect operating values, when they plan programs or studies involving pupil self-image.

Furthermore, if objectives in the affective domain are to be successfully achieved and measured, they must be related to observable pupil performance. If teachers are to design and plan classroom activities to provide opportunities through which pupils can achieve positive self-image change, they must also constantly evaluate these activities, modify them if necessary, and document their effectiveness to aid in formulating new programs. Observed and recorded change in pupil participation, contributions, self-initiated and goal-directed activity, productivity, and constructive self-criticism or self-evaluation can be interpreted as change in the Performing Self. Whether the behavior observed is directed toward academic or social goals, it can reflect positive change in pupil self-perception and increased valuing of self in the pupil role, and, as such, can be considered evidence of a changing Self-Image.

TEACHER MODELING BEHAVIORS AND PUPIL ADOPTION OF STANDARDS

In their role as advisors, guides, and evaluators, teachers can help pupils set goals appropriate to their abilities and then help them acquire goal-related skills and goal-directed behaviors. When goals, and the values associated with them, are set by the instructor, the school, or the society, the teacher's job is to communicate and help students meet the behavioral standards prescribed for them. In order to help pupils acquire a value for goals set by others, teachers must link these goals with the behaviors and skills needed to achieve them and with the positive impact on significant others and the environment which accompanies such achievement.

Skills and behaviors that bring approval from others are sometimes valued simply for that approval and sometimes for their instrumentality in achieving desired goals. In either case, the teacher's role is to reflect the positive impact of pupil performance and to organize classroom events to create an arena in which pupils can test their acquired skills and behaviors in psychological safety. The experiences provided in the classroom behavioral dialogue can offer children reinforcement and reinterpretation of their roles by allowing them the opportunity to reassess their power to control and direct their own behavior toward positive impact and an improved self-image.

Modeling—that is, performing a behavior under the observation of others who may or may not imitate the behavior modeled—is one way in which the teacher can communicate to pupils prescribed behaviors and skills. Of course, as a teaching technique, modeling involves the performance of behavior *intended* for adoption by the observing pupils. However, unless the modeled behavior is further clarified by examples of contrasting behavior or by verbal communication, modeling stimulates only an associative process of behavior acquisition. Through modeling, the teacher demonstrates "how to" respond to a specific problem in a specific situation.

The initial impact of the modeled behavior depends on the value system of the observers and their perception of the purpose and usefulness of the behavior. The associative process can be strengthened by modeling the same behavior in the same situation consistently over a period of time, and the concept of generalizability can be introduced by modeling the same behavior in similar but not identical situations. Modeling constitutes a behavioral monologue, and the effectiveness of the modeled behavior as a means of communication cannot be ascertained without evidence of its adoption by the audience. Within the behavioral dialogue, modeling becomes dialogical as the developing self adopts and imitates the modeled behavior and receives approval for its appropriate use or disapproval for its inappropriate application. Imitated behavior that does not meet with disapproval gains tacit approval until more specific evaluation is provided.

When behavior is modeled only through motor acts, there is considerable room for misinterpretation. The model depends on the context of his or her performance to communicate purpose and intent. But context and, therefore, definition of the modeled behavior, is to some extent determined by the perception of the observer. When motor acts are accompanied by explication of context, purpose, or intent (or all three), the model has greater control over the observer's perception of the behavior—which should enhance the instructional value of modeling. But explication does not entirely remove the idiosyncratic effects of perception. Thus, in examining the efficacy of any instructional method, factors related to variations in individual perception must be considered.

The adoption of modeled behavior depends primarily on the observer's perception of two power relationships: (1) the model's power in relation to the observer's power; and (2) the power of the behavior to achieve a particular effect. The modeled behavior may be imitated on the basis of the model's perceived value and authority, the kind of value and authority with which significant others are imbued. When this is the case, there may be an unquestioning acceptance of the behavior, with or without an understanding of its purpose and effect. Or the modeled behavior may be imitated because of its perceived value in producing a given effect, regardless of the model's identity or power.

Theoretically, we can expect significant correlation between the level and extent of behavior adoption in a group, and the degree of group homogeneity in regard to the characteristics affecting perception. Pupils of the same age, sex, socioeconomic status, culture, or race, for example, may show similar tendencies to imitate and adopt certain behaviors.

Research on modeling has focused primarily on its effectiveness relative to or in conjunction with direct instruction in helping pupils adopt standards and behaviors that have moral value. Though the teacher's effectiveness as a modeling agent has not been as thoroughly investigated, researchers have drawn inferences for classroom teachers from studies conducted outside the classroom. Underlying these inferences is the assumption that the teacher is equivalent to the parent, or, more often, that the investigator is equivalent to the parent or the teacher as a modeling agent. Although all of the studies reported in this section used elementary school pupils, only one, described below, was conducted in a classroom setting.

Feshbach and Feshbach (1972) report the effects of modeling by white, female teachers on stated preferences of black and Caucasian male pupils of average intelligence ranging in age from 9 to 12 years.

In the initial phase of this study, both control and experimental subjects were asked to rank ten animal pictures in order of personal preference. Four pictures from the middle preference range were enlarged, along with pictures of two other animals, and displayed in the two experimental classrooms for one week. The teachers in both experimental classrooms made specified positive comments about two preselected animals and negative remarks about the other two animals chosen from the preference listing. The comments, which took a moralistic tone designating the animals as "nice" or "not nice," failed to include reasons for the judgments rendered. Control pupils were exposed to neither the displayed pictures nor the teacher comments. After five days, the pictures were removed from the experimental classrooms, and all subjects were retested on the preference sort.

Results of the testing indicated that preference shifts among white experimental subjects did not differ significantly from those among the controls. Black experimental subjects, however, demonstrated a move toward teacher-modeled preferences that was significantly greater than that of the control group—a move which, according to Feshbach and Feshbach, illustrates the general power of teacher modeling. Since white experimental subjects were not significantly influenced by the modeling behavior of their teachers, the conclusion that these data demonstrate the teacher's ability to influence pupil attitudes through brief expression of opinions unrelated to curriculum objectives is completely dependent on the scores of black subjects. The investigators contrast the significant imitative behavior of these black subjects with that exhibited by other black males in previous research by Portuges and Feshbach (1972). In that study, eight- to ten-year-old black males in a mixed sample showed the least (and statistically nonsignificant) imitative behavior following exposure to filmed, white teacher models. Explaining these contradictory findings, Feshbach and Feshbach cite differences in the meaning of imitation from one study to the other. In the study using filmed models, imitation was assumed to reflect pupil preference for positive or negative types of teacher reinforcement. In the study of shifts in preference for animals, the imitative behavior was supposed to reflect conforming tendencies. Feshbach and Feshbach suggest that the insecurity of the subjects and the authority of the model may have been the dominant factor in producing imitative, conforming behavior among blacks in the second study.

This explanation would be more acceptable if the statements made by teachers in this study had communicated *only* preference (e.g., "I like turtles so much more than giraffes."). The insecurity demonstrated by the black subjects may have been related less to the power of the model (a condition that can be presumed for both black and white pupils) than to the content of the modeled behavior itself. Black subjects may have responded to the differentiating cues of "nice" and "not nice," not as a teacher preference or opinion, but as a *fact* of complex, white middle-class morality. White pupils, who perhaps recognized that the designations "nice" and "not nice" were arbitrary, remained unaffected by the teacher's cues. Black pupils, then, may have been more intent upon aligning themselves with whatever was considered "nice" by white middle-class standards than upon conforming to the teacher's stated preference for one animal over another. Apparently none of the pupils questioned the teacher's pronouncements. Yet, even if they were receiving and responding to her message, not all of them were internalizing it: only the black boys reached the point of significant valuing in the process of internalization. If the teacher's remarks had been more personally referenced, we might agree with the conclusion that pupil responses indicated a measure of conformity and dependence. Since they were not, however, we endorse the alternative explanation that black boys in this classroom perceived the teacher as a salient other who was providing information at a cognitive level (i.e., the classification of moral values held by white, middle-class people). The teacher's perceived power in the dialogue sanctioned the content of her message, and the pupils' value for a "good" and "nice" self-image motivated their responses in the absence of other discriminating criteria.

We have consistently stressed the critical role of valuing in the formation of self-concepts. The Sense of Self-Image is a part of the process of acquiring values, forming value concepts, maintaining value-images, and applying value judgments, but it is also the product of this process. When we examine one particular aspect of the process, such as adoption of standards, we cannot disregard the role of the individual's existing value hierarchy, which, of course, influences his or her perception and interpretation of his or her experiences. What the teacher perceives as a lesson, or what the researcher perceives as a study, the pupil perceives as an experience.

In examining the following studies, we have attempted to perceive the pupil's experience as he or she did and to identify the value concepts operating to influence his or her behavior.

Allen and Liebert (1969) investigated the effects of *modeling* versus *reporting* deviant practices on the imitative behavior of third and fourth grade pupils who had previously been given strict standards regarding the behavior in question. The female investigator, identifying herself as the representative of a toy company, briefly showed each subject how to play a bowling game and how to work an accompanying token dispenser to be used for self-rewarding. She then "explicitly instructed" each child that tokens were to be taken only for scores of 20 "because 20 is a good score and deserves a token." She also informed the subjects that tokens could be redeemed for prizes. The children were not told, however, that their scores would be dictated by a preset scoring device.

After these instructional preliminaries, three treatment groups and a control group were formed. The three treatments given were: (1) deviant symbolic modeling, in which a male model announced to the subjects that he had just played the game and had rewarded himself for scores of 15 as well as 20; (2) deviant live modeling, in which the model played the game in the presence of the subjects, rewarded himself for scores of 15 and 20, and gave verbal explanations of his behavior (e.g., "Fifteen, I'll take a token for 15," or "Five, I won't take a token for 5."); and (3) deviant symbolic and live modeling in which the model first told the subjects that he had rewarded himself for scores of 15 and 20, and then played a game in their presence, actually rewarding himself for scores of 15 and 20. In each treatment condition, the model then left the room, and each experimental subject played the game "alone" while being secretly observed. Subjects in the control group, who had been exposed to no modeling, apparently played the game by themselves without further instruction or demonstration.

Treatment conditions were designed on the assumption that there is a difference in the information value of live and symbolic modeling, and (in our opinion) on the additional assumption that instructions given briefly and "explicitly" are in fact learned by the subject. And results of the study, as anticipated and interpreted by the investigators, indicated that *observation* of deviant behavior did reduce adherence to the "learned" standard more than *announcement* of deviant behavior. Although both the verbal and combined verbal/communication modeling conditions significantly diminished fidelity to the standard, the latter did so to a significantly greater extent than the former. The authors attribute these findings to the differential information value of the three treatment conditions.

This particular study offers an excellent context for a discussion of the need to consider pupil perception in research design. If we are to obtain cumulative information on the effectiveness of behavior modeling, research reports must document rather thoroughly exactly what happened to whom. Considering the Allen and Liebert study from the pupils' point of view, one can see that it presented three "how to" behaviors to be mastered by each subject: (1) How to play the game; (2) How to score the game; and (3) How to operate the reward-dispensing machine. In regard to the first of these behaviors, bowling, though basically a middle-class game, may or may not have been familiar to most of these subjects. Yet even if understanding the game were an issue, the preset scoring device removed any real necessity for actually acquiring or exhibiting skilled behavior. Each child's performance was controlled, in spite of his or her skill. Yet the children could only perceive their scores as the result of their skill or lack of it, a perception which may have affected their self-rewarding behaviors. If some of the children already had positive concepts of their game-playing skills, for example, they may have been influenced to reward themselves in order to maintain their own standards or perhaps their need to be winners. After all, it was only a game being tested by a distant company.

The second behavior, "How to score the game," required that the subjects in both the control and the symbolic modeling groups recognize the numeral "20" and associate it with the reward condition. Subjects in the live and combined modeling groups could either recognize the numeral "20" or identify it by position since the model announced his scores during the demonstration game. Subjects in these two groups had four opportunities to note the location of 15 and 20 point scores during the model's game.

The third behavior, "How to reward," required that the subject operate the token dispenser by pressing the button and taking the released token. Subjects exposed to live modeling received additional demonstration of how, and when, to operate the token dispenser. Thus the control and experimental group means for rewarding scores of 20 actually represent differences in the informational value of direct instruction (the control group), direct instruction with verbal reinforcement (the symbolic modeling group), and direct instruction with verbal reinforcement and demonstration (the live and combined live and symbolic groups). The control group showed the lowest *rate* of self-reward—that is, control subjects didn't reward themselves when they "deserved" to. The symbolically reinforced group had a relatively higher rate of self-reward, while the remaining groups attained the highest possible self-reward rates for scores of 20. Rate of self-reward in the control group, however, does not necessarily reflect adherence to the "previously learned stringent standard" as the investigators maintain; it more likely indicates observance of a "previously explicated rule."

Furthermore, because the investigators analyzed data concerning reward behavor for scores of 15 and 20 only, we have no specific information about the children's self-rewarding activity for other scores. Although we are told that approximately 80 percent of the subjects did not reward themselves for scores "under 15 and 10," we are not told the identity of those who did. It would be interesting to know if the control subjects accounted for a significant proportion of the 20 percent who rewarded low scores.

Among the differences in pupil perception which may contribute to differential adoption of modeled behavior are those involving the power of the model and/or the power of the demonstrated behavior to produce an effect. Considering the research design employed by Allen and Liebert, and the roles they played in the experiment, one can ask, "How might the pupil have perceived these adults?" Perhaps from the child's point of view, "There was a lady from the toy company who told me about the game and a man from the toy company who knew how to play it." The fact that the male model rewarded himself for a score of 15 immediately after the "toy company lady" admonished subjects to reward only scores of 20 may have been interpreted by the children as evidence of a lapse in the woman's knowledge of the game and therefore as corrective, not contradictory, behavior on the male model's part. The subjects perhaps perceived the two adults as a single source of information from the toy company and did not concern themselves with discriminating between the power of the two models. On the other hand, if the children saw the adults as separate powers, at least two sources of perceptual variation were present: (1) the sex difference between the models, which some children may have viewed in light of the social implication that men are to be obeyed before women; and (2) evidence that the male model was the one who knew how to play and score the game and dispense rewards. Within this framework, there were any number of ways (in all treatment conditions) to interpret the model's behavior—and to devise a rationale for including 15 as a rewarded score. If the model had said, "I shouldn't but I am," the deviance of the behavior would have been unmistakable. But he merely announced that he was "going to" (or simply "did") reward himself for a score of 15, never admitting that he was breaking the rules.

Thus, pupil perception of the power of the two adult models and the content of their verbal and motor behaviors may have contributed to the adoption of deviant practices: children may have failed to differentiate early instruction from later demonstration. In that case, only the control group and the investigators actually perceived the warning to reward scores of "20 only" as a "stringent standard," and only the investigators perceived that this standard had been "learned." The experimental subjects apparently acquired a stringent criterion of their own—that only scores of 20 *and* 15 should be rewarded—and they successfully demonstrated the differential effectiveness of three modes of modeling behavior in helping pupils adopt standards.

Very similar modeling modes appear in a study by Liebert, Hanratty, and Hill (1969), who compared the effects of three levels of "rule structuring" on the rule adoption behavior of second grade pupils playing a bowling game. At the highest level of rule structuring, a model enthusiastically announced the rule governing self-reward each time a score of 20 was obtained and then rewarded himself. At the moderate level, the model simply announced that 20 was a good score, and then rewarded himself. At the lowest level of rule structuring, the model merely stated scores as they were obtained, announcing without further explanation whether he would or would not reward himself for each score. The investigators found that the highest level of rule structuring produced significantly more rule adoption. (It should be clear, however, that the three levels of rule structuring differ not only in degree but also in cognitive and affective content.)

Most reports of behavior modeling indicate that it is a very effective means of communicating standards when it is structured to interpret and define the behavior modeled. As a successful teaching technique, behavior modeling relies on consistent performance and complementary conditions to communicate and clarify the message. Adoption depends first on the individual's value for the model or the behavior, and second on the provision of a cognitive explanation of the behavior. Modeling motor behavior, for example, may stimulate associative processes which generate constructs of what to do and how to do it; but unless modeling is accompanied by the cognitive content essential for differentiation, the individual will find it difficult, if not impossible, to determine where, when, and most particularly, *why* the modeled behavior is appropriate. It is the *why* that relates the behavior or standard or rule to the individual's value system.

Yet, while valuing and cognitive understanding are essential to adoption, they do not guarantee it: various conditions and circumstances can influence the individual's decision to abide by the rules and standards governing performance of the modeled behavior. One such circumstance is value conflict—when, for example, a reward is valued as much as or more than the behavior itself or the model. Another is rule uncertainty—when the individual has only a tenuous grasp of the operating rule or standard.

Liebert and Ora (1968) report that subjects given the opportunity for self-reward under high incentive conditions abandoned strict adherence to the rules more often than subjects performing under low incentive conditions. They noted, however, that subjects exposed to direct training in or modeling of the rules governing self-reward were inclined to maintain the principle of "deservingness" even when they deviated from these rules. Hildebrandt, Feldman, and Ditrichs (1973) found that exposure to rules and modeling that were mutually supportive and reinforcing increased the tendency of subjects to adopt the rules under self-directing conditions. They also found, however, that young (7- to 10-year-old) subjects, when given the opportunity, still tended to adopt more lenient standards for their behavior.

Thus, the task of acquiring standards and values through the adoption of modeled behavior involves much more than mere imitation. Social rules and academic standards are ever present in the schools. Pupils are expected not only to learn them but also to accept, abide by, respect, and value them. These rules and standards form a part of each child's self-identity, self-extension, self-esteem, and self-image, since they are the gauge by which classroom behavior is reflected and measured. Initially, a value for authority is the source of pupil obedience. Then, as pupils begin to acquire a concept of the student role, to learn the behaviors and skills associated with the role, and to receive positive reflection from performance of the role, they develop a value for education. That is, they can and do value education when the experience of schooling is positive.

There is no disguising the imbalance of power characterizing the behavioral dialogue occurring in the school system. Of this environment, it can truly be said that obedience earns the only freedom available. The only possible means of enjoying a move toward autonomy, independence, and responsibility lies in the child's ability to understand and adhere to operating rules and standards and to contribute to the learning environment they are intended to create.

The admonition, "Do as I say," presumes all the power in the dialogue and a value for the authority of the model. It also presumes that what is said will be understood. "Do as I do" is less presumptive, but may not be as demonstrative as the model assumes. What to do and how to do it are only part of the message in communicating rules and standards. When, where, and why to behave in a given way are the elements that lead to autonomy, independence, and responsibility and encourage adoption of rules and standards.

TEACHER BEHAVIOR AND THE MORAL DEVELOPMENT OF PUPILS

> **This was the first time in my life that my fears left me. If I lived up to the rules and told the truth, there was nothing to fear.**
>
> *Eleanor Roosevelt 1961.* The autobiography of Eleanor Roosevelt, *p. 24.*

Theoretically, the foundations of moral behavior are laid in the early psychological experiences encountered by the developing self in the behavioral dialogue with significant others and the environment. When children perceive that their impact on significant others is positive, they acquire the basis for developing trusting rather than distrusting relationships. Continuing acceptance allows children to remain or become trusting and open.

Acceptance by others engenders a feeling of inherent worth and "goodness" which allows children to view disapproval realistically, as the response of others to certain of their *behaviors*—behaviors over which the children have control. Realizing this, children can eliminate disapproval either by associating it with the behavior in question and then omitting that behavior from their repertoires or by acquiring the values and standards of those persons whose approval they value.

By associating disapproval with unacceptable behavior, and acknowledging that unacceptable behavior is within their control, children develop a sense of responsibility for their actions. As children attempt to assume responsibility for their behavior, significant others can, by differentiating causal behaviors from causal circumstances, provide children the basis for a concept of "intent."

Children who experience early rejection and thus perceive that their impact on significant others and the environment is negative develop a basic attitude of distrust in relationships with others. If they continue to experience rejection, children begin to perceive themselves as unacceptable and valueless. They exist in a chronic state of disapproval. The disapproval these children suffer, however, is a reaction not only to their behavior but also to their "selves." The best they can hope for, then, is *conditional* approval, earned through performance of behaviors that are approved by those whose acceptance they value. By associating personal acceptance and worth with certain approved behaviors, children perceive their control over others' responses as limited to the ability to gain approval (conditionally). Children cannot eliminate disapproval since they perceive it as a reaction to themselves, not merely to their behavior.

As they acquire socially prescribed behaviors and standards, children's sources of approval may expand to include not only significant others but also the approved behaviors and standards themselves. This allows children to assume responsibility for both approved behavior and behavior performed in defiance of the standards they have learned. Disapproved behavior falling outside the latter category, however, remains beyond the children's control and responsibility.

> She [Eleanor Roosevelt's Aunt Bye] once gave me a piece of advice
> which must have come from her own philosophy. I was asking her
> how I could be sure that I was doing the right thing if someone
> criticized me. Her answer was, "No matter what you do, some people
> will criticize you, and if you are entirely sure that you would not be
> ashamed to explain your action to someone whom you loved and who

loved you, and you are satisfied in your own mind that you are doing
right, then you need not worry about criticism, nor need you ever
explain what you do."

Eleanor Roosevelt 1961. The autobiography of Eleanor Roosevelt,
p. 43.

The initial response of significant others to the child does not in itself
determine the morality of his or her subsequent behavior. The cognitive interpretations and information supplied by significant others are equally influential
in the acquisition of moral behavior. Children who experience initial acceptance, continuing approval, and positive self-reflections form a positive
concept of self, but do not necessarily develop a cognitive basis for differentiating themselves from their behavior. Unless children experience the consequences of their behavior, they will not recognize the existence of standards.
And in social interaction, they may perceive that the function of others is
to provide them with acceptance and approval. Children whose behavioral
dialogue offers acceptance but not cognitive interpretation may confront disapproval from others outside the home environment. But this may serve only
to reinforce the approving role of significant others and limit the children's
interaction with the environment.

Children who initially experience rejection and whose behavior is consistently disapproved and negatively reflected are of course also deprived of
the psychological experiences and cognitive content that facilitate differentiation between self and behavior. Like the accepted child who receives no
cognitive interpretation, the rejected child cannot acquire behavioral standards because he or she, too, lacks sufficient differentiating feedback.

The child who feels accepted and, in addition, receives interpretive
feedback from significant others and the environment may acquire the "how
to" behaviors and standards prescribed by society simply so that he or she
may avoid disapproval from valued others. Yet, equipped with these behaviors and psychological security, the child can investigate the environment
and risk an active role in the behavioral dialogue. From then on, even with
limited feedback from significant others, the child can seek out more frequent
and varied psychological experiences from which to formulate additional
constructs for approved, goal-achieving behavior. These psychological experiences form a value base for moral judgments. From this base, the child can
relate personal behavior to acquired moral standards. And if significant
others supply cognitive information that fosters not only acquisition, but
also *understanding* of prescribed moral behaviors, the child will expand his
or her concept of morality to include the impact of individual actions on
others in the society. The child will know "why," as well as "how to."

Significant others who answer the question "why" only in terms of the
power of enforcing agents (that is, only in terms of parental or societal

authority) encourage an associative concept of morality that focuses the child's attention on personal rather than societal consequences of individual behavior. Children who feel inherently disapproved find their own limited answer to the "why" of moral action in the rewards of acceptance and approval which follow performance of prescribed behaviors. For such children, the reason to acquire moral behavior is to gain approval. Supplemental differentiating information about "where" and "when" to perform these moral behaviors is applied to further define their appropriate use. The power of moral behavior, then, is not distinguished from the power of all prescribed behavior to help the individual avoid punishment or disapproval. On the other hand, the child who learns to view individual morality in terms of its impact on society uses such differentiating information to further his or her understanding of moral behavior and to broaden his or her basis for making moral decisions.

The moral development of *all* children, however, is approval-oriented until they internalize modeled standards and behaviors and create a construct of morality from which to form their own judgments. This being so, the acquisition of moral behavior is developmental, and the child's moral concepts and standards are closely related to his or her level of maturity and experience. One may find, then, that children in a given age group who demonstrate very similar moral behavior may be acting from very different conceptual bases.

Hoffman (1970), for example, classifying seventh grade pupils according to internal or external moral orientation, found that those who were internally directed (based on moral judgment responses) fell into two different categories, in spite of the fact that they *appeared* to have a great deal in common. They were either of two types: (1) a "humanistic" type who demonstrated concern for the human consequences of behavior and considered extenuating circumstances when making moral judgments, and (2) a "conventional" type who demonstrated rigid obedience to institutional norms, regardless of consequences or circumstances. The humanistic subjects appeared more tolerant of "antimoral impulses," were more apt to feel guilt as a consequence of their behavior and its effect on others, and tended to identify themselves with the behavioral characteristics of their parents. The conventional subjects appeared more "repressed," more apt to feel guilt about their own impulses than about harm done to others, and more likely to identify with the power of the parental role than with specific behaviors of their parents. The third group identified by Hoffman had an external–moral orientation and was motivated by fear of detection and punishment.

The classroom teacher is expected to represent and enforce the moral standards of the dominant culture in our society, modeling moral behaviors, enforcing rules, teaching values, and rewarding or punishing pupils in accordance with their obedience and compliance. Parents expect their children to "learn" honesty, respect for authority and property, responsibility, and a certain amount of social decorum. If teachers serve as significant others, they may be able to impart moral standards and behaviors to pupils who have been relatively unexposed to the core culture, and to further differentiate these behaviors and standards for pupils who have already acquired them. Teachers attempting to do so, however, will find only limited help in the research. Aside from modeling techniques, few teacher behaviors that affect the moral development of pupils have been investigated.

A study by Stouwie (1972), however, offers some insight into the relationship between obedient behavior and the perception of power on the part of younger pupils. Stouwie investigated the effect of conflicting verbal instructions given by a "dominant" adult and a "warm," nurturant adult on the moral behavior of second and third grade subjects. The two adults—a male and a female—alternately assumed the dominant and nurturant roles. The research design focused on the following variables: content of instructions; order of instructions; personality characteristics of dominance and warmth; sex of experimenter; and sex of subject. Pupils were individually introduced into an interaction with the two adults, who, following this interaction, gave each child conflicting instructions about the use of toys displayed in the room. After the two adults left the premises, the child's behavior with the toys was observed and recorded to ascertain which adult's instructions were followed.

Results indicated that pupils perceived the "dominant" and "warm" roles more accurately when the former was assumed by the male adult and the latter by the female. Furthermore, the dominant person's instructions were followed more often than the warm person's—regardless of whether they were permissive or restrictive. However, in postexperimental interviews an undesignated number of subjects reported that they had used their own judgment about whether or not to play with the toys. Apparently, some of these children were, at a relatively young age, willing to assume responsibility for their own behavior.

Focusing on another aspect of moral judgment, one that particularly distresses educators, Fischer (1970) studied the effects of five variations of teacher behavior on levels of cheating in fourth, fifth, and sixth grade classrooms at three public schools. The subjects involved were, according to their teachers, from lower to upper middle-class homes.

Groups of 10 to 15 subjects were seated for testing in a classroom situation. Pupils were widely separated, ostensibly to reduce copying, but actually to increase the opportunity for cheating. To enhance the importance of the test, they were told that scores would affect their six-week grades. Pupils were then handed a 60-item, multiple-choice achievement test and an accompanying answer sheet. Half of the questions on this test were sham items constructed so that either none or all of the response alternatives were correct. From these alternatives one answer had been arbitrarily selected for each sham question and printed on the answer sheet. The criterion for cheating behavior was the appearance of nine or more "correct" sham answers—an occurrence beyond statistical chance. The children were instructed to take the test in the 30 minutes allotted and then to score their own papers by the answer sheet. They were told not to look at the answer sheet prior to or during testing and not to alter or add answers as they scored their papers, since any of these actions would be considered cheating.

The control group received only the instructions cited above. One of the experimental groups, in the "Informative Appeal to Honesty" condition, was given these instructions along with a statement of the teacher's purpose in giving the test (i.e., to evaluate her teaching and to obtain true measures of pupil knowledge in order to improve the course). Pupils in another treatment condition, "Public Affirmation of Value," heard the general instructions as well as a discussion on cheating. These students were casually asked by the investigator to give their opinions about cheating and, after a general period of discussion, pupils were requested to give their names and the reasons why they felt they would not cheat on a test like the one they were about to take. In a third condition, "Value-Relevant Threat of Punishment," the investigator informed the subjects that since pupils "in your grade" had tended to cheat on the test, anyone who cheated would be required to write the sentence, "Although I do not believe in cheating, I cheated on this test," 50 times for punishment. In the final treatment, "Non-Value-Relevant Threat of Punishment," subjects were given the same information about previous cheating behavior, but this time the threatened punishment involved writing numbers from 1 to 100 twenty-five times. Following test taking in each school, pupils were assembled to hear an explanation of the test and its purpose. In two of the schools, pupils were asked before and after the explanation to indicate on an unsigned slip of paper whether or not they had cheated.

Although the results indicated that, at these two schools, 86 children actually cheated, only six admitted cheating on the first query and only 25 on the second (which was accompanied by a statement informing the pupils that half of them had in fact cheated on the test). Over 65 percent of the control and Informative Appeal groups cheated on the test. In the Public Affirmation and the Value-Relevant and Non-Relevant Threat groups, cheating was significantly lower.

The investigator suggests that the Public Affirmation treatment, although not statistically superior to the two Threat of Punishment conditions, is a preferable technique since it at least encouraged children to value honesty and to express this value in their behavior. The failure of pupils to acknowledge cheating was, according to Fischer, evidence of their childish understanding of ethics and their inability to apply ethical beliefs to their own behavior. Fischer suggests that teachers should make a greater effort to clarify ethical principles and to provide opportunities for children to integrate their beliefs and behaviors. This might allow pupils to see that the teacher values honesty as well as grades.

While such efforts on the teacher's part would certainly be beneficial, it appears to us that cheating may be due not only to pupils' incomplete understanding of ethical principles but also to the general nature of the school environment. The adversary relationship between pupils and teachers, pupils and tests, and pupils and school rules may be fostering conditions for unethical behavior. Very few pupils escape the fact that academic achievement, honesty, respect for authority and property, and responsibility have high priority in the system's value hierarchy. But, as teachers often say, "When you cheat, you hurt no one but yourself," and in the day-to-day battlefield of the classroom, where academic achievement is the goal and grades the representation of that goal, gaining higher marks *without hurting anyone else,* may appear to the pupil the most practical application of ethics.

Since the individual teacher cannot change the general nature of the school environment, it is particularly important, as Fischer points out, that he or she clarify ethical principles for pupils. Discussion of moral behavior beyond school regulations, and respect for authority and property is, however, not without problems. Parents have strong feelings about others appropriating their role as teachers of "morality." Even though ethics and morals (particularly those regarding sexuality and sexual behavior) are high priority concerns among teenage pupils, as topics of classroom discussion they often arouse strident conflict between parents and children, school boards and parents, and parents and teachers. Research suggests that such discussion may also produce confusion, rather than clarity, within pupils themselves.

The findings of White and Minden (1969), for example, indicate that pupil confusion about sexual attitudes may have increased following small-group discussion of moral beliefs and standards. Students in their third year at a parochial high school were each given a passage to read, covering two moral principles condemning premarital sex and endorsing the idea that sexual behavior should be confined to the "purposes of marriage and the nature of the generative act in marriage." After reading the passage, subjects were tested to establish a control for reading level and content understanding, and were then asked to indicate their agreement with each of the two principles. They were next randomly assigned to groups of five to review and discuss the material for 15 minutes. Each group was to arrive at a consensus to be reported to the total group. Prior to reporting, subjects were retested on the measures previously used.

Although the pretest did not reveal a sex difference in responses, the posttest indicated that females had significantly *increased,* while males had *decreased,* their scores on content accuracy. On measures of agreement, girls showed significantly more convergence with the "correct" responses communicated in the written material. Boys, however, shifted from convergent to more varied and "risky" (divergent) responses.

Since the boys' shift from convergent to divergent responses was accompanied by a drop in information retention, White and Minden suggest that male subjects may have been showing some cognitive withdrawal from considering the moral principles under discussion.

Amplifying this explanation, we feel that it is possible that girls, in shifting toward convergent answers, were also withdrawing from consideration of the topic—by assuming the socially acceptable stance. Both males and females may have been exhibiting different modes of self-concept sustaining behavior, the boys by avoiding and the girls by conforming. Discussion of sexual behavior in the presence of peers, under circumstances that dictated the "proper" response, may have served to increase conflict rather than clarity: perhaps the desire to avoid conflict was for both sexes more compelling in this particular situation than the need to examine sexual issues.

Moral values, standards, and behaviors are acquired the same way other social values, standards, and behaviors are learned. As a part of the Sense of Self-Image, moral beliefs assume their place in the individual's value hierarchy. When specific moral values are in conflict within a child, perhaps the most we can expect the teacher to do is to reinforce the role of values and standards as the basis of social and individual integrity.

THE SENSE OF A VALUE-BASED IDEAL SELF

> I can't hate God's pesters, definitely, because they doin what God put em here to do. The boll weevil, he's a smart bird, sure as you born. And he's here for a purpose. Who knows that purpose? And who is it human that can say for sure he knows his own purpose? He got all the wisdom and knowledge God give him and God even sufferin him to get a book learnin and like that—and what the boll weevil can do to me aint half so bad to what a man might do. I can go to my field and shake a poison dust on my crop and the boll weevil will sail away. But how can I sling a man off my back?
>
> Nate Shaw in T. Rosengarten 1974. All God's dangers, p. 228.

Whether individuals' dreams revolve around the image of "slinging a man off my back" or around something less basic, their values, goals, visions of changed circumstances and conditions, and above all, hopes for self-fulfillment are embedded in their ideal selves. Individuals whose self-ideals are anchored in the past must constantly restructure the present to maintain the valued perception of self, the "enshrined" self-image. Those whose self-ideals remain goals for the future use the Sense of Self-Image as a criterion and guide for making decisions and gauging expectations.

The teacher's function in relation to the child's ideal self is to provide accurate reflections, interpretations, and information that enable the child to base ideals, goals, and visions of self on realistic values. But here again, teachers' own perceptions, shaped by their values, can affect their performance as significant or salient others. Teachers' perceptions of what pupils can be or can hope to be should not be based on sexual, racial, socioeconomic, or other cultural stereotypes.

The child's self-ideals can be, and commonly are, used by the teacher to form a program of graduated goals and goal-directed decisions for that child. The teacher's reliance on the pupil's Sense of Self-Image and on the pupil's wish to be seen as (1) acceptable, (2) achieving, or (3) obedient to authority is clearly demonstrated by the problems encountered when pupils do *not* value these images or hope to direct their own classroom behavior.

TEACHER BEHAVIOR AND PUPIL EXPECTATIONS

Expectations of and for the self originate in the individual's operating self-image. They reflect the individual's perception and valuing of all the self-concepts the individual has developed. All individuals base their expectations on what they think they are and how they feel they should be seen, hypothesizing the effects of their attributes on others and the environment.

> **But there was so many other years the grass just et up his crops because they weren't half worked. I had all that stuck in me. I said, "Papa—" 1905 when he took me back from Mr. Knowland, "Papa—" I didn't sass him, I knowed better—"Papa, I done learnt something workin for Mr. Knowland. If you will turn your business over to my hands, I'll make you something."**
>
> **I was a stuck-up little colored boy. Looked at me and said, "Son, I'm going to do that, I'll do that. . . ."**
>
> **I got out in the yard and commenced a callin for em to come out. "Let's get in the field, children. It's time, it's time for us to go." First one come to the door was him. "Nate, Nate." I said, "Sir." "I want you to know I'm boss here. And if there's anything you want to do, you go on and do it. I'll tell these children what to do."**
>
> **Lord, I just sunk down in mind . . . I said to myself, "Went back on his word that quick, won't keep hisself under a muzzle; just actin triflin and parleyin off and comin up in the fall of the year with no crop . . . I shied my mouth and let the tail lead the head from that day . . . 1905, he just disrecognized me, discounted me; wouldn't turn nothin over in my hands like Mr. Knowland did. Good God, my feathers fell then.**

Nate Shaw in T. Rosengarten 1974. All God's dangers, *pp. 54–55.*

As self-concept changes with experience, expectations for the self also change, with varying difficulty depending on the degree to which the hypothesis is valued. Verification of expectations reinforces the particular self-perception and affirms self-knowledge, as well as perceptual accuracy in general. Contradiction of hypothesized outcomes causes self-doubt—again to an extent determined by the value invested in the expectation.

Pupils who expect to fail may find more self-confirmation in continued failure than in unexpected success. A child who has not regularly experienced success may consider it imprudent to begin changing self-concepts and behavioral schema after a single experience of success. On the other hand, pupils who expect to succeed may be more willing to revise or change their behavioral schema in order to replicate the circumstances that accompanied past success and may revise their self-concepts only when alternative behavioral schema fail to produce expected success. Failure in the face of expected success may have greater impact on self-image than unexpected success, because of the greater investment of self-value.

Crandall, Good, and Crandall (1964) investigated the relationship between children's expectations of success and adult reaction to their performance. After testing a sample of eighth grade boys, they identified those who had high expectations and those who had low expectations of successfully performing a specific task, and then grouped the boys accordingly. The performances of boys in one High- and one Low-expectancy group were given a positive response from an adult. The efforts of subjects in the remaining High and Low groups were met with a negative adult reaction. At this point, expectations of success were again measured. Then boys in the subdivided groups performed either alone or in the presence of an adult who gave them no response. Following this, expectations were measured a third time.

Results supported the investigators' two major hypotheses: (1) children with high expectations reduced those expectations considerably more after a negative adult response than subjects with low initial expectations; and (2) children with low expectations of success significantly raised those expectations after receiving positive responses. The investigators concluded that children are very sensitive to adult responses that are not consonant with their expectations. They also note that the negative treatment used in this experiment was much more effective in reducing expectations than the positive treatment was in raising them, and that subjects tended to interpret silence from adults as a reaction opposite to that previously experienced. That is, pupils who initially received negative responses interpreted adult silence as an indication of approval, while pupils who initially experienced positive reaction interpreted the silence as criticism or disapproval—at a statistically significant level. Pupils who worked in the absence of an adult evaluated their performances in accordance with the response they had received earlier.

Comparative analyses indicated that adult silence following negative reinforcement was significantly stronger in its continuing effect than that following positive reinforcement. The fact that adult silence was interpreted as a reversal of the adult's initial reaction was cited as evidence that an effect occurs even when there is no immediate or apparent adult response to a child's performance—an effect which is dependent on the child's previous experience of positive or negative reinforcement.

The methods used by Crandall *et al.* were adapted by Hill and Dusek (1969) to test the hypothesis that after experiencing failure high test-anxious subjects raise their expectations to a greater extent than low test-anxious subjects in reaction to positive social reinforcement. Subjects were selected from a pool of fourth graders who had been assessed two weeks prior to the experiment for test anxiety, lying, and defensiveness. Pupils scoring extremely high on the lie and defensiveness scales were excluded from the study.

Each subject was assigned to one of three pretraining conditions—success, failure, or no evaluation. Subjects in the first two groups were given a puzzle to work, a puzzle which could be manipulated by the investigator to guarantee the child's success or failure. Social reinforcement was provided by the experimenters who announced to each subject that he or she either had or had not put the puzzle back together correctly. (Subjects in the nonevaluative condition were given no pretest puzzle.) All subjects were then introduced to the experimental task. Both before and after performing the task, each was asked to indicate his or her expectation of success by ranking himself or herself in relation to the other subjects on a 16-point scale. As subjects in the Social Reinforcement group performed a task, the experimenter made positive statements. As nonreinforcement subjects worked, the experimenter remained silent.

Results indicated that achievement expectations increased (especially among girls) following social reinforcement and remained stable following nonreinforcement. The investigators suggest that the apparent sex difference in relation to social reinforcement may have been the result of an interaction between sex of experimenter–reinforcer and sex of subject. It also may have reflected an interaction between sex of subject and value for approval from salient others.

The role of social reinforcer is commonly performed by classroom teachers. Teacher behaviors categorized as "approving," "criticizing," "encouraging," and "ignoring," for example, contain the elements of social reinforcement used by the investigators in the studies described above. In the classroom, however, performance and evaluation are constant. From the continuing response to his or her Performing Self, each child hypothesizes expectations of success or failure. And this response includes not only social reinforcement communicated through verbal interaction, but also performance feedback given through grading.

Pickup and Anthony (1968) found that pupils generally expected higher marks than they received, the greatest discrepancy between expected and actual marks occurring when actual marks were very low. Examining the effects of differences between expected and actual grades on the pupil's future performance, they report that low achieving pupils given higher marks than they expected improved their subsequent performance, while high-achieving pupils performed better after receiving grades lower than they expected. The authors suggested that teachers reverse the fairly common practice of grading poor students harder and granting better students the "benefit of the doubt" in order to elicit improved pupil performances.

In a study investigating the effect on actual pupil performance of feedback *intended* to alter pupil expectations, Wlodkowski (1973) divided fifth and sixth grade male subjects into two categories according to their scores on a standardized math achievement test (with "simple" and "complex" components) and their reported math performance expectations. In the "positive expectancy" group were pupils whose test results showed them to be at grade level or above in math performance and whose reported expectations were either "good" or "very good." Pupils who scored below grade level on the test and who indicated "poor" or "very poor" expectations constituted the "negative expectancy" group. The investigator intentionally selected subjects whose performances were consonant with their expectations.

Assuming that the standardized test was a reasonably accurate measure of ability, the subjects selected demonstrated fairly realistic self-knowledge and reasonably accurate perception of the task. They were, according to the investigator, pupils with "valid expectations." To reinforce these expectations, the experimenters returned test papers to the pupils, indicating the number of correct answers and including a comment that reflected the reported pupil expectancy. The investigator, who had been introduced into the school situation as a special math teacher, then gave the subjects a bogus test and announced that he would evaluate test results to ascertain each pupil's true math ability. Subjects were then randomly assigned to one of three groups: Supportive Treatment, Contra-Supportive Treatment, and Control. Professing to use information acquired from the bogus test, the investigator informed the Supportive group that he expected their performance on the next test to be at or above grade level. Subjects in the Contra-Supportive group were told that their performance on the next test was expected to be below grade level, and the Control group was simply informed that test papers had not yet been evaluated.

A posttest equivalent to the standardized pretest was then given. Analyzing pre- to posttest gain scores, expectancy categories, and treatments, the investigator found no functional combination of category and treatment that related to significant improvement in pupil performance. He found that a statistically significant proportion of the pupils in the two groups who had received dissonant feedback had improved their performances in comparison with subjects in the other treatment groups.

Initially, the performance expectations of all subjects in this study were reinforced by the scores and comments on the pretest. In addition, the expectations of low ability/low expectation pupils assigned to the Contra-Supportive treatment and high ability/high expectation pupils assigned to the Supportive treatment were again reinforced. It might even be suggested, on the basis of research reported in this section, that the control pupils, who received the initial pretest reinforcement and no subsequent conflicting feedback, also experienced some further reinforcement. Yet it was those subjects whose expectations were eventually contradicted, i.e., the low ability/low expectancy group given the Supportive treatment and the high-ability/high-expectancy group given the Contra-Supportive treatment, who improved their performance on the test component ("simple" or "complex") commensurate with their actual abilities. Given Supportive treatment, low-ability pupils improved their performance on the simple component of the test; given Contra-Supportive treatment, high-ability pupils improved on the complex component. However, only the *proportion* of pupils improving their scores was significant, not the performance *gain* itself. Apparently high-ability students were motivated to improve by the contradiction of their perceptual accuracy and low-ability pupils by the contradiction of their self-expectations.

Questions should be raised, however, about the long-range motivational effects of contradicting realistic pupil expectations. How long would such contradictions continue to function as performance motivators? Would frequent and/or persistent use of such contradictions lead to a distortion in self-perception and unrealistic expectations? Several factors (the all male sample and the failure to produce significant performance gains) make the results of this study ungeneralizable, but in conjunction with the other research reported in this section, Wlodkowski's efforts offer a basis for further investigation.

Entwisle and Webster (1973), extending a previous study in which they successfully raised pupil expectations, found that the variables, age, sex, race, locus of residence, and socioeconomic status, did not significantly affect the procedures they had developed for increasing pupil expectations of success, and concluded that these procedures could be considered applicable to all classroom situations.

Basing their experimental treatment on the assumption (derived from theory) that pupil hand raising is a behavioral indication of high expectation, Entwisle and Webster measured the rate at which each subject raised his or her hand as an indication of the child's acceptance of opportunities to participate. During phase one of the experiment, children were divided into small groups and were told that each group was to compete with the others to create the "best" story by completing a given plot skeleton. Within each group, the experimenter called on all volunteers equally and recorded the number of times each child raised his or her hand. The experimenter made no comments on the children's contributions.

In the second phase of the study, one experimental subject from each group completed the story in the absence of other group members, while the investigator provided constant positive evaluation of each word the child contributed. Children who were uninvolved in this phase of individual story completion comprised the control group. In the final phase of the study, the groups were reassembled with different experimenters (to prevent unequal treatment of the experimental child), and the phase one task was repeated.

Results showed that the selected experimental children increased their hand-raising behavior between phase one and phase three significantly more than members of the control group. In an extension of this study, a number of children individually completed stories in the presence of an investigator, but were not given positive evaluations for each of the words they contributed. The subsequent hand-raising behavior of these subjects did not differ from that of the control group. However, children who *were* reinforced in this second study again increased their hand-raising behavior—significantly more than the nonreinforced children and the control group. The investigators report that, in some instances, experimental subjects did not increase their hand raising following individual reinforcement. Explaining this phenomenon, the authors suggest that task orientation, particularly with respect to academic work, may vary among pupils.

Although Entwisle and Webster felt that the circumstances prevailing and the task performed in their experiment were similar to those naturally occurring in the classroom, it should be pointed out that while pupils were supposedly in competition to create the "best" story, no evaluation of their efforts was forthcoming. This failure to "decide" the competition, to provide the promised comparative evaluation, may have affected the behavior of some pupils in the extended study. In a regular classroom situation, teachers are usually reminded of any such omission, especially if the honor of winning "best" of anything is at stake. Merely giving children unqualified praise for their contributions might be constructive when applied to certain creative composition tasks, but it would not help pupils learn that some task situations require convergent responses or formative evaluation.

Furthermore, the experimental treatment used in this study can be viewed as a method of increasing not only pupil expectations, but also pupil risk-taking behavior (Sense of Self-Extension), self-confidence (Sense of Self-Esteem), or even self-identity. Above all, this treatment can be interpreted as demonstrating the positive effects of approval on the pupil's *value* for his or her performance—not simply on his or her performance expectations.

The role of social reinforcer is played much more elaborately by the classroom teacher than by the researcher conducting a single investigation. Teachers plan and present cognitive information and supervise skill acquisition. They are responsible for guiding and evaluating the performance of each pupil. The fact that researchers, in their limited role, can produce an effect on pupil expectations suggests that the influence of *teacher* behavior on pupil expectations must be immeasurably greater and more persistent.

Although the research results reported above are for the most part ungeneralizable to the larger pupil population, the weight of the evidence does indicate that positive social reinforcement elevates pupil expectations across a variety of sample populations and research conditions. However, while altering pupil expectations may be a reasonable objective for researchers, it is not, in itself, a legitimate end for educators.

The finding by Crandall *et al.* that negative feedback was more effective in reducing pupil expectations than positive feedback was in raising them should be considered in relation to the individual's value hierarchy—where self-expectations and the sense of self-image are involved. The effect of negative information, reflection, or interpretation from a salient other that diminishes an existing value can be expected to be more intense than that of positive stimuli which, if valued, lead to a new or revised—and generally more favorable—hypothesis about self-attributes.

The Crandall study also indicated that pupils initially given positive reinforcement were apt to interpret subsequent silence as disapproval while those given negative responses interpreted silence as approval. How do these findings relate to the classroom situation where, according to several studies (e.g., Silberman 1969; Brophy and Good 1973), teacher praise, criticism, and ignoring behavior functioned to form identifiable pupil groups that teachers either "accepted," "rejected," "ignored," or were "concerned about"? We can hypothesize that a reduction in teacher praise would be interpreted as criticism by the accepted group, and though this may appear undesirable, Pickup and Anthony (1968) found that high achieving (and thus presumably "accepted") pupils improved their performance under nonreinforcing conditions. Rejected pupils, on the other hand, might benefit from a reduction in teacher *criticism*. Meichenbaum, Bowers, and Ross (1969) report that teachers who reduced their criticism of delinquent girls produced more positive change in the academic performance of those girls, which tends to support the Crandall finding that an initial negative response led to an interpretation of silence as approval. This suggests that rejected pupils might interpret a reduction in *criticism* as an indication of approval.

While the findings cited in the preceding paragraphs suggest several ways that social reinforcement may be used to alter pupil performance and expectations, they are undermined somewhat by the Hill and Dusek (1969) research. Hill and Dusek report that girls altered their expectations significantly more than boys in response to social reinforcement. This sex difference raises the possibility that social reinforcement may act, not only on pupil expectations, but also on pupil *values*. The girls in this study may have been exhibiting a *conforming* response consistent with culturally induced values for the female role. Can any procedure as limited as that employed in a single research study really alter culturally determined and reinforced values or expectations?

The Wlodkowski (1973) study draws attention to the problems involved in raising pupil expectations without reference to pupil skills and abilities and in so doing rather obliquely points to the need to help children establish realistic expectations. Pickup and Anthony (1968) report that the pupils in their sample, particularly those of low ability, had a tendency toward inflated expectations. Apparently these children had not been provided criteria for evaluating their skills and performances. And while low ability pupils might be motivated by a more favorable evaluation from their teacher, it should be clear that the perceptual confusion which may ensue when such an evaluation is given to a child who lacks cognitive concepts, skills, or ability must also be addressed. While dissonant feedback may encourage high ability or high achieving pupils toward greater performance, the efficacy of using this practice over a long period of time should be thoroughly examined.

It is important that pupil expectations be consonant with pupil ability and that assessment of ability consider not only cognitive but also affective factors relevant to the pupil's image. The Entwisle and Webster (1970) study, while demonstrating the success of social reinforcement in altering pupil expectations, calls attention to the limitations of such procedures when used in actual classrooms where pupil expectations are tested every day.

TEACHER BEHAVIOR AND PUPIL DECISION MAKING AND GOAL SETTING

The child's first experience with goal setting and decision making occurs during the early training period and is associated with the acquisition of prescribed social behaviors and skills. For most young children, "goal setting" involves merely the mastery of behaviors and skills that have an established value in gaining approval, autonomy, or extrinsic reward. And decision making is usually confined to a choice from a limited number of broad behavioral alternatives (i.e., conformity versus deviance, and obedience versus rebellion) or from several approved options (e.g., what to play, what to play with, whether to go with daddy or stay with mommy, etc.). There are, of course, differences among families, classes, and cultures about what constitutes an approved behavior or option and about the amount of autonomy permitted and the areas in which it applies—a fact which can be a source of trouble for some children upon entering the school system. For the middle-class white child, however, there is rarely a serious break in the home to school continuum of goal-setting and decision-making experiences.

The school system's interest in promoting goal setting and decision making among children is related to two of its most commonly expressed objectives: to produce citizens capable of (1) governing themselves and (2) supporting themselves. These objectives cannot be met, however, unless students first develop a value for them and then master certain prerequisite skills and behaviors, two of which are decision making and goal setting. Where and how does a student acquire these values, behaviors, and skills?

The development of social responsibility and personal autonomy demands that the student be allowed to participate, to the extent of his or her abilities, in the decision-making and goal-setting processes that affect his or her education. House (1970) suggests four ways in which teachers can help pupils acquire a participating role: (1) by allowing students a role in planning, developing, implementing, and evaluating educational experiences; (2) by expanding the opportunities for pupils to work with one another and adults; (3) by sharing leadership responsibilities in the classroom; and (4) by utilizing the pupil's own ideas for enhancing his or her role as participator in and contributor to the school and community. The implementation of these four suggestions, in addition to allowing the child to learn prescribed behaviors and to develop autonomy, would provide the opportunity to establish value relationships between behaviors and goals and to acquire a value for the goals themselves.

In the same vein, Thelen (1966) suggests that teachers use their power to organize classroom activities to provide diverse experiences so that pupils can learn the particular advantages and consequences of various forms of organization. He also suggests that teachers include the pupil experiences as a legitimate classroom resource and that they expand the student role to perceive children not only as class members, but also (and primarily) as problem solvers and producers.

Implementing the suggestions of House and Thelen may not be as easy as it sounds, however. Nash (1968), studying eight classrooms of first through sixth graders, found that teachers perceived pupils as making more decisions than pupils perceived themselves making. While the accuracy of these perceptions was not tested by actual observation, the discrepancy between them should encourage teachers and researchers to investigate whether teachers who attempt to expand pupil decision-making or goal-setting roles actually succeed in doing so or instead unwittingly preempt these functions.

In parallel studies, Gaa (1970), Marliave (1970), and Averhart (1971) examined the effect of goal-setting conferences on pupil goal-setting behavior and goal achievement. Using a low-SES sample, they divided subjects into Unit B (third and fourth graders) and Unit D (first and second graders).

The pupils were further divided by sex and reading level and were assigned to one of three groups: (1) individual conference, goal setting; (2) individual conference; or (3) control.

Pupils in the "individual conference, goal-setting" group were asked, in conference with the teacher, to select their goals for the week from a list of reading objectives arranged in order of difficulty and to set an achievement level for that week. Teachers made sure that these pupils understood the objectives they had selected and gave them reminder sheets listing these objectives. In subsequent conferences, they gave pupils feedback on the outcome of their goal setting and achievement, a review of the skills mastered, and a preview of the next list of reading objectives.

The "individual conference" pupils were not asked to select goals, but were told to "do their best" after being introduced to the objectives of the week. In subsequent conferences, they reviewed skills acquired the previous week, but received no feedback on their achievement. The control group had no individual conferences and did not set goals. All groups received the same class instruction in reading skills. After four weeks, all pupils were asked to set goals for the upcoming week, and these data were used to compare goal-setting behavior among groups. Measures of achievement, attitude toward reading, and self-concept were also collected from all pupils.

Among third and fourth graders (Unit B), no significant differences were found in the effect of treatments on any of the dependent measures. The effect of previous level of achievement was significant for measures of attitude, self-esteem, achievement, and goal-setting behavior. Results for Unit D, the first and second graders, indicated no significant differences between treatment groups on goal-setting behavior, self-esteem, achievement, or attitudes, but analysis of the interaction of treatment and previous reading level showed a wider range of mean scores for pupils in the conference treatment than for those in the goal-setting treatment who began at a comparable reading level.

Averhart suggests that since scores on self-concept and attitude toward reading were initially very high, a ceiling effect may have occurred on these measures. He also notes that five weeks may have been too short a time for pupils to acquire significantly different goal-setting behaviors. During the first few weeks of the study, the subjects' ability to set *accurate* goals was so low that they rarely achieved these goals and thus received very little positive reinforcement. However, subjects in the goal-setting group were ultimately able to set more realistic (and fewer) goals than subjects in the other treatment groups. Apparently, these pupils did learn something about goal setting. They learned the nature of the behaviors they were to acquire and perform (information gathering); they learned that the process was difficult and minimally rewarding (assessment); and they learned that by reducing both the level and the number of goals (decision making), they could achieve the desired outcome (congruence between goal setting and goal achievement).

The fact that goal-setting subjects showed a decline in confidence from pre- to posttest in their ability to achieve set goals may indicate, as the investigator suggests, their realization of a need for assistance in achieving their goals. Or, in our opinion, this reduction in confidence may reflect either a new awareness of the poor reading skills that prevented these pupils from achieving their goals or a fear of failure. Since these pupils were evaluated on goal accuracy as well as reading performance, there were two areas in which they risked failure. If these pupils were motivated by a need for approval, or at least avoidance of failure and disapproval, they might be expected to maintain as much congruence as possible between set goals and achievement, even at the cost of reading performance.

In the classroom, goal-setting and decision-making behaviors are unfortunately often presented as powers vested in the authority of the teacher and the school administration. Teachers who view pupil participation in the educational process as a surrender of either authority or responsibility are overlooking the two processes vital to both goal setting and decision making—information gathering and assessment. If goal setting and decision making are viewed as skills and behaviors to be acquired rather than powers to be wielded, they can be properly leveled and sequenced like other elements of the curriculum. In fact, curriculum materials aimed at helping pupils clarify and explore values, set long- and short-term goals, gather, evaluate, and utilize information, examine risk-taking behaviors, and develop strategies for decision making are now available for high school use (*School Curriculum* **13,** No. 2, Oct. 1973). And instructional materials for pupil "contracting," which also incorporate goal-setting and decision-making processes, are available for use in elementary classrooms.

All pupils have a unique system of values relating to their concept of self. They do not abandon these values and self-concepts at the classroom door. Teachers who consider children's value systems along with their cognitive abilities can more effectively help children acquire realistic self-perceptions and a Sense of Self-Image that leads to achievable and positive goals. Helping pupils master and practice decision-making skills gives them not only a new cognitive tool, but also a preview of the role they are to eventually assume in society.

As a significant or salient other in the classroom behavioral dialogue, the teacher is in a position to provide reflections, interpretations, and information from which pupils can form or revise their hierarchy of values. Pupil goal setting and decision making reflect the existing Sense of Self-Image, and a change in these activities indicates a change in this particular Sense of Self.

TEACHER BEHAVIOR AND THE SENSE OF SELF-IMAGE

We have defined the Sense of Self-Image as a concept of self formed by ordering the values held by and for the self. Attributes, behaviors, and beliefs are assigned a value according to the self's perception of their impact on others and the environment. Valued standards become ideals and goals. Positive perceptions of self become manifest in the Performing Self, the self observed by others. Negative self-perceptions, whenever possible, are intentionally obscured.

The child's Sense of Self-Image is subject to change. It can be altered by the psychological experiences encountered in the behavioral dialogue of the classroom and the school environment. Teachers and other pupils, in their role as significant or salient others, and the school, acting as an environmental influence, provide reflections, interpretations, and information that are internalized by the child and incorporated into his or her Sense of Self-Image.

The paucity of school-based research in this area does not reflect a deficit of moral standards and values in our society, but rather the diversity of moral systems that our society tolerates. Furthermore, there may also be a tendency among adults to view young people, particularly school children, as an inappropriate population for investigation in this area, since the results might have less than positive implications for the adults responsible for teaching and modeling moral standards and values. Young children are rarely expected to be good representatives of society's moral systems.

However, the pupils' social and moral behavior *in relation to school rules and regulations* is a legitimate concern of the school and an appropriate concern for pupils at every grade level. Studies investigating the educational institution's role as purveyor of moral values, standards, and behaviors, such as Fischer's (1970) examination of cheating, would provide a research base from which to formulate new instructional programs that teach and reinforce the moral standards of the school, apart from the general society.

The Self-Image of the child is reflected in the child's goals, decisions, and self-expectations. Though research indicates that pupil expectations can be raised, it also suggests that this practice is justifiable only when it contributes to accurate self-perception, i.e., when the child's ability is commensurate with the elevated expectations. In some instances, lowering pupil expectations provides the psychological experiences that bring about a change in values and a more realistic self-image. Or the teacher may choose not to alter pupil expectations. Rather, he or she may choose instead to focus on pupil decision making and accurate goal setting in order to reinforce a positive and realistic Sense of Self-Image.

Teachers can have positive impact on pupil value systems and Self-Images by:

1. Recognizing that pupil perception influences pupil interpretation of modeled behavior, and that pupil valuing is essential to the adoption of rules, standards, and behaviors;

2. Realizing that moral values, standards, and behaviors are learned through the same process by which other social and academic behaviors are acquired and that pupils must therefore be given the information, reflection, interpretation, and opportunity to develop a value for these behaviors—a value linked not only to the self but to society in general;

3. Clearly communicating and interpreting the values and standards of the school and identifying the behaviors by which pupils can implement them;

4. Using evaluative feedback and constructive criticism to help pupils differentiate between appropriate and inappropriate behaviors in the school situation;

5. Creating an environment that encourages pupils to discuss their concern about moral values and standards in a context of social responsibility and providing opportunities for pupils to develop and exercise their capacity to make moral judgments on their own; and

6. Teaching pupils how to make decisions and set goals that will reinforce a positive and realistic Sense of Self-Image.

Pupils who are described by teachers as "able to work with a minimum of supervision" are those who have acquired responsible social behavior, a positive value for learning, and a measure of personal autonomy. Theoretically, these pupils also have a sense of acceptance and a sense of trust, a sense of self-identity, and a positive sense of self-esteem. They perceive themselves as participating, contributing, and achieving performers with a positive impact on others and their environment. Whatever their grade level or potential for academic achievement, all pupils should acquire from their educational experience a more positive and realistic Sense of Self-Image that includes a high value for social responsibility and personal autonomy.

REFERENCES

Ali, M. 1975. *The greatest, Muhammad Ali.* With Richard Durham. New York: Random House.

Angelou, M. 1969. *I know why the caged bird sings.* New York: Random House.

Keller, H. 1968. *The story of my life*. New York: Lancer Books.

Roosevelt, E. 1961. *Autobiography of Eleanor Roosevelt*. New York: Harper & Row.

Rosengarten, T. 1974. *All God's dangers: the life of Nate Shaw*. New York: Knopf.

Welk, L. 1971. *Wunnerful, wunnerful! The autobiography of Lawrence Welk*. With Bernice McGeehan. Englewood Cliffs, N.J.: Prentice-Hall.

THE SENSE OF PAST AND PRESENT VALUE-BASED IMAGES OF SELF

Teacher Behavior and Pupil Self-Image

Chadwick, J. A. 1967. Some effects of increasing the teachers' knowledge of their pupils' self-pictures. *British Journal of Educational Psychology* **37**: 129–131.

Gordon, I., and P. Wood 1963. The relationship between pupil self-evaluation, teacher evaluation of the pupil, and scholastic achievement. *Journal of Educational Research* **56** (8): 440–443.

Griggs, J. W., and M. E. Bonney 1970. Relationship between "causal" orientation and acceptance of others, "self-ideal self" congruency, and mental health changes for fourth and fifth grade children. *Journal of Educational Research* **63** (10): 471–477.

Staines, J. W. 1958. Symposium: the development of children's values. III. The self-picture as a factor in the classroom. *British Journal of Educational Psychology* **28** (2): 97–111.

Teacher Modeling Behaviors and Pupil Adoption of Standards

Allen, M. K., and R. M. Liebert 1969. Effects of live and symbolic deviant-modeling cues on adoption of a previously learned standard. *Journal of Personality and Social Psychology* **11** (3): 253–260.

Feshbach, N. D., and S. Feshbach 1972. Imitation of teacher preferences in a field setting. *Developmental Psychology* **7** (1): 84.

Hildebrandt, D., S. Feldman, and R. Ditrichs 1973. Rules, models, and self-reinforcement in children. *Journal of Personality and Social Psychology* **25** (1): 1–5. (ERIC Document Reproduction Service No. EJ 080 672.)

Liebert, R. M., M. Hanratty, and J. Hill 1969. Effects of rule structure and training method on the adoption of a self-imposed standard. *Child Development* **40** (1): 93–101. (ERIC Document Reproduction Service No. EJ 003 058.)

Liebert, R. M., and J. P. Ora, Jr. 1969. Children's adoption of self-reward patterns: incentive level and method of transmission. *Child Development* **39**: 527–536.

Portuges, S. H., and N. D. Feshbach 1972. The influence of sex and socioethnic factors upon imitation of teachers by elementary school children. *Child Development* **43** (3): 981–989. (ERIC Document Reproduction Service No. EJ 062 923.)

Teacher Behavior and the Moral Development of Pupils

Fischer, C. 1970. Levels of cheating under conditions of informative appeals to honesty, public affirmation of value, and threats of punishment. *Journal of Educational Research* **64** (1): 12–16.

Hoffman, M. L. Conscience, personality, and socialization techniques. *Human Development* **13** (2): 90–126.

Roosevelt, E. 1961. *Autobiography of Eleanor Roosevelt*. New York: Harper & Row.

Stouwie, R. J. 1972. An experimental study of adult dominance and warmth, conflicting verbal instructions, and children's moral behavior. *Child Development* **43** (3): 959–971. (ERIC Document Reproduction Service No. EJ 062 922.)

White, W. F., and N. Minden 1969. Risky-shift phenomenon in moral attitudes of high school boys and girls. *Psychological Reports* **25** (2): 515–518.

THE SENSE OF A VALUE-BASED IDEAL SELF

Rosengarten, T. 1974. *All God's dangers: the life of Nate Shaw*. New York: Knopf.

Teacher Behavior and Pupil Expectations

Brophy, J., and T. Good 1974. *Teacher-student relationships: causes and consequences*. New York: Holt, Rinehart and Winston.

Crandall, V., S. Good, and V. J. Crandall 1964. Reinforcement effects of adult reactions and nonreactions on children's achievement expectations: a replication study. *Child Development* **35** (2): 485–497.

Entwisle, D. R., and M. A. Webster 1973. Research notes: status factors in expectation raising. *Sociology of Education* **46:** 115–126.

Hill, K. T., and J. B. Dusek 1969. Children's achievement expectations as a function of social reinforcement, sex of S, and test anxiety. *Child Development* **40** (2): 547–557. (ERIC Document Reproduction Service No. EJ 006 484.)

Meichenbaum, D., K. Bowers, and R. Ross 1969. A behavioral analysis of teacher expectancy effects. *Journal of Personality and Social Psychology* **13** (4): 306–316.

Pickup, A. J., and W. S. Anthony 1968. Teachers' marks and pupils' expectations: the short-term effects of discrepancies upon classroom performance in secondary schools. *British Journal of Educational Psychology* **38:** 302–309.

Rosengarten, T. 1974. *All God's dangers: the life of Nate Shaw*. New York: Knopf.

Silberman, M. 1969. Behavioral expression of teachers' attitudes toward elementary school students. *Journal of Educational Psychology* **60** (5): 402–407.

Wlodkowski, R. J. 1973. The effect of dissonance and arousal on assignment performance as they relate to student expectancy and teacher support characteristics. *Journal of Educational Research* **67** (1): 23–28.

Teacher Behavior and Pupil Decision Making and Goal Setting

Averhart, C. J. 1971. *Effects of individual goal-setting conferences on goal-setting behavior, reading achievement, attitude toward reading, and self-esteem for second grade students.* (Working Paper No. 71.) Madison: Wisconsin Research and Development Center for Cognitive Learning, University of Wisconsin, June. (OE 5-10-154.)

Gaa, J. P. 1970. *Goal-setting behavior, achievement in reading, and attitude toward reading associated with individual goal-setting conferences.* (Technical Report No. 142.) Madison: Wisconsin Research and Development Center for Cognitive Learning, University of Wisconsin.

House, J. E. 1970. Can the student participate in his own destiny? *Educational Leadership* **27** (5): 442–445.

Marliave, R. S. 1970. *Attitude, self-esteem, achievement, and goal-setting behavior associated with goal-setting conferences in reading skills.* (Technical Report No. 176.) Madison: Wisconsin Research and Development Center for Cognitive Learning, University of Wisconsin.

Nash, S. 1968. Perceptions of decision-making in elementary school classrooms. *Elementary School Journal* (November): 89–93.

School Curriculum, 1973, **13** (2).

Thelen, H. A. 1966. Pupil self-direction. *National Association of Secondary School Principals Bulletin* **50:** 99–109.

TEACHER BEHAVIOR AND THE SENSE OF SELF-IMAGE

Fischer, C. 1970. Levels of cheating under conditions of informative appeals to honesty, public affirmation of value, and threats of punishment. *Journal of Educational Research* **64** (1): 12–16.

CHAPTER 8
The General Self-Concept in the Classroom

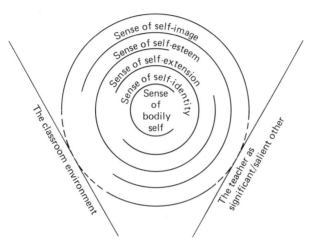

Fig. 8.1 The general self-concept.

The behavioral dialogue of each pupil in the classroom is highly individualistic and idiosyncratic because it represents that pupil's experience with "my" teacher in "my" classroom in the course of "my" education. The extent to which the pupil perceives the relationship as personal indicates the importance of the psychological events occurring within it. Although the observable teacher-pupil ratio may be one to twenty-eight, the ratio experienced by the pupil is one to one.

The crucial question for each pupil in the behavioral dialogue is: "How am I being perceived?" He or she finds an answer in his or her reflected self-image and impact on significant others and the environment—perceptions derived not only from direct, personal interaction with the teacher, but from the whole spectrum of interactive events occurring in the school situation. And it is the teacher's task to discover and understand these perceptions so that he or she may determine each child's needs.

But exactly how, one might ask, do teachers gain insights into their pupils' perceptions of their school experience? While we cannot offer specific guidelines, we can refer teachers to two aspects of self-concept that, *considered together,* suggest pupils' feelings about their role in the classroom. The *inter-*

action between the child's *sense of continuing self* (an aspect of the Sense of Bodily Self that shapes the perception of others) and the child's *past and present value-based images of self* (an aspect of Self-Image that influences how the child wishes to be perceived) offers clues to the child's view of his or her classroom experience.

The first of these two components of self-concept, the sense of continuing self, refers to the child's perception of self as fully accepted, conditionally accepted, or rejected. The child's attitude toward others and the environment is determined by this most basic perception of self.

If we consider only this component, we might find patterns of experiences and perceptions similar to those illustrated below by Pupil A (Accepted), B (Rejected), and C (Conditionally Accepted).

Pupil A is a boy who feels generally accepted. He has consistently experienced positive reflection from significant others, who have allowed him to participate in the behavioral dialogue and to assume increasing responsibility and autonomy. Therefore, he perceives adults as significant or salient others who provide information, interpretation, and approval. And he perceives the environment as an arena in which to test his mastery of skills. He has a basic attitude of trust toward others and the environment, and he brings this attitude into the school experience.

Pupil B, on the other hand, is a girl who feels generally rejected. Early in life, this pupil's basic needs were attended on a strict schedule. In learning social behaviors, she was expected to achieve perfection: effort alone did not count. Therefore, all behavior became a potential source of disapproval and punishment. In the behavioral dialogue her role was limited to conformity, and her mastery of skills was interpreted as an achievement of her significant others. Skill acquisition did not lead to autonomy or independence. Thus, Pupil B perceives adults as controllers of her existence and the environment as generally hostile unless it offers a means of hiding or minimizing her presence. Pupil B has a basic attitude of distrust toward others and fear for self, and brings this attitude to the school experience.

Pupil C is a boy who feels conditionally accepted. Early in life, he perceived that something about him was not acceptable, but in acquiring social behaviors he learned that some of his efforts gained him acceptance and approval while others did not. He was allowed limited participation in the behavioral dialogue: autonomy and responsibility were defined and circumscribed by the interpretations of the significant and salient others. Thus he perceives adults as dispensers of approval, interpretation, and information, and the environment as an inconsistent, unpredictable source of approval. He has a basic attitude of distrust toward *unknown* others and *unfamiliar* environments and in confronting new experiences he feels a sense of self-risk.

Given these three basic attitude sets, can we assume that *Pupil A* will have a positive perception of the school experience and *Pupils B* and *C* negative perceptions? We cannot make this assumption without considering the *values* that shaped these pupil attitudes. That is, the child's sense of continuing self, considered alone, may be misleading: only in combination with the pupil's values does it suggest his or her perception of school.

For example, *Pupil A*'s positive perception of self is linked to a particular value system. Suppose the child is a much-wanted boy who strongly resembles his father, after whom his Ideal Self is modeled. He has a well-defined concept of male and female roles, and he values the physical power, authority, and autonomy that he associates with the former. In the value hierarchy of Pupil A, education and aesthetics are near the bottom. Pupil A does not like school. His female teachers are "bossy," and his male physical education teacher constantly criticizes his efforts and his performance. His cognitive abilities are average, thus placing him with the classroom majority, who receive minimal teacher attention. There is very little in the teacher's learning objectives that reinforces Pupil A's existing Self-Image. Pupil A has adopted the attitude toward education expressed by his father who says "I'd rather go fishing and hunting myself than read about some other fella doin' it." Though this child feels fully accepted and has a positive self-concept, he experiences a break in the home-to-school continuum because his *values* are not particularly compatible with the school environment.

Pupil B, as a girl who feels generally rejected, has a poor concept of her Performing Self. Her most valued behavior is withdrawal. However, she recognizes certain similarities between school and her previous experience: there is a schedule of events that is reasonably predictable and an adult who has the power of approval. And while achievement brings the greatest approval and acceptance in the school setting, effort can also gain some approval. Therefore, a performance level that shows effort but leaves room for improvement is the safest choice for this child. If Pupil B is cognitively unable to achieve at a consistently approved level, the safest recourse is to exhibit a great deal of effort that will be perceived and noted as "pupil tries hard" or "applies herself." If she is able to achieve, slow achievement or underachievement will still guarantee a measure of control over her situation by her slower advance toward known and attainable goals. She will be seen as "steadily improving, but not yet working up to the level of her ability." This behavior maintains the balance of psychological safety for Pupil B, giving her a means of gaining some approval, but more important, of staving off failure, rejection, and new demands and confrontation. Pupil B neither likes nor dislikes school; her purpose is to survive it.

Pupil C, as a boy who feels conditionally accepted, has found something, a personal attribute or behavior, that has positive impact and alters his condition favorably. Where there is the possibility of disapproval, this valued behavior or attribute must be used to reduce the risk. If the valued attribute or behavior is appropriate in the school setting—if, for example it is cognitive ability, conformity, or obedience—the pupil is likely to perceive school as a friendly environment in which acceptance and approval can be gained. But if the valued attribute or behavior is something inappropriate to the classroom, such as physical aggression or total dependence, Pupil C is likely to view school in a negative light.

The point is, of course, that the basic sense of the continuing self and the value-based image of self must be served by the schooling experience or the pupil's perception of school will be negative. When a value for approval, authority, or learning is present, the teacher has a channel to the pupil's self-concept. But if the teacher hopes to have a positive effect on a pupil's self-concept, he or she must consider any planned interaction or experience in the light of that pupil's psychological safety and value-based images of self.

How can a single teacher serve as a significant or salient other to individuals as diverse as Bertrand Russell, St. Augustine, Eleanor Roosevelt, Maya Angelou, Muhammad Ali, Nate Shaw, and Helen Keller? This is an important question since it is quite possible for one teacher to have such diversity, or more, in one classroom.

In answering, let us reiterate that it is a question of *how,* not *whether,* the teacher will function as a significant or salient other. The teacher will perform the role, at least for some students, whether the teacher knows it or not. Thus, we are interested in the *quality* of the teacher's performance in this conferred role. And we believe that a good performance begins with the teacher's awareness of his or her own Self-Concept and influential role in the process of pupil self-concept formation. It continues with the realization that pupils are alike in some respects, like some others in other respects, and unique in still other respects. Finally, the teacher's performance as significant or salient other should always be guided by our traditional belief in the inherent value of each individual.

The two classroom dialogues which follow demonstrate the function of the teacher as significant other and, it is hoped, illustrate the usefulness of our theoretical framework and General Self-Concept Model to classroom teachers who wish to plan or analyze their teaching for affective content. They are *not* intended as guidelines for classroom behavior.

Both of these dialogues take place in lower-level elementary classrooms. The first occurs in a new school building, the second in an old building. Both schools are situated in a lower socioeconomic, urban setting. The lesson presented in each case is an introduction to a unit on nutrition and health.

CLASSROOM DIALOGUE NO. 1

In this first dialogue, the teacher is working with a group of eight pupils in an open classroom environment. The room is very large, with many windows and a carpeted floor. Other pupils are grouped with their teachers in other areas of the room. The eight pupils in this group are seated on the floor in a semicircle around the teacher, who occupies a low chair and holds several large posters.

Teacher Who knows what this is? [Holds up a large poster showing a glass of milk, a glass of orange juice, a bowl of cereal with fruit, a plate of bacon and eggs, and another plate with two pieces of toast. These items have been cut from magazines and pasted on the large poster board.]

Pupils [Enthusiastically] Food! Milk! Bread! A fried egg, hummm, I love eggs! I don't, I hate eggs! I'd eat the meat up! That looks good!

Teacher Yes, this is food . . . milk and eggs and cereal . . . this is a picture of a "Breakfast." All of these things are foods that are good for us and help us grow. They give us strong bones, good teeth, and good muscles. They give us the energy to do good work in school, too. Now, I have another picture here that shows us where all these things come from. Let's see if we can find something in this picture [holds up another poster showing a cow, a chicken, a pig, an orange, and a field of grain] that shows where these things [points to breakfast picture] come from. Where does the milk come from?

Pupil Milk comes from cows.

Teacher That's right. Milk comes from cows. [Points to the cow on the picture.]

Pupil Is that a cow? It doesn't look like the cows that are on TV.

Pupil This is a different cow. This cow is white and black. Cowboys don't have cows like that. They have different cows. Don't they, Miss Summer?

Teacher Well, yes—this is called a dairy cow and these cows are kept by farmers. These cows are for milk, the cows you usually see on TV are for meat.

Pupil And there's different kinds of milk, too, isn't there?

Teacher Yes, of course. Other animals give milk, too, like goats, for instance.

Pupil And some milk is dry and some milk is wet. You can add water to dry milk or wet milk to make it go further. Is it wet or dry from cows?

Teacher   Well, all milk is wet when it comes from the animals. The farmer sells it to a dairy company and they take it and put it in bottles. Or they can take some of the water out and put it in cans, or they can take all of the water out and put what is left into boxes. Then you just add water to it to make it milk to drink or use for cooking. Now, let's go on. Where do eggs come from?

Pupils   Chickens! There's the chicken right there. [One pupil leans forward and taps the chicken on the poster.] My grandpa has chickens. He's got four chickens.

Teacher   All right. Now the bacon, where does the bacon come from?

Pupil   I know where the orange juice comes from—see, there it is, a whole orange.

Teacher   Yes, that's where the orange juice comes from, but right now we're talking about the bacon. Where does the bacon come from?

Pupil   It's the pig because it's meat. I know that.

Pupil   The pig and the cow eat the grass. [Points to the field of grain.]

Teacher   Yes, we get bacon from pigs, and that leaves us the grain, here [pointing to the field of grain]. What *two* things in our breakfast come from grain? There are two—

Pupils   It's the bread!

Teacher   What else?

Pupil   We didn't find out where the stuff in the bowl came from.

Teacher   The "stuff" in the bowl is breakfast cereal. Don't you eat cereal for breakfast, like rice crispies or corn kix?

Pupil   I eat sugar flakes right out of the box all the time.

Pupil   We have oatmeal sometimes.

Pupil   I eat toast all the time. I have a piece of toast and a cup of coffee with milk in it and sugar.

Pupil   Sometimes I eat breakfast and sometimes I don't.

Pupil   I never eat breakfast.

Teacher   But you should eat breakfast. We all should. You shouldn't come to school on an empty stomach. You can eat breakfast here at school if you don't eat it at home, you know.

Pupil I don't like to eat breakfast. Sometimes I drink a coke. I like cokes.

Pupil If my mama is up, she gets me a bowl of puff rice. My mama buys puff rice. If she works at night, though, she don't get up and me and my sister, we like to fool around more so we don't eat or we'll be late.

Pupil We eat our own stuff. We don't eat stuff on that picture.

Teacher Well, the idea is to eat these things because they make you healthy. Now we're going to look at a poster that shows the food groups and you'll see which groups these breakfast foods come from. . . .

Pupil My father is sick. He doesn't have hardly any teeth, either.

Pupil You should see my mama! She has big black spots on all her teeth and they hurt. She soaks everything in her coffee—boy, is that ever sloppy looking, ugh!

Teacher That's enough, Roberto. Let's look at our food groups now and tomorrow we'll have pictures of lunch and supper.

In subsequent lessons the teacher continues to use the posters she has prepared, showing nutritionally balanced meals and the sources of selected foods. During the last two weeks of the unit, pupils work under the teacher's supervision preparing another set of posters that display model meals and food sources. The teacher chooses among the pupils' cutouts, and offers evaluative comments on the cutting and pasting skills of individual pupils. In the final week, pupils review their work with the teacher, using the posters as stimuli for naming food groups and classifying foods into the appropriate group. On the last day, the teacher gives a test on the unit and finds that all pupils have met her criterion: they can identify the four food groups, naming representative foods, food sources, and the benefits of balanced nutrition.

CLASSROOM DIALOGUE NO. 2

The second dialogue occurs in a contained classroom. Desks are arranged in rows, with a half-circle of chairs at the front of the room. The pupils are seated at their desks, and the teacher is standing at the front of the room with several large posters propped on the chalkboard rail.

Teacher [Holding up a poster with pictures of children, white, black, Oriental, Chicano, and Indian, with thin bodies and sad faces, that have been cut from magazine and newspaper advertisements for worldwide child-care, hunger, and poverty programs.] I want to show you some pictures of some children who are all having the same problem. Why do you think they look so thin and sad?

Pupils   They're poor! They don't have clothes! They don't get to eat! Their daddy is gone! They don't have any mama!

Teacher   I think you are probably all right. I thought they were probably orphans, too, and I thought they looked very hungry. So I cut these pictures out for us and left a space here under each picture so we could give each one a name. Then I thought we'd learn about what foods we should feed them to make them healthy and happy again. We will be like doctors. Of course, we'll have to find out what foods they should have and where we can get those foods. But first, we have to have names for our children. The girls can give their favorite girl's name and the boys can give their favorite boy's name. Write them on a piece of paper, just spell them the best you can, and we'll put the names in these two boxes. We'll have one boy and one girl draw out four names so we can name the four boys and four girls in our pictures.

[Pupils proceed to write names. The teacher collects the names in the two boxes. Two pupils are selected to come up and draw the names from the box for the eight pictures. Teacher takes the eight names drawn and puts them in one of the boxes.]

Teacher   Now that we have the names, we'll divide into eight groups. I'll mix these names together in this box and one person from each group can draw out a name. If it's a boy's name, this boy marked No. 1 [pointing to the poster picture] will be your group's boy. If it's a girl's name, this girl marked No. 1 will be your girl. That's the way it works for parents when they have children, isn't it? They don't know whether they'll get a boy or a girl. Let's divide up now, three people to a group. We'll count out up to eight and then start over. Everyone with the same number will be in one group. [Pupils count out and find their group members.]

Teacher   Now we'll draw the names. Let's have Group 1 come up and draw.
[Pupils from Group 1 come up and draw a name from the box. Pupils in the class are watching and commenting. "I hope we get a girl!" "I want a boy!" "Can we trade if we want to?"]

Teacher   My goodness, you do sound like parents! Some parents say "I hope we have a girl, or I hope we have a boy." But all of them hope their babies will be healthy and they love and keep whatever they get. We'll do the same. [Children finish drawing names and placing them under the pictures on the poster.]

Pupil   They didn't draw my name! Why can't they each have two names, I have three names.

Teacher   Of course they can each have two names, most of us do have two names, don't we? Let's draw out four more of each and if we have any left over—we'll just give some of our children three names.
[Children continue drawing out names, using the sequence to combine the names. The teacher writes the names drawn under each picture on the poster.]

Teacher   Now, parents and doctors, here is a chart that has four names and four columns. These are the groups of foods that we will need for our children. I'm going to ask every person in each group to name one thing he or she eats either for breakfast, for lunch here at school, or for supper at night. I'll put the food in the column it belongs in—it might even go in two columns—and that will be all we can do today. Tomorrow we'll start to learn what good things the food we have listed in the first column will do for our children when they eat it, and we'll look for more foods to put in the column we are working with. Then we'll cut out pictures in these magazines in the corner, and you can bring some from home, too, if you like, and we'll make meals for our children out of these pictures. Now, let's start with Alberto Edward Rocky's [using the three names] family. What is one food you have to eat? This will include things to drink, too.

Pupil   Beans, we have beans a lot.
[Teacher writes food names in the column on the poster.]

Pupil   Corn bread—I just love it.

Pupil   Pancakes. Let's put pancakes with lots of syrup!
[Teacher continues to write the food names under columns headed "Dairy Food, Meats, Vegetables and Fruits, and Cereals," placing each food as it is given by the pupils. She suggests that they add a fifth column for "Snacks and Coke and Candy" when they are named so that they can learn more about them and what they will do for the "children" at a later time.]

In the next lesson pupils are given a "Health Diet" guide to use in assembling meals from magazine pictures. If they want to use favorite foods from their own homes, they must have the ingredients. They will use information from parents and cookbooks. The groups prepare posters depicting three meals and one snack during each week of the unit. Poster preparation includes identification of food groups, sources, and nutritional benefits. Part of each period is reserved for group presentation of a meal poster and accompanying nutrition information. Errors are discussed by the pupils, with conflicts resolved by the teacher, who functions as consulting nutrition expert. In the last week of the unit, each group selects three meal posters and one snack poster for display, along with a picture of a child exemplifying the happy, healthy condition that their "child" has now achieved. On the last day of the unit, the pupils are evaluated to "accredit" their knowledge of nutrition and are asked to report any changes they have made in their own eating habits. The teacher finds that the pupils have met the objective criteria: they can name the four food groups and identify representative foods, sources, and nutritional benefits. Returning the test papers, the teacher suggests that the pupils now use their acquired knowledge to check school menus and select their own foods at lunchtime.

COMPARISON OF DIALOGUES 1 AND 2

The dialogues presented above do not deal with the, teachers' perceptions of *individual* pupils or with pupil needs differentiated by achievement level. They do illustrate, however, differences in teacher behavior arising from differing awareness of the General Self-Concept and *different interpretations of the pupil's role in the classroom behavioral dialogue.*

In order to compare the effect of the teacher behaviors illustrated in Dialogues 1 and 2 on pupil self-concept, we must return to the pupil's question, "How am I being perceived by my. teacher?" The answer to this question begins with each teacher's interpretation of the pupil role, which is a reflection of the teacher's perceptual set.

From the four major categories that differentiate the perceptual sets of "effective" and "ineffective" helpers (Combs 1969), we have selected statements that form a basis from which to examine the perceptual sets revealed in the lesson planning of these two hypothetical teachers.

I. General Perceptual Organization

Is the teacher more interested in people or things? Does the teacher look at pupils from the outside or does she try to see the world as they see it?

II. Perception of Other People

Does the teacher see pupils as generally able or unable to do things? Does she see them as worthy or unworthy, dependable or undependable?

III. Perception of Self

Does the teacher see herself as being with the pupils or apart from them? Does she see herself as able or unable, dependable or undependable, worthy or unworthy, wanted or unwanted?

IV. Perception of the Professional Task

Does the teacher see her job as one of freeing pupils or controlling them? Does she see her role as being involved or uninvolved? Encouraging process or achieving goals?

PERCEPTUAL SET COMPARISONS

I.   Using only the evidence supplied by the dialogue, we would conclude that Teacher No. 1 shows a strong inclination toward things rather than people. The focus of her lesson falls on "food" and the preparation of balanced meals. Teacher No. 2 focuses on the people aspects and the role of nutrition in creating a healthy child. Although the subject of the unit is one related to a basic human need and to the experiences of every school-aged child, Teacher No. 1 apparently has not considered the relevance of pupil experience except at the cognitive level ("Who knows what this is?", "Where does the milk come from?", "Where do eggs come from?"). Teacher No. 2, on the other hand, has considered the pupils' experience and has incorporated both their cognitive and experiential knowledge into her plans ("I want to show you some pictures of some children who are all having the same problem. Why do you think they look so thin and sad?").

II.   Teacher No. 1 appears to take a very limited view of pupil abilities. According to her plans, pupils will exercise a limited number of skills under close supervision. This we could take as an indication that she also has a limited view of their state of "worth" and their dependability ("Now, I have another picture here that shows us where all these things come from. Let's see if we can find something in this picture that shows where these things come from."). Her pupils are to identify and associate foods, sources, and categories already selected and pictured by the teacher. In their assigned tasks they will replicate activities the teacher has already performed. Teacher No. 2 sees pupils as able to undertake a far greater range of activities and is depending upon their ability for the success of her structured, but far more comprehensive, plans. Her pupils will also prepare posters of model meals, using the "diet" guidelines. They will need to *interpret* the guidelines and *apply* their skills without close supervision. They will *exercise their own judgment* in designing and assembling the poster to be displayed. They will need to learn the content of certain food selections, a requirement which will give them the responsibility for *collecting information* from parents, cookbooks, and labels. They will also *present* their nutritional knowledge to the class for *evaluation* and *feedback*. These people-oriented activities and the teacher's expectations of her pupils and her reliance upon their performance and participation reflect a perception of their "worth."

III.   In the role she has designed for herself, Teacher No. 1 has a very limited relationship with her pupils. The structure she has placed on her lesson plans emphasizes convergence rather than divergence in the learning process which may reflect insecurities she feels with the subject of nutrition and, therefore, the need to control the range of subject matter. Her questions are essentially "What is this?" and "What is this from?" and her comments foreclose a real relationship with the pupils. (**Pupil:** I know where the orange juice comes from—see, there it is, a whole orange. **Teacher:** Yes, that's where the orange juice comes from but right now we're talking about the bacon. Where does the bacon come from? **Pupil:** We eat our own stuff. We don't eat stuff on that picture. **Teacher:** Well, the idea is to eat these things because they make you healthy. Now we're going to look at a poster that shows the food groups and you'll see which groups these breakfast foods come from. . . .) The interaction she has planned with her students is narrow and may reflect either a limited perception of her pupils' need for her or a preference for a nonresponsive role.

In contrast, Teacher No. 2 has a broad perception of her role and her pupils' need for her. Her lesson preparation has required her to go beyond the teacher's manual and to use other resources for dealing with the subject. She has planned a variation of her role along with every instructional method employed. She perceives herself as dependable, worthy, wanted, and very much a part of the experience in which her students are engaged. She associates herself with their experiences and includes herself in their tasks. (**Pupils:** They're poor! They don't have clothes! They don't get to eat! Their daddy is gone! They don't have any mama! **Teacher:** I think you are probably all right . . . we could give each one a name . . . we'd learn about what foods we should feed them to make them healthy and happy again. We will be like doctors . . . we'll have to find out what foods they should have and where we can get those foods.)

IV.   Almost all of the dialogue for Teacher No. 1 reflects her control. She is controlling the participation, the performances, the products, the processes, and the information provided in her lessons. (**Teacher:** Yes, we get bacon from pigs, and that leaves us the grain, here. . . .   What two things in our breakfast come from grain? There are two. . . .) She is the sole source of approval or disapproval. (**Teacher:** But you should eat breakfast. We all should. You shouldn't come to school on an empty stomach. You can eat breakfast here at school if you don't eat it at home, you know.) She concentrates exclusively on the achievement of learning objectives. (**Pupil:** My father is sick. He doesn't have hardly any teeth, either. (**Pupil:** You should see my mama! She has big black spots on all her teeth and they hurt. She soaks everything in her coffee—boy, is that ever sloppy looking, ugh! **Teacher:** That's enough, Roberto. Let's look at our food groups now and tomorrow we'll have pictures of lunch and supper.)

Teacher No. 2 is concerned with the processes as well as the objectives in her lesson plans. She introduces a variety of pupil roles and provides a degree of pupil autonomy in the performance of each of these roles. (**Teacher:** Now, parents and doctors, here is a chart that has four names and four columns. These are the groups of foods that we will need for our children. . . . Tomorrow we'll start to learn what good things the food we have listed in the first column will do for our children when they eat it, and we'll look for more foods . . . we'll make meals for our children out of these pictures.)

Although in some instances we are talking about differences in degree rather than kind, we would conclude that Teacher No. 1 has an "ineffective" and Teacher No. 2 an "effective" helper perceptual set. We could also infer from the evidence of these dialogues that Teacher No. 1, who appears to have interpreted her role as one of authoritative control, may be evidencing unresolved concerns for self and concerns for self as a professional while Teacher No. 2 shows a dominant concern for pupils and her impact on pupils.

The influence of the teacher's perceptual set can also be seen in the quantity and quality of the psychological experiences provided in the classroom. The following analysis of these two dialogues guided by our theoretical framework and the General Self-Concept reveals differences in the hypothesized effect on pupil self-concept that result from the impact of the teacher's use of particular *lesson content* and *instructional methodologies*.

THE SENSE OF BODILY SELF

A positive impact on the Sense of Bodily Self is achieved by the teacher's acceptance and positive reflection of the individual and by an environment that provides psychological safety and recognition of individuality.

Teacher No. 1 is working in a small group situation which would offer considerable opportunity for individual reflection and interaction. Her response pattern, however, indicates a tendency to ignore or curtail student comments arising from individual experience which she considers non-task-related. Her responses to task-related comments are either corrective or directive with prescriptive shoulds and shouldn'ts for pupil behaviors. The environment created by this teacher would provide psychological safety for dependent, conforming, approval seeking, anxious pupils. However, pupils who venture to reveal their own eating behaviors risk disapproval and those who respond to the teacher's "who knows?" risk exposure of their inadequacies and misunderstandings without any compensating acknowledgment of their performance or participation.

Teacher No. 2 is working in a contained classroom with full class membership but she has structured the tasks to create opportunities for individual recognition. By having the pupils work in triads and structuring her role to remain accessible to them as a consultant and resource person, she has increased each pupil's opportunities for individual expression. She has also created support for dependent, anxious, and insecure pupils through her structuring and has provided psychological safety for all the pupils with a climate of mutual assistance. Using her knowledge of the varied ethnic and socioeconomic backgrounds of her pupils, she has provided additional psychological security for those who might otherwise feel threatened by the differences represented in the kinds and amounts of food used in their homes by focusing attention on the needs of the "children." She has asked the pupils to interpret the "children's" appearances sympathetically and to relate to their problem. She has used pictures of children from different racial backgrounds with obviously different physical characteristics and has modeled the same attitude of acceptance and concern toward each one. She has given a positive and affirming interpretation of each child's birth and has placed every pupil's experiences and knowledge on an equal footing. She has not defined the roles of parents or doctors by sex but by nurturant, caring, accepting behaviors.

THE SENSE OF SELF-IDENTITY

Teacher No. 1 has reflected and addressed the pupils in accordance with her interpretation of the pupil–group role and has only reinforced their identities as dependent and conforming pupils. She has not related the content of the lesson to the environment of her pupils nor to their experiences and has indirectly increased their awareness of differences in their own eating habits and "ideal" eating habits. She has structured the relationships and communications to center on herself. She has reinforced her own identity as the "teacher" with the authority to control, with superior knowledge, and the power to define and interpret both sides of the behavioral dialogue of the classroom.

Teacher No. 2 has introduced a variety of roles and affiliative relationships for her pupils and for herself. She has provided cognitive, affective, and behavioral content for the performance of all the roles as well as an arena for experiencing each role. In addition to being pupils, these students are to be parents, doctors, group members and class members. The teacher is a guide, a moderator and facilitator, a consultant, and a resource person. In her use of pupil background experience and knowledge, she has promoted an awareness of similarities rather than differences. She has also provided opportunities for a variety of communicating experiences and for increasing verbal abilities as modes of self-expression and performance. She has provided throughout her total unit plans a reinforcement of the sense of self in relation to others and the environment.

SENSE OF SELF-EXTENSION

The climate of psychological safety provided by the directiveness of Teacher No. 1 may also have been enhanced by her proximity to the children in the small group situation. However, since she was the only source of approval and audience for performance, she may have created a competitive situation that threatened those pupils who had not developed skills and competencies. She has provided clear and simple directions for the task and has utilized the pupils' known skills, but she has restricted their use of autonomy and creativity in the performance of their task. Pupil participation and contributions are confined to the teacher's dimensions for doing and learning so that all pupils are limited from the outset to self-sustaining, conforming behaviors. We have little reason to believe that the lessons of this unit will have a modifying effect on pupil eating habits. Because they were under strict supervision with immediate correction, however, pupils in this classroom will probably make few errors in demonstrating their ability to select and categorize food items and their sources. The teacher's repeated modeling of the sorting and categorizing process should have reinforced her pupils' understanding of the process, their cognitive constructs of the categories, their information, and their ability to perform on a test.

Teacher No. 2 has clearly represented her perception of her pupils as doers, knowers, and learners. She has created a learning situation that provides pupils with the opportunity to participate and contribute in small groups and through class presentations. The small group situations are somewhat vulnerable to dominance by one individual in the selection of food pictures and group representatives. However, working in triads offers the other members of the group a means of controlling dominant behavior. The task structuring has defined the autonomy and responsibility of the group and permits the pupils within each group to contribute to their own psychological safety through their self-directed use of self-revealing or self-sustaining behaviors. Since each pupil selected by his or her group was representing that group, the other members could share in the success of their presentation and products and support their representative's efforts. Pupils were not in direct competition with each other for teacher attention or approval and were, in fact, allowed to confer their attention and approval on others. These pupils were allowed to follow their own initiative, use their creativity, and control their own behavior within the limits provided by the structure of the task and the guidelines and standards provided them. Errors were *group* errors and were corrected through teacher/ pupil consultation with reference to their guideline information. The final display of prepared meals and their healthy child represented the pupils' selection of their best work, their understanding and use of the process, their skills, and their knowledge. The cause-and-effect relationship of this newly acquired information to their own health and eating habits was demonstrated to them through their nurturance and care of their "child. They now have the information, skills, and concepts necessary for applying their new competency and modifying their own eating habits for better health.

THE SENSE OF SELF-ESTEEM

Teacher No. 1 provided opportunities for recognition and affirmation of pupils only through her approval of their participation, contribution, performance, and products. The teacher is the source of all evaluation and criticism, and since she has not approached the content of the subject with the experiences and knowledge of her pupils in mind, she cannot supply positive, relevant, self-criticism. Any experience of increased status among peers is again dependent upon status conferred by the teacher in recognition of pupil skills. Those who receive specific approval for their performance may increase their self-confidence in their acquired skills, and the fact that these pupils will be able to perform well on the test at the end of the unit may increase their self-esteem as pupils. It seems unlikely, however, that these pupils will gain any self-esteem or confidence from their newly acquired information and competency. Since the products of the pupils were achieved by group effort they may each receive some affirmation from the teacher's approval of their final products. However, this is a situation in which the members of the group, while co-operating to produce a product in one sense, were still working individually and in competition with each other.

Teacher No. 2 has provided several sources of approval: (1) from their own group, (2) from the total class, and (3) from the teacher. Teacher evaluation has been formative and constructive and pupil evaluation has been incorporated into the task. Pupils have been given an informed basis for evaluating and criticizing their work and have been allowed to reward themselves as well for their efforts. There have been opportunities for pupils to increase their self-confidence through their participation in the task and their exercise and demonstration of acquired skills and competencies. They have not had their tasks defined as competitive and have experienced the satisfactions of goal-directed cooperative efforts. Each pupil has completed this unit with an "accreditation" of his or her new skill and knowledge with a clear idea of how, why, and where to use it.

THE SENSE OF SELF-IMAGE

In Dialogue No. 1 the teacher reflected her value image of the pupil as obedient and conforming. Therefore, only pupils with a value for obedient and conforming behaviors were positively reflected. The teacher modeled behavior which the pupils could imitate in those circumstances, but the relationship of the behavior to other conditions and circumstances was not clear. The standards and behaviors implicit in the unit on nutrition could only be adopted and simulated in the classroom. Pupil decision making was limited to a correct sorting and associating process for which they received immediate corrective feedback. In defining the pupil role, the teacher had placed very low expectations on her pupils. They were given an opportunity for only limited and conditional positive impact upon their immediate environment through their preparation of model meal posters and were not given any relevant image of the impact they could have upon their own conditions.

Teacher No. 2 encouraged pupils to acquire ideal images of themselves as parents and professionals and gave them simulated experiences of the positive impact they could have on their own and others' conditions. She modeled behavior that had relevance in the immediate circumstances and in their other environments. She modeled a nurturant, caring role and a value for others. She helped pupils to experience the fulfillment of their expectations for their roles as pupils, parents, and doctors and to see the lesson content in terms of their own values and impact. Pupils were allowed to make decisions and to relate these decisions to the achievement of a goal other than academic performance. The pupils in this dialogue encountered an environment that reflected them as worthwhile, contributing, responsible, and relatively independent members of this small community, and they experienced a relationship between their present and future images of self from which they could form a realistic Ideal Self-Image.

In light of our comparative analysis, the reader may now wish to review the dialogues before proceeding to our concluding comments.

CONCLUDING COMMENTS

The teacher's preparation of lesson plans and selection of instructional methods and classroom activities is the first evidence of his or her perception of the pupil. Teachers may carefully adapt learning objectives and activities to the achievement levels of different pupils without realizing that their efforts may consistently reflect their preference for one group over another. Teachers who feel that they spend too much of their time working with their "slow" groups while their high achieving pupils work on their own should consider that, as far as self-concept development is concerned, there is more *personal interaction* between teacher and pupil involved when high achievers work independently than there is in the group work done with low achievers, even though the teacher is in constant attendance. The high achiever experiences an individualized reflection of a "self" while the low achiever gets an occasional reflection of a "self" in a crowd.

The psychological constructs of self as we have defined them can be used to examine both teacher and pupil behaviors in all classroom dialogues. Differences in academic content influence, to some extent, the teacher's opportunity to plan psychological experiences through which pupils can acquire positive concepts of self. In the light of our conceptual framework, however, we are convinced that in every classroom dialogue, the teacher can create at least some experiences designed to encourage or enhance positive self-concepts.

We would like to suggest that researchers investigating teacher behavior and pupil self-concept view classroom interaction in terms of the behavioral dialogue and the five concepts of self. There is, of course, the problem of designing instruments sensitive to the affective content of the behavioral dialogue. While we can hypothesize that the teacher in Dialogue No. 2 had a more positive effect on pupil self-concept than the teacher in Dialogue No. 1, we cannot be certain until the five aspects of the General Self-Concept can be reliably and validly measured. Moreover, the legitimacy of research on teacher behavior and pupil self-concept is still the subject of debate. At present, such research is conducted primarily in the name of cognitive achievement—in an attempt to identify those teacher behaviors that enhance or inhibit the pupil's *academic* growth. The rationale for such investigation appears to be based upon three research hypotheses.

1. Teacher behavior affects pupil cognitive behavior;

2. Pupil self-concept affects pupil cognitive behavior;

3. Teacher behavior affects pupil self-concept.

Unfortunately, the last of these hypotheses has been of limited interest to educational researchers. It generally appears only in studies relating teacher motivating behavior to the pupil's academic self-concept (through its effect on pupil self-concept), or teacher bias to pupil learning. It is parents, and the larger society, who appear to be concerned with this third hypothesis, but not as a research topic. Parents react to perceived changes in the behavior of their children, attributing these changes to the influence of a particular teacher; and society condemns both the permissiveness and the stifling rigidity of our schools. Yet both fail to recognize, or at least to express, the fact that society as a whole is affected not only by the literacy but also by the self-concepts of its members. It is self-concept that shapes attitudes toward others, cultural standards and values, and individual participation in and contributions to society.

Teachers are the largest body of representatives that our society places in contact with its future citizens. It is well worth the time and effort required to investigate the relationship between the teacher's classroom behavior and the pupil's self-concept—*apart from academic achievement*. Research studies which relate self-concept to academic, and especially cognitive, achievement at a single point in time may obfuscate the true role of self-concept in the long-term development of the child. It is our belief that pupils who are perceived as worthwhile, participating, and contributing members in the classroom will eventually reflect that image of self not only in academic achievement but also in their role as members of society.

REFERENCE

Combs, A. W. 1969. *Florida studies in the helping professions* (Social Science Monograph No. 37). Gainesville: University of Florida Press.

AUTHOR AND SUBJECT INDEX